A VOICE THAT COULD STIR AN ARMY

RACE, RHETORIC, AND MEDIA SERIES
Davis W. Houck, *General Editor*

A VOICE THAT COULD STIR AN ARMY

FANNIE LOU HAMER
and the Rhetoric of the
BLACK FREEDOM MOVEMENT

Maegan Parker Brooks

UNIVERSITY PRESS OF MISSISSIPPI • JACKSON

www.upress.state.ms.us

Designed by Peter D. Halverson

The University Press of Mississippi is a member of the Association of American University Presses.

First printing 2014

∞

Library of Congress Cataloging-in-Publication Data

Brooks, Maegan Parker.
A voice that could stir an army : Fannie Lou Hamer and the rhetoric of the Black freedom movement / Maegan Parker Brooks.
    pages cm. — (Race, rhetoric, and media series)
Includes bibliographical references and index.
ISBN 978-1-62846-004-9 (cloth : alk. paper) — ISBN 978-1-62846-005-6 (ebook) 1. Hamer, Fannie Lou. 2. African American women civil rights workers—Biography. 3. Civil rights workers—United States—Biography. 4. African American women civil rights workers—Mississippi—Biography. 5. Civil rights workers—Mississippi—Biography. 6. Civil rights movements—United States—History—20th century. 7. Civil rights movements—Mississippi—History—20th century. 8. African Americans—Civil rights—History—20th century. 9. African Americans—Civil rights—Mississippi—History—20th century. I. Title.
E185.97.H35B76 2014
323.092—dc23
[B]   2013039752

British Library Cataloging-in-Publication Data available

To my dear husband, David W. Brooks, who encourages me to follow my dreams and enables me to do so

Contents

INTRODUCTION
"I Don't Mind My Light Shining"   [3]

CHAPTER 1
A Rhetorical Education, 1917–1962   [11]

CHAPTER 2
Through the Shadows of Death, 1962–1964   [44]

CHAPTER 3
"Is This America?," 1964   [86]

CHAPTER 4
"The Country's Number One Freedom Fighting Woman," 1964–1968   [121]

CHAPTER 5
"To Tell It Like It Is," 1968–1972   [167]

CHAPTER 6
The Problems and the Progress   [208]

AFTERWORD
"We Ain't Free Yet. The Kids Need to Know Their Mission," 2012   [237]

ACKNOWLEDGMENTS   [247]

CODA
Listen to the "Voice That Could Stir an Army"   [251]

NOTES   [253]

BIBLIOGRAPHY   [298]

INDEX   [309]

A VOICE THAT COULD STIR AN ARMY

"I Don't Mind My Light Shining"

"I NEVER THOUGHT IN A MILLION YEARS THAT FANNIE LOU HAMER WOULD be on a postage stamp," Vergie Hamer Faulkner exclaimed as the United States Postal Service included her mother among the twelve civil rights pioneers honored in celebration of the NAACP's one hundredth anniversary.[1] The previous week, on February 17, 2009, the International Slavery Museum recognized Hamer as a "Black Achiever," hanging a portrait of her in their permanent exhibit next to one of President Barack Obama.[2] For many, placing Hamer's portrait next to Obama's made good sense—during his 2008 presidential campaign, national commentators pointed out that Obama's successes were made possible by the forerunning dedication of activists like Hamer.[3] Her tireless advocacy of voting rights was also recognized in 2006, when Congress named the reauthorization of the 1965 Voting Rights Act after Fannie Lou Hamer, Rosa Parks, and Coretta Scott King. A decade earlier, Bill Clinton invoked Hamer's trademark refrain, "I'm sick and tired of being sick and tired," to roaring applause when he accepted the Democratic Party's 1992 presidential nomination.[4]

Closer to home, the Mississippi State Legislature formally recognized Hamer as a "symbol for people in Mississippi and across the nation who struggled for human dignity and government open to all its citizens."[5] A few miles from the capitol building, at Jackson State University, Dr. Leslie McLemore cofounded the Fannie Lou Hamer National Institute on Citizenship and Democracy to "nurture a generation of young people engaged in and committed to discourse" about "civil rights, social justice, and citizenship."[6] And in her hometown of Ruleville, a memorial garden replete with a nine-foot-tall bronze statue of the civil rights stalwart pays tribute to her legacy.

Friends, fellow activists, and historians alike define that legacy in terms of representation. Famed singer and Student Non-Violent Coordinating Committee (SNCC) supporter Harry Belafonte contends that in Hamer's voice he "could hear the struggle of all black America." "When she sang," he continues, "there was indeed a voice raised that was, without compromise, the voice of all of us."[7] Mississippi native and Freedom Democratic Party (MFDP) member McLemore concurs, claiming that although Hamer "was telling *her* story," the very nature of her testimony was "a commentary on the national scene."

There was at once something so personal and yet so inescapably political about Hamer's narrative. "It was her story," Belafonte reasons, "but she captured the conditions of the time."[8] Historians John Dittmer and J. Todd Moye have drawn related conclusions about Hamer's symbolic legacy. Moye contends, "Hamer flourished in the democratic atmosphere that SNCC created, and she would go on to become the absolute personification of 'Let the people decide,' the archetype of SNCC's organizing strategy."[9] Having attended a series of gatherings among movement veterans, Dittmer writes furthermore: "At each of the movement reunions . . . the person most fondly remembered was Mrs. Fannie Lou Hamer. More than any other individual, Mrs. Hamer had come to symbolize the black struggle in Mississippi."[10]

A Voice That Could Stir an Army, written as a rhetorical biography, both reconstructs and critically considers Hamer's symbolic legacy.[11] Although the term "rhetoric" is often used disparagingly in popular parlance to mean inflammatory or vacuous speech, the discipline of rhetorical studies has a rich history, extending across cultures and dating back to at least the fifth century BCE, as one of the original liberal arts.[12] Rhetoric, as I employ the concept in this book, can be understood as the practice of using symbols—images, words, and even material objects like the ballot, food, and clothing—to influence others. Similarly, the term rhetorical is descriptive of a mode of analysis concerned with understanding where advocates derive the substance of their appeals, how the symbols they use operate (e.g., create unity and division, frame ideas, transmit ideologies, inform and persuade) within particular contexts. Rhetorical analysis also considers what effect the use of these symbols has on audiences, both immediate and removed. This book is a rhetorical biography, therefore, in two senses of the genre. First, because Hamer understood her life's calling in fundamentally rhetorical terms—often assuming a prophetic post and claiming that she was sent by God "to preach deliverance to the captives"—this book seeks to enrich the study of Hamer's biography by examining how she used symbols to influence audiences.[13] It also traces what about those symbols changes and what remains consistent in response to shifts in her personal life and changes in historical context. In a second vein, this study is guided by questions about Hamer's symbolic legacy, asking: what is rhetorical about her biography? How has Hamer's life story been used to persuade, which audiences, for what purposes? What is the potential and what are the limitations of her symbolic status as aspects of her persona continue to circulate within society?

Nearly twenty years after Kay Mills first published *This Little Light of Mine: The Life of Fannie Lou Hamer* and a decade after Chana Kai Lee's *For Freedom's Sake: The Life of Fannie Lou Hamer* was released, this rhetorical biography has benefited from previous biographies' success in popularizing Hamer's story.[14] Mills's and Lee's seminal work has enabled me to move beyond a retelling of Hamer's story to ask questions about how that story has been adapted in American culture. Similarly, thanks to the groundbreaking work of her previous biographers, I can delve more deeply into particular aspects of Hamer's discourse and rhetorical events that define her legacy.[15] Put simply, the core difference between a traditional biography and a rhetorical biography is acknowledgment versus analysis. Mills and Lee both acknowledge Hamer's rhetoric but, given their biographical focus, they rarely offer analysis of how her discourse operated in context, shaped/was shaped by her activism, and conveyed her sense of self.

Hamer's affinity for the spoken word, her self-perception as a prophet, and the lasting impact her use of symbols had upon those who experienced her discourse suggest that a sustained rhetorical analysis of Hamer's contribution to mid-twentieth-century human rights struggles is due.[16] Up until the last few years, however, surprisingly little has been written about her discourse.[17] And what had been written focused on a relatively small sample of Hamer's expansive rhetorical career, engendering critical claims that mischaracterized her signature.[18] For example, Bernice Price and Annie Pearle Markham suggest that "As a speaker, Townsend Hamer used no elaborate lines of argument or ornate stylistic devices. Her rhetoric was straightforward and simple but extremely powerful."[19] Characterizations such as Price's and Markham's reflect a popular misconception of Hamer as "some romantic grassroots person who didn't consciously think about what she was doing"—someone who stood and spoke and stumbled upon greatness.[20] Her close personal friend and fellow activist, Reverend Edwin King, bristles at such depictions, suggesting instead that Hamer "was aware, she had a mission, she was self-conscious and knew that hers was a voice that needed to be used." King and others close to Hamer tell me that she was constantly revising her message to more effectively reach her audiences, engaging in revision that, as this rhetorical biography demonstrates, involves complex lines of argument and utilizes a range of stylistic devices.[21] Hamer's careful rhetorical consideration invites a similarly sustained scholarly approach to understanding the richness of her discourse.

The dearth of rhetorical scholarship about Hamer, the mischaracterization of her rhetorical signature, and the related apocryphal conceptions about how she gained and sustained a platform for her expression can be largely attributed to the limited number of her published speeches that existed prior to the 2011 publication of *The Speeches of Fannie Lou Hamer: "To Tell It Like It Is."* Although both historical and rhetorical scholars had included Hamer's texts within their anthologies, up until Davis W. Houck and I published this anthology only four discrete published texts existed.[22] To compile *The Speeches of Fannie Lou Hamer*, we combed ten archival collections in seven US cities and culled the private holdings of Hamer's family, friends, and fellow activists. This research yielded nearly thirty previously unpublished texts, many of which were speeches that Hamer delivered in over eight states and which span thirteen (1963–1976) of Hamer's fifteen years (1962–1977) as a civil rights activist. The fuller account of Hamer's rhetoric and activism provided within the pages of *A Voice That Could Stir an Army* was made possible, in large part, by the recovery of these texts. My consideration of these speeches—and the wide range of symbols Hamer utilized—is further informed by close readings[23] of the symbolic acts themselves, by oral history interviews with audience members who experienced Hamer's discourse first-hand, and by the growing cache of historical scholarship that comprises the bottom-up approach to studying black freedom movement struggles.[24]

Featuring Hamer as exemplar, this rhetorical biography provides a glimpse into the complex role rhetoric played within various aspects of mid-twentieth-century civil and human rights struggles in the United States. Just as this study stands on the shoulders of previous biographical works about Hamer and is informed by advances in rhetorical studies, it is also influenced by the historiographical shift away from the conservative master narrative of civil rights history.[25] Over the last two decades, the bottom-up approach to studying black freedom struggles has compelled scholars to rethink widespread assumptions about the movement and to redefine frameworks for studying it. This reorientation, in particular, engendered a "long view" of black freedom struggles, which stretches well beyond (in each direction) the traditional 1954–1968 time frame.[26] It has inspired students to reconsider "the movement" as a plurality of local struggles at times attached to, and others independent from, national mobilizing milestones.[27] The bottom-up orientation also decenters the emphasis on pulpit-driven mass mobilization, marked by grand orations, legislative victories, and Supreme Court decisions, considering, instead, the widespread organizing tradition in places like the American South. Community studies that investigate the organizing tradition, furthermore, feature local leaders—ordinary people, oftentimes women, empowered to discover and articulate solutions to their problems by radically democratic organizations like SNCC.[28]

Informed as they are by oral histories of movement participants and its detractors, studies written in the bottom-up vein are recovering the nuance and complexity of local struggles by revealing differences among black freedom advocacy groups, as well as detailing arguments between advocates of social change, white supremacist resisters, and governmental actors.[29] Perhaps most significantly, many of the studies that constitute the bottom-up approach to studying black freedom movement history are mindful that the way the story is told holds implications for how lessons from the struggles inform contemporary politics.[30] The master narrative's focus on a few larger-than-life leaders, its emphasis on national victories, and its triumphalist overtones belie the work that remains to be done, conceal the range of advocates with the potential to participate, and mask the ideologies that perpetuate white privilege and continue to disempower African Americans.

The bottom-up approach to studying the civil rights movement frames this study, which begins by taking a long, localized, and nuanced view of the traditions of white supremacy and black resistance in which Hamer was reared. Considering the significant spaces Hamer occupied—her home, the plantation, and the black Baptist church—chapter 1, "A Rhetorical Education, 1917–1962," examines Hamer's life from birth to age forty-four, when she became involved with SNCC. This examination reveals that though she never received a formal education, Hamer patched together a remarkable rhetorical education that she later transferred to her voter-registration, community-organizing, and fund-raising efforts.

Chapter 2, "Through the Shadows of Death, 1962–1964," focuses on the symbiotic relationship that developed between Hamer and SNCC in the midst of white supremacist backlash to the budding voting-rights movement SNCC spearheaded in the Delta. A dual focus on Hamer's rhetorical signature and SNCC's cultivation of local leadership help explain how Hamer—whose age, gender, class, and level of education made her a nontraditional black freedom movement advocate—ascended to local prominence and national platforms.[31]

"'Is This America?,' 1964," the project's third chapter, compares Hamer's famous 1964 Democratic National Convention (DNC) testimony to an equally riveting, yet lesser known, speech she delivered just weeks later in Indianola, Mississippi. Analyzing the two texts in their historical context explains what was memorable, compelling, and persuasive about each. It also reveals how she adapted the Jeremiadic rhetorical structure, which was becoming her signature mode of reasoning, to appeal to markedly different audiences. Comparing the two texts to each other, furthermore, sheds light on the construction of Hamer's plainspoken sharecropper persona as well as the ways in which this symbolic status belied her intellect and the complexity of her activist message.

Through the analysis of Hamer's mid-decade speeches and other symbolic action, the book's fourth chapter demonstrates how Hamer contributed to the transformation of her public persona from that of a plainspoken sharecropper to a warrior. Chapter 4, "'The Country's Number One Freedom Fighting Woman,' 1964–1968," also considers how this newly fashioned persona was propagated by movement activists and organizations who utilized Hamer as a symbol to argue for a broad spectrum of causes. As powerful and useful as Hamer's symbolic warrior status is, like her image as a simple honest sharecropper, the warrior persona overlooks core aspects of who she was and what she was struggling with during this tumultuous period in her personal life, in movement politics, and in American history. By bringing to light the hardships that Hamer was silently enduring, chapter 4 rounds out her warrior persona with a more realistically human depiction. Ultimately, I suggest that the composite portrait that emerges from layers of rhetorical, contextual, and biographical consideration is actually more empowering than Hamer's larger-than-life warrior persona.

Extending the traditional movement chronology, the study's fifth chapter, "'To Tell It Like It Is,' 1968–1972," traces the final transformation in Hamer's public persona from a plainspoken sharecropper to a warrior and ultimately to an uncompromising truth-telling prophet. This turn-of-the-decade transformation occurred during the period in Hamer's career when she was most highly sought after as a speaker. Hamer was in high demand as a symbol of earlier resistance among the increasingly integrated state and national Democratic parties. The burgeoning second-wave feminist movements also laid claim to Hamer's legacy and solicited her insight regarding their struggles for equality between the sexes. I analyze Hamer's speeches and writings in relation to feminism and formal party politics, considering both how Hamer employed her signature Jeremiad and truth-telling persona, as well as how her story was appropriated for a variety of political ends. The bulk of Hamer's energy during this portion of her activist career, however, was expended in the ongoing fight against poverty. This chapter concludes with an examination of the Freedom Farm Cooperative that Hamer organized in the Delta, considering the enterprise's rhetoricity—what it symbolically stood for, how Hamer represented it, and how she built it with the funds she gained from national speaking tours.

The book's sixth and final chapter, "The Problems and the Progress," acknowledges the many needs surrounding Hamer as she struggled with the increasingly poor state of her own health. In a vain attempt to keep Freedom Farm financially solvent, Hamer undertook a few more national speaking trips, but after 1972 her poor health did not permit much travel. This chapter challenges the triumphalist tenor of the conservative master narrative with the details of Freedom Farm's failure as well as the lonely and penniless state in which Hamer died. Chapter 6 pays close attention to the details surrounding Hamer's

demise, before analyzing the eulogies of several different speakers at her funeral. Hodding Carter III, Stokely Carmichael, and Ambassador Andrew Young
each offered funeral orations that connected Hamer's life to a particular set of
political commitments. When read alongside one another, these addresses reveal the range of Hamer's contributions. The study's final chapter also considers
the telegrammed condolences that poured into the Hamer household in the
weeks following her death. The funeral orations and telegrams offer a sense of
how her postmortem symbolic legacy was initially constructed. I compare this
initial legacy to the way in which public memory of Hamer is broadly crafted in
our contemporary context—through representations in widely used American
history textbooks, at national political conventions, and in the public speeches
of national leaders, among other symbolic renderings.

"'We Ain't Free Yet. The Kids Need to Know Their Mission,' 2012," the book's
afterword, concludes the study with a more detailed consideration of public
memory about Hamer.[32] Focusing specifically on the 2012 Fannie Lou Hamer
Statue and Museum dedication, which brought both local and national figures to her hometown of Ruleville, Mississippi, the afterword examines what
remains rhetorical about her biography. This weekend-long tribute provides a
complex contemporary instance to consider what about her biography gets emphasized and what gets overlooked as well as to examine what the larger social,
political, and historiographical implications are for remembering and forget-
ting particular aspects of Hamer's legacy.

A Voice That Could Stir an Army takes seriously Hamer's rhetorical contributions to several mid-twentieth-century struggles for social change in the
United States. Sustained consideration of her wide-ranging symbol use coupled
with a reconstruction of her symbolic legacy enriches our understanding of
Fannie Lou Hamer, even as this book contributes to the larger historiographical
conversation about bottom-up approaches to studying black freedom struggles.
By featuring an unlikely leader whose activist career provides a long view of the
black freedom movement, who combined the power of mass mobilizing with
diligent organizing work, and whose symbolic legacy represents both the potential of empowering local persons, but also the danger of misappropriation,
this rhetorical biography challenges central aspects of the conservative master
narrative. This book also demonstrates the fecundity of rhetorical analysis as
a mode of examining, understanding, and rearticulating the array of symbols
used by movement participants to influence local and national audiences. Rhetorical analysis, as this book demonstrates, works well in concert with historical
reconstruction to explain how particular strategies for social change are invented, to recognize how these arguments function in context, and to learn

what they have left to teach contemporary audiences. Such explanations not only engender greater appreciation for individual advocates and organizational approaches, they provide more complex and nuanced accounts of how social movements actually move.

CHAPTER 1

A Rhetorical Education, 1917–1962

The people are our teachers. People who have struggled to support themselves and large families, people who have survived in Georgia and Alabama and Mississippi, have learned some things we need to know. There is a fantastic poetry in the lives of the people who have survived with strength and nobility. I am convinced of how desperately America needs the blood transfusion that comes from the Delta of Mississippi.

—PRATHIA HALL

OVER FIFTY YEARS AFTER PRATHIA HALL EXPRESSED THIS CONVICTION, America still has much to learn from people who not only carved out an existence in the Mississippi Delta, but who also left an indelible mark on this nation.[1] I traveled to the Delta in search of one particular source of this wisdom. On a humid June morning in 2007, I first made the two-and-a-half-hour trek from Jackson. That day, I brought flowers to set upon Fannie Lou Hamer's grave—a small cement headstone with a marble placard echoing her now famous words of determination—"I'm sick and tired of being sick and tired." That same day, several other people braved the heat and humidity to beautify her memorial site. Hattie Robinson Jordan, a Ruleville alderwoman, and Mary Moore, a relative of Hamer's who proudly donned a t-shirt embossed with a black and white image of Hamer speaking at the 1964 DNC, greeted me as I approached. Not long after I told the two women about my project, I was settled comfortably in the backseat of Jordan's black Buick Lucerne witnessing all the Hamer-related landmarks their town had to offer. And there was no shortage of these. It would be impossible to drive through Ruleville and not realize that this was where Hamer lived and worked, that she played a pivotal role in redefining race relations in this small Delta town, and that she is sorely missed. The post office, local day care center, and a side street are named after her. The memorial site where she and her husband are buried sits on forty acres of land, adjacent to the town's recreational center. And many of the hundreds of houses for low-income residents that Hamer worked tirelessly to fund still provide shelter to Ruleville residents.

Although Hamer emerged as Ruleville's most famous and beloved inhabit-ant, the road to that status was often blocked by retaliation, fear, and resent-ment: like the time Hamer's home was firebombed by white supremacists, or when few of Ruleville's black citizens would provide her a safe harbor, or even as her Freedom Farm food cooperative for the Delta poor—black and white alike—failed to take root. When Hamer's parents, James Lee Townsend and Lou Ella (Bramlett) Townsend, moved their twenty children to Ruleville in 1919, it would have been difficult for them to predict that their youngest daughter would fundamentally challenge the segregated structure of this city. In fact, when Fannie Lou Hamer was born Fannie Lou Townsend on October 6, 1917, in the city of Tomnolen, Mississippi, the Townsends were grateful for another healthy child and the fifty dollars landowners typically paid sharecropping families to swell their workforce. The Townsends, like so many other poor black families in Mississippi, desperately needed the money and welcomed the ad-ditional labor this child would provide.

Fannie Lou was only two years old when her parents packed up their six girls and fourteen boys and moved from Montgomery to Sunflower County. Sunflower County attracted a large number of displaced sharecroppers, who came seeking work and higher wages after being pushed off farms that had been devastated by the boll weevil. A small beetle that feeds on cotton, the boll weevil migrated to the United States from Mexico and infested cotton crops across the South. Sunflower County was largely spared from its infestation and, as a result, the county experienced a population explosion during the 1910s—"growing by more than 60 percent to exceed 46,000 inhabitants," and becom-ing the state's fourth largest county.[2] Once the Townsends arrived, the family found work and lodging at E. W. Brandon's plantation along the Quiver River a few miles east of Ruleville. The city was named after the Rule brothers, who built the town's first cotton gin in 1886, some forty years after the Choctaw In-dians had been forced from the land. The dwellings for black families on these plantations were typically two- or three-room wood huts, built from old boards nailed to rickety frames or held up by logs. The sole source of heat and light within these huts usually came from an open fireplace in the center of the makeshift structure. The children's "beds" consisted of no more than old cotton sacks filled with grass or cornhusks.

Spared from the boll weevil's destruction and with the influx of new labor, Sunflower County quickly became "the most productive cotton-growing area in the most productive cotton-growing state in the most productive cotton-growing country in the world."[3] This distinction connected Delta planters to a global economy that yielded considerable profits for them—these profits were not, however, passed down to the sharecroppers who labored in the hot, humid, mosquito-ridden, and snake-infested fields. In fact, sharecroppers were often kept in the landowners' debt through an exploitative credit-based system, against which blacks had no recourse.

The Townsends arrived in Sunflower County during a particularly tumultuous period with regard to race relations. Black veterans who returned from fighting the Great War abroad joined blacks who were generations removed from slavery and who began to grow more outwardly resentful of their miserable living conditions, exploited labor, and lack of opportunity. Some blacks left the state for northern cities as part of the Great Migration; those who stayed created pockets of resistance across the Delta. Anthropologist Hortense Powdermaker observed in her 1930 study of the region that the children born two generations removed from slavery—the generation to which Hamer belonged—"exhibited a great deal more resentment at their station in life. They considered themselves entitled to equal treatment and were much less comfortable than their parents had been with the elaborate codes of ritual deference."[4] Dissenting views about the imbalance of power between the races grew alongside traditional lessons of pride and perseverance, which were passed down through generations of black sharecropping families. Knowledge of the white supremacist ideology and skills of interracial communication also developed as a necessity for blacks who lived and worked in the homes and on the fields of whites. Sharecropping communities, moreover, were sustained through sermons and spirituals delivered in small plantation sanctuaries throughout the South.

In light of all that was withheld from black sharecropping families, therefore, it is still possible to discern the lessons, skills, and strength that members of this Delta community shared with one another. To do so, however, requires looking outside formal institutions of learning and to consider, instead, spaces like the home, the plantation, and the black Baptist church. As Afrocentric scholars Molefi Asante and Maulana Karenga emphasize, in the Ancient Egyptian rhetorical tradition, "eloquent and effective speech" is a "practice carried out with skill, artistry and precision," but it is not the sole possession of the formally learned person. Good speech "can also be found among the women at the grindstone," because they too "are hearers and participants in the rhetorical and political project of creating and sustaining a just and good society."[5] Revisiting the spaces Hamer traversed, with a focus on the rhetoric she heard and the lessons she learned within them, reveals where she derived the substance of her appeals and honed her widely celebrated delivery. A look back at Hamer's early years before she became involved in SNCC's voting-rights campaign suggests that long before she received civic training from leaders within the struggle, she was developing rhetorical skills from her family, her life on the plantation, and her church. When Hamer's path eventually intersected with SNCC's, she needed only the empowerment and citizenship training that the organization provided to local people to become an asset to their voter-registration, community-organizing, and fundraising efforts.

LESSONS FROM FAMILY AND FIELD

The region of Mississippi known as the Delta sits between the Yazoo and Mississippi Rivers. In this area of the state, where the well-nourished soil yields cotton, corn, rice, and soybeans, and where the black population outnumbered whites—constituting 75 percent of Sunflower County's population in 1920—the exploitative system of sharecropping thrived during Hamer's formative years. Sharecropping or "halving," as it was often called, replaced slavery after the Civil War as a means of controlling the black population and securing cheap labor. On the fields in and around Ruleville, plantation owners fostered dependency by encouraging black families to live on their land and by loaning them small amounts of money for living expenses throughout the year, to be paid back at harvest. When that time came, the plantation owner ostensibly split the proceeds from the season's yield with the sharecroppers. The main catch, however, was that the seed and fertilizer for planting, in addition to the family's medical expenses, food costs, cash advances, and whatever else the plantation owner reckoned to be fair, was paid out of the cropper's half. The sharecropping system was thereby maintained in such a way that the workers remained indebted to the landowners and, on a good year when a large and industrious family like the Townsends could pick fifty or sixty bales of cotton, they still were not likely to turn a profit.

"Sharecroppers were strictly prohibited from taking any part whatsoever" in the profit calculations, notes historian J. Todd Moye in *Let the People Decide*, wherein he offers the extended example of how L. C. Dorsey's family was manipulated by the sharecropping system.[6] Dorsey grew up in a sharecropping family in the town of Drew, seven miles outside of Ruleville. One year, Dorsey defied this prohibition and took it upon herself to meticulously track the family's shares. From the initial loan amount to the harvest, Dorsey documented all the family's expenses and listened to the radio during harvest to learn what cotton was selling for in their area. According to her math, the family's haul minus their legitimate expenses should have earned them $4,000; at settlement time, however, the plantation owner gave her father $200 for an entire year of labor. With no recourse for the injustice, Dorsey realized first-hand how blacks "were locked into this system, and the fear and lack of control made them take" what they could get.[7]

As patently unfair as the system was, it had to be continuously reinforced and defended by its beneficiaries. The most ubiquitous line of defense was rooted in the popular Social Darwinist ideology, which combined ostensible laws of nature with the historical advances of the Anglo-Saxon race to suggest that the white race was the most fit for survival and, thus, whites' social dominance was warranted. White supremacists ignored advances made by the African race and held fast to the consequent of their natural dominance argument, declaring that blacks were biologically inferior to whites. Stretching back to the days of slavery, white slave-owners-turned-landowners propagated similar beliefs, most commonly that "the Negro is congenitally lazy and must be kept in debt in order to be made to work."[8] Landowners typically provided housing, healthcare, and food—substandard as it was—in return for the sharecroppers' hard labor and deference to the system. In some cases, this relationship engendered for blacks a "plantation mentality," defined by historian Chris Meyers Asch as "an outlook on life that encouraged immediate gratification and deference while discouraging individual responsibility and collective protest. Because black workers were not allowed to make decisions or wield any power on the plantation," he reasons, "over time they were conditioned to defer to authority and accept (and sometimes even prefer) powerlessness."[9]

Although the absence of any incentive to effort and the perceived futility of protest did lead to a plantation mentality among many black sharecroppers, there were certainly exceptions. Though rural and remote, Sunflower County was not immune to the national trends in rising black consciousness that occurred following WWI. Black servicemen returned from war embodying the spirit of the "New Negro," no longer deferent to exploitation and eager to advocate for the same rights they had fought to secure for others in Europe. Marcus Garvey's United Negro Improvement Association (UNIA) was also formed in 1917, the year of Hamer's birth, and a local chapter of the UNIA cropped up in Sunflower County in 1921, just two years after the Townsends moved their family there.

To quell resistance, white beneficiaries of the sharecropping system would make horrid examples of those blacks who threatened racism's stronghold on the region. Lynching was the most barbaric method white supremacists deployed to maintain the region's racial hierarchy and to ensure cheap labor. Though extreme in nature, lynchings were not all that uncommon—in 1919

alone there were eighty-nine reported lynching victims across the South. Between 1882 and 1951, furthermore, there were nearly five thousand reported
lynchings in the United States. And nearly every state in the union was home
to at least one race-based lynching, with 90 percent occurring in the South and
the largest percentage taking place in Mississippi, Georgia, Alabama, Louisiana,
and Texas. In the state of Mississippi, in particular, at least six hundred blacks
were lynched between 1880 and 1940.[10]

One such instance of white-inflicted terrorism on the Delta's black sharecropping community remained with Hamer throughout her life. When she was
just eight years old, a black sharecropper named Joe Pulliam was murdered in
a violent confrontation with a lynch mob. The mob descended upon Pulliam,
who managed to kill several of his assailants with a Winchester rifle, before
the group murdered him. Pulliam was lynched over a dispute with his landowner involving no more than $150; the mob drug his corpse behind a truck
for all the town's black inhabitants to see. After the beastly parade, the killers
went a step further in intimidating the black community by cutting off Pulliam's ear and displaying it in a store window. The Pulliam lynching happened
in the neighboring town of Drew. The message of intimidation it sent quickly
reached the Townsend's plantation dwelling and deeply attached itself to young
Fannie Lou's consciousness, as she invoked the horrid tale decades later in au-
tobiographical accounts.[11]

Even before the Pulliam lynching, young Fannie Lou became personally
familiar with sharecropping's exploitative nature. The system not only targeted her parents, but the landowner also enlisted Fannie Lou—at the young age
of six. While she was playing beside a gravel road near Brandon's plantation,
the owner drove up and asked her if she could pick cotton. Fannie Lou was
unsure, so Brandon encouraged her by saying: "Yes. You can," and if you do
"I will give you things that you want from the commissary store."[12] Tempting
her with treats she rarely enjoyed—sardines, Crackerjacks, and candies like
"Daddy Wide-Legs"—the plantation owner persuaded Fannie Lou to pick thirty pounds of cotton in her first week. Hamer later explained that through the
promise of goods from his commissary, Brandon "was trapping me into beginning the work I was to keep doing and I never did get out of his debt again."[13]

This was just one of the many injustices that Jean Sweet, a northern activist
with whom Hamer stayed when she traveled to Madison, Wisconsin, recalls.
"So many injustices were done to her from day one," Sweet remembers. "She
was tricked and lied to so she began to learn early. And no doubt she learned
to trust her own judgments very well because of all those experiences."[14] The
experience of being tricked into an exploitative system of sharecropping at

such a young age led Hamer to distrust the white power structure and to advocate black self-reliance, as she later wrote: "The question for black people is
not, when is the white man going to give us our rights, or when is he going to
give us good education for our children, or when is he going to give us jobs—if
the white man gives you anything—just remember when he gets ready he will
take it right back. We have to take for ourselves."[15] Before Hamer turned her
experience of exploitation into wisdom for the movement, however, the pitiful
remuneration she received for her labor led young Fannie Lou to question the
southern racial caste system. Rather than breed deference, Brandon's exploitation incited further interrogation from young Fannie Lou.

"One time," Hamer remembered, "I asked my mother why wasn't we white?"
"The reason I said it," she explained, was "we would work all summer and we
would work until it get so cold that you would have to tie rags around your feet
and sacks . . . to keep your feet warm while we would get out and scrap cotton."
After all this work, she insisted, "we wouldn't have anything; we wouldn't have
anything to eat; sometime we wouldn't have anything but water and bread." The
white landowners, however, "would have very good food" and yet "they wasn't
doing anything," she observed. To her child's mind, the solution seemed simple:
"to make it you had to be white, and I wanted to be white." Her mother quickly challenged this desire, telling Fannie Lou "there was nothing in the world
wrong with being black."[16] "Be grateful that you are black," Lou Ella Townsend
instructed her daughter, "If God had wanted you to be white, you would have
been white, so you accept yourself for what you are and respect yourself as a
black child." Reasoning further, Lou Ella advised, "when you get grown . . . you
respect yourself as a black woman; and other people will respect you too."[17] As
an adult, Hamer often recited this instruction, noting the transformative impact it had upon her perception of race relations. Through her response, Mrs.
Townsend had helped her daughter "see that it wasn't because this cat was the
best," that he could relax and enjoy the fruits of blacks' labor, rather "it was
because of the kind of crook that he was . . . the white man was such a crook."[18]
Her mother's belief that black people were oppressed by no fault of their own
ran directly counter to the widespread Social Darwinist explanation of black
inferiority that served to justify the exploitative sharecropping system. Arguing
further that white oppressors deserved no envy, Lou Ella's alternative explanation really "sank down in" young Fannie Lou's mind.[19]

This message was further reinforced by particular verses of songs Mrs.
Townsend would sing to her children. Hamer remembered her mother working in the fields or cleaning their small shack while singing, "I would not be a
white man / White as a drip in the snow / They ain't got God in their heart /

To hell they sure must go," which she would follow with the related stanza, "I would not be a sinner / I'll tell you the reason why / I'm afraid my Lord may call me / And I wouldn't be ready to die."[20] Beyond restoring a sense of race pride in her daughter, Lou Ella's allusion to divine justice, left Fannie Lou with an understanding that the sharecropping system did not leave white people unscathed. Years later, Hamer would draw upon this reasoning to suggest that the races were inextricably bound—both ensnared by segregation and in need of each other to liberate themselves from its effects. Hamer not only carried the content of her mother's lesson forward, but she also adapted her mother's mode of teaching, often using song to reinforce movement messages.

Just as Hamer carried the lessons of self-respect and race pride with her throughout life, she was also particularly inspired by how hard her parents worked to meet the family's most basic needs of safety and survival. "My mama and daddy were some great folks," Hamer maintained; "Daddy was a minister— a deeply religious man. My mother was a fantastic woman, I used to hear her get on her knees and pray that God would let all of her children live."[21] Faced with white violence and hunger pangs, this prayer was a desperate and constant plea. She did more than just pray, however. Day in and day out, Mrs. Townsend would carry a covered bucket into the field with her. "One day," Hamer ex- plained, "I kind of peeked in that bucket, and mama had a 9mm Luger in there." Lou Ella armed herself to protect her children from the physical threats planta- tion owners wielded against them while they worked. "No white man was go- ing to beat her kids," Hamer remembered her mother exclaiming.[22] Like many blacks across the rural South, Hamer clung to this protective spirit of self-de- fense well into her activist career; Stokely Carmichael remembers Mrs. Hamer handing him a loaded pistol when he stayed at her home.[23]

Lou Ella Townsend and her husband also shielded their children from de- spair by finding joy in the least likely of places. To make the long workday go by faster for her children, Lou Ella would initiate races to see who could pick cotton the fastest—all the while singing a lighthearted song: "Jump down turn around pick a bale of cotton / Jump down turn around pick a bale a day / Ohhh, Lord pick a bale of cotton / Ohhh, Lord pick a bale a day."[24] Songs and games like these would help the children pass the twelve to fourteen hours they typically worked on Brandon's plantation. At night, the children would hud- dle around their father, roast peanuts, and enjoy his endless arsenal of jokes.[25] Hamer characterized these fond memories amid trying times as the only things that "kept her going," the small moments of pleasure her mother and father provided for the Townsend children also kept the resentment they felt toward white people from turning to hatred. Hamer later remarked that in spite of her experience with racism in Mississippi, she really did not "hate any man." As she saw things, hate was like a cancer that "eats away at a human being until they become nothing but a shell."[26] In small yet significant ways, therefore, Hamer's parents protected their children both from imminent physical danger and from the looming risk of being consumed by hatred.

Mr. and Mrs. Townsend were commonly seen around the Brandon plantation clearing new ground for planting by raking and burning brush, picking cotton in the fields from sun up to sun down, and running farm machinery—both working as hard as they could to make life easier for their twenty children. This work was rarely enough to meet their large family's needs, however. Fannie Lou's father also ran a small juke joint, bootlegging liquor to supplement their income. Her mother would ask neighboring plantation owners if she could "scrap" their cotton, which entailed gathering what was left after sharecroppers harvested the fields. Lou Ella Townsend would even offer to wash and iron white families' clothes or slaughter their hogs in return for milk, butter, or leftover pieces of meat like the hog's head, feet, and intestines. When all else failed, Fannie Lou's mother would cut the tops of greens, beets, and white potatoes or she would try to make gravy out of leftover grease and flour. In spite of her parents' best efforts, however, Hamer remembered that the sharecropping system often left the Townsends hungry; "I know what the pain of hunger is about," she informed audiences later in life.[27]

By the time Fannie Lou reached adolescence, the Townsends' resourcefulness and drive to break free from the sharecropping system seemed to have paid off. Her parents managed to save up some money. "It must have been quite a little bit," Hamer gathered, because her father bought wagons, tools, cultivators, and even some livestock. She remembered that, for once, the Townsends were "doing pretty well" for themselves. They left the plantation shack and rented a house of their own; they even bought a used car. Their relative affluence, however, tipped the carefully regulated balance of power between the races. Once the Townsends began farming and providing for themselves, they were no longer beholden to the white power structure and it was just a matter of time before whites reasserted their dominance over the family. The Townsends had just managed to fix up their rented home "real nice," in fact, when a white man snuck onto their lot and mixed an insecticide called "Paris Green" into the livestock's food trough. This killed all the mules and the other precious animals the Townsends had struggled to accumulate, reversing the strides the family made. "That poisoning knocked us right back down flat. We never did get back up again," Hamer admitted.[28]

Unable to overcome the deeply entrenched sharecropping system themselves, both James Lee and Lou Ella Townsend encouraged their children to get an education. "My parents tried so hard to do what they could to keep us in school, but school didn't last but four months out of the year and most of the time we didn't have clothes to wear," Hamer explained. Devoted to her children's well-being, Lou Ella Townsend would wear threadbare clothes herself, heavy with patches "done over and over again," so that her children could have "decent" clothes to wear to school.[29] The decent clothes the Townsends could provide for their children, though, were not warm enough to withstand Mississippi's coldest months, when temperatures can dip below freezing. School was only provided for sharecropping children from December to March, when there was little work to do in the fields, and since two of those months—December and January—were too cold to walk to school without shoes or a coat, Fannie Lou was like most other blacks in the state whose education was cobbled together from a few months over the course of a few years.[30]

The segregated school that the Townsend children were able to attend for those few months a year was inadequately funded, staffed, and supported. Operating under the "separate but equal" doctrine, the state of Mississippi spent "about $6 annually per black pupil, less than 20 percent of what it spent on each white pupil."[31] Black schoolhouses were rundown and black students of all ability levels were taught together. Black students got the discarded books and materials from Mississippi's white schools and black schools "often lacked enough basic amenities such as desks and seats."[32] By the age of twelve, Hamer dropped out to "cut corn stalks and help the family."[33]

Fleeting and relatively poor as her educational experience was, it left a permanent impact on Hamer. She excelled in reading and in spelling and she learned that her excellence was quite pleasing to her teacher, Thornton Layne, as well as to her parents. The pleasure young Fannie Lou's success gave these people that she respected encouraged her to work harder. Before long she was winning spelling bees and performing poetry for her parents and their adult friends. The pride that her performances gave her parents, who would show her off by setting her atop their table to sing, recite, and spell, also encouraged young Fannie Lou.[34] She not only enjoyed displaying her lessons through performance and competition, she also reveled in the self-satisfaction that literacy incited. "When I was a child, I loved to read. In fact, I learned to read real well when I was going to school," Hamer boasted to one interviewer.[35] Reading was a skill that Hamer honed throughout her years and it was one that she urged all those around her to acquire. "She told us 'read something every day,'" Dorsey, recalls. "'Don't worry if you didn't get an education. Educate yourself. Read something everyday . . . Go use the libraries! Find out what's going on,'" Hamer would implore.[36] Northern activists who met Hamer later in her life reason that, in light of the "little formal education" she received, "she had to be a fast learner and really intelligent." Based on the time they spent with her, these activists reiterate: "There was no way she wasn't naturally really intelligent."[37]

Despite her love of learning, her natural intelligence, and her parent's best efforts to help their children break free from the sharecropping system, Hamer remarked: "My life has been almost like my mother's was because I married a man who sharecropped."[38] In 1944, Fannie Lou Townsend married Perry "Pap" Hamer, who lived on W. D. Marlow's neighboring plantation. At the age of twenty-seven, Fannie Lou Townsend became Fannie Lou Hamer and moved to Marlow's plantation where she and Pap lived and worked for the next eighteen years of their lives. The couple was well respected among the other sharecroppers and instrumental to the landowner, as Pap drove tractors and Fannie Lou recorded the workers' harvest. Her formal title was "timekeeper" on Marlow's plantation and she was chosen for this leadership position, in part, because of the reading and writing skills she gained during her several years of schooling. As a plantation timekeeper, she was a liaison between the Marlows and the other sharecroppers; thus, Mrs. Hamer must have also had "trust on both sides," reasons McLemore. He explains that her position as a timekeeper reflected the confidence that the Marlows had in her, otherwise they would not have given her the job. Concomitantly, this position enabled her to help other sharecroppers, who respected her "because they knew when Marlow was not around she would use a different kind of 'p,' [a device used] to weigh cotton, to give them a full measure for the cotton they had picked." Hamer excelled in this role, McLemore posits, because of "her great ability . . . to talk to both the white boss man and to talk to her friends and neighbors on the plantation."[39]

Hamer's own reflections about her work as a timekeeper on the plantation support McLemore's contentions. To one interviewer Hamer explained how she transformed her responsible position into an outlet for her rebellious desire: "I would take my 'p' to the field and use mine until I would see him coming, you know, because his was loaded and I know it was beating people like that."[40] Through her small act of providing sharecroppers with a fair measure for their harvest, Hamer worked to balance the scales that had been tipped against blacks in Mississippi for hundreds of years. Hamer's mutinous behavior extended into all aspects of her labor, as she told a northern audience that although she became formally involved in politics in 1962, she had been acting out against exploitation for many years. When Hamer was not working in the fields of the plantation, "I always had to work at white folks' houses," she explained. "They would tell me that I couldn't eat with them or that I couldn't bathe in their tub, so what I would do was eat before they would eat and bathe when they was gone." This subversive act elicited wild applause from her Wisconsin listeners—clearly she had perfected the delivery of a punch line from years of listening to her father's fireside jokes. Hamer continued: "I used to have a real ball knowing they didn't want me in their tub . . . just relaxing in that bubble bath." Similarly, "when they was saying that I couldn't eat with them, it would tickle me because I would say to myself, 'baby I eat first!'"[41]

Through these everyday acts of resistance, Hamer explained, "I was rebelling in the only way I knew how to rebel."[42] Hamer's actions were also an indication that she did not internalize white supremacist arguments about black biological difference, arguments that maintained the black race was more prone to disease and could spread these diseases to whites if strict separation of the races was not maintained.[43] While Hamer's subversive behavior helped temporarily balance the unequal plantation scales and restore her sense of human dignity, she declared: "I just steady hoped for a chance that I could really lash out, and say what I had to say about what was going on in Mississippi."[44]

Hamer's compelling drive to speak out about the injustices she faced, coupled with her natural and nurtured talents of expression, distinguished her among her peers. It was not the case, for instance, that Hamer and her family had it particularly worse than other sharecropping families living on Marlow's plantation. In fact, Vergie Hamer Faulkner, the Hamers' second-oldest adopted daughter, remembers that because her mother was the timekeeper, the plantation owner "made sure we was in a nice house." She described their living conditions: "no running water . . . but it was alright, we didn't have to worry about it raining inside. We had windows and doors, that kind of thing." She concedes that "it could have been better," but notes that "we had no need to complain because it was better than the house we had been living in" before Hamer assumed the timekeeper role.[45]

As evidenced by the children they were entrusted with, the Hamers' distinguished position extended beyond Marlow's plantation and into the larger Ruleville community. The couple never had children of their own. Perry Hamer had children from his two previous marriages and Fannie Lou reportedly gave birth to two stillborn children before she was forcibly sterilized at the age of forty-two.[46] The couple, nevertheless, reared two children from their community. Dorothy, their eldest, was given to the couple by a single mother in the mid-1940s, shortly after the Hamers wed. About ten years later, the couple took in Vergie, a baby who was badly burned when she was five months old and whose biological parents had so many other children that they were unable to provide her with proper medical care. The doctor treating Vergie for the burns called upon the Hamers, trusting that the couple would be able to more adequately care for Vergie. And Vergie certainly remembers this being the case. "My daddy was a provider," she declared proudly. "He made sure we had plenty of food to eat. We raised our own garden, and daddy would raise hogs, chickens . . . They would make long sticks of bologna, and stuff I could eat while they were working in the fields."[47] Fannie Lou and Perry Hamer cared for Dorothy and Vergie, even as they welcomed Lou Ella Townsend into their home. Fannie Lou's mother moved in with the Hamers in 1953 and lived there until she passed away in 1961.

During a typical day in the Hamers' family life, Fannie Lou, Perry, and Dorothy would work in the fields from four or five o'clock in the morning until it was dark outside—from "kin to kant" (can see to can't see)—as the fieldworkers referred to their seemingly interminable schedule. Season by season the work varied from chopping the cotton stalks to planting the seed to picking the harvest. The harvest work was perhaps the most grueling. The workers had to stoop down to reach the boll, the oppressive sun bearing down on their backs, as they struggled to retrieve the fluffy fiber from a sharp spikey stalk. When Vergie reached the age of five, she began caring for her grandmother, who was now blind and confined to a wheelchair, while the rest of the family labored in the fields. Fannie Lou made the most of the time Lou Ella Townsend spent living with the Hamers, using the opportunity to fulfill a promise she made to herself as a child. Witnessing her mother's self-sacrificing devotion to their family, Hamer vowed that if she "lived to get grown and had a chance," she "was going to try and get something for [her] mother." To keep this promise, however, Hamer had to work so hard she "couldn't sleep at night," explaining, "I was determined to see that she did have something in her last few years. I went almost naked to see that my mother was kept decent and treated as a human being for the first time in all of her life."[48]

Through the Hamers' backbreaking efforts, they managed to create a decent life for Lou Ella. Vergie recalls that Fannie Lou was "grandmama's *heart*, she didn't want to stay with nobody but my mama and my dad."[49] The couple also succeeded in shielding Vergie from the harshest aspects of their impoverished and exploited existence. Looking back on her childhood, Vergie characterizes their life on the plantation as "nice—everybody was family people," she remembers; "Back then everybody had enough food; you could leave your house unlocked. It was nice," she repeats.[50] "Nice" was certainly not how Fannie Lou Hamer recalled this period on Marlow's plantation, however. Struggling to provide for Dorothy and Vergie, her mother, her husband, and herself brought Hamer to a tipping point as she became "sicker and sicker of the system."[51]

CHALLENGES TO THE SYSTEM

Hamer was certainly not alone in her resentment of the white supremacist system. Even as she tirelessly labored on Marlow's insular plantation, national race politics and race relations in the community surrounding her family were in flux. About the time she and Perry Hamer married, black servicemen were again returning from war—this time WWII and like the WWI veterans before them, these servicemen "*return[ed] fighting.*"[52] Their insistence on the freedoms they had fought for abroad dovetailed with the rising expectations of equality engendered by New Deal era activism. By the time the Hamer's children were attending school, the *Brown v. Board of Education* decision had passed, though it would be another ten years before the ruling had any impact on Mississippi's segregated school structure. *Brown* did, however, have an immediate impact on white resistance to black organizing in the state.

During the 1950s, the National Association for the Advancement of Colored People (NAACP), the Regional Council of Negro Leadership (RCNL), and the Mississippi Progressive Voters League were the primary avenues for black empowerment, and their membership consisted of "the small number of middle-class blacks who had managed to remain financially independent of local whites."[53] Though Hamer did not fit within this narrow constituency, she was likely aware of their activity, and there is some evidence that she may have even been involved with the NAACP and the RCNL in a limited capacity throughout the 1950s.[54] Even with a relatively small constituency, the early civil rights organizations could boast impressive results; in the four-year period between "1948 and 1952, the number of black voters in the state nearly tripled, reaching twenty thousand."[55] Minor political gains made by middle-class blacks through voter-registration campaigns coupled with the Supreme Court's 1944 *Smith v. Allwright* decision, which outlawed the all-white Democratic primary, were somewhat tolerated by local whites up until the *Brown* ruling fundamentally challenged the segregated structure of their society.

In response to what segregationists branded "Black Monday"—May 17, 1954—the day the *Brown* verdict was handed down, Mississippi white supremacists banded together. Legislation swiftly passed that promoted white racial superiority through the educational system and permitted spying on Mississippi citizens by governmental agents serving the newly formed State Sovereignty Commission.[56] On July 11, 1954, Robert "Tut" Patterson, a Leflore County farm manager, WWII paratrooper, and Mississippi State University football star, "gathered the pillars of Indianola society to form a patriotic society dedicated to the preservation of white supremacy by legal means only."[57] This collective of well-educated prominent members of society—lawyers, bankers, and government officials—formed the Citizens' Council in Indianola, no more than thirty miles from Hamer's home in Ruleville. In the months following their inaugural meeting in the Delta, local council chapters formed all over the region, then the state, and soon Citizens' Councils could be found throughout the South; by October 1954, "the council claimed 25,000 dues-paying members."[58] Although the council never grew to represent a majority of southern citizens, "the organization did become the mouthpiece of southern defiance," posits historian Neil R. McMillen.[59]

Maintaining white dominance through the ideology of white supremacy was the common purpose binding councils across county and state lines. This ideology rested on those Social Darwinian beliefs that "Negroes were inherently different from Caucasians and that this difference, this hereditary inferiority, rendered them unsuitable for free association with white society."[60] Arguments about blacks' inherent criminal tendencies, the diseases they carried, and their lower intelligence all related back to what councilors contended were fundamental differences in the Caucasian and Negroid species.[61] They broadcast messages of racial difference in their own pamphlets and newsletters in addition to outlets like the *Jackson Daily News* and the *Clarion-Ledger*, two popular newspapers controlled by the Hederman press, which supported the council. National politicians, state legislators, local elected officials, psychologists, and sociologists promoting the segregationist agenda were also featured on the council's weekly radio and television show, *The Forum*. Throughout these varied media, the message that integration meant miscegenation was widespread; councilors exploited whites deep-seated fears when they suggested, "the way to the bedroom was through the schoolhouse door."[62]

Fears about miscegenation stoked by the council's pervasive propaganda coupled with anxiety concerning federal intervention spurred by the Supreme Court's *Brown* decision were most gruesomely manifest in the lynching of fourteen-year-old Emmett Till. A Chicago native, Till was visiting relatives in Money, Mississippi, during the summer of 1955, when he allegedly "wolf-whistled" at Carolyn Bryant, a white woman who was working alone in the grocery store she ran with her husband. Upon learning about the encounter, Roy Bryant and his half-brother J. W. Milam kidnapped Till from his uncle's home, tortured him, and disposed of his body in the Tallahatchie River. In the midst of her mourning, Mamie Till-Mobley sought purpose from the tragedy and displayed her son's mutilated corpse for the world to see—first during a two-day open-casket viewing at Roberts Temple Church of God in Chicago and later through the images of Till's disfigured face she permitted the *Jet* and the *Chicago Defender* to publish. News of Till's lynching and the widely publicized murder trial, which was held in Sumner, Mississippi, doubtlessly reached Hamer's plantation. Learning about Till's lynching and the historic attempt by the NAACP to prosecute his killers likely planted seeds of disgust and resistance in the hearts of the sharecroppers, just as it compelled people across the nation to commit themselves to the struggle for black freedom.

A longtime activist for black equality, Rosa Parks remembers that she was thinking of Till when she refused to give up her seat in Montgomery. Parks's bravery and the commitment of the majority of Montgomery's black citizens who carried out the thirteen-month boycott, from 1955 to 1956, was not unlike the bravery exhibited by the Little Rock Nine, who integrated Central High School in the face of Arkansas's National Guard in 1957. That same year, President Eisenhower signed into law the first civil rights legislation passed by Congress since Reconstruction. In 1960, college students began sitting in at lunch counters across the segregated South. Furthermore, the Congress for Racial Equality's (CORE) Freedom Rides and the violence with which the riders were subjected captured both national and international attention—shining a spotlight on the brutality with which segregation was enforced. The sit-ins and Freedom Rides are also significant because they brought a different type of movement for social change into Mississippi. These demonstrations inspired the formation of SNCC, which sought to organize a people's movement among Mississippi's masses of sharecroppers, domestics, and day laborers.[63] Until Hamer's path intersected with the burgeoning struggle for black equality surrounding her, however, she sought refuge from segregation's pervasive force in the black Baptist church and prayed that change would soon come.

LESSONS FROM PEW AND PULPIT

Like her mother and father, whom Hamer remembered singing spirituals in the plantation fields late into the evening when "they would be looking for something better," she, too, was brought up and sustained by the promise of the black Baptist church.[64] Amid all of the things blacks did not have in Mississippi, the church stands out as one thing that black Mississippians could, in Hamer's words, "really call our own."[65] And the parishioners relished this space, often spending three to four hours of their Sunday at church enjoying the freedom. Hamer's connection to the church ran deep. She was baptized in the Quiver River at the age of twelve and her Bible study at the Stranger's Home Baptist Church provided the sole avenue to continue formal learning after she left her one-room schoolhouse.

Fannie Lou's father, and his strong ties to the black Baptist church, further reinforced the lessons of self-respect and race pride Lou Ella Townsend taught her daughter. In addition to sharecropping, Mr. Townsend also served as a minister. As the child of a black Baptist preacher, Hamer was not unlike scores of notable male civil rights orators who grew up learning lessons from the Bible in their home and hearing their fathers preaching the Word from the pulpit. This familial connection to the church later revealed itself in her public addresses, as Hamer would often couple her mother's transformative lesson—that God intended for her to be black and that she should not covet the station of her white oppressor—with biblical verses such as Galatians 6:7, "Do not be deceived, God is not mocked; for whatever a man sows, that he will also reap" (NKJV). This biblical instruction, combined with her mother's wisdom, endowed Hamer with an abiding sense of divine justice, giving her the faith she needed to persevere in the face of gross inequality.

The biblical verses Hamer chose, which feature actions common to sharecroppers like sowing and reaping, also reflect her upbringing in a religious tradition that preferred "useful, concrete visions to learned abstractions."[66] The tradition of black preaching in the United States evolved within the context of slavery, which gave rise to a core set of common characteristics. Most noticeable among the characteristics Hamer adopted are an emphasis on relevant theology, content rooted in the "images and idioms of the people" and oriented toward meeting the daily needs of those parishioners enduring exploitative conditions. For generations, black preachers worked to establish a new orientation, understanding, or vision through their sermons, one that provided strength "for extended survival in an absurdly trying existence."[67] This orientation was often constructed by drawing upon biblical touchstones such as the Exodus narrative. A story of the Israelites' bondage in Egypt, their journey out of slavery, and onto the Promised Land where they enter into a covenant with God, the Exodus narrative is more than a tale of divine deliverance. It also provides a resource for oppressed persons to imagine overcoming the confines of institutionalized power and to see themselves as moral agents of change within a corrupt political system.[68]

Hamer's words both instructed and inspired through what her audience members describe as an unparalleled ability to "cast the struggle that blacks had against the role of the church in the human struggle."[69] This competency was likely cultivated within her particular religious community, as black Baptist preachers in the South were known for emphasizing the "practical rather than the theoretical aspect of Christian theology." As a collective, moreover, black Baptists also commonly relate "a relevant theology to slavery in the South and white racism throughout the nation."[70] During the course of Hamer's speaking

career, one can see traces of this influence as she was often praised for making biblical allusions "clear so that all could understand."[71] In her speeches to
black Mississippians, for example, Hamer would often draw connections to the
Exodus narrative that embodied this sense of relevant theology. "God made it
so plain," Hamer was fond of saying, "he sent Moses down in Egypt land to tell
Pharaoh to let my people go." Explicating the connection, she reasoned, "And
he made it so plain here in Mississippi the man that [is] heading the project is
named Moses, Bob Moses . . . He sent Bob Moses down in Mississippi, to tell
all of these hate groups to let his people go."[72] As Hamer interpreted it for her
audience, Bob Moses's presence in Mississippi was surely a sign from God that
deliverance was near. Relating the struggle in Mississippi to the Jews' struggle
in Egypt imbued the act of registering to vote, an incredibly risky endeavor for
black Mississippians, with even grander significance. Employing biblical typology this way, Hamer moved beyond illustration to prediction in such a manner that constructed a prophetic persona for herself, elevated the significance
of black Mississippians' civic struggle, and reassured her audience of the righteousness of their cause.[73]

The strength of Hamer's message lies not only in the content of the biblical types she adopted. Her fellow activists maintain that the depth of Hamer's
faith, conveyed through the delivery of her speech, was contagious. Central aspects of Hamer's delivery can be traced to her religious upbringing in the black
Baptist tradition. Though led by the preacher, the experience of worship for
most African American denominations developed as a communal participatory event propelled by both the rhythmic tonal quality of the preacher's call as
well as the parishioners' spontaneous responses. The call-and-response format
of the black church experience necessitates a flexible approach to preaching,
one that relies upon oral editing and impromptu redirection to meet the needs
and interests expressed by a particular audience in a given setting. If facilitated
successfully, the black preacher's sermon engenders an emotionally transcen-
dent experience—a temporary escape from the harsh realities defining the parishioners' existence.[74] Such an experience, though fleeting, is believed to "plant
the Word deep in the human consciousness" where it can grow to be "real and
life-changing."[75]

Those who witnessed Mrs. Hamer speak remember the experience vividly.
Owen Brooks, who worked for the United Church of Christ's Delta Ministry
during the civil rights movement, describes the experience: she "didn't just sing
about 'We shall overcome.' She believed. She believed it with all of her might."
Brooks elaborates, "She was able to make it clear for all who listened what she
stood for, what she in fact believed in, and that her faith was strong."[76] Central

to both the clarity and the long-lasting appeal of Hamer's messages was the fact that she "declared the gospel in the language and culture of the people—the vernacular." Employing the local vernacular is foremost among the principles of black preaching that create a transformative experience for the audience.[77] Because Hamer's rhetorical education developed outside formalized centers of higher learning, because it grew out of and represented the community from which she came, and because this community largely existed outside of, and often was set in opposition to, institutionalized centers of power, Hamer's discourse can be considered "vernacular" in several senses of the term.

Etymologically speaking, rhetorical scholar Robert Glenn Howard suggests, "the word 'vernacular' has its origins in the concept of 'the local' or 'home grown.'" In classical Greek, furthermore, the corresponding adjective is "*oiko-genes* or 'home-genetic.' For the Greeks and Romans, the marks of this 'home genetic' nature were found in the language with which a person spoke."[78] Describing Hamer's speech as vernacular in the sense of being "home grown" and located in the spoken word helps capture the southern black quality of her discourse. Her clearly discernable regional accent and phrases she commonly used like "raising Cain" are employed by southerners of all races.[79] The designation "black" acknowledges the aspects of Hamer's speech that reflect characteristics of African American Vernacular English (AAVE), including the consistent use of double-negation, over-pluralization, as well as use of the verbs "been" and "done" to indicate habitual or recently completed action.[80] Grammatical and lexical markers such as these combine with a distinct syntactical pattern, in which there is no marked beginning or end to sentences that are commonly linked to one another in a *hypotactic* fashion, with an abundance of connectives like "and" as well as "but."[81] These features, furthermore, support the trademark structural and stylistic elements of Hamer's rhetoric—including image making, testifying, mimicry, and verbal wit—all commonly observed aspects of AAVE.[82]

From its roots in the ancient Greek and Roman eras forward, however, vernacular has always meant more than just accent, colloquial phrases, speech patterns, syntactical, and stylistic features. As Howard observes, Cicero "understood the 'vernacular' as set in opposition to what he and other Roman politicians saw as the universalized and institutional elements of persuasive communication codified in textbooks." The vernacular "flavor," as Cicero described it, "existed and was learned outside of formal Roman education."[83] Because vernacular speech sits outside formal education, as a means of communication that is "commonplace" and "accessible to all," its use holds the potential to reaffirm a sense of shared knowledge and community.[84] By drawing upon the wells of cultural sentiment flowing through the sounds and style of the southern black vernacular, Hamer established her credibility among audiences of black Mississippians and her vernacular speech patterns also endowed her with a representative significance when she addressed crowds outside of her home state.

Both in terms of content—"a heritage of biblical teaching applied to this world"—and style "that came from the preachers down at the churches," posits Reverend Edwin King, Hamer's religious and cultural background echoed through her discourse.[85] Dorsey explains further that, the church functioned as a "training ground" for Hamer.[86] McLemore agrees, placing Hamer's experience within the larger context of southern African American culture. "Her experience was like so many experiences of African Americans in the South who were church-going people," McLemore clarifies, "you learn how to preside over meetings. You learn how to conduct meetings. You learn how to give a speech. You learn all of this stuff in the church . . . so she had all of that training."[87] Although her training was common to many African Americans who grew up in the South, and the biblical types she utilized were part of a shared black Baptist heritage, Hamer did emerge as a distinctive voice within her community. "She had a way that only a few people that I met had" of linking the struggle in Mississippi to the struggles of all oppressed peoples. "She was able to do that," Dorsey remembers specifically, "with her song."[88]

By adapting the songs and lessons she learned from her parents at home, in the fields, and as a parishioner and choir member in her Baptist church, Hamer's message and modes of delivery became highly sought after within movement circles. Just as in her speaking, Hamer did not sing to simply please an audience. Hamer, wrote one reporter, "sings as if the entire world depends on it."[89] Belafonte concurs: "I have got to always talk about Fannie Lou Hamer singing." He especially notes "the *power* of her voice because there was a mission behind it and in it."[90] Belafonte suggests that Hamer's use of song was fundamentally purposive, "I don't think there was ever a wasted hum when she sang."[91] The songs she became best known for were spirituals that she "reshaped into local statements," explains SNCC Freedom Singer and historian Bernice Johnson Reagon. Just as Hamer's speeches featured biblical teachings applied to contemporary phenomena, her songs utilized the familiar form and content of hymns to connect particular civil rights struggles to the larger human struggle for freedom. When Hamer sang the recognizable Christmas carol, "Go Tell it on the Mountain," for example, she changed the lyrics: "Go tell it on the mountain that Jesus Christ is born" to "Go tell it on the mountain to let my people go."[92] As Hamer sang it, the song held even greater salience for the civil rights movement: "Who's that yonder dressed in red? Must be the children that

Moses led."[93] Featuring Bob Moses's name in her speeches and songs "was a powerful way of articulating that this was surely a sign from God that it was time for Mississippi Negroes to move."[94] Hamer's rendition became the Mississippi movement anthem, as folklorist Worth Long recalls, each struggle could be identified with its own particular song and "the song in Mississippi was Fannie Lou Hamer's 'Go Tell it on the Mountain.'"[95]

On a more personal plane, Hamer often began the speeches she delivered at mass meetings with what became her signature song, "This Little Light of Mine." Reagon describes one mass meeting, in which, even "before she completed the first two phrases of the song, 'This little light of mine, I'm gonna let it shine,' she was joined by others in the congregation."[96] Hamer's songs not only conveyed political messages, they also created an atmosphere of connection among her listeners. The lyrics Hamer added to "This Little Light of Mine" further reveal core aspects of what she and others considered to be her prophetic purpose. Edwin King recalls how she built upon the verse "I've got the light of freedom," by adding "Jesus gave it to me. I *have* to let it shine." This addition, he explains, changed the tenor of song from "I've got it, *whoopee*, I'm going to let it shine" to "a much deeper thing."[97] The way Hamer amended "This Little Light of Mine" demonstrated her belief that she was given a gift and therefore had a responsibility to spread God's word. Hamer bolstered this assertion in her speeches with biblical references, often quoting Matthew 28:19: "Go therefore and make disciples of all the nations" (NKJV). This verse connected well to Luke 4:17–19, which she commonly invoked:

> The Spirit of the Lord is upon me, because He has anointed me to preach the gospel to the poor; he has sent me to heal the broken-hearted, to proclaim liberty to the captives, and recovery of sight to the blind, to set at liberty those who are oppressed, to proclaim the acceptable year of the Lord. (NKJV)

Taken together, these core verses express Hamer's belief that she had a divine responsibility to use her gifts of speech and song to bring about change in Mississippi.

Such a conviction inspired Hamer to take her speaking engagements quite seriously. Though she would rarely speak from a prepared manuscript, Hamer's apparent spontaneity should not be mistaken for careless speechmaking. In fact, careful consideration of her extant corpus of speech texts, in addition to the memories of those close to her composition process, suggest that Hamer critically and continuously thought about how she could best convey her message.[98]

She revised core aspects of her message over time and, like any good preacher, Hamer reflected often about how she could "give God her best"—commonly advancing the belief that "God will surely not do for us what we cannot do for ourselves."[99] This belief connected Hamer to generations of black preachers, even as it placed her within a long line of African American women activists who saw themselves as "doers of the Word."[100]

Armed with the conviction that she was spreading God's word, Hamer used speech and song to convey a message rooted in the equal dignity of all human beings, black and white alike. This was a religious belief, which was fundamentally democratic in nature and reconciliatory in practice. Though she was steadfast in her faith, expressed by Proverbs 14:34, that "righteousness exalts a nation but sin is a reproach to any people," and that "there is nothing covered that will not be revealed, nor hidden that will not be known," Hamer did not take refuge in the prospect of retributive justice (Luke 12:2, NKJV). She was not comforted by the idea that segregationists would be made to suffer for their treatment of blacks. Quite conversely, these scriptural references grounded her plea for white and black people to work together to solve the country's problems. From Greenwood, Mississippi, to Berkeley, California, Hamer could be heard informing audiences that God "has made from one blood every nation of men to dwell on all the face of the earth." This scripture, taken from Acts 17:26, tugged at the root of white supremacists' arguments against integration (NKJV). Countering such widely circulated supremacist claims as "God was a segregationist," manifest in the natural separation of the species, Hamer proclaimed the unity of the human race and the righteousness of integration.[101] She reasoned further: "a house divided against itself cannot stand and that same thing applies to America."[102] The emphasis Hamer placed on the interconnection of all human beings revealed the incongruity between segregation and Christianity, even as it mandated an interracial movement for social change. "Until we consider that all of us are God's children and we can work together and really have democracy in this country," Hamer predicted, "we're going to have problems, we're going to have riots, we're going to have, what you call, human sickness."[103] For these principled and pragmatic reasons, Hamer told an audience in Madison, "I never been hung up in all of my work in just fighting for the black." "Your freedom," she informed her predominantly white audience, "is shackled in chains to mine. And until I am free, you are not free either." Challenging them further, she suggested: "if you think you are free, you drive down in Mississippi with your Wisconsin license plate and you will see what I am talking about."[104]

While Hamer's adoption of many of the black preaching tradition's core sermonic characteristics—an abiding faith in divine justice, a pragmatic theology comprised of relevant connections to daily life and delivered in the community's vernacular—suggests an affinity to the church, the content of her speeches and songs occasionally belied this sentiment. "Christianity," Hamer explained, "is being concerned about your fellow man, not building a million-dollar church while people are starving right around the corner. Christ was a revolutionary person, out there where it was happening. That's what God is all about, and that's where I get my strength."[105] Hamer modeled her own activism after Christ's example and was quite critical of religion that conflicted with the Bible's basic teachings. Careful to note that she was "not anti-church" nor was she "anti-religious," Hamer admitted that she would often "get so disgusted with . . . chicken eatin' preachers"—those religious leaders who were well taken care of by their congregation and who were content to stay out of the risky movement for social change.[106] The phrase "chicken eatin' preachers" was an especial-ly relevant one for Hamer, as Moye notes that a preacher in her hometown of Ruleville refused to open his church doors to the movement until the women in his congregation "threaten[ed] his fried chicken."[107] Hamer tried a different tack: public shaming. "Every church door in the state of Mississippi should be open for these meetings," she told an audience of black sharecroppers in Indi-anola, "but preachers have preached for years what he didn't believe himself. And if he's willing to trust God . . . he won't mind opening the church door."[108] In light of her biblical knowledge, it seemed plain to Hamer that religious lead-ers, if they were true to their faith, would be vociferous advocates in the fight against discrimination.

Ironically, she observed, many of the clergy were too scared to stand up and speak out against segregation. Their reluctance revealed what Asch rec-ognizes as "the double-edged sword" of the black church in the rural South.[109] Inasmuch as parishioners like Hamer used lessons from the Bible to challenge segregation and imagine liberation, and even as the black-controlled church provided a transformative experience for its parishioners—a space where they could worship freely and control their own affairs—the institution was not en-tirely free from the specter of white dominance. Anthropologists and historians alike have noted, "Sunflower County planters supported black churches as a means of pacifying their laborers."[110] More than just an avenue to emphasize the biblical instruction propagated during slavery: "Bondservants, be obedient to those who are your masters according to the flesh . . . in sincerity of heart, as to Christ," Powdermaker recognized the church as a "conservative force, tending to relieve and counteract the discontents that make for rebellion" by providing "an antidote, a palliative, an escape" (Ephesians 6:5).[111] Furthermore, black preachers often relied on funding and protection to run their parishes, which bound these ministers to their white benefactors. This was especially the case in Mississippi. Dittmer argues that "employing religion as a means of social control and using black preachers to patrol the color line were tactics not peculiar to Mississippi, but the practice lingered there after it had begun to break down in other areas."[112] Dittmer chalks up the sticking power of this practice to the predominantly rural composition of the state and explains further that black Mississippi ministers on the whole were reluctant to act because those most likely to assume leadership posts were also those most susceptible to the "economic warfare that was the trade-in-stock of the Citizens' Council."[113] Regardless of the reasons for black preachers' reluctance to lead, Hamer remained outspoken about her disappointment in the church, offering criticism of the breach between what the clergy preached and what they practiced in her speeches, interviews, and even in one stanza of her "Go Tell it on the Mountain" rendition, in which she sang: "Who's that yonder dressed in black? Must be the hypocrites turning back / Let my people go."[114]

TRANSFERRING HER ABILITIES

Not all preachers and churches shied away from civil rights activity. While some high-profile ministers like Martin Luther King Jr. were leading marches, boycotting segregated establishments, and delivering grand orations that began capturing the nation's attention, other preachers like James Bevel were speaking in small rural churches and cultivating local leadership across the state of Mississippi. In the summer of 1962, members of the Council of Federated Organizations (COFO)—a coalition formed in February of that year and comprised of the major civil rights groups operating in the state, including the Southern Christian Leadership Conference (SCLC), SNCC, and CORE—traveled throughout Mississippi holding meetings in churches to inform local people of ways to secure their voting rights. These "mass meetings" were part and parcel of COFO's new strategy. As Dittmer recalls, "voter registration had been the staple of black political activism in Mississippi for nearly half a century" before COFO began their campaign in the Delta. The constituency COFO sought, however, was fundamentally distinguished from the target of past NAACP campaigns.[115]

Unlike the NAACP's decades-old strategy of developing leadership for their voter-registration campaigns among educated middle-class blacks, COFO targeted the masses of poor blacks living in the vast rural areas throughout the state. And unlike direct-action protests that were popular among the younger

generation of activists, Bob Moses—one of the initial SNCC activists to enter the Magnolia state—followed the advice of Greenwood native and veteran
organizer Amzie Moore, who suggested focusing on voting rights. As SNCC
soon learned, given the state's viciously racist and violently retaliatory climate,
in Mississippi, "voter registration was direct action."[116] Though dangerous, the
voter-registration approach made strategic sense—especially in places like Sunflower County, where blacks outnumbered whites two-to-one and yet "of the
more than 13,000 blacks eligible to vote, fewer than 200 were on the books."[117]
The Kennedy administration also supported a voting-rights focus over direct-
action campaigns. Eager to avoid the violence engendered by the Freedom
Rides, the Kennedy Justice Department pledged their support by promising to
accept collect calls "at any hour from civil rights workers involved in voter registration."[118] What's more, through the Voter Education Project (VEP), which
the administration helped establish, SNCC received the initial $5,000 it needed
for an expanded voter-registration drive across the Delta.[119]

To gather a base of support for this project, which began in June 1962, SNCC
followed longtime movement activist Ella Baker's model of cultivating grassroots leadership among locally respected community leaders. Baker, whom
Hamer celebrated as "the most important black leader in the United States,"
was largely responsible for undermining the traditional racial uplift ideology
rooted in oppressive class and gender hierarchies.[120] Working with SNCC activists, Baker persuaded "talented and educated young black people . . . to forfeit
their privileged claim to leadership of the race," and to "instead, defer to the
collective wisdom of sharecroppers, maids, and manual laborers."[121] As Baker's biographer, Barbara Ransby, also notes, "Her way of being a black woman
challenged men in SNCC to rethink manhood and masculinity, just as it gave
women in the movement a widened sense of their own possibilities as doers,
thinkers, and powerful social change agents." Baker's "uninhibited occupation
of predominately male spaces," for instance, provided "a different model of gender identities" within movement activism.[122] Baker's alternative mode of being
enabled SNCC activists to look past the traditionally defined role of leader as a
black male preacher and to see, for instance, Hamer's gift of linking the gospel
to present movement circumstances. Baker also held the firm conviction that
"the people should speak for themselves"—often contending: "it was not ur-
bane articulateness that was needed; the people who were suffering could say
it better."[123]

Rather than dominating the registration projects themselves, therefore,
SNCC fieldworkers like Moses, a Harvard-educated schoolteacher from New
York, or Charles McLaurin, a self-described "renegade" plucked from a Jackson

ghetto, would don overalls, work shirts, and boots as they entered rural communities in search of local leadership.[124] These fieldworkers learned time and again that the older people, independent farmers, struggling entrepreneurs, even those well into their seventies and too old to work, provided key points of entry to gain broader access to the larger community. SNCC organizer Sam Block remembers that after spending a good deal of time in Greenwood's "laundromats, grocery stores, pool halls, and juke joints," he discovered it was the "older people who were most receptive" to the topic of voter registration. He explains that adults in their fifties, sixties, and seventies "were angry, [they] were looking for somebody who could give form and expression to ideas and thoughts that they had in their mind for years."[125] What's more, they had slightly less to lose. By contrast, middle-aged ministers and teachers, the core of the black middle class, became targets for the Citizens' Councils' economic terrorism whenever they dared engage with SNCC fieldworkers.

Although older black Deltans' pent-up anger often overshadowed their trepidation, blacks of all ages and occupations had good reason to fear for their lives. As Dittmer put it, "standing up for your rights in southwest Mississippi could get you killed."[126] This ugly truth was woefully exposed during SNCC's previous campaign. In the fall of 1961, Herbert E. Lee a black farmer and father of nine, who was involved in the McComb voter-registration drive, was shot and killed in broad daylight. The fact that E. H. Hurst, a member of Mississippi's state legislature, shot Lee with impunity, made it plain to would-be activists and SNCC workers alike that one had to be willing to die to bring about social change in this state. "I wanted to challenge the status quo in some kind of way," McLaurin recounts his attitude of fearless determination; "I wanted to let white people know that there was one nigger who didn't mind challenging them. And I didn't care what the consequences were, whether I got killed or not."[127] Though not all of the community leaders SNCC cultivated were as fearless as fieldworkers like McLaurin, SNCC did search for well-respected local people who were sick of the system of segregation and who could also withstand the constant threat of white supremacist backlash.

In Ruleville, voter-registration fieldworkers found several such people. Longtime residents like Herman and Hattie Sisson, Robert and Mary Tucker, and Joe McDonald were among the first to welcome the young activists into their community. With the help of these brave and well-connected community leaders, COFO organized a mass meeting at William Chapel Missionary Baptist Church in Ruleville. Fannie Lou Hamer learned about this meeting during her Sunday service, when Reverend J. D. Story notified his parishioners that the first-ever mass meeting to be held in their town would take place at their church the following evening. However, it was not until Mrs. Mary Tucker encouraged Hamer to attend the meeting that the skeptical sharecropper took an interest. Tucker had been like a mother to Hamer in the time since Lou Ella Townsend passed, so when Tucker explained that mass meetings taught people about their rights and encouraged them to vote, Hamer agreed to talk it over with her husband.[128] Though initially leery of the danger surrounding voter registration, Fannie Lou consulted with Perry Hamer, who assured her that if the couple could pick enough cotton the next day, then he would accompany her to the meeting that evening.[129]

In the cotton fields on Monday, August 27, 1962, Fannie Lou Hamer labored determinedly to ensure that she could attend. When the Hamers entered their humble sanctuary that late summer evening, they were introduced to local and national civil rights activists like Amzie Moore, James Forman, Reggie Robinson, Bob Moses, and James Bevel. The meeting's agenda featured two orations, one religious and the other secular. Bevel began the program with the sermon portion, entitled "Discerning the Signs of the Time." Years later, Hamer recalled the moral of Bevel's oration: "He talked about how a man could look out and see a cloud and predict it's going to rain, and it would become so; but still he couldn't . . . tell what was happening right around him."[130] Bevel derived this theme from Luke 12:56, in which Jesus proclaims boldly: "Hypocrites! You can discern the face of the sky and of the earth, but how is it you do not discern this time?" (NKJV). As a native Mississippian and a trained Baptist theologian, Bevel used scripture to connect with his Ruleville audience, priming them with broad biblical instruction that Forman applied more directly to the immediate political situation they faced.[131]

After Bevel's sermon, "Jim Forman got up, and he talked about Voter Registration," Hamer remembered, "that was the next strange thing to me. I never heard about that."[132] She confessed that up until this moment, as a forty-four-year-old woman, she was unaware of her constitutional right to vote.[133] While it seems somewhat unbelievable that anyone living in the United States in 1962 would be unaware that African Americans could vote, McLaurin—who devoted his early adult life to promoting black suffrage in the Delta—explains the unawareness by pointing to the insular nature of plantation life. Like Mrs. Hamer, most black sharecroppers he met in the Delta were surprised to learn that Mississippi even had a constitution; "all people knew about Mississippi was racism, brutality, harassment, violence, intimidation—they never thought about Mississippi being a state." He reasons further, "because to them what was a state? The whole plantation they lived on was all-inclusive of everything they needed. The plantation owner owned them, in a sense." Elaborating on the paternalistic nature of the system, McLaurin specifies that the owner "was their boss man, he signed for them at the bank; he signed for them at the store; he saw to it that they had food and clothing; and he whooped their behinds when they acted up . . . All they knew was this man."[134]

Offering a slightly different explanation, Asch reasons that though television had "penetrated much of America" by 1962, and while radios were "prevalent on the plantation," Hamer might have been isolated from civil rights gains because sharecroppers "seldom had the time to listen to news broadcasts."[135] Given the closed nature of plantation society within the larger closed society of Mississippi, it seems possible that Hamer learned about black suffrage for the first time when Forman told the William Chapel parishioners "that we had a right to register and vote to become first class citizens" and that with the ballot "we could vote out people like hateful policemen." The idea that, through the vote, black Mississippians had the power to transform the exploitative conditions surrounding them really resonated with Hamer, who had previously remarked exhaustedly: "hard as we have to work for nothing, there must be some way we can change this."[136] To someone who had been looking for an opportunity to more boldly rebel against the sharecropping system, Bevel's and Forman's messages of hope "seemed like the most remarkable thing that could happen in the state of Mississippi."[137] After these two civil rights workers finished speaking, in fact, Hamer was among the eighteen people who raised their hands, indicating her willingness to try to register at the county courthouse that Friday.

On Friday, August 31, 1962, eighteen of Ruleville's black residents boarded an old school bus for the twenty-six-mile trip to the Indianola courthouse. Upon their arrival in the county seat, Cecil Campbell, the county registrar, informed the group that they would have to pass a literacy test before registering. Literacy tests, like the grandfather clause, poll taxes, and the widespread practice of publishing registration applicants' names in the newspaper, were strategies that white leaders devised at Mississippi's constitutional convention of 1890, in an attempt to curtail political advances made by blacks during Reconstruction. Though seemingly "race-neutral on the surface," the new Mississippi Constitution effectively "made black voting a thing of the past."[138] In the spirit of their grandparents' generation—a generation in which newly freed blacks exercised their freedom by voting in droves and electing blacks to such posts as lieutenant governor, secretary of state, and Speaker of the House of Representatives—the Ruleville registration hopefuls marched forward.[139] Two at a time, the applicants were given exams, which involved reading section sixteen of the Mississippi Constitution, copying it, and providing an interpretation of the passage that met the registrar's approval.

Hamer, who was one of the first two people to attempt this exercise in futility, remembered that the constitutional passage dealt with *de facto* laws. "And I knowed as much about a facto law," admitted Hamer, "as a horse knows about Christmas Day."[140] While the other Ruleville sharecroppers tried their hands at the test, Campbell called in police from the neighboring city of Cleveland. By four o'clock that afternoon, when Hamer and the others boarded their bus for the return trip to Ruleville, they were surrounded by more "policemen with dogs and guns" than they had ever seen before.[141] Warily, the bus took off toward Ruleville only to be stopped several miles down the road by a state highway patrolman and a city police officer. The group was ordered back to Indianola where the bus driver was charged with "driving a bus the wrong color." The policeman argued that the bus was "too yellow" and thus resembled a school bus. Ironically, the same vehicle had been used for years to drive migrant workers to and from Florida without incident. Initially the driver's charge was coupled with a $100 fine, but this was soon reduced to $50, and then to $30, which the eighteen passengers were able to gather.[142]

Hamer's trip to the Indianola courthouse, her initial foray into civil rights activity, conveys the harassment and intimidation that commonly befell African Americans who exerted their constitutional rights in the state of Mississippi. Recognizing the way in which her personal story functioned as a gauge of the larger political climate, Hamer included this anecdote in many speeches, most famously in her 1964 testimony before the credentials committee at the DNC. Through this experience of intimidation, Hamer's strength as a local leader also became apparent. McLaurin, who accompanied the Ruleville group to the Indianola courthouse, remembers how anxious and scared people became once the police began to surround them. Some worried that they would be put in jail; others expressed their eagerness to return to the relative safety of their homes. "In the midst of all this grumbling," he remembers, "a voice, a song, a church song, just kind of smoothly came out of the group."[143] Charles Cobb, a SNCC organizer originally from Washington, DC, shares a similar recollection. "From the back of the bus this powerful voice broke out in song. I remember hearing 'this little light of mine' and 'ain't gonna let nobody turn me 'roun.'" The voice, Cobb clarifies, "was Mrs. Hamer, until then, just one of 17 or 18 people . . . With the power of her voice alone she shored up everybody on the bus."[144] As both McLaurin's and Cobb's reflections intimate, Hamer's adept use of song distinguished her as a leader, capable of both inspiring people to act and reinvigorating them in the face of fear and disappointment. In this tense moment, Hamer, like her mother before her, used the power of song to distract the group from the fear they faced and to assure them that God was on their side. In this moment, Hamer also offered a glimpse into the leadership abilities she had been cultivating on the plantation and in her church for years.

When Hamer made it home that night, her family informed her that the plantation owner was infuriated by her registration attempt. Their words of warning quickly jogged Hamer's memory. She recalled that on the top of the registration test she filled out that day, Campbell had asked her to write the date, her full name, and "to whom [she] was employed," which, she now knew, "mean' you would be fired by the time you got back home."[145] The fact that Marlow knew about Hamer's registration effort even before she returned to his plantation suggests that he received a phone call from the registration office. The phone call, in turn, conveys just how threatened white Mississippians were by the prospect of black voters, how organized they were in response to the challenge, and how white supremacy bound the freedom of even its supposed beneficiaries—Marlow had little choice in the matter of firing one of his best employees. Before long, Marlow arrived at the relatively nicer plantation dwelling he reserved for his timekeeper and tractor driver and told Fannie Lou that she needed to withdraw her registration paperwork, informing her that if she did not withdraw the application she would have to leave his property. "Then if you go down and withdraw," he continued, "you still might have to go because we are not ready for that in Mississippi." To which Hamer boldly retorted: "I didn't try to register for you. I tried to register for myself."[146]

She later explained that she did not intend for her reply to come off as "nothing smart," but that she simply "answered in the only way [she] could."[147] In fact, her response quite cleverly carried forth the meaning of an old spiritual her parents sang when she was a child. Hamer recounted the lyrics of this song in an interview, noting, "this song seemed like this would be about the way they felt when they would have to stand a test before they could cross the river Jordan . . . I'm going down to the river of Jordan / Yes, I'm going down there for myself. There's nobody else that can go there for me / I'm going down there for myself. Oh, I got to stand my test in the judgment / Oh, I got to stand it for myself. There's nobody here that can stand it for me / I've got to stand it for myself."[148] Perhaps the test Hamer struggled through that day, with the possibility of political power hanging in the balance, reminded her of these lyrics from her childhood and gave her the strength to respond assertively to the enraged plantation owner. Whatever the source of her brazen behavior, Hamer's retort incited Marlow to fire her on the spot. He ordered Hamer to immediately leave the plantation where she had labored for the last eighteen years, the community of workers among whom she had risen to a position of leadership, and the home she made with Pap while caring for her mother and raising two children.

Although Marlow sought to deter Hamer from pursuing the vote by punishing her, his actions bound her closer to the movement, enabling her to devote all of her energy to civil rights activity. Being banished from his plantation was undoubtedly devastating for Hamer. Getting fired, explains Ambassador Andrew Young, did, however, give "Hamer the freedom to become a voter registration worker and leader."[149] In 1962, Young was working as an administrator for the United Church of Christ, which had recently aligned itself with the Highlander Folk School's citizenship program. Young's duties as administrator included "recruiting people for the citizenship training centers," developed by Septima Clark at Highlander in Tennessee and later held in Dorchester, Georgia. To find trainees, Young would drive "across the South looking for people who had PhD minds, but who had never had an opportunity to get an education." "There are people like that in every community," he asserts; "there are people who are really bright that everybody looks up to for their opinions, but they may not have had any formal training or schooling. Mrs. Hamer was that way."[150]

Movement mentors like Septima Clark, the SCLC's education director who had long shared Baker's passion and radical vision for empowering the masses, encouraged Hamer to recognize her own potential. Clark's program for social change took shape in literacy-based citizenship pedagogy oriented toward poor uneducated blacks who were brave enough to accept the risks associated with civil rights activism. Clark worked to build these budding activists' confidence through improved literacy with the hope that they would, in turn, become leaders and teachers within their own communities. Outlining her alternative approach to empowerment, Clark contended: "I don't think that in a community I need to go down to city hall and talk," she explained further, "I think I train the people in that community to do their own talking . . . I would not have ever been able to work in Mississippi and Alabama and all those places if I had done all the talking."[151] SNCC members who worked closely with Mrs. Hamer adopted this approach; Hamer remembers McLaurin, in particular, being "so forceful" in his affirmation of her ability that he made her believe "you're somebody, you're important."[152] By empowering, enabling, and allowing the people in the local communities they served to do the talking, visionaries like Baker and Clark challenged the prevailing sexist and classist conceptions of leadership within the black freedom movement and, in so doing, paved the way for a different type of activist—older, female, impoverished, and not formally educated—to emerge.

The COFO activists who came into Hamer's small Delta town were well versed in Baker's and Clark's radical visions of social change. They quickly recognized that Hamer had the trust of her fellow sharecroppers, that she had the confidence to speak widely about the injustices she endured, and that her discourse conveyed a vernacular flavor, which represented not just the speech patterns of her local community, but their shared experiences, viewpoints, and modes of reasoning as well. Exiled from the Marlow plantation and threatened by members of Ruleville's white community, Hamer committed herself to bettering her life and the lives of those around her. And movement organizers needed someone like Hamer, a brave and well-respected local leader from whom they could learn about the community's needs and with whom they could work to encourage civil rights activity. Hamer's vernacular education and the Mississippi movement's reoriented focus on cultivating grassroots leadership converged to secure an initial platform for her rhetorical expression.

CONCLUSION

A closer look at Hamer's formative years in the Mississippi Delta helps explain how she achieved a platform for her expression. Though Hamer did not have the luxury of much formal education, the rhetorical education she received from her family, her work on the plantation, and her connection to the black Baptist church imbued her with confidence, a keen understanding of race relations, and a mastery of biblical allusion. Hamer needed a crash course in citizenship rights when she first became active in the Mississippi struggle, but she brought to the cause a shared background from which to craft appeals to Delta blacks and an intimate familiarity with the rhetorical styles through which to best deliver these arguments. What's more, because she was reared in a tradition of resistance to dominant white supremacist ideologies she knew how to confront and challenge their oppressive logic. The early relationship between Hamer and the movement was precisely the type of symbiotic bond envisioned by longtime activists like Baker and Clark: Hamer learned about her rights and means to secure them from more seasoned movement participants. In return, those activists learned about life in the Mississippi Delta, about how to best undermine the pervasive white supremacist ideology, and about how to inspire rural communities from Hamer.

Hamer was initially launched into the limelight of the civil rights movement because of her life experiences growing up as a child of sharecroppers on a Mississippi plantation, with little formal education, but a nuanced understanding of divine justice and a belief in the equality of all people—and not in spite of these defining qualities. Her rhetoric reflected her connection to the spaces of invention she inhabited, as the education she received would echo through the substance of her discourse for the remainder of her activist career. Alongside the content of her testimony, vernacular aspects of her delivery also functioned as arguments about injustice and exclusion that conveyed many other African Americans' experiences.

Chapter 2, "Through the Shadows of Death, 1962–1964," explores Hamer's representative nature through the analysis of her early speeches, testimonies, campaign platforms, and grassroots activity. From August 1962, when she first realized her political subjectivity, to August 1964, when she delivered her famous testimony before the credentials committee at the DNC, Hamer wove the verbal and visual aspects of her vernacular identity into an appeal for representation—using her experiences to represent the simultaneous need for southern black civic assertion and for federal intervention into Mississippi politics. White supremacist retaliation to Hamer's early activism drew her closer to the movement, even as she used this suffering to enrich her personal narrative. "Through the Shadows of Death" explicates the finer points of what became Hamer's Jeremiadic rhetorical signature, as it was constructed against a backdrop of both organizational support and virulent white supremacist resistance.

CHAPTER 2

Through the Shadows of Death, 1962–1964

"'THE SPIRIT OF THE LORD IS UPON ME BECAUSE HE HAS ANOINTED ME TO preach the gospel to the poor. He has sent me to heal the brokenhearted, to preach deliverance to the captive . . . to set at liberty to them who are bruised, to preach the acceptable year of the Lord.'" This verse, taken from the fourth chapter of Luke, serves as both the introduction to Fannie Lou Hamer's first recorded speech and as her personal conviction for joining the ranks of prophetic movement orators. Addressing an audience of black Deltans at a Freedom Vote rally in Greenwood, Mississippi, in the fall of 1963, Hamer testified to God's grace and challenged those in her community to interpret the signs of change that surrounded them. Like most Delta sharecroppers, Hamer's life was filled with suffering. Hard work, hunger, and racist oppression were mainstays of her existence. "But all them things was wrong, you see," she contended. Out of despair, Hamer admitted, "I have asked God, I said, 'Now Lord'—and you have too—ain't no need to lie and say that you ain't," she admonished those who might outwardly scoff at her desperate plea. "Said, 'Open a way for us.' Said, 'Please make a way for us, Jesus . . . where I can stand up and speak for my race and speak for these hungry children.' And he opened a way and all of them mostly backing out." The opened way was "so plain" for Hamer to see—"He sent a man in Mississippi with the same name that Moses had to go to Egypt. And tell him to go down in Mississippi and tell [Governor] Ross Barnett to let my people go." Hamer interpreted the presence of SNCC leader Bob Moses, along with the scores of fieldworkers and college students he enlisted, as an answer to her prayers.

Hamer told the audience of black Deltans that voter-registration work was "working for Christ," and suggested that God had both provided for her and protected her since she began "fighting for freedom." Drawing upon the biblical knowledge she shared with this audience—most of whom were reared in the black Baptist tradition—Hamer explained: "it's kind of like in the twenty-third of Psalms when he says, 'Thou prepareth a table for me in the presence of my enemies. Thou anointed my head with oil and my cup runneth over.'" Hamer's basic needs were met by movement organizations, and fighting for freedom was much more gratifying work than sharecropping, but she was never one to gloss over the dangerous aspects of voter-registration advocacy when persuading others to join the cause. "I have walked through the shadows of death," she informed them, "on the tenth of September '62 when they [white supremacist night riders] shot sixteen times in a house and it wasn't a foot over the bed where my head was. But that night I wasn't there—don't you see what God can do?" Hamer did not interpret threats on her life as signs that she should abandon civil rights activism or as proof that God was not on her side; even when she "was beat in a jailhouse until [she] was hard as metal," Hamer espoused scripture to her assailants and remained convinced that God spared her life so she could share her experience. She boldly attested, "I never know today what is going to happen to me tonight, but I do know as I walk alone, I walk with my hand in God's hand."

White supremacist retaliation to black attempts at civic engagement did not deter Hamer's activism; instead, their resistance underscored the need to keep on fighting. "You know the ballot is good," she reasoned. "If it wasn't good how come he trying to keep you from it and he still using it?" The sheer number of whites outraged by increased black registration activity and the presence of guards and dogs to bar blacks from participating in the democratic process only stressed the significance of the vote. "Now if that's good enough for them, I want some of it too," Hamer insisted during the rally.[1]

Blending the sacred and the secular during this particular meeting in the SNCC-headquartered town of Greenwood, Hamer helped convince droves of people to cast ballots in the Mississippi Freedom Vote election. This mock election, the joint creation of Moses and Allard Lowenstein—a well-connected white Democratic Party liberal from New York, who borrowed the idea from mock elections he observed in South Africa—was designed to dramatize the fact that disenfranchised Mississippi blacks would cast ballots if given the opportunity. And it worked. Nearly 80,000 people voted for the alternative candidates SNCC ran in the election lasting between November 2 and 4, 1963. Beyond the immediate success of this demonstration, the long-range canvassing and organizing work that COFO was conducting across the Delta combined with mass meeting speeches, like the one Hamer delivered at the Freedom Vote rally, were beginning to reshape the self-conceptions of Delta blacks. "Fannie Lou Hamer," suggests Moye, "had a unique ability to define the problems that affected African Americans in the Delta in their own vernacular. Hamer was a leader awaiting a movement," he insists, "and she . . . settled into the role of what one magazine termed 'The Prophet of Hope for the Sick and Tired.'"[2] This chapter explores the initial phase of Hamer's prophetic outreach, describing how she became a symbol for the "sick and tired," analyzing the discourse that helped construct her symbolic status, and considering how this status worked toward the rhetorical purposes of the burgeoning movement for black freedom in the Mississippi Delta.

Rooted in the core themes of Hamer's first recorded speech—that the black freedom movement was divinely mandated to free southern blacks from racist oppression, and that God would provide for as well as protect those who "let their light shine" by participating in the movement—Hamer developed a *Jeremiadic* appeal.[3] Her overarching claim that black activism was vital to the nation's survival relied upon the argument that the oppressed, by virtue of their subjugation, possess experiential wisdom and, hence, moral authority. Hamer extended the biblically rooted conviction that "unearned suffering is redemptive" from generations of African American activists who came before her. As did Hamer, these activists reconciled their reality of enslavement and subsequent discrimination with their Christian faith by championing the "social messianic" potential of the "rejected and disinherited."[4] The biblical parallel upon which Hamer drew to make sense of her oppressed existence was the Exodus narrative and, more specifically, the belief that bondage in Egypt provided the Israelites a training ground, "schooling the soul," for the reparative work that lay ahead. In *Exodus and Revolution*, philosopher Michael Walzer notes that Egyptian oppression has also been characterized as an "iron furnace," interpreted in the rabbinic tradition as "a cauldron for refining precious metals: what emerges . . . is pure gold." Hamer's faith, that "spiritedness is born from affliction," dovetailed with the logic underpinning SNCC's radically democratic approach to civil rights advocacy in the nation's most segregated state.[5]

Just as Hamer likened her experience in Mississippi to the Israelites' enslaved existence in Egypt, black freedom movement activists also recognized Mississippi as the worst state with regard to its treatment of African Americans and held it up as "the standard by which this nation's commitment to social justice would be measured."[6] Influenced by their mentor, Ella Baker, and by their training at the Highlander and Dorchester Centers for Citizenship Education, SNCC fieldworkers believed that those who had endured this unjust treatment, "the oppressed themselves, collectively, already have much of the knowledge needed to produce change."[7] SNCC's role in Mississippi, therefore, was to empower the oppressed to recognize their own potential, to teach them how to analyze the conditions that kept them bound, and to work collectively with local people to find solutions. The ballot became the primary symbol of empowerment for the protracted rhetorical encounter known as canvassing. As movement historian Wesley C. Hogan describes in *Many Minds, One Heart: SNCC's Dream for a New America*:

The Freedom Ballot had been useful at the local level, as volunteers can-vassed house-to-house persuading people to envision themselves as voters. At that point, Afro-Mississippians became citizens in their own minds and gave substance to that transformation by attending small community meet-ings at local churches or halls. There, people learned how to act as if they were free to act as full citizens.[8]

Hogan alludes to the rhetorical elements of canvassing in her description of the practice. Fieldworkers engaged in *conversations* with local people using the ballot as a *symbol* to *persuade* them; this persuasion materialized when Delta blacks began attending movement meetings where they were exposed to more discourse in the form of speeches and songs, which taught about citizenship and inspired them to take action.

The emphasis Hogan places on the contingent and experimental nature of SNCC's activity also underscores rhetoric's vital role in this organizing tradi-tion. "The young people of SNCC," she writes, "invented particularly ingenious experiments in freedom. In so doing, they caught a glimpse of an America not-yet lived."[9] Her description of local people "acting as if they were free to act as full citizens," and her emphasis on invention and the "glimpse of an America not-yet lived," suggest that SNCC operated in a realm of contingent possibil-ity. This is rhetoric's realm. Rhetoric operates in the midst of contingency, it is concerned with what is possible; it is an art, writes rhetorical scholar Thomas B. Farrell, "not of being but of becoming."[10] SNCC's activity in the Delta was fundamentally rhetorical in the senses that the organization featured symbols like the ballot, the constitution, and the example of local people like Mrs. Ham-er, during their persuasive encounters such as canvassing and mass meetings, to constitute black Deltans as citizens of the United States. Such an identity sought to empower local people in a manner that would transform their self-conceptions from victims of an oppressive system to agents of change within a more just nation. Such a transformation rested upon the belief that, by virtue of their subjugation, black Mississippians held the wisdom necessary to under-mine segregation and, in so doing, to democratize the nation.

As SNCC enlarged its voter-registration campaign across the state of Mis-sissippi, the organization targeted multiple audiences. They sought to persuade blacks to overcome their fear and to act as citizens; they challenged white seg-regationists' exclusive grip on the franchise; and they urged the federal gov-ernment to live up to its ideals. Hamer was pivotal to each of these efforts, concurs Asch: "As a sharecropper-turned-voter, she became a vivid symbol of what SNCC believed Mississippi blacks could achieve; as a candid and forceful

speaker, she articulated the moral imperative of the movement often more effectively than SNCC's organizers could." "[O]ne of Hamer's most important
contributions to SNCC," Asch notes furthermore, "was her ability to articulate
the depths of Delta suffering to people outside the region."[11]

Hamer's early relationship with civil rights organizations, thus, conveys a
clear convergence of interests. In working within the movement, Hamer became educated about her rights and ways to secure them, thereby discovering
the very opportunity she had been searching for to challenge the exploitative
system of white supremacy. Likewise, in Hamer, civil rights organizations found
an activist who could work with local community members to inspire change
and who could also garner support from national audiences, as she symbolically represented the masses of disenfranchised and dissatisfied blacks—the
new constituency that activists in Mississippi were organizing. SNCC provided
Hamer a platform for her expression while historians and activists alike agree
that she "conferred legitimacy" on the organization; her "presence gave SNCC
efforts authenticity and inspiration."[12]

From the fall of 1962, when Hamer became SNCC's oldest fieldworker,
through the end of the summer in 1964, when she departed for the DNC in
Atlantic City, she joined the battle against the system of white supremacy by
advocating voter registration, by testifying in a federal trial against state officials who used violence to deter her activism, and by opposing the Second
Congressional District's representative in Mississippi's primary election. Hamer
also helped train Freedom Summer volunteers, while inspiring Delta blacks to
overcome their fears and assert their rights as US citizens. Records from the
first two years of her activist career, including transcripts of her testimonies,
campaign and movement speeches, interviews, and eyewitness accounts of her
grassroots efforts to encourage voter registration, suggest that whether Hamer
was addressing Mississippi sharecroppers or attorneys from the Department
of Justice, she represented her history of oppression, her ongoing experiences
of exclusion, and the violent retaliation she suffered at the hands of white supremacists. By telling her story, Hamer inspired Mississippi blacks who had
been intimidated into submission for centuries. Toward national audiences less
familiar with the extent of this oppression, her message provided perspective
about the rampant "deprivation and dissatisfaction" in the Magnolia state.[13]

By using her life experiences to connect to local blacks and to expose the
brutal, illegal, and unconstitutional conditions under which blacks suffered to
national audiences, Hamer developed a vernacular persona. The image of herself that Hamer featured in her speeches is best described as a persona because
it is a mediated implied presence. As rhetorical scholar Karlyn Kohrs Campbell

posits, the "culturally available subject positions" rhetors occupy are themselves "constituted and constrained by externals that are material and symbolic," and thus the concept of "*personae . . .* comes closest to capturing the shifting but central character of the roles we assume in the plays in which we participate."[14] Like *ethos*, which rhetorical scholars from Aristotle onward have recognized largely as a symbolic construction, Hamer's persona is not a static given; rather, it is something she continuously built, reiterated, and reinvented through rhetoric.[15] Moreover, Hamer linked this vernacular persona—the image of herself as an oppressed other sitting outside of, and in opposition to, formalized institutions—to the deeper cultural resonances of the Exodus narrative and its Jeremiadic extension in a manner that transformed the experience of powerlessness into a source of moral authority and experiential wisdom. The first two years of her civil rights activism provide the opening salvo to this complex rhetorical strategy, which develops over the course of her career into a powerful Jeremiadic appeal.

RACIAL ADVANCEMENT AND RETALIATION

From the moment Hamer attempted to register on that fateful Friday afternoon in August 1962, she became a prime target of white supremacist terror. After she was fired from Marlow's plantation, she sought refuge with friends in Ruleville. Robert and Mary Tucker, the elderly couple who arranged the mass meeting at William Chapel on the night of Hamer's political awakening, welcomed her into their home until Perry (Pap) Hamer began to fear for his wife's safety. Mr. Hamer was forced to remain on the Marlow plantation through the harvest or else sacrifice the couple's belongings (and risk imprisonment) as payment for the lost work. Mississippi native, personal friend, and fellow SNCC activist Dorie Ladner recognizes that this separation happened "almost at gunpoint," because "Mrs. Hamer was strictly a family person. She loved her Pap dearly."[16] For Pap to be required to stay on the Marlow plantation after Fannie Lou had been fired was a cruel punishment indeed, but his position on the plantation did prove serendipitous. One afternoon he noticed newly purchased buckshot shells in the plantation's maintenance shop. Fearing that the shells were intended to hunt down his wife and not meant for any game this early in the hunting season, he convinced Fannie Lou to take their two daughters and flee to her niece's home in Tallahatchie County.[17] Pap's suspicion, fueled in large part by the retaliatory campaign of terror ravaging their small town, was well founded. "On the 10th of September 1962," Hamer famously recalled two years later in her nationally televised testimony before the credentials committee, "sixteen bullets was fired into the home of Mr. and Mrs. Robert Tucker for me." "That same night," just days after Hamer left town, "two girls were shot in Ruleville, Mississippi."[18] Marylene Burks and Vivian Hillet, the two victims to whom Hamer would often refer when recounting her own narrow escape from terror, were visiting their grandparents, Herman and Hattie Sisson. "Burks was shot in the head; Hillet was wounded in the arms and the legs" by the same occupants of the speeding car that had fired shots into and then fled the nearby McDonald home.[19]

The shootings sent chills through Ruleville's black community, freezing the budding registration campaign. Since the organized Delta campaign began in June 1962, SNCC fieldworkers like Charles Cobb and Charles McLaurin had encouraged close to fifty local blacks to try their hand at voter registration. But after the early September shooting, nobody wanted to be seen talking to SNCC workers and it was months, remembers Cobb, until they could convince anyone to try to register. Local blacks' leeriness of civil rights activity was only compounded by the end of the month when white supremacist backlash to federal intervention reached a fever pitch. In September 1962, James Meredith's integration of the University of Mississippi left the Oxford campus in shambles. Two people were killed, nearly two hundred injured, and it took twenty-three thousand soldiers to quell the riots spurred by white segregationist resistance to Meredith's admission.

To regain black Deltans' confidence and help overcome their fears of white retaliation, SNCC workers remained in the community and dug into local affairs. When they found that no one was willing to talk to them on their front porches or attend meetings at local churches, Cobb and McLaurin offered to take people to the store in town, to help them pick cotton, or to chop wood. The larger act of staying in the community coupled with the smaller everyday interactions that this proximity afforded helped establish SNCC's ethos, a touchstone in any persuasive encounter. These actions conveyed a spirit of goodwill, trustworthiness, and commitment to the local community, which imbued the voter-registration project with credibility. SNCC workers "gradually, very gradually," movement scholar Charles M. Payne suggests, won "back the town's confidence."[20]

While Cobb and McLaurin were embedding themselves into the Ruleville community, Hamer was living in exile. Fired from her job, evicted from her home, and scared for her life, Hamer and her daughters began picking cotton on the plantation where her niece worked. This is where McLaurin found Hamer and convinced her to accompany him to a civil rights meeting in Nashville. On a stormy night in a little cabin at the top of a hill in the small town of Sumner, McLaurin located the woman who had motivated the Ruleville group of registration hopefuls and who later calmed them through song. To McLaurin's surprise, Hamer was eager to accompany him to the SNCC rally. Taking only a few moments to gather her belongings, almost as if she had been expecting him, Hamer left her life of exile and traveled on with McLaurin first to Tougaloo College and then to the conference at Fisk University in Nashville, Tennessee.

On their way to Tougaloo, McLaurin remembers inquiring curiously: "Mrs. Hamer, how did you know I was coming?" To which she unabashedly replied: "God sent you." McLaurin admits that her reply "scared the hell out of me!" And he corrected her, "Bob Moses sent me." Hamer remarked consistently, "Well, he told Bob to tell you to come."[21] Hamer had long believed that God was on the side of the oppressed and her upbringing in the black Baptist tradition taught her to look for signs of God's will in everyday life. To Hamer, McLaurin's ability to track her down at her niece's cabin in Tallahatchie County was surely a sign that the time for exile was over. This was a realization that Hamer had reached even before McLaurin arrived. Vergie remembers how miserable the living conditions were in Sumner. It was cold and the house where they stayed was drafty. She would cry out in the middle of the night to her mother, "I want to go home; I miss my Dad." And even though the separation from Pap was painful for Hamer as well, she tried to assure her homesick daughter that "it's going to be alright."[22] Hamer also objected to the exile on principle. She believed that she was in the right and should not be the one hiding out like a criminal. By the time McLaurin came, Hamer's practical desires to reunite their family, her principled objections to the forced separation, and her strong spiritual belief in the righteousness of the struggle compelled her to leave the relative safety of an anonymous life in Tallahatchie County.

The conference McLaurin brought Hamer to was organized by SNCC for local leaders whom registration fieldworkers discovered in communities across the South. Hamer was invited to attend, in particular, "because of her singing and her ability to communicate."[23] Once she arrived in Nashville, Hamer did not disappoint. Young activists and older local leaders alike were eager to hear her sing and to learn about the retaliation she endured after attempting to register. Beyond sharing her own story, Hamer learned from the student activists, as she attended a politics and voting workshop that engaged the "topics of nonviolence, communications, and economics."[24] Hamer became so comfortable amid this group that, immediately following the Nashville rally, she went on touring college campuses, speaking and singing to raise awareness and money for SNCC.

During her time on the road, Pap worked the harvest on Marlow's plantation and was able to reunite with his wife when she returned to Ruleville. The Hamer family took up residence at 626 East Lafayette Street, a small three-room white house near William Chapel with no indoor plumbing, but with a screened porch and a large pecan tree in the front yard. A little over two months after those sixteen bullets left their mark a foot over the Tucker's guest bed, Hamer was back in Ruleville telling her fellow Mississippians to "quit running around trying to dodge death because this book said: 'he that seeketh to save his life, he's going to lose it anyhow.'" While in Sumner, Hamer had reached the conclusion that "as long as you know you going for something, you put up a life that it can be like Paul, say 'I fought a good fight.' And 'I've kept the faith.'" Rather than protect herself from white segregationists' violence by remaining in exile, or by living under their radar in Ruleville, she decided to "fight the good fight," which, for Hamer, meant securing citizenship rights.[25]

Armed with this renewed sense of determination and supported by SNCC workers like McLaurin and Cobb, Hamer helped revitalize the voter-registration campaign in Ruleville. She returned to the Indianola courthouse the day after she and her family moved into town. "We moved in on the third of December," Hamer remembered, "and I went back on the fourth of December to take the literacy test again."[26] This time Hamer was presented with section forty-nine of the Mississippi constitution, which deals with the Mississippi House of Representatives. Just as before, the registrar asked her to copy the passage and provide a "reasonable interpretation." Although she was able to copy the selected passage during both of her registration attempts, this second time Hamer felt far more comfortable interpreting the text because she had been studying the Mississippi constitution with SNCC workers. In some recollections, Hamer explained that the studying paid off as she passed the literacy test, becoming only the sixth black registered voter in Ruleville, on this, her second try.[27]

In other recollections, however, Hamer's account of her success is more realistically mindful of the fraudulent registration system that was set up to keep blacks powerless, not to reward competence. In these accounts, her successful registration attempt is linked to a promise she made to the Indianola registrar. "You'll see me every 30 days till I pass," she informed him with allegedly convincing determination, as she was never pressed to make good on that threat.[28] Regardless of the cause—whether the studying did indeed pay off or the registrar simply did not want to deal with Hamer each month—her success at the registrar's office and her renewed determination to combat oppression helped revitalize SNCC's voting-rights campaign, which soon saw a marked increase in registration hopefuls. "In February 1963 alone," observes Moye, "400 Ruleville residents traveled to Indianola to take the registration test."[29]

Motivating poor black Mississippians to risk their jobs and to put their lives and the livelihood of their families on the line, Hamer admitted was "really rough" and often "very disappointing" work.[30] She traveled around the Delta talking with black sharecroppers who expressed interest in learning about their citizenship rights only to return to their community days later and find that these people had been threatened by their bosses and warned not to talk to her. Similarly, SNCC would hold mass meetings at local churches and then those churches would be firebombed or stripped of their tax-exempt status.

Voter intimidation took on a variety of forms in the Mississippi Delta during this time—from the more calculated efforts of the Citizens' Council, whose well-connected members would bar active blacks' access to bank loans or would have those involved with the campaign fired from their jobs, to everyday forms of harassment. Hamer remembered truckloads of white men with gun racks circling the houses that held registration meetings. She also recalled white men menacingly walking the streets with large dogs while she tried to canvass small towns. Those brave few whom Hamer did persuade to register would often return home from the courthouse to threats of termination or violence and eventually withdraw their applications. The very rare people like Hamer who were able to withstand this pressure and become registered voters "were punished to the fullest to keep other [black] people disgusted" and "to keep them from going" down to the courthouse and following suit.[31]

On June 9, 1963, on her return trip from a weeklong voter-registration and community-development workshop, Hamer and her fellow registration workers suffered abuse so severe that it would have dissuaded most people from future activism. Being wrongly imprisoned and brutally tortured, however, emboldened her fight. Interpreting her deliverance from the depths of the Winona jailhouse as divinely sanctioned, Hamer's resolve to testify about black life in Mississippi was strengthened and her testimony grew even more prophetic following the experience.

HAMER'S WINONA NIGHTMARE

The voices of ten black passengers—June Johnson, James West, Ruth Davis, Rosemary Freeman, Euvester Simpson, Annell Ponder, Fannie Lou Hamer, Bernard Washington, Mr. Palmer, and Miss Ford—rose above the noise of State Route 82 as their Continental Trailways bus made its way west toward Greenwood from Columbus, Mississippi. It was early in the morning, just after eight o'clock, when the bus driven by Billy Eugene Haithcock departed the terminal. Perhaps Hamer initiated the singing of spirituals, as she had the previous

August to quell the fear and disappointment of the eighteen registration hope-fuls who had been turned away at the county courthouse and threatened by state highway patrolmen. That memory could not have been far from Hamer's mind now as those with whom she traveled had been roughly ordered by an enraged bus driver to sit in the back of the bus. Haithcock was infuriated by their attempt, unsuccessful as it was, to integrate a lunch counter during the bus's brief layover in Columbus.[32] The activists had been traveling all night on a return trip from the weeklong civic education and voter-registration train-ing session spearheaded by Septima Clark and Bernice Robinson. The training, cosponsored by the SCLC and the Highlander Research Center, was held at the Sea Island Center on Johns Island, South Carolina.

Hamer had attended a similar workshop just a few months earlier in Dorchester, Georgia, led by Clark, Dorothy Cotton, and Andrew and Jean Young. Having emerged as one of their "star" graduates, Hamer returned to share her inspiring testimony with a new group of trainees and to gather strength for her continued activism.[33] At these five-day residential training ses-sions, the SCLC's Citizenship Education Program (CEP) leaders taught the fifty or sixty workshop participants about all aspects of voter registration—from canvassing rural communities to teaching literacy skills required for filling out registration forms to interpreting their state's constitution. This type of train-ing intended to make it much more difficult for registrars to withhold the ballot from blacks on the basis of incompetence. Consonant with her radical social vision of empowering masses of local people, Clark encouraged those participants who attended her workshops to go back to their own communi-ties and hold similar training sessions, thereby multiplying the number of well-equipped black registrants across the South.

Cotton, the director of the CEP, also envisioned these workshops transform-ing the participants' self-conceptions. The curriculum was designed to move the participants from feeling like victims of racism, poverty, and other unjust systems under which they suffered toward recognizing themselves as citizens of the nation. Furthermore, Cotton emphasized that with citizenship came both entitlements and responsibilities. This pivotal transformation involved undo-ing the "programming" and "brainwashing" instilled in blacks through what Cotton refers to as "our American-style apartheid."[34] This perspective shift was sparked through celebrations and affirmations of black southern culture. Songs, food, and storytelling were mainstays of the CEP training sessions. These cel-ebrations were coupled with a re-education of what citizenship is, who is en-titled to it, and what role citizens play in a democratic government. During her years as CEP director, Cotton witnessed heartening results. Of the nearly eight thousand participants who graduated from the CEP training sessions, most left with a "new consciousness" and a "redefinition" of self:

> [P]eople who had lived for generations with a sense of impotence, with a consciousness of anger and victimization, now knew in no uncertain terms that if things were going to change, they themselves had to change them. They now had the consciousness of a firm philosophical as well as legal basis for challenging oppressive systems and even accepted the obligation to work to change such systems.[35]

The ten activists aboard the bus headed for Greenwood that fateful Saturday morning were chosen to attend the CEP workshop in South Carolina because of their dedication to the cause and their potential to engage others in their community. They were returning now armed with a renewed sense of self and clearer ideas about how to effect the change they sought.[36]

Just one stop, a mere thirty miles, away from the group's final destination, Haithcock pulled his bus into the terminal adjacent to Staley's Café. This establishment, and the city of Winona in which it is located, was a hotbed of racial tension. Winona was home to the organizational headquarters of the Citizens' Council, which had been operating for nearly nine years by this time and had spread its white supremacist ideology across the region, the state, and the South, boasting more than 200,000 members. Staley's Café, in particular, had been the site of several attempts at desegregation since the Interstate Commerce Commission's (ICC) 1961 ruling, which outlawed segregated interstate buses and travel facilities. The café and the bus terminal remained strictly segregated despite the edict and in the face of CORE's widely publicized Freedom Rides.

Illicit segregationist policies were supported and brutally enforced by local police. In sifting through Mississippi State Sovereignty Commission reports, rhetorical scholar Davis W. Houck discovered at least three instances in two years wherein the Winona sheriff, Earl Wayne Patridge, had taken the lead in arresting and torturing those who dared violate the now expressly outlawed racial customs. What's worse, Patridge and the police force he led did so with impunity. "And so on the morning of June 9, 1963, Sheriff Patridge had good reason to believe that he and his fellow officers were above the law," contends Houck.[37] In fact, they were prepared for another showdown. Someone aboard the Continental Trailways bus alerted the officials in Montgomery County that "trouble" was making its way to Winona. It's unclear if the caller was a white passenger who phoned from a previous stop, perhaps following the group's unsuccessful attempt to integrate the bus station food counter in Columbus, or if it was the bus driver himself who called in the news. In any case, the Montgomery County chief of police Thomas Herod Jr. and Mississippi state highway patrolman John L. Basinger were at Staley's by the time Haithcock's run number 1729 pulled in. Sheriff Patridge, accompanied by his deputy, Charles Perkins, arrived soon after.

To make the most of a short twenty-five-minute stop in Winona, six of the black activists with whom Hamer was traveling hurriedly exited the bus. Two of the female passengers, Euvester Simpson and Ruth Davis, visited the restroom, while Annell Ponder, James West, June Johnson, and Rosemary Freeman headed toward the lunch counter. Hamer and three other black passengers remained on the bus. Those who went into the restaurant seeking food were met by an aggravated white waitress, who threw a wadded dishtowel against the wall and declared: "I can't take it no more!" when she saw the group of African Americans approach her counter.[38] Her outburst caught the attention of Chief Herod and Patrolman Basinger, who were seemingly waiting for such provocation and who quickly advanced upon the registration workers. "Get up and get out of here," Chief Herod ordered as he tapped the black activists' shoulders with his billy club. Thirty-one-year-old Georgia native and Clark College graduate Annell Ponder was quick to respond to the encroachment by citing the ICC's 1961 ruling and informing the policemen that it was unlawful to discriminate against her and her fellow travelers on the basis of their race. Herod's retort came swiftly, "Ain't no damn law, you just get on out of here."[39] The group of registration fieldworkers left the counter and congregated outside the diner. By that time, Simpson, whom Basinger had ordered to use the "colored" restroom, rejoined her compatriots. Hamer saw the group gathered outside and asked what happened. Ponder told her that the policemen would not let them eat and Hamer replied simply, "Well, this is Mississippi," as she returned to her seat on the bus.[40]

Several others were less resigned to the policemen's unlawful behavior. After some discussion, they decided to copy down Herod's and Basinger's license plate numbers along with brief physical descriptions so they could later identify the culprits in this discriminatory encounter. Their actions did not go unnoticed by the officers who were now joined by Sheriff Patridge and Deputy Perkins. The four Montgomery County officials placed the five activists gathered in the parking lot under arrest. Stirred by the commotion, Hamer shouted from the door of the bus asking Ponder if the rest of the group should travel on to Greenwood. At that moment, Herod spotted Hamer and exclaimed: "Get that one there!"[41]

The policemen roughly loaded the group of six activists: Hamer, Ponder, Simpson, Johnson, West, and Freeman into their patrol cars. Hamer remembered being kicked and called names by Perkins as he shoved her into his backseat and drove to the Winona jailhouse. As soon as the group arrived, the officers began questioning them. What did they know about the Greenwood voter-registration project? Had they been trying to demonstrate at Staley's Café? What was this "voter education workshop" they were returning from? Did they meet Martin Luther King Jr. there? When the group tried to answer the policemen's barrage of questions, they were told to "shut up" and called names like "nigger," "fatso," and "bitch." Officer Surrell, who joined the policemen harassing the activists at the station, slammed his own foot down on top of James West's feet before transporting the teenager to the black area of the jail, known as the bullpen. Once there, West noticed three inmates: Roosevelt Knox, Sol Poe, and Willie Kidd, who sat fearful of the foreboding commotion.

Hamer was placed in a cell with Simpson; Ponder and Freeman were taken to another room in the women's quarters. Johnson, a fifteen-year-old Montgomery County native, stayed in the booking room only to suffer the first blows from both Basinger and Perkins, who took turns punching her in the face. The officers asked Johnson if she was a member of the NAACP. To which she replied, "yes," further stoking their sadism. The officers called her a "nigger," and Perkins beat the young woman with a blackjack, a two-foot-long leather baton loaded at both ends with metal weights. Eventually, they brought a battered Johnson to the cell shared by Ponder and Freeman.

The bloodthirsty officers then set their sets on the group's leader, Annell Ponder, the southwide supervisor for the SCLC. It was Ponder who initially organized the group, selecting which activists would attend the training workshop and it was Ponder to whom Chief Herod now demanded threateningly: "You come on out here. You the boss of these people. We want to talk to you." Ponder's torturous investigation took place in the booking room where Johnson had just been assaulted. The officers wanted to know why Ponder had copied down their license plate numbers, and she told them plainly that was her job: to report civil rights violations to federal authorities. This admission, along with her refusal to address the men by the title "sir," elicited punches in the stomach and the head from Surrell, Basinger, and Perkins. The jailhouse was small enough that Hamer could hear Ponder's refusal to use the courtesy title they demanded of her, claiming she "didn't know them well enough" to call them "sir." Ponder drew upon a tradition of defiance established by activist forerunners like Reverend C. T. Vivian and Hollis Watkins, whose own refusals to use courtesy titles while imprisoned were well known in movement circles.[42]

Hamer could also hear Ponder praying for God to forgive her assailants.[43] Soon Hamer and Simpson watched in horror as Ponder passed by their cell barely able to stand; she tried to stabilize her ravaged self by holding onto the jail walls, her clothes torn, her mouth swollen, and her eyes bloodied.

Before the officers made their way back to Hamer's cell, they took a rest from assaulting the prisoners and ordered the black inmates Knox, Poe, and Kidd to beat their cellmate, James West. Herod, Patridge, and Basinger supervised as the frightened prisoners followed orders to "whip this nigger's ass."[44] For over a half an hour the black inmates beat West with a blackjack until the nineteen-year-old lost consciousness and Basinger rewarded Knox, Poe, and Kidd with corn whiskey.

Then Basinger approached Hamer's cell. The Mississippi state highway patrolman asked where she was from and Hamer replied honestly: Ruleville. He went to "check this out" and returned, declaring, "You damn right you from Ruleville. We going to make you wish that you were dead, bitch."[45] One phone call to local officials and Basinger surely discovered that Hamer was an active voter-registration worker, on the SNCC payroll, revered among black Deltans and civil rights workers alike—"the big shit," Basinger branded her as he led her out of her cell and into the bullpen.[46] Once there, officers Basinger, Surrell, and Perkins ordered the black inmates, who were fatigued from West's beating and now inebriated from the moonshine given as a reward for their violence, to exact similar "punishment" upon Hamer. "You mean for me to beat her with this?" Roosevelt cried out, staring incredulously at the two-foot-long leather blackjack Basinger thrust upon him. "You damn right. If you don't you know what I'll do to you," was Basinger's menacing reply.[47] Basinger ordered Hamer to lie face down on a bunk bed in the small cell, surrounded by three officers of the law and the black prisoners they now controlled.

The torture began. There, in that Winona jail cell, in the county of her birth, Hamer was beaten by Roosevelt until he was too tired to continue. Then, on strict orders from Basinger, Poe took over the assault. Hamer cried out to the black teenager imploring, "you mean you would do this to your own race?"[48] To which Poe could only plead with her to move her arm away from the side of her body she was shielding—it had been affected by the bout of polio she suffered as a child—because he didn't want to hit her hand. Hamer claimed to have endured the first beating rather well, but remembered how she was unable to stop writhing in pain and screaming in agony during the second. To keep her still while Poe beat her, Roosevelt was commanded to sit on Hamer's legs. Surrell, whom Hamer remembered "got so hot and worked up off" the beating, soon joined in—hitting her in the head and shouting at her to stop screaming.[49]

Amid the torture, Hamer sought to preserve her dignity by pulling down her dress, which had slid up high. Just as she managed to smooth the dress back down, however, Surrell pulled it up over her head, exposing her bare flesh to Poe's blows. Not only was Hamer debased by the exposure of her naked body before the policemen and male prisoners surrounding her in the bullpen, she also remembers one of the officers "trying to feel under my clothes," while the black prisoner beat her.[50]

The abuse continued for nearly half an hour. Hamer had difficulty accounting for the precise amount of time that passed as she lost consciousness, only to be awakened by Basinger cussing at her and telling her to "get up, fatso."[51] Barely able to move, feverish, bloody, and severely bruised, Hamer was dragged back to the cell she shared with Simpson. During that first night in the Winona jailhouse, Hamer's debilitating physical pain was not all that kept her from the rest her battered body so badly needed. The ongoing screams echoing through the jailhouse as the remaining group members received their beatings made sleep impossible.

The four remaining black passengers aboard Continental Trailways run 1729, Washington, Davis, Palmer, and Ford, escaped the notice of the Winona policemen and traveled on to Greenwood. Once there, they informed SNCC headquarters about their traveling companions' arrest. Lawrence Guyot, a Mississippi native, Tougaloo College graduate, and one of SNCC's first fieldworkers in the state, was the first person to reach the Winona jail in hopes of securing their release. Not only did Guyot fail to rescue the group, but he was taken into custody and tortured by the Winona policemen as well. By Monday, June 10, with Guyot now imprisoned, Willie Peacock among other SNCC officials escalated the matter to the Department of Justice; before long, Attorney General Robert Kennedy, who claimed a personal interest in the matter, as well as FBI director J. Edgar Hoover were on the case. And by Tuesday, June 11, FBI special agents had made their way to the Winona jailhouse to meet with the group of victimized civil rights workers. The agents returned again on Wednesday afternoon to take color pictures of the victim's battered bodies. Though Kennedy and Hoover were apparently on the case and while the presence of FBI special agents certainly made it clear to local jailers that they were under federal surveillance, the government's response—to send agents in to investigate, but not to intervene on behalf of the battered civil rights workers—was emblematic of a larger pattern of surface level "assistance" that contributed to SNCC's growing disaffection with the federal government. Sensing that the agents would do little to protect their coworkers, members of SNCC and civil rights supporters across the country began phoning the Winona jailhouse asking to speak with the prisoners. Ladner remembers demanding to talk to Guyot and thinking he was "some impostor," his "voice was so halted," she recalls. "I said 'If you are Guyot, you will answer this question.' And so he answered in the affirmative and I knew it was he . . . and I said 'Oh my God!'"[52]

During the four days that the group remained in prison, as the pressure of the federal investigation and civil rights activists' inquisitions bore down upon local officials, Hamer overheard the policemen discussing what they should charge the group with, if they should throw their bodies in the Big Black River or, if not, how they could avoid taking responsibility for beating the activists? Late one night, the police guards offered to let the group go, which Hamer and the others clearly recognized as a trap that would indeed end with their bodies being disposed of in the river.

All seven captives were tried at the Winona courthouse the morning of Tuesday, June 11, each pleading "not guilty" to the spurious resisting arrest and disorderly conduct charges leveled against them by their assailants. The activists were also forced to sign a release indicating that they had not been harmed. Hamer remembered that Basinger—gun in tow—"told me to write that since I had been in jail I had been treated good; I had been fed, and had nobody mistreated me." She confessed to writing the statement because she felt that she "didn't have no other choice," but Hamer said she wrote it "terrible. I wrote it just real bad," in protest of the forced lie and as an indication of her duress.[53]

Just as those four days would forever shape the lives of the seven prisoners tortured in the Winona jailhouse, the larger movement for racial equality in the United States also underwent momentous changes during this brief time period. On the same day that the activists were arraigned on spurious charges, President Kennedy delivered his "Civil Rights Address," announcing the federal push to desegregate all public facilities and provide greater protection for voting rights. Early the next morning, less than one hundred miles away from Winona, Klansman Byron de la Beckwith shot NAACP leader Medgar Evers in the back as Evers returned from a late-night meeting to his suburban Jackson home. Guyot insists that if it were not for the national pressure exerted on the state of Mississippi following the assassination of Evers, the prisoners would not have been released and would have likely faced more torture and perhaps death. "I think the only thing that saved our lives was Medgar Evers was killed while we were in there," insists Guyot.[54]

Cotton's account of the prisoners' release supports Guyot's contention. Evers was shot in the early morning hours of Wednesday, June 12, and Dr. Martin Luther King Jr. quickly got involved with the Winona imprisonment. He had heard about the group's arrest, remembers Cotton, and now "after hearing about the shooting of Medgar Evers, he called from Atlanta advising some of us to go to Winona and see if we could get them out of jail."[55] He phoned Young to inform him that SNCC leaders had been unable to secure the groups' release—in part because they did not have access to the set bail of $1,400. The SCLC was able to wire the necessary funds from their headquarters in Atlanta to Young, who was in Birmingham, alongside activists Bevel and Cotton. The three embarked on the two-hundred-mile drive from Alabama to Mississippi on Wednesday morning and made it to Montgomery County by four o'clock that afternoon. To secure the civil rights workers' release, the SCLC representatives assiduously adhered to southern customs. Young, Bevel, and Cotton, all outsiders to the Winona area, were mindful to stop at a local gas station and make their presence in town known before they approached the jail. When they did arrive, Bevel, Young, and Cotton addressed the policemen with respect, conveying self-confident yet nonconfrontational personae.[56] However, Cotton—a committed student and avid proponent of the nonviolent philosophy of social change—recalls that sitting in the foyer of the jail, "was the first time I felt that I could have done physical damage to our opponents." "I was angry at them when I realized that they had abused our friends and yet could stand there making small talk with us," she recalls.[57]

In public speeches and interviews Hamer gave after her Winona experience, she would commonly note that she was released from the jailhouse where she had been savagely beaten on the same day Evers was gunned down in his front yard. She would leave it up to her audience to consider the significance of this connection, to ponder what her experience in Winona and Evers's assassination in Jackson said about life in Mississippi and about civil rights in the United States. Regarding the irony of her particular experience, though, she was far more explicit. Hamer's narrative describing her time in Winona prominently featured two common aspects of the African American oral tradition: testifying and image making.[58] These rhetorical aspects not only describe the particular school of the soul that gave rise to Hamer's prophetic wisdom, they also "season" her discourse. "In African-American culture," explains Bernice Johnson Reagon, "the text is assessed through taste." Audiences assessing the value of a text and the uniqueness of a rhetor's signature, commonly ask such questions as: "Is it seasoned? Has it been through life's experiences . . . Is it a creation that has been weathered by the life and struggle of the one who is offering it up for sharing?"[59] Hamer's Winona narrative, described through the tradition of testifying and brought to life through image making, became a central tenet of her rhetorical signature and established her credibility as one who has walked through the shadows of death. The tradition of testifying is quite popular in southern black churches, but it has also been appropriated by speakers of Black English and used in other contexts. Hamer testified about her Winona beating at mass meetings held in southern black churches across that region of the country, and she also verbally witnessed to her experience of torture in venues as diverse as the Democratic National Convention, the halls of the US Congress, a rally in Harlem with Malcolm X, and at college campuses across the United States. Hamer offered an official testimony, moreover, to the FBI and to the all-white jury at the trial the Justice Department brought against her assailants.

Hamer's Winona testimony was a significant feature in her political discourse both because of what it represented and also because of how she presented it. Hamer's story about police brutality and white segregationists' abuse of the legal system was not hers alone. In testifying about Winona, Hamer was bearing witness to experiences that were all too common among blacks in Mississippi. At the Winona jailhouse, in particular, the same assailants who ordered her sadistic beating had tortured at least four other blacks before the registration workers in Hamer's group arrived on the scene.[60] In fact, the mass arrests of demonstrators and imprisonment in places like the infamous Parchman penitentiary, where officers were known to use cattle prods and sexually abusive strip searches in their dealings with the protestors, were not uncommon retaliatory efforts deployed by the Mississippi establishment.[61] So, when Hamer said, "I have walked through the shadows of death" before a congregation in Greenwood, her audience's outpouring of verbal feedback, choruses of "amen," "mhmm," and "tell it!" indicate the black Mississippians gathered there empathized with this allusion to white supremacist terror.[62] To impart this perspective to northern audiences who had not shared her lived experience, Hamer's testimony featured vivid images that recreated searing depictions of her abuse. Image making in the African American oral tradition is commonly constituted by "figures of speech [that] . . . tend to be earthy, gutsy, and rooted in plain everyday reality."[63] These characteristics are readily apparent in Hamer's testimony, and they seasoned her discourse with a corporeal quality that imparted the visceral nature of her experience.

In fact, Hamer's testimony typically engaged all of her audience's senses. Her claim that the "white men had made [the black prisoners] drink corn whiskey before they beat us" suggested a bitter taste filled the mouths of her assailants and a sour odor pervaded the bullpen where she was violated.[64] When Hamer described how she buried her "head in the mattress and hugged it to kill out the sound of [her] screams," her audience could visualize the image of a defenseless Hamer writhing on a dirty jailhouse cot and hear the muffled sound of her pain.[65] Once the horror was over, she recalled the way this abuse left her body looking and feeling: "My body was real hard-feeling like metal. My hands were navy blue—and [I] couldn't bend the fingers."[66] The beating's details: the taste of the corn whiskey that fueled it, the way it smelled, looked, sounded, and felt, not only helped bring her experience to life, but they established her credibility as someone who had lived through this iron furnace. The details also affirmed the veracity of her testimony for those auditors who might believe the white establishment's denial of wrongdoing or who simply considered her story too awful to be true. "I'm not lying," she told one movement activist who recorded her testimony, "because I just can't sit down. I been sleeping on my face because I was just as hard as a bone . . . when they turned me loose, I was hard as a bone."[67]

Hamer's common comparisons and sensory descriptions also enabled her to keep a verbal record, preserving those aspects of the abuse that faded from her body over time. The importance of incontrovertible evidence in the black freedom struggle was not lost on Hamer, who—like her rhetorical forbearers Sojourner Truth and Frederick Douglas—used her body to testify. Even in her ravaged condition, Hamer chose exposure over quiet convalescence. "I was begging somebody . . . I told them, I wanted to go to Washington to show in person what had happened to us," she declared when pressed about the national travels she undertook immediately following the beating.[68] Hamer informed the court during her federal trial that she traveled from Greenwood, where she finally received medical attention and where movement supporter Dr. Mabel Garner took more pictures of Hamer's battered body for the FBI, on to Atlanta, where she met with King as well as other members of the SCLC and the VEP. From Atlanta, Hamer and Ponder made their way to Washington, DC, to meet with Justice Department officials including attorneys St. John Barrett and John Rosenberg, who filed suit against Hamer's Winona assailants.

While her body provided incontrovertible evidence of the abuse she suffered, Hamer's discourse worked to transcend the particularity of her experience. The SCLC, VEP, and Justice Department officials to whom Hamer testified were doubtlessly moved not only by the physical markers Hamer's body bore, but also by the way she linked the details of her abuse to the perpetrators' violation of US principles. Connecting the truth of her experience to the larger African American struggle, Hamer testified, "I have a blood clot now in the . . . left eye and a permanent kidney injury on the right side from that beating. These are the things that we go through in the state of Mississippi just trying to be treated like a human being, but still this is called a part of America."[69] Illustrating the tragic irony, state-sanctioned officials savagely beat her on her return trip from a voter-registration workshop, Hamer's individual story functioned as a compelling commentary on the larger disease ravaging the nation.

Hamer's testimonies often moved beyond this secular appeal. In all of Hamer's speeches of which I am aware, she never mentioned that the group of registration workers with whom she was traveling attempted to integrate the food counter during their Columbus layover before coming to Staley's Café. During the federal trial, furthermore, Hamer denied allegations that the group was demonstrating in Winona. In her trial testimony, Hamer paraphrased a conversation she had with Basinger. "'What was you all trying to do? Demonstrate or something?'" she remembered him asking. "'No sir. I was not off of the bus,'" and "'they was just trying to get food,'" was her reply.[70] When asked a similar series of questions during cross-examination, Hamer held fast to her account— the group was not trying to "integrate the lunchroom," because "we knew from the ICC ruling in 1961 that had already passed," that "they had a right to eat in the bus terminal."[71] In this manner, Hamer not only underscored the guilt of her assailants, who fought to uphold outlawed racial customs, she exacerbated their offense by portraying the total innocence of the registration workers. They were simply trying to get food—she never even left the bus—and yet state-sanctioned officials treated them so savagely.

The fact that Hamer chose to depict the registration workers as wholly innocent victims attacked without provocation creates an even more dramatic narrative than portraying the group as victimized for asserting their rights. Her Winona testimony—particularly, the narrative line of bondage and freedom—thus functioned not only as evidence of the compelling need for federal intervention into roguish Mississippi politics, it was also a story about divine deliverance, proof that God was indeed on the side of the oppressed. Before an audience of Delta sharecroppers gathered in Indianola, Hamer made this biblical allusion explicit. Leading into her Winona testimony with a hint of mystery, she said that while local clergy preach about "[w]hat God has done for Meshach, Shadrach, and Abednego," they don't even know that "God has done the same thing for Fannie Lou Hamer, Annell Ponder, and Lawrence Guyot."[72] Just as Meshach, Shadrach, and Abednego kept the faith and were delivered from King Nebuchadnezzar's fiery furnace, Hamer held fast to her belief in God's deliverance while in captivity.[73]

She even challenged her assailants, telling them "'It's going to be miserable when you have to face God . . . Because one day you going to pay up for the things you have done,'" reasoning that "Scripture says, 'Has made of one blood all nations.'" To which Hamer claimed the policeman "pitifully" responded, "It's a damn lie . . . Abraham Lincoln said that."[74] Much like Ponder's evocation of Jesus Christ through her prayer that "God would have mercy on these people because they didn't know what they was doing," Hamer was testifying to "the truth

... it's pitiful, you see—that people can have so much hate that will make them beat a person and don't know they doing wrong."[75] By combining the group's absolute blamelessness and their eventual deliverance with scriptural evidence of the races' interconnection, Hamer elevated their narrative of victimization to biblical heights.

From the movement lore that preceded her involvement, Hamer was aware that the few black Mississippians who initially began challenging their society's unjust configurations—forerunners like Reverend George W. Lee, Gus Courts, Lamar Smith, and Herbert Lee—were severely, sometimes fatally, punished as a means to both deter their activism and to discourage others from joining the struggle. Her reaction to the Winona beating, however, defied all expectations of deterrence. "If them crackers in Winona thought they'd discouraged me from fighting," she proclaimed, "I guess they found out different. I'm going to stay in Mississippi and if they shoot me down, I'll be buried here."[76] The strength carried through her words belied her body's weakness. The Winona beating left Hamer's body permanently damaged. "Mrs. Hamer came out and she was never the same," Ladner recalls:

> I remember she had that red eye for a long time, long time. And she had, a face was like beef that had been beaten. I mean this face was so battered, it was like a piece of beef . . . And you know she walked with a limp and that limp became more manifest after the beating and her health seemed to have started deteriorating after that. But I remember those eyes, oh my God. They were bloodshot; they had blood clots in them. Her face, oh my God, and that's something that I never want to see again.[77]

Though Hamer did suffer from the blood clot, the kidney damage, and the exacerbated limp for the rest of her life, living through the torture in Winona emboldened Hamer's faith in the divine purpose of the civil rights struggle and strengthened her resolve to share her testimony.

Compelling as Hamer's account of injustice in America was, her federal trial testimony—combined with testimony from all seven victims, from the black prisoners who beat West and Hamer, and from the FBI special agents who visited their cells—did not move the all-white jury who assembled in Oxford, Mississippi, from December 2–6, 1963, to acknowledge the guilt of their peers. The twelve jurors heard the case, *United States of America v. Earle Wayne Patridge, Thomas J. Herod, Jr., William Surrell, John L. Basinger and Charles Thomas Perkins*, deliberated for seventy-five minutes, and found the Mississippi law enforcement officials "not guilty" on all counts brought before them.

EXPOSING MISSISSIPPI'S "WICKEDNESS BEFORE THE ASSEMBLY"

No more than three months after the Winona verdict was handed down, Hamer was busy working on another campaign to right the rampant wrongs in her community. By the spring of 1964, she had been active in the movement for over a year, canvassing small rural towns in the Mississippi Delta and speaking at mass meetings in local churches to encourage voter registration. Hamer now announced that she would provide those who managed to register with something significant to vote for, namely, Fannie Lou Hamer for Second Congressional District representative. The Second Congressional District included twenty-four counties in the northwest corner of the state, encompassing the region known as the Mississippi Delta. COFO was especially interested in running a candidate in this district, explains McLaurin, because "this was our district. Historically, the Second Congressional District was our district—John R. Lynch was the last [black] person who held it. We wanted to take it back because they [white segregationists] had gerrymandered our district and taken it from us."[78] Not since Reconstruction had a black person represented this district, which was home to an overwhelming black majority, in the US Congress. COFO wanted to run a candidate who had a fighting chance against Representative Jamie Whitten. Since Fannie Lou Hamer lived within its perimeters and since she made such strong impressions on COFO activists and Delta blacks alike, the conglomerated civil rights organization promoted her candidacy.

When Hamer qualified to run in March 1964, she became the first African American woman in the state of Mississippi to run for Congress. McLaurin will never forget the day they went to the secretary of state's office in Jackson to get her qualified. "It was a spectacle," he remembers, "when we went up to the counter and told the white lady, she said: 'what do you niggers want?'" McLaurin responded assertively, "said, 'First of all, we reject what you just called us, but since there's nobody else standing here you must be talking to us. We want this lady to run for Congress!" The woman at the counter went to the back office and brought out "ten to fifteen more white people" to witness the scene of qualifying Hamer to run for public office. The woman asked Hamer to provide her campaign manager's information and Hamer momentarily froze, before muttering nervously under her breath, "Shit, Mac, will you be my campaign manager?"[79] However intimidated, McLaurin and Hamer stood their ground and she went on to challenge the seat that Representative Jamie Whitten had held since 1941.

Whitten, a Tallahatchie County lawyer and chairman of the House Appropriations Subcommittee on Agriculture, ran unopposed in the previous election and had been serving a narrow set of interests for quite some time. In fact, Whitten had served his post as chairman "for so long that Washington wags knew him as 'the permanent secretary of agriculture.'"[80] He used this powerful position to support policies that enriched Delta planters at the cost of the majority of the region's inhabitants. In the early 1960s, for example, Whitten "killed a federal program to teach unemployed black farmworkers how to drive tractors."[81]

Covering the twenty-four counties that comprised Mississippi's Delta region, the Second Congressional District was the largest district in Mississippi. In 1964, African Americans constituted 59 percent of this district and yet they made up a dismally small proportion of the registered voters. In Sunflower County, 4,500 whites were registered to vote—51 percent of the voting-age population—whereas only 114 blacks were registered, 0.9 percent of the total voting-age population. In Whitten's home territory, Tallahatchie County, the figures were even more astounding: 4,334 whites, nearly 85 percent of the voting-age population were registered, in contrast to just 5 registered blacks, which amounted to 0.8 percent of that voting-age population.[82] On the basis of these figures alone, Whitten could not claim to represent the people of the Mississippi Delta. Further, only 20 percent of voting-age whites bothered to vote for him in 1962, when he ran unopposed.[83] The majority of whites in the Delta, in fact, had little reason to vote for Whitten, as he consistently advocated against the interests of poor white laborers. By opposing Whitten, Hamer's campaign was more than just an effort to encourage black civic participation in the Mississippi Delta. It was also an attempt to give voice to the needs of the Second District's impoverished inhabitants, black and white alike, whose interests had gone unrepresented and even lobbied against for years.

From the evening of March 20, 1964, when Hamer first announced her candidacy, until June 2, when the Democratic primary was held, she and McLaurin scoured the Delta region. Traveling from Clarksdale to Mayersville (and everywhere in between), Hamer spoke during mass meetings at churches and in front of courthouses, canvassed small towns and remote rural areas, held picnic gatherings on college campuses and near popular lakes, spoke to people at juke joints, and organized "freedom day" rallies.[84] Her hectic campaign schedule included multiple events each day, often in different cities, and allowed for only one day of rest per week. Even more strained than Hamer's time and physical energy was her meager campaign budget. COFO provided Hamer with $38,000 for all expenses. With these funds, COFO managed to circulate campaign literature, run radio, newspaper, and television advertisements, and rent meeting halls for rallies and picnics. McLaurin and Hamer spent no more than five dollars a day on food for themselves, often splitting a soda pop and a bologna sandwich or a hot dog for dinner so that they could reserve the remainder of their campaign finances for "harassment expenses." This money was earmarked for "making bond and paying fines" in the case of arrests. It was a vital reserve considering that Hamer's campaign challenged not only the racial caste system so pervasive in the Delta, but class-based oppression as well.[85] The first night Hamer announced her candidacy, two of her campaign workers—Mendy Samstein and George Greene—were arrested in Ruleville. "We don't have no nigger politics in Ruleville," the policeman told them. The workers were charged with violating a local "midnight curfew law" and when the campaigners responded that the federal courts had deemed adult curfew laws unconstitutional, the town's mayor, who was also present, informed them, "That law hasn't reached here yet."[86]

In the face of constant harassment, Hamer insisted that she had the right to run a political campaign just as any other American had the right to run for public office. Hamer's primary bid itself was symbolic, demonstrating to black Mississippians that it was possible to get involved in the political process and that involvement was one way to alter the oppressive social structure. McLaurin claims that though many blacks across the Delta were afraid to attend the events they held and while most whites were threatened by the radical change about which she spoke, her campaign was "introducing them to the future."[87] To empower Delta blacks in the face of harassment and to publicly oppose white supremacist and classist rule, Hamer had to not only deliver compelling speeches, she also had to exude bravery. "What was so killing about hearing Mrs. Hamer speak," contends McLaurin, was "when she come into a space she never act as if she was afraid!"[88] This fearlessness both inspired McLaurin—"she gave me some courage a lot of the time," he remembers—and was itself inspired *by* him. In an interview later in life, Hamer cited McLaurin as one of the most influential black leaders with whom she had worked because he "was just so forceful that he made me believe, 'you're somebody. You're important.'"[89] McLaurin admits that he "told everybody that. 'You're great, you can be great, you need to tell your children that they're going to be great,'" he remembers saying. "The idea is if you've got fear you're going to overcome it by facing it."[90] In a time of great turmoil, Hamer enacted this very idea—a cornerstone of SNCC's empowerment strategy in the Delta—through her campaign as she coupled her bravery with engaging extemporaneously delivered speeches.

Hamer rarely spoke from a manuscript and her Second Congressional District campaign speeches were no exception. COFO "would send out a speech," recalls McLaurin, and the two would work through it together, Hamer asking, "Give me the high points of it, Mac." If she found aspects of it confusing, she'd consult him and "if it didn't make no sense to" him either, McLaurin would instruct her to "leave it out. Keep doing what you been doing. Use what you're comfortable with." So, they would pick out important statistics and relevant points about the area they were visiting from the materials COFO sent and Hamer would combine these facts with the overall platform she was crafting.[91] Although researchers have been unable to locate complete transcripts from these campaign addresses, newspaper accounts, speaking notes, and Sovereignty Commission files indicate that Hamer's speeches promised to "undo everything Jamie Whitten has done in Washington."[92]

What Whitten did in Washington, Hamer underscored, was further isolate their district from the mainstream of American politics. Once a leader in the world's cotton production profits, the Delta had faced a series of challenges to its prominence. Asch suggests that a combination of factors including the growing supply of synthetic fibers and foreign cotton-growing competitors drove down the value of the crop. To remain competitive in the global market, American cotton producers had to drive down labor costs and the most efficient way to accomplish this was through mechanization. Advances in the mechanical cotton picker and in chemical weed killers precipitated a "gradual agricultural revolution" in the American South. Within a generation, "the people who had been the economic foundation of the region had become economically expendable."[93] Many sharecroppers left the Delta in search of work in the North or in southern cities. Between "1940 and 1980, the total African American population of Sunflower County dropped from 43,477 to 21,591." Those who stayed had few job prospects and began to increasingly rely on federal programs for survival.[94] As a representative of what became the poorest region in the poorest state of the union, Whitten consistently voted against programs to improve laborers' wages, secure food subsidies for the Delta, and improve their educational system.

Throughout her campaign, Hamer commonly combined specific examples of Whitten's political decisions with her verbal wit, using mimicry to cast herself as a more representative candidate. The rhetorical strategy of mimicry, commonly evoked in the African American vernacular tradition, functions as a form of what literary critic Henry Louis Gates Jr. identifies as "Signifyin(g)." He defines this practice as a tropological confrontation in which black vernacular discourse calls the white linguistic circle into question.[95] Such a rhetorical strategy reinforced the vernacular persona Hamer was building, by demonstrating her credibility as an in-touch member of the Delta community. Her strategic use of mimicry also embodied the very attitude of critical examination that COFO was cultivating among the citizens it empowered.

"Back in late 1961," explained Hamer on the stump, "the United States government wanted to start a program training tractor drivers so they could command good wages from the planters." She introduced the program and detailed its widespread benefits for her audience, "About 2,400 of the workers to be trained would have been Negroes and the other 600 would have been whites. The classes would have been integrated. Negro and white workers would have the chance to get to know and understand each other." In response to this program that would garner higher wages for three thousand workers in the Delta, while bringing poor blacks and whites in closer contact with one another, Whitten declared: "this is the entering wedge into the Labor Department's supervision of wage rates and hours in agriculture, which would upset the local economy." Hamer interpreted Whitten's reaction for her audience, suggesting: "What he meant was that he was afraid there'd be more money for the workers and less for the planters—that's what he calls 'upsetting the local economy.'"[96] Hamer mimicked Whitten's phrase in such a manner that cast his interests as inimical to those of the Delta laborers who came to hear her speak. By imitating Whitten's out-of-touch phrases in her campaign discourse, Hamer reflected her own connection with the poor majority. Mimicry projected her authenticity by ridiculing Whitten, which, in turn, elicited connection from an amused audience.[97]

Hamer also employed mimicry to engage her audience by drawing upon aspects of their shared experience.[98] "Jamie Whitten is up there in Washington trying to get the Congress and the President to keep the price of beef high so the big cattlemen in the district can make more money," Hamer explained; "He calls this 'aiding the livestock industry.'" Translating this statement for her audience, Hamer ridiculed Whitten: "What he really means is that he wants his rich cattlemen friends to be able to charge more money for their beef." She then highlighted the negative effects of "aiding the industry," while speaking to the shared experience of hunger among the Delta poor: "He doesn't seem to care what this does to the poor people who have to get along on rice and beans and fat back because the price of beef is just too high." Contrasting their insufficient food staples to the "rich cattlemen's" profit motive, Hamer exposed the interests Whitten actually represented.

This rhetorical strategy can be found in her critique of Whitten's stance on government labor regulations and on educational aid as well. Hamer acknowledged that the Delta planters, like the rich cattle ranchers, were outspoken in their opposition to "federal control" when it meant paying "their workers a decent wage and giving them decent housing." Hamer remarked, however, "it's funny they don't worry about 'federal control' when it comes time to get their subsidy money every year from the United States Government." Whitten also claimed that he was "afraid" of federal aid to education inevitably leading to "federal control." By contrast, Hamer surmised that "the fact is he's afraid if federal money comes in to help Mississippi people get educated, it won't take them long to learn that they don't want the likes of him representing them in Congress!"[99] Although none of these allegations—that Whitten sought to keep Delta laborers untrained, unorganized, unfed, and uneducated as a means to maintain the cattle ranchers', planters', and politicians' control over the region—were humorous, Hamer's use of mimicry revealed Whitten's narrow constituency while fostering connections between herself and the Delta's laboring class. What's more, this rhetorical strategy of signification embodied a spirit of engagement with politics as Hamer's criticism of Whitten enacted the type of critical questions COFO encouraged Delta blacks to ask of their government: whose interests are elected officials representing? How can these interests be better served? The concerns Hamer raised throughout her candidacy and her historic campaign bid itself demonstrated for Delta blacks what all citizens of the United States are entitled to require of their government, as well as the responsibility that all citizens have to engage with the systems that affect their daily lives.

On June 2, 1964, in the first election that Hamer was able to cast a ballot, she voted for herself. Nevertheless, Whitten ostensibly received 35,218 votes to Hamer's 621. It is not surprising that Hamer lost to Whitten considering white supremacists' widespread use of terror to suppress black civic participation—fewer than 1 percent of blacks of voting age were registered in her district. This coupled with the reluctance of poor whites to cross over the color line and vote for black candidates, even for those candidates who promised to better represent their interests, could easily explain Hamer's defeat. Her loss was difficult to verify, though, without the presence of federal examiners or even the ability for a neutral party to oversee the ballot-counting process. As Hamer testified before the US Congress a year later, poll workers told her campaign representatives that they needed to stand at least "50 feet away and watch through a concrete wall."[100]

Hamer's loss in the Democratic primary may have made her campaign promise to expose injustice and represent the laboring class's needs seem unattainable, but no more than two weeks after the June primary she was in

Washington, DC, testifying about her home state's climate of racial oppression. Hamer's testimony was an integral part of a panel that COFO organized to inform the nation about the problems their Freedom Summer campaign would soon confront. The hearing took place at the National Theatre on June 8, 1964. The panelists, who witnessed testimony from twenty-four Mississippians, included Justice Justine Wise Polier; novelist Joseph Heller; the president of the American Sociological Society, Gresham Sykes; Harvard research psychiatrist Robert Coles; journalist Murray Kempton; and Harold Taylor, the former president of Sarah Lawrence College. They compiled their findings into a report, titled "Summary of Major Points in Testimony by Citizens of Mississippi," and recommended that federal authorities provide protection for the voter-registration project in Mississippi. US representative William Fitts Ryan, who was among the hearing participants, moved to have the proceedings read into the *Congressional Record* on June 16, 1964—a motion that received unanimous consent.

The proceedings capture Hamer's first attempt to share her personal account of terror and injustice in Mississippi with a national audience. As such, her testimony helps chart the development of her rhetorical signature. At the outset of Hamer's testimony, she was asked, "What is it that brings you before the panel today?" To which she replied plainly, "To tell about some of the brutality in the state of Mississippi."[101] Hamer began with her registration attempt in 1962, and her subsequent termination and eviction from the Marlow plantation. She spoke of the white supremacists' retaliatory violence, the Ruleville shootings, and her Winona beating. Adding recent events to this unfolding narrative, Hamer testified about the white power structure's response to her political campaign, reporting that her husband lost his job, their phone line was monitored, and their house invaded by policemen in the middle of the night. In offering this testimony about her own experience, Hamer also represented larger social problems like police brutality, white supremacist retaliation, and the invasion of privacy that kept African Americans in the Delta from challenging the imbalance of power.

Hamer did not stop there. Before her turn to air these grievances was over, she presented an aspect of her personal experience about which she rarely spoke. "One of the other things that happened in . . . the North Sunflower County Hospital, I would say about six out of ten Negro women that go to the hospital are sterilized with the tubes tied."[102] The issue of forced sterilization was an even graver example of privacy invasion than a telephone operator's inquisition into her correspondence and a policemen's unlawful entry into the Hamers' home. Just like police brutality and segregationists' retaliatory violence, though, forced sterilization was also part of Hamer's lived experience.[103] Taken together, Hamer's overall testimony revealed the range of injustices perpetrated against Mississippi blacks, even as it conveyed the need for federal intervention into the state's violent and oppressive structure. Her personal experiences supported her prescient declaration: "I can say there will be a hot summer in Mississippi and I don't mean the weather."[104]

FREEDOM SUMMER: "THE NEW KINGDOM RIGHT HERE ON EARTH"

By the summer of 1964, white supremacist backlash to incremental strides made in the struggle for black freedom had reached hysteric levels. "Newspapers and politicians were whipping whites into this kind of frenzied anger," Cobb describes, "it was a real white hysteria and the history was that when you had that kind of white hysteria there almost certainly was going to be violence."[105] The Ku Klux Klan, an organization that Dittmer notes "had not been active since the 1930s," revived with a vengeance by late 1963. Cross burnings, nightriders shooting into and bombing black churches, businesses, and homes, all tragically demonstrated white supremacists' "frustration, a gut feeling that the battle for white supremacy was being lost."[106] Louis Allen, a logger from Amite County who witnessed the 1961 murder of Herbert Lee and had spoken to the Justice Department about it, was gunned down by two loads of buckshot on January 31, 1964. Dittmer connects Allen's murder to the Klan's revival across the state. De la Beckwith, Evers's assassin, also had Klan ties. Not long after John F. Kennedy's November 22, 1963, assassination, President Lyndon B. Johnson began pushing the civil rights legislation his predecessor advocated through Congress. By the spring of 1964, while the Civil Rights Bill was hotly contested in the Senate and voter-registration activity in the Magnolia state was on the rise, white supremacists became fiercely defensive. In preparation for Freedom Summer, what many Mississippi whites referred to as an "invasion," they bought tanks, armored cars, swelled their police force, and passed legislation designed to impede voter-registration projects.

Meanwhile, SNCC assembled a Mississippi Summer Project Committee, composed of Dona Richards, Bob Moses, Ella Baker, Casey Hayden, and Mendy Samstein. Freedom Summer was the culmination of the voter-registration and community-development work that SNCC, and later COFO, had been conducting in Mississippi since Moses's 1961 arrival in the state. Inspired by the success of the 1963 mock election, Moses proposed extending these efforts into the realm of actual politics. The summer of 1964 proved fitting for the operation as it would prepare Mississippi voters for the fall's presidential election. The summer project would redouble voter-registration efforts, organize Freedom Schools and local adult community centers, in addition to orchestrating a national challenge to be held at the DNC in Atlantic City. Much like the Freedom Vote election, therefore, Freedom Summer would rely on student volunteers to work with local Mississippians and the COFO activists. Nearly 650 students, primarily from the North and the West, came to Mississippi to live and work in rural black communities for the summer-long registration effort. Joining the student volunteers were "nearly 150 lawyers and law students who took on civil rights cases . . . 300 ministers representing the National Council of Churches . . . and some 100 physicians, nurses, and psychologists," who "came to offer their services to movement workers."[107]

In addition to canvassing, volunteers also organized "Freedom Schools," in which they taught basic skills like reading and writing as well as courses about black history and culture. Cobb, the SNCC volunteer who initially conceived of the schools, recognized the "disparity in the Mississippi school system," the myriad ways in which "the educational system was designed to instill in black students a belief in their own inferiority."[108] Ladner, a Palmer's Crossing native, testifies to this systemic discrimination when she recalls: "One of the things that made me aware of who I was, was always in school we would get second-hand books with children's names being written in them. We were told they were the white children's names and I resented that, that our school was inferior. Meaning that the toilet would run over and the feces was running outside on the ground."[109] Hamer's daughter, Vergie, also attended these inferior schools. "We always got passed down books, used books, they was raggedy." Beyond poor supplies, "these regular schools, [it was shameful] what they was doing to the students—taking them out of school, taking them into the fields."[110] McLaurin shares this recollection, explaining that the administrators would take the black students out of school and into the fields "to raise money for the school!" "'Course the students felt that the money never got spent on things that they wanted," McLaurin clarifies.[111]

The Freedom School model challenged all of this. In a big old house on the corner of Center Street and Highway 8 in Ruleville, COFO organized a school with new books sent from northern supporters to form a respectable library where adults and children were taught to read and write. What's more, Freedom School pupils were taught about black history and the contributions African Americans made to literature and science. The celebrated author and dramatist Endesha Ida Mae Holland was transformed by what she learned during her Freedom Summer experience. She remembers asking the volunteers: "you mean, black folks can write books?"[112] Many of the summer volunteers did not know much about the black history they were charged with teaching and thus, after the summer's end, they were compelled to go back to their own colleges and spread their newfound knowledge.[113] These Freedom Schools became community centers and they empowered pupils to take pride in their black heritage, even as the volunteers taught Delta blacks the requisite skills to become more engaged citizens. Approximately 2,500 students attended the forty Freedom Schools COFO established across Mississippi. US representative Bennie Thompson is among the schools' notable alumni.

Given the scale of these Freedom Summer projects, COFO certainly needed the white college students' help to canvass and to teach classes. But Moses also sought the national attention that was bound to follow a group of privileged young people who opted to spend their summer vacation fighting racism in America's most segregated state. The selected students were carefully screened. Psychiatrists and veteran civil rights workers eliminated personality types that were unstable, overly idealistic, or domineering, as they searched instead for "realistic, responsible, flexible, and understanding" volunteers. Beyond these personal characteristics, the volunteers' economic status mattered. They had to "forgo summer jobs, to pay for their own transportation, and to provide their own bond money in the event of an arrest," thus "affluent students predominated."[114] Not surprisingly, financial affluence corresponded with national influence. Moses explained that because the students were "from good schools and their parents are influential," the country's interest would be "awakened, and when that happens, the Government responds to that interest." In this sense, Moses reasoned, the white volunteers brought "the rest of the country with them" when they came to Mississippi.[115]

On a pragmatic plane, Moses's plan played into America's racism—the nation's proclivity to pay more attention to the actions of economically privileged white young people than to either economically oppressed southern blacks or to the black civil rights workers (from a variety of backgrounds) who had been empowering the state's oppressed blacks for the previous three years. Though logical, Moses's plan incited tension between the new batch of volunteers and the movement veterans. Rita Schwerner Bender, who volunteered alongside her husband, Michael Schwerner, in Meridian, Mississippi, the year leading up to Freedom Summer, remembers "there was a lot of distrust, hesitation, and outright opposition to the project from some of the long-term staff for months and months before it happened."[116] In fact, Cobb insists that one of the most vital roles Hamer played in Freedom Summer was her unrelenting promotion of bringing outsiders into the state, which "contributed as much to there being a Summer Project as any proposal Bob Moses or Jim Forman [executive secretary of SNCC] put forward."[117]

Arguments among COFO organizers were widespread. They were concerned that the student volunteers would take too long to train and would therefore divert resources away from the important focus on local people. Others worried that the new volunteers would "trample on the very fragile grassroots we were trying to cultivate," or that their presence was a sign of COFO workers' failure, and that capitalizing on their national influence only reinforced the very racism that COFO fought to combat. Nevertheless, Hamer held fast to her principles. Arguing that white students coming down to help offered the possibility to "live in the solution—black and white together," an embodiment of SNCC's own logo of a black and a white hand clasped together.[118]

Hamer also welcomed the presence of outsiders because her experience had proven their influence to be positive and liberating. Cobb, who had worked in the state for nearly two years prior to the summer project, but who originally hailed from Washington, DC, admits that even he was opposed to the influx of outsiders. That is, until "Mrs. Hamer had me up in the corner and she told me, she said, 'Well, Charlie I'm glad *you* came.'" At which point, Cobb realized that "there's absolutely no argument to that."[119] In promoting the presence of outside volunteers, Hamer represented the stance of all the local people Cobb can recall. Explaining that though Hamer was the most outspoken and "influential" in her advocacy of the project, he remembers that Annie Devine, Victoria Gray, E. W. Steptoe, Lawrence Guyot, and Amzie Moore, among scores of other native Mississippians, "held the same position."[120] And their promotion of the project struck a chord with even the most reticent COFO organizers because it stood as a call to conscience. SNCC had spent the last three years advancing a "let the people decide" philosophy, so organizers could not have it both ways. "You can't, on the one hand say that people have a right to . . . make the decisions that affect their lives and then turn around and say, 'Well I don't like your decision. I won't work with you,'" reasons Cobb.[121] If, as Moye suggests, Hamer was the "embodiment" of SNCC's philosophy, then as Cobb puts it, "Who is going to argue with Mrs. Hamer about the Summer Project?"[122] Hamer was, thus, influential in securing the Freedom Summer volunteers' entrance into Mississippi, in the first place, and she would continue to promote their presence as the summer unfolded.

Though COFO organizers were persuaded by the arguments of local people to go forward with the Summer Project, tension between those initially opposed to the idea of outsiders and the actual student volunteers themselves remained well into the initial phase of the project. This tension boiled over during a meeting at the Western College for Women in Oxford, Ohio, where two weeks of volunteer training sessions took place. A group of new volunteers erupted in laughter during the screening of the CBS documentary, *Mississippi and the Fifteenth Amendment*. The film featured a rotund white segregationist registrar with a thick southern drawl barring black registrants from applying at the courthouse and explaining that Mississippi blacks did not really want the franchise. The registrar donned a shiny black belt along the perimeter of his large waist line and appeared as a caricature of southern segregation. Six staffers walked out of the meeting because they saw nothing funny about the stark symbol of white oppression he represented; the volunteers' laughter brought to the fore feelings of resentment tied to the fact that COFO needed to enlist the help of these college students.[123] There was "this sense that this would be a whole bunch of kids coming in, primarily white, very well educated, who wouldn't be able to understand—wouldn't be able to relate to the people they were supposed to be working with," Bender explains the movement veterans' complex feelings, claiming: "there was a fair amount of discomfort from the start of the Oxford training, from a significant number of COFO workers, about who these kids were and what they could do."[124]

Because many COFO workers were suspicious and some were resentful of the volunteers, the Oxford training sessions were strained to say the least. The first session focused on community canvassing and the second on teaching in the Freedom Schools. Both sessions sought to familiarize volunteers with Mississippi politics and nonviolent methods of protest. By the second session, which Hamer attended, it was no longer necessary to explain to volunteers that their activism would be met with violent opposition for volunteers were well aware that three workers who had attended the first training session, Michael Schwerner, Andrew Goodman, and James Chaney, had disappeared in Philadelphia, Mississippi. Schwerner had been working in Mississippi with his wife for several months, Chaney was an African American who grew up in the state, but Goodman was fresh out of the first training session and had never before entered the Magnolia state. As the specter of these three missing activists— Goodman, in particular, so similar to themselves—hung over the second training session, Hamer's warm and disarming personality brought some comfort to this new batch of volunteers, even as she taught them about her own experiences with Mississippi terror.

"Part of what I think has happened over the years in talking about Fannie Lou Hamer is that she has become somewhat of an iconic figure and the result of that is [she] becomes two-dimensional," suggests Bender. Part of what gets lost in this symbolic status, according to Bender, is Hamer's "humanity . . . her warmth and caring." Bender can remember exactly where she was when she learned that the charred remains of the blue Ford station wagon her husband, Goodman, and Chaney had been driving through Mississippi were found. She was in the Cincinnati airport returning to Mississippi from Oxford; so was Hamer. Bender was sitting on a bench talking with Hamer and Bob Zellner when a group of reporters who recognized Bender came "racing up to us and told us that the burned car had been found." Wasting no time, "Fannie Lou literally took me . . . in her arms, took me over to another space. Shooed everyone else away and sat and held me while I cried." Bender characterizes this as the "most intimate moment" she had with Mrs. Hamer during her years of activism in Mississippi.[125] It also is a revealing moment to consider the broad scope of contributions Hamer made to the Freedom Summer project.

More seasoned activists like Bender and fresh Freedom Summer volunteers alike found much-needed comfort in Hamer's warm and caring personality. In their activism, Hamer saw the promise of "the New Kingdom right here on earth." Hamer compared the student volunteers' willingness to help black Mississippians to the Good Samaritan's action in the biblical story where this character stops to help a wounded stranger. Like the Good Samaritan, Hamer reasoned, "these people who came to Mississippi that summer—although they were strangers—walked up to our door. They started something that no one could ever stop. These people were willing to move in a nonviolent way to bring a change in the South." Characterizing the summer volunteers' action as selfless and devoted, Hamer compared them to Jesus Christ. "If Christ were here today," she contended, "He would be just like these young people."[126]

Though Hamer lavishly praised the volunteers in the introduction to Tracy Sugarman's Freedom Summer memoir, *Stranger at the Gates*, Sugarman acknowledged that Hamer could also be quite critical of their behavior. In particular, he recounted Hamer's frustration with the white women volunteers' disregard for the rigidly defined, and brutally enforced, social mores of her small Mississippi town. "They sit out under the trees in the backyard playing cards with the Negro boys . . . Some of them even wave at cars as they drive by! They cut through white property to get to town. And they go to town to buy curlers and cokes," Hamer ranted.[127] Sugarman, an illustrator and a WWII Veteran who traveled south to capture scenes from the summer, became fast friends with Hamer. He characterizes their relationship as "beautiful," and suggests that their proximity in age made it easier for the two to confide in each other. With Sugarman, she shared "her worries about these kids. Her frustration with trying to get through to Washington, her fears and her hopes."[128] The summer volunteers were by no means perfect and Hamer's affinity for them did not blind her to their transgressions. Her instinct to instruct and protect them, though, brought these strangers close to one another. "All of the students who went south were just in love with Mrs. Hamer," Sugarman attests, "they would have gone through fire for her! They still talk about her."[129]

Out of admiration, many students flocked to her small Ruleville home once they arrived in Mississippi and their lively presence quickly transformed her old frame house into a hub of activity. The Hamer home was not the only one so transformed. There is perhaps no clearer sign of local people's support for the Summer Project than the fact that they opened their homes—at great risk to their lives and livelihood—to the volunteers. The act of living with one another, eating together, and talking with one another as equals fundamentally altered the self-conceptions of both parties. Relatively affluent outsiders, who bathed in ponds or with buckets of water in the backyard, used outhouses, endured chigger bites, and enjoyed the food that was available to them while in Mississippi, got a small taste of what life was like for blacks in the region. Years later, volunteer Heather Booth reflected on her own naïveté, suggesting that prior to Freedom Summer she "thought the police were our friends." She soon learned that Mississippi blacks "never ever thought that," as Hattiesburg native Victoria Gray Adams put it: "anytime they show up in our community it meant trouble."[130] For blacks, who had been expected to address even white children as "sir" and "ma'am," who had been prohibited from sharing meals with whites, and whose viewpoints and rights had never been respected within Mississippi's racial caste system, being treated with dignity and respect by the white volunteers helped reinforce COFO's message that they were entitled to and deserving of such treatment.

That summer, Hamer's singing and impassioned testimony about her own efforts to break through the repressive system of white supremacy inspired Freedom Summer volunteers as well as black Mississippians. Beyond inspiration, however, there was a much more practical side to her advocacy which revealed her strong connection to those she tried to persuade. A poor woman herself, Hamer understood that political strategies remained secondary to Sunflower County residents' immediate physical needs for clothing and food. So Hamer used discourse to forge a symbolic link between the two. By the summer of 1964, she was becoming widely recognized in her community and in activist circles as a community leader who could connect local people to one another and to larger national organizations.[131] As such, northern civic and religious organizations sent food and clothing to Hamer's Ruleville home for her to distribute among those in need and those punished for trying to register. Soon after these large shipments began to arrive (one weighed upwards of 30,000 pounds) Hamer's Freedom Summer activity grew to include the position of goods distributor.[132] She used this post, in turn, to encourage Delta blacks to assert their rights as American citizens.

The goods were sorely needed as local officials often withheld federal subsidies and surplus commodities from blacks in retaliation for increased civil rights activity. Ruleville mayor Charles M. Dorrough attempted to derail the donation distribution by taking to the airways to announce the arrival of the goods and encouraging listeners to flock to Hamer's home. Thinking that Hamer and the Freedom Summer workers would be so overwhelmed by those in need that the program would somehow implode, Durrough's strategy backfired as word of the donations secured a large audience for Hamer's registration advocacy. During these impromptu addresses, Hamer would commonly link the distribution of material resources with Freedom Summer's voter-registration efforts. Sugarman recounts one day when Hamer was unabashed in connecting COFO's political strategy to the donations from northern organizations. "No food and no clothes was going to be distributed," Hamer told a group of women gathered on her front yard at seven o'clock in the morning, until they went to the Indianola courthouse "to try and register to help themselves!" Beyond promising material goods to motivate these women, Hamer enlisted SNCC workers to drive them twenty-six miles to the Indianola courthouse. Hamer did not stop there. After loading these women into cars bound for Indianola, she interrupted a Freedom School class. Witnesses say she "roared up to the group of local women like a locomotive," stunning the class leader into silence. Hamer faced them, declaring, "Now, I know that you ladies that's here in the Freedom School understand how important it is for us to keep pounding on that registrar's door. It's even more important," she insisted, "than class." Scanning the faces of the women in attendance, Hamer confronted them even more directly: "Some of you . . . hasn't been down for a long time. Like you," she pointed, "Mrs. McDonald. And you, Mrs. Davis." Before the women had a chance to explain themselves, Hamer was ushering all of them in the direction of the remaining volunteers' cars, pausing only to ask them who preferred to ride with whom.[133]

By midafternoon, the group of women Hamer convinced to try to register gathered once again in her front yard. Perched on her front porch step, Hamer welcomed them back with an impassioned speech, in which she proclaimed: "These thirty women know that the way we're going to change things here in the Delta, here in Mississippi, is by getting the vote." Referring specifically to the link between material resources and voter registration, Hamer reasoned, "Folks up North want to help us free ourselves, and that's why they send these boxes."

Informing her audience that northern organizations were enabling them to take the risks involved with voter registration, she continued. "Anybody who loses his job because he tries to register to vote is gonna be helped." Hamer assured the women further, "Anybody who tries to help by standing up—going to Indianola—is gonna be helped." Looking out onto the crowd of local women, most of whom were disappointed after failing to pass the rigged registration test, Hamer pointed to the volunteers' cars and asked: "Who's gonna go with us tomorra when we drive down to the county seat?"[134]

In direct contrast to the uncompromising manner in which Hamer motivated these Sunflower County residents, Freedom Summer volunteers who canvassed the state typically followed Moses's more subtle approach to voter-registration advocacy. Payne describes what Moses came to recognize as the "most effective way to canvass." When going door to door, Moses would "introduce himself to people and show them a registration form, asking if they had ever tried to fill one out. Then he could ask if they would like to try it right there in their own homes." Believing that there "was psychological value in just getting people to imagine themselves at the registrar's office."[135] This approach held rhetorical value as well. By introducing Delta blacks to the franchise in the comfort of their own homes, by working with them to fill out the form, and by encouraging them to picture themselves registering to vote, SNCC workers were demystifying the process. What's more, the registration form and the ballot became symbols of citizenship through which the process of enfranchisement was made tangible—if not readily attainable.

Moses and other non-Mississippi natives were reluctant to go to the persuasive lengths Hamer traveled because they realized that local people's jobs, lives, and the lives of their family members were at stake. Hamer, however, seemed to justify her bold approach through personal experience. She amplified aspects of her common identity to relate to Delta blacks in a vernacular sense, while also standing—from her front porch perch—both literally and figuratively outside of the collective and above them as a prophet, preaching her enlightened perspective. Hamer often recounted how empowered she had felt upon first learning of her right to vote, "I could just see myself voting people out of office that I know was wrong and didn't do nothing to help the poor."[136] She viewed this awareness as a moment of conversion in her own life and, as her speech to the women in her front yard suggests, she worked brazenly to prompt this transformation in the lives of others.

While the use of material resources might seem like a forceful way to foster civic engagement, within Hamer's discourse these resources function rhetorically rather than coercively. The food and clothing she distributed served not only to satisfy immediate physical needs like cold and hunger, these goods also functioned as symbols used to overcome her audience's fear of reprisal and to spark their political imagination. The link she drew between her audience's physical need for these resources and the need to secure political power suggested that one was just as dire as the other. Hamer contended further that acquiring political power would enable those in the Delta to restructure the system so that they would no longer need to rely on donations from outside sources. Connecting their attempts at political representation to the need for the redistribution of resources, Hamer maintained that registering to vote is the means by which people can help themselves. Food and clothing, thus, functioned as promises of the privileges associated with citizenship. The goods are sent by people in the North, she reasoned, as tools to enable oppressed people in the South to free themselves. Mindful of the purpose for which the goods were sent in the first place, Hamer used them even more creatively as vehicles for those in her community to imagine a better life, as she had, where they would be able to meet their families' physical needs by exercising their suppressed political power.

In addition to sparking her audience's political imagination, the food and clothing Hamer distributed served as symbols of security and promises of protection against the risks associated with voter registration. Hamer knew firsthand the reprisals that would befall those she persuaded to register. She understood the danger associated with black civic assertion and yet she encouraged all those she encountered to register. More than this, Hamer preempted any possible reservations that people in her community might have about going to the courthouse. If they had no transportation, she would arrange to have a Freedom Summer volunteer drive them. If they could not read or write, she would inform them about Freedom School programs that could help prepare them for the registration test. If they feared for their livelihood, she assured them that "anybody who loses his job because he tries to register to vote is going to be helped." More than a comforting statement, Hamer used the large amount of donations sent to her community by northerners to support her assertion. Further, she described the unity fostered by those affiliated with COFO's Freedom Summer: "Anybody who tries to help by standing up . . . is gonna be helped." Simply put, Hamer did everything short of registering Mississippians herself—an action she later claims to have attempted. Hamer told one interviewer that COFO had "been screaming federal registrars ever since we heard of them and even asked them to deputize us . . . Let them deputize me as a federal registrar," Hamer challenged. "In a week I would have all these folks registered, 'cause I would be zooming everywhere. Like out in the rural areas where they're scared to come in from the fields."[137] In these ways, Hamer's discourse surrounding the act of voter registration reveals that she reasoned from her experiences of political assertion—aligning her own physical needs and emotional fears with the protection fostered by the movement and the excitement associated with political power—to persuade those in Sunflower County to join in the push for change.

Although her heavy-handed tactics did convince some to register, Sugarman remembers that Hamer "was not loved by a lot of her neighbors." He explains that some were turned off because "she called it like it was and it was not endearing" and others were just plain "jealous." Living in the Ruleville community that summer, Sugarman heard a lot of local people say with envy, "oh, Fannie Lou, everyone knows Fannie Lou, well what makes Fannie Lou so special?" In a "poor parochial agricultural black community," Hamer had made scores of northern "white friends. She had connections to congresspeople—imagine that!" Sugarman exclaims. In response to these critics, Sugarman contends that Mrs. Hamer "*was* special." Conceding that "you're not a prophet in your own land," he agrees with Edwin King that Hamer was indeed a prophet and that her great gift was her ability "to communicate what people in her community felt to people like *me* who didn't know shit about these people, who never could empathize" before Mrs. Hamer began describing their plight.[138] Soon, she would be given the opportunity to display this gift on a grand scale.

After two months of voter-registration canvassing and Freedom School teaching, the Freedom Summer activists managed to register twelve hundred new voters, but they did not secure the federal oversight and intervention for the registration process that Mississippi needed. What's worse, the summer of 1964 turned out to be "the most violent since Reconstruction: thirty-five shooting incidents and sixty-five homes and other buildings burned or bombed, including thirty-five churches. One thousand movement people were arrested, and eighty activists suffered beatings." In addition to the lynching of Goodman, Schwerner, and Chaney, "there were at least three other murders" on record.[139] As the summer came to a close, the energy and attention of these beleaguered activists turned to their final hope: the Freedom Democrats' challenge to unseat the segregated Mississippi delegation at the Democratic National Convention.

CONCLUSION

Movement scholars and activists agree that Fannie Lou Hamer was a powerful symbol of what Mississippi blacks could achieve if informed of their rights and empowered to act as citizens of the nation. She became a registered voter in the most segregated state in the union. She even ran for political office against a US congressional representative and testified before a national panel on civil rights. Hamer endured white supremacist retaliation and violent retribution for her accomplishments. But she lived to testify, transforming the oppressive experiences she suffered—being fired, arrested, and savagely beaten—into powerful arguments about the need for federal intervention into Mississippi politics and about the sacred stakes of the struggle COFO waged. Hamer's testimony, built as it was from her background growing up in Mississippi's violently controlled racial caste system, was both rendered in the vernacular traditions of her community and also represented the very discrimination civil rights organizations came to Mississippi to combat. In this sense, Hamer's symbolic status might appear coincidental. She was looking for a way to challenge the oppressive system that bound her potential just as COFO was spearheading a voting-rights campaign in the Delta. Such an interpretation, while true on the surface, does not tell the whole story. It overlooks Hamer's intellect, ignoring the fact that she had a hand in crafting her symbolic status through the vernacular persona she projected. In constructing her persona, Hamer selected which aspects of her life experiences to amplify before which audiences and toward what rhetorical purposes. Hamer also decided how to best present her testimony—the biblical parallels to pair it with and the tropes and linguistic traditions to draw upon. Her complex rhetorical strategies convey forethought and reflection, indicating that Hamer took her role as a prophet quite seriously and that she both understood, and is partially responsible for, the persuasive potential of her symbolic status.

From the cotton fields of Mississippi to the boardwalk of Atlantic City, as the next chapter will explore, Hamer continued to develop her rhetorical signature as COFO projected her symbolic significance. And she continued to face fierce opposition not only from white supremacists, but also from more polished African American leaders and members of the political establishment. Nevertheless, Hamer held fast to the firm understanding of who she was and what she was entitled to, which COFO had helped to cultivate. Illustrating her leadership ability, her strong desire to participate in the political process, and her faith that God was on the side of the oppressed, Hamer's steadfastness defied the insultingly stereotypical traits of submissiveness and contentment that were negatively associated with the image she projected. Her spiritual argument for social and political change also expanded beyond the realm of testifying to God's grace and encouraging her peers to read the divine signs that surrounded them. Chapter 3 not only analyzes Hamer's nationally televised testimony before the

DNC's credentials committee, it also explores how Hamer appropriated the Jeremiadic tradition to move Delta blacks to action by transforming their past of exploitation into a powerful source of experiential wisdom. This perspective, she argued, imbued the most oppressed with the moral authority necessary to save the crumbling nation.

CHAPTER 3

"Is This America?," 1964

Fannie Lou Hamer did national work from the deep most point of the pit. Mississippi was the pit; she was the canary in the mine. She was the voice in the hole crying out to those above, "Hey there's danger down here, there's violence down here, there's unfinished business down here."

—REVEREND JESSE JACKSON SR.

IN THIS CHAPTER I SLOW DOWN THE CHRONOLOGY OF HAMER'S LIFE BY pausing at two significant rhetorical moments in the late summer and early fall of 1964. Focusing specifically on the MFDP's 1964 challenge to be seated at the DNC, this chapter provides both the context for Hamer's memorable testimony and a sustained analysis of the testimony itself. My analysis of Hamer's most famous speech does not just argue that it was compelling. In contrast to past accounts, I provide a detailed consideration of Hamer's visual image, the vernacular quality of her speech, and the content of her testimony to demonstrate how and why this was so. I also consider varied reception to Hamer's testimony to explain for whom her rhetorical strategy of representation, and the larger vision of social and political change she symbolized, did and did not resonate. Such a multifaceted consideration of Hamer's DNC speech is key to understanding how Hamer became a national symbol, of what, as well as what about her biography gets compressed by such symbolic status. In particular, I suggest that while the MFDP was ultimately unsuccessful in replacing the segregated delegation sent from their state, through her testimony, Hamer developed a compelling national reputation as a simple and sincere poor black sharecropper who spoke truth to power. While this symbolic status opened doors for Hamer both locally and nationally, it concomitantly belied Hamer's intellect and the complexity of her message.

To recover these central aspects of who Hamer was and how she approached her activist career, chapter 3 moves from the political defeat in Atlantic City to Hamer's newly won celebrity back home. Unpacking the Jeremiadic structure of "We're On Our Way," a less well known speech Hamer gave at a mass meeting in Indianola, Mississippi, chapter 3 recovers the depth and complexity of her activist approach. Illustrating how she expanded and altered core themes from her DNC testimony to persuade a markedly different audience, analysis of this speech reveals what was becoming Hamer's rhetorical signature. Underscoring what remained consistent about Hamer's message throughout time, space, and toward varied audiences suggests that the Jeremiad was an integral feature of her persuasive efforts. The comfortable local setting for Hamer's Indianola speech, in addition to the lengthy, nearly forty-five-minute, nature of the address permitted her to set forth the most developed and nuanced account of her Jeremiad to date. Analyzing the core features of this appeal, furthermore, helps restore a sense of depth and intellect to Hamer's legacy that often gets stripped away through a myopic focus on her DNC testimony. Reflecting on audience reception to "We're On Our Way," in particular, and Hamer's mass meeting orations, more generally, also provides a glimpse into the vital role mass meetings played in propelling SNCC's grassroots campaign for social and political change in Mississippi.

FREEDOM SUMMER'S FINAL PHASE

The MFDP, founded in April 1964, was a nondiscriminatory biracial political organization formed in line with COFO's primary Freedom Summer objective: expand the possibility of political participation to all Mississippi's inhabitants. In a state with 480,000 blacks of voting age, but only 26,000 registered black voters, COFO leaders needed a multipronged strategy.[1] The Freedom Schools, voter-registration rallies, and community canvassing efforts, however, took a backseat to the MFDP challenge by midsummer. The Freedom Democrats first tried to work within the existing Democratic Party structure, but on June 16, when Mississippi blacks tried to participate in many of the state's 1,884 precinct meetings—where delegates were chosen to go on to the district and statewide caucuses—they were systematically excluded. Dittmer acknowledges that while a "few blacks were admitted in larger cities such as Greenville and Jackson . . . the vast majority of blacks who showed up for the meetings either were turned away at the door, found that the meeting site had been changed, or learned that no meeting was held in their precinct."[2] As a result, the official delegation to be sent to the DNC from Mississippi—the state with the highest percentage of black people in the Union—was lily white.

    In an effort to represent the state's population at the DNC and to encourage broad participation in the political process, the MFDP formed its own delegation, working from the precinct to the district and onto the statewide level.

The key differences between the MFDP and the "official" delegation was that the MFDP opened its doors to all races and remained loyal to the Democratic Party's nominee, sitting president Lyndon B. Johnson. By contrast, the Mississippi "Regular" Party (as the official delegation was dubbed) opposed recent federal civil rights measures like the Civil Rights Act of 1964. James O. Eastland, longtime US senator from Sunflower County, Mississippi, referred to the act as "the most monstrous and heinous piece of legislation that has ever been proposed in the entire history of the US Congress."[3] When Johnson signed the bill into law on July 2, Mississippi Democrats began shifting their allegiance to the Republican Party's nominee for president—the conservative senator from Arizona, Barry Goldwater.

Although the segregated Mississippi delegation rejected core aspects of the National Democratic Party's platform and were wavering in their support of Johnson, they were vehement in their opposition to integration and African American civic participation. The Regular Party passed a resolution at their statewide meeting promoting the "separation of the races in all phases of our society."[4] What's more, Mississippi's segregationist lawmakers were busy passing legislation to halt the strides made by Freedom Summer volunteers working in their state, including a riot control law, a curfew law, an antipicketing law, a law banning the distribution of boycott literature, and legislation aimed to criminalize the act of teaching at a school not licensed by the state, such as COFO's Freedom Schools.[5] Whatever their issues with the National Democratic Party, the Regulars were not going to step aside and voluntarily allow an integrated delegation to represent their state—a state that had voted for the Democratic ticket in every election since its formation in 1817.

With their exclusion from the official delegation well documented, the MFDP set its sights on challenging the legitimacy of this delegation before the eyes of the nation. The Freedom Democrats knew their challenge was audacious. So they appointed seasoned activist Ella Baker to set up an office in Washington, DC, and to seek national support for their cause. Baker also assembled a legal team spearheaded by the United Auto Workers of America's head legal counsel, Joseph Rauh. The Harvard-educated Rauh was a longtime civil rights supporter, who worked alongside Eleanor Roosevelt and Hubert Humphrey to insert a strong civil rights plank into the 1948 Democratic Party platform. Attorneys Eleanor Holmes Norton and H. Miles Jaffe joined Rauh, and together they submitted a legal brief to the credentials committee. This brief challenged the legitimacy of the Regular Party sent from Mississippi, explained the formation of the MFDP, and argued for the merits of seating the integrated coalition in place of the segregated delegation; the brief also provided historical and legal precedent for such a motion.

While Baker and Rauh worked at the national level, Moses redirected local Freedom Summer efforts to focus intently on the challenge. In an emergency memorandum dated July 19 and sent to all COFO field staff, Moses ordered "*everyone* who is not working in Freedom Schools or community centers" to "devote all their time to organizing for the convention challenge."[6] This redirection was necessary, he reasoned, because the MFDP needed to demonstrate its broad membership base for the party to claim representative legitimacy at the convention.

By August 6, when the MFDP held their statewide convention at the Masonic Temple in the capitol city of Jackson, the mood was hopeful. Moses's redirection of Freedom Summer efforts had borne fruit: eight hundred delegates from forty Mississippi counties came to Jackson to participate in the election of the thirty-four delegates and thirty-four alternates who would represent their party in Atlantic City. Nearly seventeen hundred additional supporters, excitedly waving American flags and holding signs bearing their county's names, joined these delegates at the temple. As sweat poured down her cheeks and welled up on the thick white beaded necklace she paired with a black sheath dress for the occasion, Hamer vigorously clapped her hands and determinedly shook her full head of dark hair, leading this group in a powerful rendition of "Go Tell It On the Mountain."[7]

Rauh assured the empowered crowd that the Baker-led lobbying efforts in Washington were paying off, as they had already garnered significant national support. He detailed their "eleven and eight" convention strategy: the MFDP would bring their case before the 108-member credentials committee, of which they needed only eleven committee members (10 percent of the committee) to vote on their behalf in order to bring the issue before the larger convention. Once the issue was introduced on the convention floor, the MFDP needed eight states to support a roll call vote, which would force every delegation to go on record—before a nationally televised audience, no less—for or against the MFDP.

The enthusiasm generated by Rauh's confident oration and Hamer's passionate song leading was tempered by Baker's pragmatic and, at times, mournful keynote address. Donning black cat-eyed glasses, her hair pulled back in a tight bun, Baker urged the energized crowd seated before her on that sweltering August afternoon to be careful to elect people "who represent us" and not those "people who, for the first time feel their sense of importance, and will represent themselves before they represent you." She charged the jubilant audience to remain fastidious and committed to the struggle. "I'm not trying to make you feel good," she confessed. "We have to know what we are dealing with and we can't deal with things just because we feel we ought to have our rights. We have to deal with them on the basis of the knowledge that we gain." That knowledge is derived from reading, "through sending our children through certain kinds of courses," and through remaining mindful of "this South we live in."[7] Modeling this mindfulness for her audience, Baker connected the MFDP's struggle to the lynching of Goodman, Schwerner, and Chaney, eulogizing the three civil rights workers whose bodies had been found just two days earlier buried in an earthen dam on a Neshoba County farm. National reaction to the deaths of two white volunteers and one black civil rights worker revealed the painful truth that, in America, black lives were perceived to be less valuable than white. Baker doubtlessly had in mind the somber image from Chaney's funeral of his grief-stricken mother, stone-faced behind a black veil, his sobbing younger brother by her side when she incited her audience: "Until the killing of black mothers' sons is as important as the killing of white mothers' sons, we who believe in freedom cannot rest."[8]

Carrying forth the legacy of these martyred activists, the MFDP delegation traveled to Atlantic City with "the confidence that the righteous have," explained one Freedom Summer volunteer.[9] The integrated sixty-eight-member coalition consisted of sixty-four black members and four whites. Among those members were blacks who had traditionally held leadership roles in their communities as teachers, clergy, and members of the NAACP, in addition to whites like Reverend Edwin King and Father William J. Morrissey, who fought for freedom within their closed society. The delegation also included a significant contingent of the rural poor "accurately reflect[ing] the socioeconomic composition of the state's black population."[10] Dorie Ladner remembers that "people like Mrs. Hamer and others," who were inspired by COFO's voter-registration campaigns, came "from the plantation, walked off their maid jobs, their waitress jobs, their fieldwork, their ditch-digging jobs . . . to say: 'I'm going.'"[11] Dittmer notes that grassroots activists like "E. W. Steptoe, Winston Hudson, Hazel Palmer, and Fannie Lou Hamer" represented the new constituency that COFO's registration and empowerment campaign elicited, specifically the type of "men and women who had little formal education or social status but who spoke—with authority and from experience—in the name of the dispossessed."[12] Guyot and McLemore were elected as chair and vice chair of the MFDP, respectively. NAACP activist and pharmacist Dr. Aaron Henry of Clarksdale was chosen as chair of the delegation, and Hamer was chosen as vice chair.

The MFDP delegation, accompanied by over one thousand supporters, made the 1,200-mile trip from Mississippi to New Jersey. Most of the MFDP members traveled by Continental Trailways bus, many had never been out of the state, and some had never left the county of their birth. All made the nearly twenty-hour voyage only to arrive at the rundown Gem motel, a mile from the convention headquarters. The party was operating on a limited budget; they slept five and six people to a room, while subsisting off little more than crackers and soda. Nevertheless, the group's spirits were high and they were determined; they got right to work painting posters and lobbying delegates.

The MFDP's approach in Atlantic City was multifaceted. The delegates and supporters held a round-the-clock vigil for Chaney, Schwerner, and Goodman on the boardwalk outside of the convention center. Backed by the SNCC Freedom Singers, Hamer belted out movement anthems as casual onlookers stood stunned at the charred remains of Schwerner's blue Ford station wagon. The group also displayed the bell from a church that was burnt to the ground by white supremacists in Philadelphia, Mississippi, set against a backdrop of a "We Shall Overcome" banner. This vigil-turned-political-rally contrasted with the jovial preconvention atmosphere—delegates driving around the boardwalk on go-carts, sporting "All the Way with LBJ" t-shirts and cowboy hats, riding the Ferris wheel, and purchasing kitschy political figurines from sidewalk vendors. The marked contrast drew attention to the MFDP challenge not only from other delegates, but also from television networks eager to reflect convention tumult and from an anxiety-ridden President Johnson.

Johnson was so preoccupied with the MFDP challenge, in fact, that he resorted to extralegal tactics to survey the delegation, ordering the FBI to tap Martin Luther King Jr.'s hotel room and to bug the SNCC headquarters at Union Temple Baptist Church. Johnson received frequent updates about the Freedom Democrats' activity through the wiretaps and from the thirty special FBI agents devoted to information gathering. Some agents posed as reporters to glean information, while others infiltrated key civil rights groups to learn more about their strategies.[13] Not only were the MFDP members disrupting what was to otherwise be a coronation ceremony for Johnson, they were forcing the Democratic Party to show its hand. Would the party take a stand for civil rights and democracy, extending upon the gains made earlier in the summer by the passage of the 1964 Civil Rights Act? Or would they succumb to southern pressure and avoid a walkout, the likes of which the party had not seen since 1948? Johnson called preconvention strategy sessions with his advisors and with civil rights leaders in a desperate attempt to avoid a floor battle that was sure to be captured by the television cameras surrounding the convention.

Just days after James Farmer of CORE, Roy Wilkins of the NAACP, and long-time movement stalwart A. Philip Randolph met with Johnson in Washington, the civil rights leaders were in Atlantic City holding meetings to garner support for the Freedom Democrats' cause. Black Mississippians like McLemore and

Hamer were often brought along with more notable leaders like Martin Luther King Jr. and Wilkins to meet with other states' delegates and credentials committee members. McLemore explains, "Mrs. Hamer did a lot of that because she was obviously a great spokesperson representing the Mississippi soul. She represented the heart and soul of the delegation."[14] By Saturday, August 22, two days before the convention's opening ceremony, the MFDP moved their protest from the boardwalk to a ballroom where they made their official case before the credentials committee.

In a crowded and smoky room at 2:55 in the afternoon, Chairman David Lawrence called the hearings to order. The room was set up in a rectangular configuration with the 108-committee members lining the perimeter. Witnesses testified from a chair in the center of one end of the room. The press was situated at the opposite end and there were "lots of press," remembers Michael Schwerner's widow, Rita Schwerner Bender.[15] The press had to fight to be there. The hearings were originally to be held in a small room, just big enough to seat the committee and those testifying. Confident that the MFDP's case would make for dramatic television, Rauh worked with the press to lobby the committee for a larger venue. Once the ballroom was secured, the MFDP rolled in three large gray filing cabinets each overflowing with sworn affidavits from Mississippi blacks excluded from participating in the democratic process. Flanked by these cabinets, the embattled Mississippi delegations sat facing one another as they waited to offer their respective arguments for why they should be seated as the legitimate delegation sent from the Magnolia state.[16] Bender, who testified on behalf of the MFDP that day, characterizes the Regular Party's behavior as "hostile," noting that they sat with arms crossed over their chests as they stared over at the MFDP delegates. When asked if she felt intimidated by them, though, her response came swiftly: "No, I felt angry."[17]

Rauh, Norton, and Jaffee, the team of lawyers Baker assembled, channeled that righteous indignation into compelling testimony against the Mississippi Regulars. Bender remembers that the witnesses met with the legal team beforehand to go over the order of the testimonies and to ensure that each speaker contributed to the overall case they were fashioning, while sticking within the tight time constraints imposed by the committee. Each side was given just one hour to make their case. Rauh garnered an impressive roster of witnesses, which included Mississippians directly affected by the reign of terror designed to bar black political participation, people like Hamer, Henry, and Edwin King. The roster also featured Rita Schwerner's (Bender's) testimony, which provided the emotionally laden perspective of a northern volunteer who had recently lost her husband in the battle for civil rights. To put these local testimonies in a broader movement context, the MFDP's case against the Regulars also featured national figures like Farmer, Wilkins, and Martin Luther King Jr.

In all, eight witnesses spoke on behalf of the MFDP that Saturday afternoon. To ground the MFDP's appeal, Rauh alluded to evidence from the forthcoming testimonies, read quotations from Regular Party members who denounced President Johnson, and cited legal precedents for unseating illegitimately constituted delegations. Rhetorical scholar Morgan Ginther suggests that the Freedom Democrats' case advanced a "moral and political perspective," rooted primarily in exposing the reign of terror used against blacks in Mississippi to deny their political participation.[18] The MFDP reasoned, most prominently, that the all-white delegation was not legitimate because it denied black participation. What's more, the Mississippi Regulars opposed Johnson's domestic agenda and they openly supported the Republican candidate. Some delegates even drove their personal cars emblazoned with pro-Goldwater bumper stickers to the convention. Because the official delegation from Mississippi was both illegitimately constituted and disloyal to the party, argued Rauh, the Freedom Democrats who had opened their doors to all races, sworn loyalty to Johnson, and supported the party's policies should be seated in their place.

After Rauh outlined the Freedom Democrats' case, he called forth the witnesses to testify about the unlawful acts that inhibited black political participation in Mississippi. At the end of his roster, following emotional testimonies delivered by Henry and by Edwin King, Chairman Lawrence directed the remaining witnesses to narrow the scope of their speeches. He asked them to focus only on problems with the election machinery, rather than on general life in Mississippi. Rauh immediately countered this instruction, arguing: "It is the very terror that these people are living through that is the reason Negroes aren't voting. They are kept out of the Democratic Party by the terror of the Regular Party," he maintained. Continuing with the testimonies as planned, Rauh suggested, "what I want the credentials committee to hear is the terror that the Regular Party uses on the people of Mississippi . . . which is what the next witness will explain—Mrs. Fannie Lou Hamer."[19]

"REPRESENTING THE MISSISSIPPI SOUL"

Hamer made her way to the dais, white purse clutched in her right hand and her MFDP badge prominently displayed across her chest. She took her seat as camera crews attached a microphone to the collar of her short-sleeved polyester dress. Hamer wore her hair down and curly, sweat gleamed on her cheeks, and her gold-plated front tooth caught the light in the ballroom once she opened her mouth to speak. Even before her testimony began, the image that Hamer conveyed stunned many to silence. Reagon, who sang alto to Hamer's contralto on the Atlantic City boardwalk, remembers that it was unusual to see a woman like Hamer projected nationally as a leader of a political party. Reagon describes Hamer: "she looked like all the black women *I* knew—she was hefty, she was short . . . she didn't look like my teacher. She looked the usher on the usher board at church. . . . She looked real regular."[20] The ordinary and representative quality of Hamer's image was certainly something that civil rights organizations hoped would resonate with national audiences. The MFDP promoted her individual testimony as emblematic of the sworn affidavits within their three file cabinets of evidence—a representation of the 93 percent of adult black Mississippians who met the requirements, but were denied the right to vote. Ladner suggests, furthermore, that Hamer did not just represent regular people, she represented the politically and economically disenfranchised, the "other, other America."[21] Bender agrees, remembering that Mrs. Hamer "wore old tattered clothes and she was not physically attractive and she didn't move in circles of educated and refined people—those were not her people. And she didn't speak for those people. When she spoke . . . she spoke for the wretched of the earth, she knew who they were."[22] MFDP member L. C. Dorsey reasons further that Rauh, the MFDP, and the other civil rights supporters championing their cause "successfully used Mrs. Hamer . . . in a clever way to force white America to look at what the Democratic Party was doing to women, to blacks, and to rural America."[23]

The vernacular quality of Hamer's image, which was unusual in this setting, both captured her audiences' attention and also lent credibility to her message. Much to the chagrin of the Regular Party, who challenged the veracity of the Freedom Democrats' claims to state-sponsored discrimination, Hamer's "unpolished" image conveyed honesty and sincerity.[24] Dorsey suggests that Hamer came across as the "true grit. The real McCoy."[25] Sugarman maintains that Hamer's image reflected that of a "black farmwoman, ill-educated, Christian, who believed in America, who believed in the Constitution, who believed that black people were as good as white people and it was wrong for them to be denied the benefits of American society." As such she functioned as "an honest spokeswoman for the dispossessed"; Sugarman remembers that in front of the credentials committee she "spoke truth to power," without script or notes, just telling them "what was in her heart."[26]

The sincerity and truthfulness of her message indicated by the lack of polish Hamer's image projected was reinforced by what several audience members refer to variously as her "ungrammatical profundity" and her "grammatically incorrect honesty."[27] Throughout Hamer's address, she repeated two different sentence constructions that violate Standard English rules of grammar. Specifically, Hamer used the singular form of the verb "to be" when the subject was plural, as in the second sentence of her testimony: "We was met in Indianola by policemen . . . ."[28] This under-pluralization of the verb "to be" is a frequently featured aspect of Hamer's address, occurring seven times within a relatively short, 1,100-word, speech. Hamer's verb conjugation is also consistent with what linguist Geneva Smitherman recognizes as one of "the most distinctive differences in the structure of Black Dialect," namely, the "patterns of using *be*." "When the forms of *be* are used" within African American Vernacular English (AAVE), explains Smitherman, "they are simplified so that *is* and *was* usually serve for all subjects of sentences, whether the subjects are singular, plural, or refer to *I, you, we* or whatever."[29] Perhaps most memorably, in the last line of Hamer's testimony—delivered through a cracking voice with tears welling in her eyes, she asked—"Is this America, the land of the free and the home of the brave, where we have to sleep with our telephones off of the hooks because our lives *be* threatened daily, because we want to live as decent human beings, in America?"[30]

While two of Hamer's commonly used verb constructions violated rules of traditional grammar, they both comported with traditions of AAVE and, in so doing, their violation conveyed additional meaning. As Reverend Jesse Jackson Sr. asserts, "the southern verb conjugation is important, but the mission statement is even more important."[31] And as Smitherman's explanation alludes, the mission statement behind Hamer's use of *be* in the place of "are"—in the example of "our lives be threatened daily"—"convey[ed] habitual conditions." Through this verb construction, Hamer was conveying that death threats were a mainstay of black Mississippians' existence.[32] Furthermore, Hamer's use of "was" in the place of "were" does more than simplify the sentence construction; it also intimates a unity among subjects. When Hamer makes such statements as "we was met in Indianola by policemen," or "we was held up by the city police," she is syntactically demonstrating both the cohesion of the group and the representativeness of their experiences. They share the same verb, their actions are unified, and repression to these actions is both common and widespread.[33]

Hamer's use of AAVE, the colloquial phrases like "raising Cain" that her testimony featured, her tendency to drop the "g" in gerunds such as "drivin," "talkin," "returnin," and the thick southern accent through which she delivered the address, all contribute to the image of Hamer as a representative of disenfranchised poor black southerners. As Jackson describes Hamer's speech patterns, "she came from brokenness and all the time she spoke in a broken way." He suggests, moreover, that the brokenness itself represents life's "highs and lows, the risks and the suffering."[34] Young remarks similarly that Hamer's rhetoric was "total folk speech," claiming further, "there was nothing polished about it."[35] Ladner also observes that Hamer's testimony was both distinctive and simultaneously representative because, unlike the other witnesses who had "little prepared statements," Hamer "spoke from her heart and from her mind and from her many years of vexation."[36] Through this nationally televised address, which enabled millions of Americans to both see and hear Hamer, she became emblematic of the radical delegation SNCC helped build within the MFDP.

What's more, the content of Hamer's testimony explicated SNCC's radical vision of social and political change before the nation. In his brief introduction to her testimony, Rauh made Hamer's rhetorical purpose clear: she was to testify about the terror she endured in Mississippi. By this point in her life, Hamer had plenty of material upon which to draw. She told the committee about being fired from Marlow's plantation immediately following her initial registration attempt. She exposed the retaliatory efforts of Ruleville's white supremacists who shot into the Tucker's home where she stayed after her eviction, and she shared her experience of being beaten with a blackjack in a Winona jail cell on her way back from a voter-registration workshop. These instances of terror led to the climactic conclusion in which Hamer questioned, "Is this America?"

Beyond using her experiences of exclusion as evidence for the Regular Party's illegitimacy, Hamer's speech offered a reflection of American political life that demanded corrective action. Notably, most of the perpetrators in Hamer's testimony were not hooded Klansmen or even ordinary citizens, she was careful to specify that those who prohibited her from registering—those who harassed, kicked, and ordered her brutal beating—were the very people entrusted with the responsibility to uphold law and order. Eleven times within her testimony, Hamer specified her antagonists as "policemen," "highway patrolmen," "city police," and even the "chief of police." Repeatedly designating these posts revealed that the terror faced by blacks in Mississippi often occurred at the hands of those who should be protecting their rights. By emphasizing this tragic irony, furthermore, Hamer began to chip away at conceptions of America as a just and moral nation. As Freedom Summer volunteers' stunned reactions to state-sanctioned violence in Mississippi demonstrated earlier in the summer, many Americans honestly thought the police were "our friends," there "to serve and protect."[37]

When she specified the official positions held by those who inhibited and punished her for political assertion, Hamer called America's moral stature into question. She simultaneously established her own moral authority, and the authority of those she represented, by describing the type of civic activities with which she was involved in noticeable detail. Her testimony began, for instance, with the attempt "to try to register to become a first-class citizen." Alluding here to the centuries-long struggle of African Americans, Hamer underscored the modest desire for which public officials repeatedly harassed her and her fellow would-be registrants. Furthermore, Hamer specified that she was returning from "a voter registration workshop" when she was arrested and tortured in a Winona jail cell. Her traumatic encounters with Mississippi law enforcement, Hamer made lucid, coincided with her attempts to assert rights guaranteed to her by the federal Constitution. Far from seditious or criminal endeavors, these examples of civic assertion and the corresponding reprisals further dramatized the irony of being punished for trying to participate in the political process.[38]

Though victimized in the narratives she recounted, Hamer did not emphasize her victimhood. Instead, she made several efforts throughout her testimony to establish agency—her own and the agency of those with whom she worked closely. When Hamer recounted the retaliation she suffered after her initial registration attempt, for example, she moved beyond the offense of being fired from the plantation "where [she] had worked as a timekeeper and a sharecropper for eighteen years," and featured her empowered response. Reacting to the plantation owner's instruction that she had to withdraw her registration attempt and that even if she did withdraw she might still have to leave his plantation "because we're not ready for that in Mississippi," Hamer claimed she "addressed and told him . . . 'I didn't register for you, I tried to register for myself.'"[39]

Hamer's accounts of agency also ground her appeal to moral authority, as manifest in the exchange she recounted between Annell Ponder, southwide supervisor for the SCLC, and the Winona police who attacked her friend.[40] Hamer recalled that from her own jail cell, she could "hear the sound of licks and horrible screams," and she could "hear somebody say, 'Can you say, "yes, sir," nigger? Can you say "yes, sir?"' To which Ponder replied, "Yes, I can say, 'yes, sir.'" "So, well, say it," was the officer's response. And Ponder replied, "I don't know you well enough." This defiant retort incited further beating, during which time Hamer told the committee she could hear Ponder "pray, and ask God to have mercy upon those people."[41] In passages such as these, Hamer alluded to the moral righteousness of the oppressed, the greater perspective held by those who lived through the fiery furnace of life in Mississippi and who held fast to their religious faith and their belief in American principles.

Questioning, "Is this America, the land of the free and the home of the brave," Hamer moved from the specific instances of discrimination she and her fellow registration workers endured to larger American principles. Her use of this rhetorical question is what makes her appeal both shocking and potentially transformative. In the conclusion of her address, Hamer takes her testimony beyond demonstrating civil rights abuses in Mississippi and toward a reflection of the gap between American principles and her lived experience. In issuing a question as her conclusion, more specifically, Hamer relied upon the moral authority she established throughout her testimony to sit in judgment of the nation, demanding a corrective response to the fundamental ruptures she recounted. If her previous depictions of the vengeance with which public officials in Mississippi counter black civic engagement were inconsistent with the hallowed American principles that her various audiences held, then corrective action should be taken. She even prescribed the necessary remedy within her speech, her husky voice near shouting, as she proclaimed: "if the Mississippi Freedom Democratic Party is not seated now, then I question America." In this passage, Hamer raised the stakes of dismissing the Freedom Democrats' challenge by establishing the members of the credentials committee, surrounded by the national press, as stalwarts of the nation's principles. If the committee sided with the Regular Party and refused to seat the MFDP delegates then, Hamer's concluding challenge suggested, America condoned state-sanctioned discrimination and torture. If the committee seated the MFDP, however, they could reaffirm America's reputation as "the land of the free and the home of the brave." Thus, Hamer positioned the credentials committee as not only audience members, expected to absorb the evidence of her oppression, but also as agents of change, imbued with the power to counteract its exclusive influence.[42]

Of all the testimonies offered, the opening and closing arguments advanced, the rebuttals and the refutation that took place during this two-hour credentials committee hearing, the eight minutes and ten seconds of testimony delivered by Fannie Lou Hamer is what people remember most. Nan Robertson of the *New York Times* referred to the "confrontation of the two forces" as the "most spellbinding event so far in the convention preliminaries" and singled out Hamer's testimony as "the most dramatic."[43] Arthur Waskow, an MFDP supporter, proclaimed, "Fannie Lou Hamer was agreed to have been the star."[44] The US senator from Minnesota and credentials committee member Walter Mondale recalled: "Hamer transfixed the room."[45] One need only observe the countless committee members who were left in tears when Hamer finished speaking to prove that her speech deeply touched many who heard it.[46]

Even before Hamer brought members of the committee to tears on that August afternoon, the MFDP knew that if the speakers before her could just "lay out" the case for seating their party, then Hamer "would get people's ear" as her experiences tugged at their hearts.[47] The Freedom Democrats were heartened by how their approach played out in practice. Ladner remembers the group "watching her speak"—pointing out that they "already had a good idea of the flavor of her tone and so forth" from speeches Hamer had given throughout Freedom Summer—but "when she spoke" that afternoon, Ladner still gasps as she describes the experience, "I was amazed again!" She gushes, "It was like, 'Oh, my God! Tell it! Tell it!'"[48] Hamer's ability to articulate southern black Americans' experience, as manifest in this testimony, is precisely what Sugarman identifies as her "great role for the movement." Arguing that "black people had been shut the hell up for a hundred years. They couldn't say what they wanted to say; they couldn't say what was in their hearts. They were intimidated; they were harassed; they were beaten; they were killed for saying what was in their heart."[49] Sugarman claims though that Hamer "could articulate what black people felt . . . she had the guts to say, 'hey, this isn't right!'"[50] Hamer's bravery certainly enabled her to speak with such conviction on that August afternoon, but it was ultimately SNCC's campaign of empowering ordinary people to assert their citizenship rights that catapulted her onto the national stage.

Through Hamer's visual image and the vernacular quality of her discourse, through what Dorsey refers to as "the truth and passion of her speech . . . the sincerity and the integrity and the dignity of her carriage," Hamer symbolized SNCC's radical vision.[51] Instead of grounding her plea for human rights and citizenship privileges in the ostensible similarity, and hence, equality of the races, Hamer's visual and verbal characteristics affirmed both race- and class-based differences as well as her entitlement to the privileges of American citizenship. Up to this point, "if we wanted white folks to pay attention to us," Dorsey explains, "we've had the burden of having to be Yale and Harvard-educated. Not just Yale or Harvard. You got to be both! And then you have to be able to look like them and to talk like them. And to be able to metaphorically deal with all of them at their level." Hamer stood out from those African American activists who came before her emanating middle-class respectability—women like Mary McCleod Bethune, whom Dorsey points out "had been talking to Presidents for years"—but Hamer held fast to who she was and what she was entitled to.[52] As her testimony indicates, Hamer did not come before the credentials committee to request the favor of being seated, nor was she looking for political compromises. Instead, she and the other poor black Mississippians the MFDP spoke on behalf of demanded the right to be represented. The basic truth Hamer both symbolized and proclaimed, that all Americans regardless of their level of education, the color of their skin, or the amount of money in their bank account are worthy of citizenship rights, astounded her varied audiences. McLemore characterizes Hamer's message as "overwhelming in the sense that she was able to begin to change the mindset of a political culture."[53]

REALPOLITIK

Although the reception of Hamer's speech was overwhelmingly positive, her testimony's potential to reshape American political culture was curbed by several audiences who felt threatened by her image, her message, and the larger vision of political change she represented. NAACP executive secretary Roy Wilkins, for instance, objected to the fact that Hamer did not disguise her lower-class standing when she addressed the nation. Wilkins pleaded with Edwin King to "do something about her dress," particularly "ugly flowery thing she wore to the Convention."[54] What's more, he confronted Hamer directly, telling her: "'Mrs. Hamer, you people have put your point across . . . You're ignorant, you don't know anything about politics. I have been in the business over twenty years. You have put your point across, now why don't you pack up and go home?'"[55] Although he was highly critical of Wilkins's derisive remarks, King later tried to contextualize the offensive comments, maintaining that Wilkins had spent his whole life telling "white middle class Americans that blacks are middle class, too" and then Mrs. Hamer, "who's a stereotype," came along and threatened to undermine Wilkins's claim to equal rights rooted in the similarity of the races. "Because of 200 years of white racism," which propagated the perception that "all blacks are backwards" as evidenced by the fact that "they can't speak the language. Don't know how to dress" and would therefore "embarrass you if they came to your church, much less your country club, especially your political party," King reasoned that Wilkins became quite nervous about catapulting someone like Hamer into the center of the struggle.[56]

Symbolizing SNCC's valiant efforts in Mississippi as she did, Hamer might have also received the brunt of NAACP's feelings of displacement. Dittmer explains the inter-organizational tension that arose between SNCC and the NAACP during Freedom Summer and suggests that "State NAACP leaders," though ostensibly included under the COFO umbrella, "felt shut out from the decision making."[57] Though the NAACP was the civil rights organization with the longest history in Mississippi, their traditional approach to activism—cultivating leadership among the black middle class—was being overshadowed by SNCC's radical grassroots approach. Members of the SCLC were closely aligned with the NAACP's position. These alliances came out most clearly in the days after the credentials committee hearing when local people like Hamer were barred from negotiation meetings to consider the compromises that the MFDP was offered. Seasoned activists like Bayard Rustin also urged the rank-and-file MFDP members to accept a political compromise, lecturing them on the difference between protest and politics.[58]

Young, the newly appointed executive director of the SCLC, was also someone who tangled with Hamer at the DNC and who favored reigning in the broad scope of SNCC's radically democratic vision. He mentioned that Hamer "got very upset with us" because of the SCLC's willingness to compromise and avoid a southern walkout. Suggesting that the MFDP had begun as a "demonstration party," Young nevertheless acknowledges that "they were more successful than anybody thought they could be," but that their insistence on "totally unseating the Mississippi Regulars" would have "lost the South to the Republicans." He referred to the totalizing position of "some people in the student movement" as "sophomoric," claiming that they wanted to force "a crisis that would have crushed the Democratic Party" because their position was "none of the parties were any good." Instead, Young saw the SCLC's willingness to work within and preserve the system as an integral step to achieving the subsequent voting-rights legislation.[59]

The threat of crisis did loom large over the preconvention proceedings. Although Ginther characterizes the arguments proffered by the Regular Party during the credentials committee hearings as primarily "legal and technical" in nature, their addresses also included appeals to fear in the form of thinly veiled threats of a southern walkout.[60] State senator and DNC delegate, E. K. Collins, along with the assistant attorney general of Mississippi, Ruble Griffin, were the only two representatives to speak on behalf of the Regular Party. Both the quantity of representatives testifying and the quality of their speeches indicate that the Regular Party did not take the challenge as seriously as had the MFDP. Rabid white supremacist and Mississippi Supreme Court justice Thomas P. Brady conveyed the Regular Party's irreverent attitude toward the MFDP's challenge when he commented on the Citizens' Council radio show that the hearing was "one of the most trying and uncalled for debacles that has ever been my duty to witness. Mississippi has been libeled before the nation," Brady maintained, "by a motley crew of agitators calling themselves the Freedom Democrats."[61] Throughout the program, he referred to the MFDP variously as "troublemakers" and "agitators," calling their charges against the Regular Party "ludicrous" and branding the multifaceted aspects of their challenge "jungle antics."[62]

The case the Regulars built for their own legitimacy and against the MFDP centered on the claims that the MFDP "represented no one" because the credentials committee had no proof that the Freedom Democrats followed the appropriate procedure for founding a political party; thus, the Regulars represented the only "lawful" delegation. The Regular representatives reminded the committee of their loyalty to the Democratic Party over the years, noting that the state had voted the Democratic ticket in every election since their inception. Collins and Griffin criticized the MFDP's case as "all emotion and no evidence," while pleading with the credentials committee members not to "kill our party"—an unnecessary reminder about the potential for a southern walkout.[63]

President Johnson was so determined to avoid such a crisis that he worked tirelessly to repress the radical vision SNCC espoused and to silence the organization's most persuasive advocate. Contrary to the widespread myth that surrounds Hamer's DNC testimony, it was not the case that Johnson interrupted the live television broadcast of her testimony by calling a spurious impromptu press conference. As Houck has discovered, Johnson did not call a press conference on August 22, and the address the president did deliver that afternoon, the speech that redirected the media's attention during Hamer's testimony, was a scheduled address delivered to an assembly of thirty governors who had gathered from all over the United States in the East Room of the White House. Johnson's short speech, filled as it was with vague proclamations of American greatness and Americans' obligations to retain this status, paled in comparison to Hamer's heart-wrenching testimony. Most of the major news networks realized this and therefore replayed Hamer's speech during their evening broadcast. This exposure succeeded in placing Hamer squarely at the center of the challenge, bringing her into the homes of Americans who, in turn, flooded the convention with telegrams of support for the MFDP.[64] And yet, Johnson adamantly refused to let Hamer participate in the convention, declaring that he would not allow that "illiterate woman" to be seated on the convention floor; "we cannot have her speaking again," King remembers vice presidential hopeful Hubert Humphrey insisting on the president's behalf.[65] If not through the intentional disruption of her testimony, then at least through his determination to exclude her from participating in the convention, Johnson, like Wilkins, tried to silence the very voice and vision that SNCC was amplifying.

In the end, it was Johnson who triply insulted the MFDP delegates by first offering them two at-large seats on the floor of the convention and then suggesting that the remainder of the party sit in the balcony as "honored guests." Johnson later specified that the two seats must go to Dr. Aaron Henry and Reverend Edwin King. Hand picking an African American pharmacist and a white college chaplain to represent a delegation in which poor sharecroppers, maids, and day laborers predominated was an affront to the MFDP members. Although Martin Luther King, Wilkins, Rustin, and other prominent civil rights leaders urged the delegates to accept the compromise, SNCC leaders held fast to their "let the people decide" philosophy and encouraged the MFDP delegates to make the decision for themselves.

Upon consideration, Hamer rejected the compromise, famously decrying: "We didn't come all this way for no two seats."[66] Her position was both practical and principled. In an initial closed-door meeting where political power players like the US representative from Michigan, Charles Diggs, Martin Luther King, Henry, and Rauh gathered to discuss options, Hamer remembered that Humphrey pleaded with her, his eyes filled with tears.[67] He told her that his chance to become vice president rested upon his ability to keep the party united, to which Hamer responded: "Well, Mr. Humphrey, do you mean to tell me that your position is more important to you than 400,000 black people's lives?" Edwin King remembers Hamer exhibiting her moral authority and telling Humphrey that she had been "praying about" him, insisting, "you're a good man and you know what's right," but the "trouble is, you're afraid to do what you know is right," Hamer told him. "I'm going to pray for you again."[68] Ladner suggests that the "other side" of Hamer's compelling sincerity was that "there was no compromise." The people Hamer represented had "put down their hoes . . . walked off their jobs . . . they have given up a whole lot" and "they didn't know what was going to meet them when they came back" to Mississippi.[69] In light of these sacrifices, Hamer was fundamentally opposed to cutting deals and striking insulting compromises.

There was no shortage of ideas floating around about how to both recognize the legitimacy of the MFDP's claims to discrimination and to simultaneously placate the Regulars—from the simple proposal of seating half of each delegation, "anyone who would take an oath of loyalty to the convention nominee," that Congresswoman Edith Green from Oregon suggested, to the more complex idea of splitting the two seats and corresponding votes proportionally between additional members of the MFDP, advanced by Edwin King.[70] In the midst of late-night political strategy sessions, backroom dealings, and pressure from the administration, Hamer's gift for distilling complex ideas to their essence stood out. "To me it's very simple," she told one interviewer, "if we was free almost a hundred years ago and if we are really free citizens, then what is we going to take a little something for?" She continued, offering an analogy to illustrate her position, if "the pie is mine . . . well then you don't take it and dish out how much I should have of my own pie. You just don't issue me my portion of pie if it's my pie."[71] This statement aptly conveys what was so fundamental, yet so profound, about the Freedom Democrats' strategy that Hamer symbolized. Her credentials committee testimony proved that Hamer did not need well-educated politically savvy African American activists to represent the MFDP's cause to the nation. Instead, to ground their plea for representation she used her life experiences, which were described through her words, reflected through the vernacular in which they were spoken, and indicated by her appearance. Presenting herself as herself—replete with dark sweating skin, an inexpensive dress, and a markedly southern black vernacular—Hamer demanded her fundamental right, and the rights of those she represented "to live as decent human beings in America."[72]

Upon rejecting Johnson's insulting compromise, the MFDP had no official representation at the 1964 DNC, although some delegates did unofficially attend the gathering using borrowed passes from other states' delegates. A handful of these MFDP members, including Hamer, Mrs. Annie Devine, and Edwin King, even tried to take the seats left vacant by the members of the Regular Party, who were offended by the compromise to seat two Freedom Democrats along with their delegation and who refused to sign an oath swearing loyalty to Johnson. Prominent white segregationists such as Justice Brady, Mississippi governor Paul Johnson, and former governor Ross Barnett referred to the loyalty oath request as a breaking point between white Mississippi Democrats and the National Democratic Party. Brady suggested that the Regular delegation was stripped of their freedom of choice "and thus became . . . with all the other national Democrats, second class citizens."[73] What's more, he threatened that there would not be a "white backlash" to the Democratic National Party, which he began referring to as the "National Negro Party," but rather a "white tornado" in response.[74] White southern democrats did vote for Goldwater in droves, many officially severing their ties with the National Democratic Party after the 1964 convention.

Unofficially occupying the seats left vacant by the Regular delegation was little consolation to the MFDP leaders whose challenge never even made it to the floor for debate. Their actions provided broader exposure for the MFDP's mission, though, as they caught the attention of the media. When asked by one reporter, "Where did you get the credentials to come into the building tonight? Do you have any credentials to sit in these seats tonight?" Hamer responded plainly, "No, we don't, only as American citizens."[75] When an NBC reporter asked Moses how he felt about the compromise, he angrily responded: "What is the compromise? We are here for the people and the people want to represent themselves. They don't want symbolic token votes. They want to vote themselves."[76] Moses's anger, argues historian Wesley C. Hogan, stemmed not from the Democratic Party's failure to "recognize the moral nature of the MFDP's cause," but rather from their failure to "follow their own rules."[77]

Even in the midst of anger and disappointment, the impact of the MFDP's protest at the DNC was clearly discernable. Though their challenge did not succeed in unseating the Mississippi Regulars in Atlantic City, it did prod the National Democratic Party to officially pledge that they would never again seat a segregated delegation, a promise that changed the face of southern politics. The MFDP's insistence on representation and the importance of the franchise, furthermore, pushed prominent civil rights leaders who were "relishing the victory of the public accommodations act" to see that, as Jackson put it: "the absence of barbarism is not the presence of franchise." Jackson credits Hamer with sparking this realization, "she fought for the franchise," he recalls, suggesting further: "her uncompromising stance on voting rights paved the way for Selma, to be honest."[78]

For her testimony and her participation in the convention more broadly, Hamer became widely revered as "the symbol of grass-roots activism in Mississippi."[79] And Sugarman insists that since Hamer's testimony people have "learned how to listen in ways that they never really listened before. You know you can look and not see; you can listen and not hear? I think the voices that came out of Mississippi, which were inarticulate voices—by and large—but honest voices, American voices that hadn't been heard before, she made us capable of hearing those voices and that's a gift to the country . . . A great gift," he reiterates.[80]

The convention also prompted political realizations with consequences for the direction of SNCC and the MFDP. SNCC fieldworker Joyce Ladner referred to the Atlantic City disappointment as "the end of innocence." Moses characterized it as a "watershed in the movement," reasoning that before Atlantic City, SNCC thought they "were working more or less within the Democratic party," but their experience at the convention revealed the party's support was only "puddle deep." Cleveland Sellers, also of SNCC, described the strategic shift that accompanied this realization: "Never again were we lulled into believing that our task was exposing injustices so that the 'good' people of America could eliminate them . . . After Atlantic City, our struggle was not for civil rights, but for liberation."[81]

Members of the MFDP interpreted their experience in Atlantic City quite differently. Dorie Ladner, the older sister of Joyce, considers the 1964 DNC "seasoning" for the work the party continued to do in the state. Arguing that the convention disappointment "didn't stop anything," she suggests instead, that it was simply "fodder to keep moving." "If we had thought that that was a disappointment," Ladner elaborates, "then we would have stopped much earlier . . . That was nothing that would stop people" because "people had laid down their hoes and their cotton sacks, their ironing boards . . . to go. So when people make those type of commitments they are usually committed." She views Atlantic City as "a taste . . . a learning experience for everybody. They went back to their communities and told what happened and they were prepared for the next go-round."[82] Guyot, chair of the MFDP, concurs, claiming that unlike "SNCC's position on the MFDP," which was that "it failed in Atlantic City so therefore it should be disbanded," the MFDP members "considered ourselves a newfound organization, an organization that SNCC certainly helped create, but we were not SNCC." By contrast, Guyot recalls, "we took the position that since we were going to be the Democratic Party in the state of Mississippi we were going to support publicly the election of Lyndon Johnson, Hubert Humphrey just like the Democratic Party should do."[83]

The 1964 DNC also marked a shift in Hamer's political ideology that manifest itself in her discourse. From the time young Fannie Lou became cognizant of the exploitative nature of the sharecropping system up until the time when she received this formal introduction to American politics, she held the faith that if the truth were revealed—if she could just demonstrate the narrow set of interests Representative Whitten was serving or if she could just expose the unrepresentative nature of the segregated delegation from Mississippi—then principled American people and institutions would move to rectify the injustices. Before Atlantic City, like Sellers and other members of SNCC, Hamer viewed discourse as a means to expose Mississippi's civil and human rights abuses before the eyes of the nation. After the convention, it became increasingly clear to Hamer that many Americans already knew the truth, and yet they failed to ameliorate the inconsistencies that racist- and class-based injustices posed to their prized principles of "liberty and justice for all." The discourse Hamer produced after this realization attests to the fact that although she did not give up on rhetoric's potential to spark political change, she did alter her rhetorical strategy. Hamer continued to represent American injustice through embodiment and testimony, yet she began accompanying this demonstration with a more incisive and provocative Jeremiadic appeal.

HOMECOMING

Inasmuch as the symbolic status Hamer attained through her DNC address opened doors for her both nationally and locally, as much as it promoted the MFDP's case and testified to the significance of SNCC's radical democratic vision, and even as Hamer's testimony exposed the state of Mississippi for failing to live up to American principles, it also severely compressed the complexity of her image. The flip side of celebrating Hamer's honesty and sincerity as conveyed through her image, vernacular, and the content of her testimony, is the mistaken understanding that "she spoke from her pain and from her suffering and she just let it speak, however it came out."[84] This characterization of Hamer's testimony, advanced here by Young but widely shared among those who heard her speak, suggests that Hamer did not consciously consider her rhetorical approach. It intimates, furthermore, that while her DNC testimony was significant in its context, Hamer's rhetorical corpus does not warrant the type of sustained consideration given to speeches whose rhetors imbue their texts with purpose and forethought. Similarly, much of what gets lost about Hamer as a historical figure can be attributed to a preoccupation with those eight minutes and ten seconds of her fifteen-year career as an activist. The surface level simplicity of Hamer's DNC speech, suggests Jackson, belies the fact that "she was an intellectual. If intellectual means thinking through and processing options." What's more, Hamer "was a visionary, she saw around the curve," Jackson insists.[85]

There is no better speech to recover the complexity, what Jackson and others maintain is "missing about her," than the forty-five-minute address Hamer delivered at the Negro Baptist School in Indianola, Mississippi. "We're On Our Way," delivered in September 1964, is among the greatest of all the speeches she gave during her activist career.[86] Several factors contribute to its exceptional status. The forty-five-minute recording of Hamer's address is the longest speech of hers thus preserved, and the recording itself permits one to consider both her vocal range as well as the audience's reception to her message. Such consideration suggests, in turn, that "We're On Our Way" was even more passionately delivered than Hamer's DNC testimony. The length of the Indianola address also provides Hamer the space to fully develop her complex Jeremiad, an argument strategy that she had been building over the last two years and which would go on to serve as a touchstone for the remainder of her activist career. Hamer's critique of the southern system of exploitation is even more incisive here than in her campaign speeches challenging Representative Whitten. And the lengthy nature of this address coupled with its setting enabled her to foster more meaningful connections with her audience of black Mississippians than was permitted by the Freedom Summer speeches she had been delivering from her front porch. Because this speech was delivered before a markedly different audience than her DNC testimony, moreover, one can take stock of the similarities between the two to describe Hamer's rhetorical signature, the core sense of self that emerged even while appealing to, in Reagon's words, "dual and antagonistic cultural systems."[87]

The mass meeting setting for this speech contributed to its greatness as well. Hamer's light shone most brightly when reflected back from the supportive faces of the community out of which she emerged. The supportive faces in this particular audience were also quite curious to see this woman from their neighboring town who had recently captivated the nation with her widely broadcast testimony. Hamer alludes to her local celebrity within the speech, mentioning that she and her campaign manager, McLaurin, had been trying without success—"for the past two years"—to secure a speaking venue in Indianola. Deriding those who just came "to see what I look like," Hamer nevertheless acknowledged that her DNC testimony "helped people wake up" and now hopefully they will "do something about the system here."[88] In fact, Payne contends that many Delta blacks were initially drawn to mass meetings "out of sheer curiosity," but once there, the movement songs and featured speakers held the audience.[89] In this respect, Dittmer surmises that mass meetings were "perhaps the movement's most effective organizing tool."[90] Moses referred to the gatherings as the "energy machine" of the movement.[91] Historian Emilye Crosby observes similarly that the "spirit and fervor of these meetings was contagious," and adds that they also "helped combat fear and break the paralyzing grip of white supremacy."[92] Cobb's memories support Crosby's observations, even as they attest to the significant role Hamer played in this movement setting. He suggests "people forget that as much as the movement was about challenging white supremacy . . . the movement was also about challenging black people within the black community," acknowledging what "Mrs. Hamer could do very, very effectively was push black people into action, challenge them."[93]

Those who witnessed Hamer speaking at these mass meetings agree that her political sermons were particularly powerful for members of the local community "because she could explain fairly complex phenomena in very straightforward terms that the people she represented, the people that she emerged from, could understand."[94] Young remembers, "from the minute she got up everything was silent because she spoke with such . . . she spoke with a spiritual authority."[95] In fact, Alan Ribback, later known as Moses Moon, traveled all the way from Chicago for this particular meeting in Indianola—expensive recording equipment in tow—to capture the voice of the woman who had come to symbolize SNCC's efforts in Mississippi.[96] Ladner agrees that Hamer's mass meeting orations were uniquely moving, suggesting that although the movement had "so many people" like Mrs. Hamer whose lives had been transformed by SNCC's empowerment campaign, "she stood out." When pressed to describe why this was, Ladner responded plainly: "Everybody doesn't have it." "Mmhmm, Everybody doesn't have it," Ladner repeats for emphasis. Illustrating her point by comparing Hamer to such oratorical greats as Frederick Douglass, Ladner suggests that like Hamer, Douglass "was one who had the ability to translate his bondage into the word that could capture what had happened to him and many others."[97] Ladner and countless others posit that Hamer was born with this gift; nevertheless, she coupled her natural abilities with concentrated effort—forethought and revision—to most effectively achieve her rhetorical purposes.

"WE'RE ON OUR WAY"

Put simply, Hamer's rhetorical purpose in this speech was to encourage black Mississippians to register and vote. As her own experiences with voter registration attested, if you were black in Mississippi, there was nothing simple about voting. To promote voter registration among an audience that had been exploited and intimidated for centuries, Hamer not only had to inform Delta blacks of their rights and encourage them to see themselves as agents of change, she also had to undermine the plantation mentality and the white supremacist terror that bound their potential. Confronted with this multifaceted rhetorical challenge, Hamer "don[ned] the mantle of the prophet," and advanced a Jeremiadic appeal.[98] The appeal itself was delivered in a circumlocutory style as opposed to a linear structure, but the major premises Hamer advanced and reiterated throughout the speech were: first, that Mississippi blacks are God's chosen people; God was on the side of the oppressed and would ultimately deliver them from captivity. Second, Hamer argued that God was not pleased by the ill treatment of his people; segregation had so weakened the nation that without a dramatic change America would crumble. Third and finally, Hamer coupled the assurance that God was on the side of the oppressed with pitiful depictions of white supremacists to strip their terror of its intimidating force. Hamer urged black Deltans to exhibit a charitable attitude toward their fallen white brethren, challenging black Mississippians to fulfill their moral responsibility as God's chosen people in an effort to save their crumbling nation.

"Blessed Are Those That Moan"

Leading into the body of her Indianola address in much the same way as her previous DNC testimony, Hamer declared: "My name is Mrs. Fannie Lou Hamer and I live at 626 East Lafayette Street in Ruleville, Mississippi."[99] After establishing herself as a fellow Mississippian, and a resident of Sunflower County no less, she forged an even closer connection to the mass meeting attendees by sharing the story of her first registration attempt at the local Indianola courthouse. As in the DNC testimony she delivered the month before, Hamer described the mistreatment that she and the Ruleville group endured at the registrar's office, and later, at the hands of the highway patrolmen. Further, she told the audience that she was fired from the plantation where she and her family worked and lived, that bullets were shot into the home of her friend's house where she sought refuge, and that she and her husband had been continually harassed by city officials since her initial registration attempt. Beyond this, Hamer went into even greater detail about her Winona beating here than she had during her DNC testimony.

Though it might seem counterintuitive for Hamer to promote voter registration among Delta blacks by recounting the brutal retaliation she suffered for her civic assertion, Hamer utilized her experiences with white supremacist terror to firmly establish her vernacular identity as someone who had been oppressed and brutally excluded from the promises and privileges of American citizenship. This first premise in her Jeremiad pulled through arguments she had been making for the last two years about walking through the shadows of death, about Mississippi being the iron furnace—like Egypt, providing schooling of the soul for the oppressed. Historian David Howard-Pitney explains that the Jeremiad, "meaning a lamentation or doleful complaint," is a term "derive[d] from the Old Testament prophet, Jeremiah, who warned of Israel's fall and the destruction of the Jerusalem temple . . . as punishment for the people's failure to keep the Mosaic covenant."[100] An extension of the Exodus narrative, the American Jeremiad has deep roots in the discursive traditions of both Anglo and African Americans. Each of these traditions feature a characteristic rhetorical structure: namely, a reminder of the chosen people's covenant with God, a critique of their failure to live up to this promise, and the prophecy that society will fulfill its promise and return to both God's favor and their exceptional destiny. The "black Jeremiad," in particular, adapts the familiar Western rhetorical structure to reveal the paradoxes embedded in the African American experience. In a twist of signification, "blacks are [characterized as] a chosen people *within* a chosen people." Though intertwined, the roles assigned to black and white Americans within the black Jeremiadic framework are distinct; "by virtue of their unjust bondage," argues Howard-Pitney, blacks claim "a messianic role in achieving their own and others' redemption."[101]

In "We're On Our Way," Hamer began crafting this messianic identity for her audience of Delta blacks by moving beyond her own testimony of enduring oppression and injustice toward indicating the widespread and ongoing nature of the abuse. "'Blessed are those that moan, for they shall be comforted.' And we have moaned a long time in Mississippi," she asserted. Suggesting that God is on the side of the oppressed, Hamer demonstrated the depths of oppression Delta blacks suffer: "He said 'the meek shall inherit the earth.' And there's no race in America that's meeker than the Negro":

> We're the only race in America that has had babies sold from our breast, which was slavery time. And had mothers sold from their babes. And we're the only race in America that had one man had to march through a mob crew just to go to school, which was James H. Meredith.[102]

Since she began speaking for the movement, Hamer had been comparing black Mississippians' experience to the oppression the Israelites suffered in Egypt. In this speech, Hamer similarly emphasized the exceptionally oppressive nature of their experience to establish Mississippi blacks as God's chosen people and to indicate why he is angered by their mistreatment. "God is not pleased," Hamer insisted, connecting centuries of injustice to recent events:

> God is not pleased at all the murdering, and all of the brutality, and all of the killings for no reason at all. God is not pleased at the Negro children in the state of Mississippi suffering from malnutrition. God is not pleased because we have to go raggedy each day. God is not pleased because we have to go to the field and work from ten to eleven hours for three lousy dollars.[103]

To draw out the broader implications of their localized abuse, furthermore, Hamer moved from her individual testimony to the broader experience of suffering in Mississippi and on to its national consequences.

"A House Divided Against Itself Cannot Stand"

Delta blacks' exclusion from the promises and privileges of American citizenship was not just unfortunate for them, argued Hamer; their exclusion threatened the nation's survival as it defied America's covenant with God and weakened the very principles on which the nation stood. To demonstrate this second premise to an audience she constituted as chosen people within a chosen people, Hamer prodded her Indianola auditors first with a familiar question, "is this America, the land of the free and the home of the brave?" Altering her now-famous refrain, she pushed this particular audience further than she had the credentials committee in Atlantic City, "where people are being murdered, lynched, and killed, because we want to register and vote."[104] Hamer returned to this central question later in the speech, this time yielding an answer: "I want to say tonight, we can no longer ignore the fact, America is not the land of the free and the home of the brave when just because people want to register and vote and be treated like human beings, Chaney, Schwerner, and Goodman is dead today."[105] Invoking the names of the three civil rights workers who were found dead in early August—less than two hundred miles away from where she spoke—Hamer related local and recent events to make the case even more relevant for her audience of Delta blacks.

More than passively agreeing that the nation has failed to live up to its principles, Hamer encouraged this audience to recognize the dire implications of America's failure. "Righteousness exalts a nation, but sin is a reproach to any people," Hamer repeated this Proverb twice within her speech, prophesying: "Sin is beginning to reproach America today."[106] Hamer paraphrased Abraham Lincoln and Jesus Christ, contending: "A house divided against itself cannot stand. America is divided against itself and without their considering us human beings, one day America will crumble."[107] These passages, in which Hamer set biblical scripture in dialogue with ubiquitous aspects of American mythology, dramatized the distance between American promises and the African American experience. More than pointing out America's failure to live up to its principles, the biblical scripture that Hamer summoned forces a choice: either America will recommit itself to its principles by making democracy a reality for all its inhabitants or the nation will crumble.

The "shared myths, symbols, and rituals" that constitute America's "civil religion" support African Americans' hope that the nation will choose repair over destruction. As Howard-Pitney describes this creed, the country's civil religion rests upon "the idea that Americans are in some important sense a chosen people with a historic mission to save and remake the world."[108] This concept of American Exceptionalism is codified in such founding myths as the story of the New England Puritans, who escaped a "hopelessly corrupt European religious and social establishment" to "found a holy society in the American wilderness."[109] American leaders like Washington and Lincoln are praised as "patriarchs and saviors" within this pervasive mythology, while founding documents such as the Declaration of Independence and the Constitution are revered as "scripture."[110]

In her discourse, Hamer does not simply adopt the myths, symbols, and rituals that constitute America's civil religion; instead, she adapts them— *Signifyin(g)* upon their meaning to demonstrate America's declension and to promote repair. As Gates further describes the double-voiced practice of Signifyin(g), it is a process of revising in which "black vernacular discourse proffer[s] its critique of the sign as the difference that blackness makes within the larger political culture and its historic unconscious."[111] This critique works through the act of adaptation and reinterpretation, a practice not unlike literary theorist Kenneth Burke's notion of "perspective by incongruity." Burke acknowledges that this method of creating new meaning through juxtaposition can serve activist ends. Perspective by incongruity, which Burke likens to "verbal atom cracking," is designed to "'remoralize' by accurately naming a situation already demoralized by inaccuracy."[112]

Hamer's critique of America's failure to live up to its principles, and the prophecy that such a breach in the nation's covenant with God will ultimately end in destruction, are significant components of the Jeremiad she advanced. But the most pivotal aspect of her argument is the moral responsibility she assigns to Delta blacks. As chosen people within a chosen people, she contended, African Americans have a moral imperative to liberate themselves, free the nation from its affliction, and restore America's covenant with God. As she had for the previous two years, Hamer imbued the suffering of African Americans with meaning and purpose. Being excluded from centers of power granted them superior perspective in remaking the crumbling nation. In "We're On Our Way," Hamer took this argument a step further. The third premise of Hamer's Jeremiad is that Delta blacks have a divine responsibility to deliver the nation from an otherwise imminent demise.

"God Is Not Going to Put It in Your Lap"

To compel the action advocated in this final premise, it was not enough for Hamer to inform her audience of their special position and their corresponding divine responsibility; Hamer had to overcome two powerful psychological obstacles: namely, fear of white supremacy and the plantation mentality that this ubiquitous ideology engendered. Though centuries of oppression imbued Delta blacks with moral authority over their white oppressors, it also fostered for blacks envy of whites' privileged station in life and feelings of helplessness in the face of their own disadvantaged situation. Hamer acknowledged these destructive sentiments head on:

> [T]o be truthful to you, tonight, I first wished I was white. Some of you've wished the same thing. The reason I wished it was they was the only people that wasn't doing nothing, but still had money and clothes. We was working year in and year out and wouldn't get to go to school but four months out of the year because two of the months we didn't have nothing.[113]

Countering this widespread desire to switch places with the white oppressor, Hamer invoked scripture that appealed to the natural sensibilities of those who spend their days tilling the land: "The 37th Psalms says 'Fret not thouselves because of evildoers, neither be thy envious against the workers of iniquity for they shall be cut down like the green grass and whither away as the green herb.'"[114] Through this biblical passage, Hamer carried forth the lesson she gleaned from the songs her mother sang to her as a child. Expressing the conviction that whites were in no position to envy, even as she reassured her black audience that they would be cared for if they trusted in God. Arguing that the experience of slavery and continued forms of oppression should not be reasons to feel disempowered, Hamer reiterated: "*We* don't have anything to be ashamed of. All we have to do is trust God and launch out into the deep. You can pray until you faint," she charged, "but if you don't get up and try to do something, God is not going to put it into your lap."[115]

Continually guarding against the complacency that promises of divine intervention risk promoting, Hamer balanced claims that reassured her audience God was on the side of the oppressed and God would bring relief to the captive with claims that reversed internalized feelings of helplessness by challenging her audience to act. Questioning their faith, Hamer stood apart from the congregation and remarked, "Now you can't tell me you trust God and come out to church every Sunday with a bunch of stupid hats on seeing what the other one have on and paving the preacher's way to hell and yours too."[116] Although the comment was highly critical of her immediate audience, many recognized the truth of her critique and responded with roaring applause. A similar claim Hamer made in the middle of her address was met with comparable enthusiasm. She contended boldly: "You have a responsibility . . . to walk in Christ's footstep and keep his commandment . . . to launch into the deep and go to the courthouse, not [to] come here tonight to see what I look like, but to do something about the system here."[117] In these passages, Hamer confronted those churchgoing people who keep up with appearances, but not with the scripture's convictions.

As Hamer expressed it, the songs sung and the scripture read at mass meetings should be purposeful and provocative, not just palliative and oriented toward socializing. "I believe tonight, that one day in Mississippi—if I have to die for it—we shall overcome. We Shall Overcome means something to me tonight," she told her audience. "Because He said 'seek and ye shall find, knock and the door would be opened, ask and it shall be given.' It was a long time, but now we see. We can see, we can discern the new day."[118] Hamer moved along with her audience from the past where their ability to act was clouded by the pervasive plantation mentality to a pivotal moment of recognition and empowerment that prompted action in line with the scripture's challenges.

Hamer's personal testimony coupled with the scriptural reassurances and the direct challenges she advanced all worked to overcome the engrained feelings of powerlessness she shared with her audience. To quell Delta blacks' fears of white supremacy, moreover, Hamer turned their attention to signs of *white* Mississippians' trepidation. She accomplished this shift by proclaiming: "We don't have anything to be ashamed of here in Mississippi . . . we don't carry guns because we don't have anything to hide. When you see people packing guns and is afraid for people to talk to you, he is afraid something is going to be brought out into the open on him."[119] She echoed the reversal of fear throughout her address, asking her audience at one point: "Do you think anybody would stand out in the dark to shoot me and to shoot other people, would you call that a brave person?"[120] Without hesitation, her audience shouted: "No!" Using the example of night-riding white supremacists as a thermometer to measure the nation's health, Hamer altered her house divided refrain: "It's a shame before God that people will let hate not only destroy us, but it will destroy them. Because a house divided against itself cannot stand and today America is divided against itself because they don't want us to have even the ballot here in Mississippi."[121] According to Hamer, white Mississippians are afraid of black suffrage for the same reason they worry about their actions being brought out into the light of day. "If we'd been treated right all these years," she reasoned, "they wouldn't be afraid for us to get the ballot."[122]

Hamer explained that blacks have been systematically deprived of their constitutional privileges because of white shame and white panic over black retaliation. This interpretation of the political situation in Mississippi also contributed to overcoming the plantation mentality as it specifically targeted allegations of African American apathy. "People had said for years and years 'the Negroes can't do anything.' That's the report they was sending out about the people of Mississippi," reiterating, "'The Negroes are ignorant,' But just who is acting stupid now?" she asked her audience of black Mississippians.[123] Interpreting white violence as a sign of shame, fear, and stupidity weakened the terrorist power that white supremacists held over the lives of black Mississippians. Hamer weakened the common adversary she shared with her audience by establishing the righteousness of black Americans' struggle for suffrage and contrasting it to the white segregationists' deplorable motives for suppressing black civic assertion. Exposing white supremacists as shameful, fearful, and ignorant, Hamer encouraged blacks to exhibit a charitable attitude toward their pitiful white brethren.

From abolitionism onward, advocates of social and political change in the United States have featured the messianic characterization of American blacks to establish a moral imperative. "Messianic themes of coming social liberation and redemption have deep roots in black culture," observes Howard-Pitney, who also notes that for generations blacks have championed their unique role in bringing about larger national redemption.[124] Hamer was, thus, following in a long line of activists when she imbued Delta blacks' participation in the black freedom movement with salvific significance: "[W]e are not fighting against these people because we hate them." Quite conversely, "We are fighting these people because we love them and we're the only thing can save them now. We are fighting to save these people from their hate and from all the things that would be so bad against them. We want them to see the right way."[125] African Americans' struggle against white supremacy, as this final plea made manifest, was a struggle not only *for* recognition—for blacks to be recognized as citizens worthy of, and entitled to, rights and protection—the struggle was also one aimed at prompting segregationists *to* recognize the way their oppression of blacks affected themselves and the nation at large.

Acknowledgment of the interconnection between the races was central to this recognition. Exposing white hypocrisy, Hamer insisted: "Some of the white people will tell us, 'Well, I just don't believe in integration.' But he been integrating at night a long time!"[126] Though white men's sexual exploitation of black women was no joke in the Mississippi Delta, the audience laughed and applauded Hamer's audacity in pointing out the reality of their experience. She drew her audience in through this bold allegation and deepened their adherence through a well-known scriptural reference: "The seventeenth chapter of Acts and the twenty-sixth verse said: 'Has made of one blood all nations.' So whether you black as a skillet or white as a sheet, we are made from the same blood and we're on our way!"[127] The races' interconnection was not just a fact of life in the Delta; Hamer contended that it was divinely sanctioned. In order to prompt such recognition within the minds of whites, she encouraged her black audience to love their enemy. Embodying such an attitude herself, she told her audience that "Every night of my life that I lay down before I go to sleep, I pray for these people that despitefully use me."[128] In this culminating thought, Hamer advocated a selfless, morally superior type of love, one that is rooted in the promise of the gospels and in the inescapable interconnection between the races.

In "We're On Our Way," Hamer deployed rhetoric to incite directed action from her audience. She used the relational quality of speech to challenge Delta blacks. She worked to overcome the deeply engrained plantation mentality, to move her audience beyond their fear of political assertion and toward their obligation to help themselves, their white brethren, and the larger nation to which they belonged. By linking black Deltans' struggle to the familiar Exodus narrative and its Jeremiadic extension, Hamer began cultivating the will to change among an audience who had been subjugated for centuries. Assuring Mississippi blacks that God was on their side and imbuing their fight with biblical significance, moreover, Hamer encouraged her audience to see liberation as imminent, but not inevitable. She signified upon celebrated American refrains, marking them with the difference of black Deltans' experience in such a way that revealed the nation's failure to live up to its principles. Bringing biblical prophecy to bear on this declension, Hamer forced a choice: the country could either reaffirm its covenant with God by extending the privileges of citizenship to all Americans or it could continue dividing against itself and ultimately crumble. Since white Americans broke the initial covenant with God, they lacked the moral capability to direct a reparative effort. Black Americans' position as the most oppressed race in the nation secured God's favor and imbued them with the perspective necessary to take a leading role in fostering national change.

Analysis of the content of Hamer's speech reveals the complexity of her message. Consideration of its reception—the roaring applause she received upon hitting particular punch lines, calling out hypocrites, and speaking candidly about controversial topics—suggests that her message also resonated quite powerfully with her audience. This powerful resonance was derived in no small part from Hamer's familiarity with the shared black Baptist tradition in which the majority of her audience was reared. As folklorist Worth Long notes, those movement speakers with "very good, traditional . . . oratorical skills" would incite action by drawing upon sermons that were "encoded" within the community. Given a sermon's widespread familiarity, the speaker would not have to "preach the sermon" in its entirety, but she could simply "refer to it because people know it and they believe it."[129] The Exodus narrative and the Jeremiad are sermonic frameworks that would have been well known among Hamer's audience of Delta blacks. By invoking these traditions to urge civic assertion, Hamer made voter registration—a strange and fear-inducing practice—more familiar and more significant.

Hamer's rhetorical power was derived from her familiarity with and proximity to her Indianola audience, as well as from the distinctive qualities that set her apart from them. When asked about other local people who spoke at mass meetings, Bender suggests Hamer was without comparison: "I can't think of anybody else, frankly, who I've ever known who had the ability to speak and move people the way Mrs. Hamer did." Her ability to move people, posits Bender, came in part from her frank speech in these and all other movement settings, "she wasn't polite necessarily. I mean she called it as she saw it . . . she was plainspoken," Bender explains.[130]

Reagon's reflections about Hamer's rhetorical power speak to the range she exhibited in lengthier mass meeting orations. There was strength in Hamer's plainspoken orations, Reagon remembers: "What I saw was the clarity. She was so clear and there was such a breath of fresh air and she was so powerful, she described people shooting at her, beating her, and she was fine." And there was love, Reagon recalls, "I really liked the feeling that in the midst of the most intense danger there could be a sense of peace and safety. That you really could speak about the immense anger, but what people listening to you felt was how much love you had in you. Those are not lessons you get often." According to Reagon, Hamer was both clear—plainspoken—and distinctively complex: "She was always so clear, strong, insistent. And she was so mad and she was so loving," Reagon pauses, "I really needed to meet a black woman like that."[131]

Even as Hamer inspired others through the rhetorical range exhibited in her powerful mass meeting orations, the speeches she delivered fostered her own personal transformation. Payne describes the way in which mass meetings functioned as inventive spaces for speakers to rehearse the empowered identities they were fashioning. "Mass meetings," he posits, "created a context in which individuals created a public face for themselves, which they then had to try and live up to." Not wanting to contradict the powerful image they projected, the speaker continually endeavored to embody the new role. Eventually the identity, which was first fashioned rhetorically, becomes a habit of character: "After playing the role he has defined for himself for a while—and getting patted on the back for it—he may find that the role becomes natural," reasons Payne.[132]

For Hamer, donning the mantle of the prophet was something she infused into all aspects of her life. Guyot characterizes Hamer as "a religious fanatic in the most positive sense. She took her religious beliefs and parlayed them into all of her politics."[133] In many ways, SNCC had given her the extra push, the confidence in herself that she needed to take the religious beliefs, knowledge, and principles she already possessed and apply them to political situations that would alter the direction of her life here on earth. And this was precisely SNCC's aim: "The whole freedom movement for me was to have people determine and define their lives," contends Long.[134] In the sense that Hamer's "We're On Our Way" oration urged a transformation in blacks' self-conception, even as it crafted her own empowered persona, the speech provides a telling glimpse into Hamer's unfolding biography, her rhetorical influence, and the larger purpose of the Mississippi freedom movement.

CONCLUSION

Whether she was addressing Mississippi sharecroppers or delegates to the Democratic National Convention, Hamer represented her history of oppression, her ongoing experiences of exclusion, and the violent retaliation she suffered at the hands of white segregationists. By combining her personal testimony, blacks' collective suffering, and the Jeremiadic rhetorical tradition, Hamer inspired poor southern blacks who had been intimidated into submission for centuries. Toward audiences less familiar with the extent of this oppression, furthermore, Hamer's message provided a unique perspective about the rampant deprivation and dissatisfaction in the Mississippi Delta. For SNCC, and other civil rights organizations that sought to expand the franchise to all America's inhabitants, Hamer functioned as a symbolic representative—offering personal accounts of much larger phenomena that illustrated the need for federal intervention into Mississippi politics.

The DNC testimony and Hamer's 1964 Indianola speech offer insight into Hamer's developing rhetorical signature. After her nationally televised testimony, remembers McLemore, "Hamer got invitations to speak everywhere," she and her campaign manager, McLaurin, were literally "overwhelmed" with the speaking requests that came pouring into the Hamers' Ruleville home.[135] Living and working in Ruleville, while traveling and speaking across the country, Hamer became, in Reagon's words, "a straddler." One who is "born in one place . . . and sent to achieve in the larger culture, and in order to survive [straddlers] work out a way to be who we are in both places or all places we move."[136] Sustained consideration of these two speeches that Hamer delivered just weeks— but worlds—apart from one another suggests that the Jeremiadic rhetorical tradition was a core feature of Hamer's rhetorical signature. Hamer imbued the Jeremiadic framework with contemporary significance by inserting her personal testimony within its structure to adapt the traditional political sermon to the activist ends she represented.

Over the next four years of her career, Hamer traveled from the West Coast of Africa to Harlem and on to Washington, DC. Her core message and activist mission was enriched by these travels, but she held fast to the Jeremiadic frame. Chapter 4 considers the influence that Hamer's trip to Africa, her newfound relationship with Malcolm X, the MFDP's congressional challenge, and reelection campaigns, as well as poverty politics in the state, had upon Hamer's ideology as communicated through her discourse. The next chapter will also analyze the symbolic transformation in Hamer's image from a plainspoken sharecropper to a warrior, noting how Hamer contributed to this change, why her warrior image was propagated by others, and what about Hamer's biography this powerful symbolic status overlooks.

CHAPTER 4

"The Country's Number One Freedom Fighting Woman," 1964–1968

IN THE YEARS FOLLOWING HER NATIONALLY TELEVISED CREDENTIALS COM-
mittee testimony, Hamer crisscrossed the United States and ventured all the
way to the West Coast of Africa. She shared platforms with Malcolm X in Harlem and challenged the US congressional representatives sent from her state.[1]
She filed a lawsuit against the Sunflower County registrar, which helped secure reelections in the Delta towns of Sunflower and Moorhead. She became a
spokesperson for, and an inspiration to, the striking farmworkers who formed
the Mississippi Freedom Labor Union (MFLU). And she was instrumental in
coordinating local poverty programs made possible by the hard-fought federal dollars that came into her state from the Office of Economic Opportunity
(OEO). Hamer's valiant efforts—relentlessly fighting battles on multiple fronts,
displaying courage in the face of dispiriting odds, holding fast to principles
and promoting enhanced awareness—transformed her symbolic status. Among
Mississippi blacks, movement activists, and the broader American public, Hamer became increasingly revered as a *warrior*.

"She looked strong," remembers Edwin King; Hamer exuded an "inner
strength, an inner dignity, and I looked upon her as a religious prophet. And
she saw herself as called by God for what she was doing," he recalls.[2] "She was
a warrior," Sugarman repeats for emphasis, "She was a *warrior*. I think she
thought of herself as on a mission. And she was."[3] Guyot contends that Hamer
was, in fact, "considered a warrior of warriors," remembered because "she was
beaten; she was remembered because she stood up after being beaten; she was
remembered because her life was threatened and she never let that stop her."[4]
Reagon suggests, furthermore, that viewing Hamer as a warrior relieves the tension implicit in deciphering the roles—a singer, a speaker, or an organizer—that
Hamer fulfilled in the service of her activist mission. Rather than approaching
Hamer's career from the compartmentalized "Western perspective," argues Reagon, "if you just look at her you see she is a warrior, who could sing, who could
speak, who could organize. She was a multitalented fierce fighter: a warrior."[5]

This chapter traces the transformation of Hamer's symbolic status from a simple honest and plainspoken sharecropper to a warrior, demonstrating how Hamer contributed to the construction of this powerful persona through speech and symbolic action. Building upon the dual senses in which Hamer's biography can be considered rhetorical, I also analyze how Hamer's warrior image was propagated by movement activists and organizations who utilized Hamer as a symbol to argue for a broad spectrum of causes including retributive violence, voting rights, and economic justice. As powerful and useful as Hamer's symbolic warrior status is, like her image as a plainspoken sharecropper, the warrior symbol overlooks core aspects of who she was and what she was struggling with during this tumultuous period in her personal life and in American history. Considering how Hamer's persona was constructed through both discourse and silence develops a fuller and more empowering historical picture of her. This picture comes into focus through the rhetorical analysis of her wide range of activities and struggles during the middle period of her activist career.

In this chapter I closely consider three speeches Hamer delivered: an address she gave with Malcolm X at the end of 1964, her 1965 congressional challenge testimony, and a speech she delivered before the National Council of Negro Women (NCNW) in 1967. The analysis of these speeches is set against a historical backdrop of movement activity and inspiration. Hamer traveled to Africa in the fall of 1964; she campaigned for the historic 1967 reelections in the towns of Sunflower and Moorhead; she served as an inspirational figurehead for the MFLU. What's more, she spoke out about Black Power during the Meredith March and at a CORE convention in 1966. Chapter 4 unpacks the rhetorical nature of her involvement with these activities, while also bringing to light personal hardships she was silently but simultaneously enduring. The composite portrait of Hamer that emerges from this layered consideration of text, context, and biography is a more human depiction of a strong but wearied woman, a woman who fought through pain and who also battled doubt and despair within a rapidly shifting historical milieu.

"THE TIMES THEY ARE A-CHANGIN'"

The period between the end of 1964 and the early part of 1968 was a time of significant changes within the black freedom movement, the state of Mississippi, and the national political scene.[6] The 1964 DNC proved to be a watershed event in several respects. The tensions between SNCC and more moderate organizations like the NAACP and the SCLC reached a boiling point at the convention. To many members of SNCC, the leaders of these organizations' willingness to compromise with the political establishment and to go against the Democratic Party's own principles suggested that the social and political change SNCC activists sought would not come within the confines of a corrupt system. At a SNCC meeting in the fall of 1964, Moses urged an alternative: "We have to ask ourselves what is the government? Who sets it up? The people set it up . . . Why can't we set up our own government? So that in 1967, if we get organized enough between now and then, we can set up our own government and declare the other one no good. And say the federal government should recognize us."[7]

The idea of a third party system was implemented most successfully by Stokely Carmichael, Willie Ricks, and the other SNCC field secretaries who began working in Lowndes County, Alabama. As historian Hasan Kwame Jeffries illustrates in his work on the Lowndes County Freedom Organization (LCFO), SNCC organizers took the lessons they learned about the "black traditions of self-reliance" and "self-determination" from their fieldwork in Mississippi and brought that experiential wisdom to Alabama's black belt.[8] They coupled this knowledge with wisdom gleaned from their experiences in Atlantic City, namely, that the Democratic "party's liberal leaders were not just slow to move, they were unwilling to change the political status quo."[9] Instead of continuing to work within a political party that they "had no heart for"—through efforts like the MFDP, which sought to establish itself as the legitimate Democratic party in the state of Mississippi—SNCC organizers helped establish the LCFO. This party was an "all-black, county-wide third-party that fielded a full slate of African American candidates for local office in 1966 in a bold bid to wrest political control of the county courthouse away from white supremacist Democrats."[10] SNCC's organizing experiences in Alabama's black belt, furthermore, "gave form to their version of Black Power. It becomes clear," posits Jeffries, "that SNCC activists connected the slogan to a concrete organizing program of forming all-black third-parties as a first step toward creating independent power bases."[11]

The Black Power slogan, however, was not widely understood as such in its immediate context. Confusion surrounding the slogan led liberal whites to withdraw their financial support from organizations like SNCC, which they perceived as militant and antiwhite. Allegations of communist infiltration also plagued the group; the NAACP listed "Chinese Communist elements" within SNCC among their reasons for publicly withdrawing from COFO, the umbrella organization through which the NAACP and SNCC had (more or less successfully) combined their activist efforts in Mississippi.[12] Allard Lowenstein, who had helped attract Freedom Vote and Freedom Summer volunteers to Mississippi earlier in the decade, made similar accusations. Lowenstein warned northern students to avoid working with SNCC when he returned to Yale in the fall of 1964.[13] SNCC did accept support from organizations with well-known communist ties like the Lawyer's Guild and the Southern Conference Educational Foundation. Members of SNCC were also interested in global liberation movements, some of which promoted communist ideologies. And many of the new student volunteers, who were drawn to the organization toward the middle part of the decade, were well versed in the works of Mao Zedong, Karl Marx, and Fidel Castro.

All of this made the organization susceptible to allegations of a communist conspiracy, a popular attack white supremacists issued against "outside racial agitators," and an all-consuming suspicion that goaded FBI director J. Edgar Hoover's efforts to sabotage SNCC. Eastland, the US senator who hailed from the Delta, was so virulently anticommunist that he was branded the "Mississippi McCarthy." From the *Brown* decision forward, elected officials in the state like Eastland and Governor Ross Barnett (1960–1964) propagated the conspiratorial charge that communists were stoking racial agitation to weaken the nation into a vulnerable state susceptible to a takeover. This line of conspiratorial reasoning could be heard from the halls of Congress to the airwaves, as Mississippi representatives and Citizens' Council members alike—provided with support and classified information from the FBI—broadcast the accusation of communism to undermine their opponents' success.[14] Drastic decreases in financial support for SNCC, combined with faltering alliances between national movement figures and organizations, as well as "FBI and state police agencies' [efforts] to destroy the organization, stripped it of its capacity to grow," argues Jeffries.[15]

Communist presence within SNCC was not the only point of contention between mainstream civil rights organizations and the more radical collective, as the civil rights attorney from Alabama, Charles Morgan Jr., quipped in 1966: "Would to God there were communists in SNCC. They would be a moderating influence."[16] Though SNCC did grow more extreme in its politics as the decade wore on, Wilkins's reaction to the image Hamer projected at the 1964 DNC intimates that the NAACP was never as comfortable as SNCC was with cultivating leadership among the nation's most oppressed blacks. Longtime NAACP activist Gloster Current expressed the organization's reluctant position in a meeting of black moderates and white liberals held in New York City three weeks following the 1964 convention. "I have been listening to the crying of people from

Mississippi for seventeen years. I don't want to listen to [E. W.] Steptoe. We need high-level meetings so we can cut away the underbrush," Current proposed.[17] Current, and most other mainstream civil rights leaders, certainly realized the influence Mississippi now exerted on the national scene. Hamer and the MFDP had captured the nation's attention, but more moderate organizations feared that the radically democratic demands and unconventional strategies SNCC advanced would undermine the political progress that the more conservative organizations desired. Though the Atlantic City experience had turned SNCC away from working within the Democratic Party, black moderates saw promise in the convention's negotiations and redoubled their efforts to work within existing political structures as the movement's legitimate representatives.

The national struggle for civil rights and entitlements was emboldened by President Johnson's landslide victory over Senator Barry Goldwater in the 1964 election. The fact that Johnson trounced Goldwater, even in the face of southern white fallout over the MFDP challenge, gave him the political clout necessary to push the Voting Rights Act (VRA) of 1965 through Congress. Johnson also began advocating his Great Society programs, which included Medicare, Medicaid, Job Corps, and expanded welfare. These programs were sorely needed in the Delta where synthetic alternatives to cotton, chemical weed killers, mechanical pickers, the 1965 federal farm bill (which awarded subsidies to farmers who slashed their cotton acreage), and the minimum-wage requirement (which made it far more profitable to hire day laborers) displaced thousands of sharecroppers. Without access to low-skill agricultural jobs—the only jobs for which the majority of black Deltans were trained—starvation and malnutrition plagued the region. A Department of Agriculture study noted that the majority of Sunflower County residents "received less than two-thirds of the minimum dietary allowances recommended by the federal government." A reporter visiting the region observed, "'Children with the great swollen bellies that mark the protein deficiency disease called kwashiorkor dot the countryside . . . these children live in Mississippi on a diet of cornbread, grits and Kool-Aid.'"[18]

The War on Poverty, a central plank of Johnson's Great Society initiative, was limited in its ability to meet the Delta's pressing needs, however, as resources and attention became increasingly diverted to the war in Vietnam and to race riots erupting in northern cities like Harlem, Watts, and Detroit. Efforts to relieve the endemic poverty within the Delta were also stymied on the ground by fierce competition to control the influx of federal funds. Although many within SNCC viewed OEO programs like Head Start as a "blatant move to co-opt the movement" and therefore "opposed participation," the founders of these initiatives looked to the networks that civil rights activists in the state had previously established to get their poverty programs started. For instance, New York psychoanalyst and Freedom Summer volunteer Tom Levin, who organized the Child Development Group of Mississippi (CDGM), tapped into COFO's rich network of community leaders and even managed to sign SNCC field secretary Frank Smith on as their director of community staff. The CDGM faced opposition from white supremacist state leaders like Governor Paul Johnson (1964–1968), as well as Mississippi's US senators and congressional representatives, who considered a federally financed poverty program committed to racial equality to be a direct threat to their increasingly tenuous racial and class-based caste system. Early programs like the CDGM were also opposed by more moderate and middle-class blacks and whites who began jockeying for control and positions of power in distributing the "[p]overty gold . . . falling all over Mississippi."[19]

Against this backdrop of local, national, and international tension—wars for both liberation and dominance raging abroad, riots erupting in northern cities, and quarrels in Mississippi that threatened the lives of its most impoverished inhabitants—Hamer expanded her fight for citizenship rights to explicitly include basic entitlements like food, education, and healthcare. The broader perspective she gained from traveling nationally and internationally echoed through her appeals for these entitlements. Rather than flee the state in search of a better life, as many white supremacists encouraged Mississippi blacks to do, Hamer insisted on her right to stay in the state and her mission to improve the quality of life for its inhabitants. As she communicated it, Hamer's decision to stay—her commitment to the local struggle—was a central aspect of her Jeremiadic appeal and her activist mission. She decided to fight, instead of to flee, both because she had a right to stay and because she believed in the possibility of change. In fact, Hamer felt that it was the mission of those chosen people within the land of chosen people to spark the awareness that would lead to a restoration of founding principles, making those principles a reality for all Americans.

Though she held fast to her religious frameworks, her faith in moral suasion, and her belief that integration held the solution to the nation's woes, Hamer's rhetoric and her symbolic status did transform in line with the tumultuous times. Hamer's discourse became more militant and confrontational even as she remained committed to an interracial solution to the nation's problems. The result was a distinctive brand of tough love through which Hamer promoted aspects of the Black Power philosophy while holding fast to her belief in moral suasion and her commitment to working within the system—sick as it was—to restore the nation's founding principles.

AFRICAN EPIPHANY

When SNCC fieldworkers returned to Mississippi from Atlantic City, the feeling of total exhaustion was widespread. Harry Belafonte encountered the group upon their return and recalls their rough state: "I saw Julian Bond looked terrible, John Lewis was just . . . really stressed" and "Fannie Lou, whom I thought . . . would never wear out on any level" was showing signs of battle fatigue.[20] As the MFDP geared up for the fall election by attempting to run a slate of candidates and holding mass meetings to encourage voter registration, many SNCC activists were dealing with utter disappointment and uncertainty about their organization's next steps. To provide well-deserved respite for the weary SNCC fieldworkers, Belafonte proposed a trip to Africa. Traveling to the West African nation of Guinea, Belafonte reasoned, would put enough distance between the war-torn activists and the problems that remained in Mississippi and the United States at large. What's more, Guinea, a former French colony that had gained its independence in 1958, would provide the American freedom fighters an opportunity to internationalize their perspective by learning more about this African-led socialist society. With these arguments, Belafonte convinced the deeply committed leaders James Forman, John Lewis, Bob Moses, Dona Richards, Prathia Hall, Julian Bond, Ruby Doris Smith Robinson, Bob Hansen, Donald Harris, and Fannie Lou Hamer to leave their work behind and join him in Africa from September 11 to October 4, 1964.

For the poetically inclined like Julian Bond, who remembers the tranquility and harmony of "canoes going out in the morning and the fishermen" coming back at night, the trip to Guinea provided much-needed relaxation and rejuvenation.[21] For other activists, such as John Lewis and Donald Harris, the initial stop in Guinea was just the beginning of a longer tour through the African nations of Liberia, Ghana, Zambia, Kenya, Ethiopia, and Egypt.[22] For Hamer, the three weeks in Africa instigated deep personal growth, imbuing her with an even stronger sense of racial pride and entitlement as she saw connections between herself and the powerful, intelligent, and beautiful Guinean people. This exposure both empowered Hamer and saddened her as she grappled with the fact that white Americans not only enslaved her ancestors and oppressed her, but they also severed her family from their relatives and stripped away their cultural heritage. Hamer's trip to Guinea, therefore, incited reflection about the core aspects of who she was and who she, and all blacks living in America, had the potential to become.

Hamer found many connections and similarities with the African people she encountered, especially the African women. Hamer described the women in Guinea as "so graceful and so poised." They reminded her of her mother in the way Lou Ella Townsend would carry things: "[she] could have two pails in her hand and a pail on her head and could go for miles and wouldn't drop them." Most of the women Hamer saw there "wear their heads tied up," and she found this "so similar to my own family because it's very seldom that anybody see me without something tied on my head."²³ The poise and grace of these women and the connections she saw between Guineans, herself, and her family, had a lasting impact on her, as she would continue to talk about the bond in interviews for years to come. In 1973, for instance, Hamer told Neil McMillen that what was "really beautiful" to her about Guinea was watching the African people act so freely and so naturally. She remembered them "just being their real selves and not having to pretend to be somebody else."²⁴

Hamer was clearly moved by the self-confidence and race pride the Guinean people emanated, but she was also emotionally struck by the positions of power and prestige they held. "I saw black men flying the airplanes, driving buses, sitting behind the big desks in the bank and just doing everything I was used to seeing white people do," Hamer remarked. Adding that, "for the first time in my life [I saw] a black stewardess walking through the plane," Hamer declared: "that was quite an inspiration for me."²⁵ The delegation was not only exposed to black bankers, pilots, and flight attendants, President Sékou Touré himself paid them several visits. Belafonte remembers the first time the president met with the group of SNCC activists, explaining that he came unannounced, surprising the SNCC members who were not expecting to see him until the following day. Hamer was actually in the bathtub when the president arrived. When Belafonte told her that President Touré was at the house where the group was staying, a submerged Hamer replied: "Harry, you funnin' me?" After Belafonte convinced her that the president was indeed there, Hamer rushed out to greet him; "[S]he at first went to just shake hands and [then] he just opened up and enveloped her." Belafonte distinctly recounts Hamer's reaction to the embrace: "I'd never known her to be inarticulate," he explains, "but she was absolutely dumbfounded" by this "strikingly handsome man" clad in a white robe "against this very black skin and these gleaming white teeth and these flashing eyes, this fez that he had on which was white."²⁶ The regal image of President Touré was also seared into Hamer's memory, as she shared years later: "I had never seen nobody black running the government in my life. So, it was quite a revelation to me."²⁷

Most of all, the beauty, the power, and the ability of the Guinean people challenged Hamer to interrogate the preconceptions she held about Africans based on widely circulated white supremacist arguments about the racial inferiority of the "Negroid" race. Though most popular among segregationists in the South, Citizens' Councilors also found northern voices propagating vestiges of the Social Darwinian philosophy well into the 1960s. In 1962, for example, the *Forum* featured Princeton graduate, author, and CEO of Delta airlines Carleton Putnam, whose 1961 book *Race and Reason: A Yankee View* won broad acclaim among southern whites. Both Mississippi and Virginia made *Race and Reason* a required read within their statewide high school curriculum and Governor Barnett declared October 26, 1961, "Race and Reason" day in the state he led.

In his book, and during his 1962 interview broadcast on the *Forum*, Putnam insisted that the races were not equal. "Negroes have certain genetic limitations," he maintained, but scientists across the globe have been forced to suggest the equality of the races to justify economic social welfare policies.[28] On an episode of the *Forum* broadcast later that year, Dr. Robert Gayre advanced a similarly polygenic and Social Darwinist view of racial difference, suggesting further that the Negroid race—unlike the Mongoloid and Caucasoid races—never experienced the weaning process of natural selection because the Ice Age did not affect people living on the African continent. As a result, the "weak and stupid" were not killed off from their race, whereas the Mongoloid and Caucasoid races had been left with only the "strong and able."[29] Beliefs such as these were not only taught in school and broadcast over the airwaves, they were also widely subscribed to by those who drafted legislation and enforced laws in Mississippi.

"Being from the South," Hamer explained, "we never was taught much about our African heritage. The way everybody talked to us, everybody in Africa was savages and really stupid people."[30] Through the absence of information and the presence of racist and woefully misinformed stereotypes, Hamer developed a sense of shame surrounding her African ancestry. During her stay in West Africa, however, Hamer quickly learned "that [she] sure didn't have anything to be ashamed of from being black." It was in Guinea that she learned for the "first time" to "never, ever" be "ashamed of [her] ancestors and [her] background."[31] Beyond divesting herself of this shame, the Guinean people revealed the African people's inherent potential. To Hamer, the people she encountered demonstrated "what black people can do if we only get the chance in America. It is here within us," she declared.[32] The trip to Africa prompted Hamer to carefully examine and ultimately disregard the negative stereotypes she held about the continent and about her ancestors. She was able to let go of the shame she was taught to carry about who she was because of where she came from. This shame was replaced with a sense of connection to a beautiful and capable people who lived in a nation where they were allowed to be their "real selves" and

empowered to reach their full potential. Even in the absence of traceable ances-
tral ties, Hamer saw unmistakable similarities and glimpsed her own potential
in the Guinean people. Her trip to Africa was a form of self-discovery, offering
a type of recognition that fostered a deep sense of racial pride. This recognition
manifest itself in her discourse as she worked with renewed zeal to encourage
all Americans to recognize the value and the potential of African Americans.
What's more, she used this enhanced awareness to more forcefully argue for
blacks' status as chosen people, vital to the nation's survival.

By this point in her career, any illusions Hamer held about the country of
her birth had been replaced by harsh realities of injustice—the federal government's failure to provide protection for civil rights activists in Mississippi, the
Democratic Party's failure to live up to its principles at the 1964 convention, and
even the lies she discovered the nation propagating abroad about its treatment
of African Americans. While in Guinea, the SNCC delegation came across a
periodical published by the United States Information Agency. The magazine
featured pictures of Moses and Hamer "over some such caption as 'Bob Moses
and Mrs. Hamer leading delegates of the Mississippi Freedom delegation to
their seats at the Democratic National Convention,'" recalls scholar and activist Staughton Lynd.[33] Lynd posits that this propaganda pamphlet, in which the
United States not only lied about the MFDP being seated at the convention, but
also used Moses and Hamer to falsely suggest its commitment to civil rights,
further turned Moses away from working within the corrupt system. Hamer
was also disgusted by the lies and deceit represented in the pamphlet, but she
was not surprised. She knew America was a sick nation, but the pamphlet also
demonstrated to her that the nation ultimately knew what was right, they just
needed to be goaded back into affirming their founding principles. As she
would go on to tell an interracial audience in New York, "there's so much hypocrisy in America and if we want America to be a free society we have to stop
telling lies, that's all. Because we're not free and you know we're not free. You're
not free in Harlem."[34] Hamer carried this realization and an enhanced sense of
race pride with her as she returned to the United States, committed to securing
freedom for all the country's inhabitants.

"I'M SICK AND TIRED OF BEING SICK AND TIRED"

As Belafonte had hoped, sending the delegation of SNCC workers to Guinea to
see a black-led socialist state and to meet with African leaders like Touré did internationalize their perspective regarding liberation struggles. The delegation's

time in Africa also helped strengthen ties between SNCC and the well-known African American activist Malcolm X. Lewis and Harris did not return to the states with the rest of the delegation; instead, these two SNCC activists extended their stay and traveled through other parts of the continent. Their decision to remain proved serendipitous when they unexpectedly encountered Malcolm X in Nairobi, Kenya. SNCC historian Clayborne Carson refers to this encounter as "[p]erhaps the most significant episode of their stay in Africa," because the "Nairobi meeting was followed by a series of attempts by Malcolm to forge links with SNCC."[35] SNCC was quite receptive to Malcolm's overtures as the organization's ideological transformation, from an explicitly nonviolent collective working within established political channels to an organization whose leaders began to increasingly champion self-defense and promote third-party alternatives, occurred around the same time as Malcolm's break from the Nation of Islam and his creation of the Organization of Afro-American Unity (OAAU). In fact, Jeffries insists that while "SNCC activists' experiences in the field caused them to look anew at the work of black nationalists and Pan-Africanist theoreticians and practitioners," such as Marcus Garvey, Kwame Nkrumah, Elijah Muhammad, and Frantz Fanon, "it was the rhetoric of Malcolm X that most encouraged their expanding black nationalist consciousness."[36] This convergence of interests and ideologies led to mutual support for SNCC programs and OAAU causes. On December 20, 1964, Hamer and Malcolm shared a platform at Williams Institutional Christian Methodist Episcopal Church in Harlem, which housed a political rally in support of the MFDP's upcoming congressional challenge.[37]

During the Harlem rally, the SNCC Freedom Singers performed and both Hamer and Malcolm addressed the crowd. The purpose of Hamer's Harlem speech, "I'm Sick and Tired of Being Sick and Tired," was to drum up support for the challenge the MFDP would bring before the US Congress on January 4, 1965. Closer analysis of the speech reveals that Hamer worked not only to encourage her Harlem auditors to support the challenge—"morally, politically, and financially"—but that she also incited this audience to "wake up" and recognize America's declension from its espoused values, to acknowledge the ways in which this hypocrisy affected all Americans, and to band together to "make democracy a reality."[38] She sparked this deeper sense of recognition by Signifyin(g) upon central tenets of America's civil religion and by foregrounding the interconnection and interest convergence among all Americans' freedom struggles. In so doing, Hamer contributed to the rhetorical construction of her warrior persona and distinctively situated herself within a rapidly evolving context of movement oratory. Her distinction becomes all the more apparent when comparing Hamer's "I'm Sick and Tired of Being Sick and Tired" to the address, "With Mrs. Fannie Lou Hamer," that Malcolm delivered immediately following her oration.

In Harlem, Hamer spoke before an integrated northern audience of approximately three hundred attendees, one hundred of whom were white, and the remainder reportedly black.[39] Though the modes of proof she used in this Harlem speech were far more secular than previous addresses she delivered in southern black church settings, there were some noticeable similarities in content. Hamer began with the story of her first registration attempt, for instance, which led into a discussion of being fired from the Marlow plantation. She then described her experiences as the target of white supremacist retaliation, using both the bullets fired into the Tucker's home and her brutal Winona beating as vivid and visceral evidence for her claim. These personal experiences both demonstrated her strength in the face of adversity and brought Hamer to her larger political objective: "What I'm trying to point out now," she informed her audience, "is when you take a very close look at this American society, it's time to question these things . . . this whole society is sick."[40]

To broaden the scope of her indictment, she moved past her experiences in Mississippi, leading the audience through her more recent, national battles with discrimination. "And to prove just how sick [America] is," Hamer contended, "when I was testifying before the credentials committee, I was cut off." She interpreted President Johnson's remarks to the governors assembled in the East Room of the White House in a manner consistent with her plea for recognition: "I was cut off because they hate to see what they been knowing all the time and that's the truth."[41] This passage illustrates a central aspect of Hamer's evolving rhetorical strategy. Following Atlantic City, Hamer moved beyond using speech to represent the injustice she experienced in hopes that once revealed national leaders would be prodded to restore their principles. She now moved toward employing rhetoric to incite a deeper sense of recognition, explicating the way in which injustice in Mississippi affects all Americans, and enlisting all the nation's citizens in the reparative effort.

A core aspect of her expanded rhetorical mission, therefore, entailed encouraging Americans to "wake up" to the hypocrisy and injustice that surrounded them, to "take a very close look at this American society" and "to question these things."[42] To prompt this recognition, Hamer signified upon refrains from American scripture in a manner that underscored the ways in which the country's defining principles were violated. Before her Harlem auditors, for example, Hamer altered her trademark introduction, declaring, "My name is Fannie Lou Hamer and I *exist* at 626 East Lafayette Street . . ." Explaining the alteration from "live" to "exist," Hamer contended, "The reason I say 'exist' [is] because we're excluded from everything in Mississippi but the tombs and the graves." Instead of the "'land of the *free* and the home of the *brave*,' it's called in Mississippi 'the land of the *tree* and the home of the *grave*.'"[43] Signifyin(g) upon the national anthem by alluding to Mississippi's bloody history of lynching and racially motivated killing, Hamer vividly illustrated the distance between her lived experience and America's professed values. By opening her address this way, furthermore, she established a tone of critical questioning and examination for the address.

Hamer's critically inquisitive tone—the attitude she displayed toward her topic and her audience—continued throughout the speech. For instance, she returned to Signifyin(g) upon the *Star Spangled Banner* later in her address, suggesting: "we can no longer ignore the facts and getting our children to sing, 'Oh say can you see, by the dawn's early light, what so proudly we hailed.' What do we have to hail here?," Hamer asked an audience whose city had recently erupted in riots following the murder of a black teen by the New York Police Department.[44] She stressed the interconnection of northern and southern struggles for freedom, noting that in all the big cities she traveled—places like Harlem, Chicago, and Philadelphia—the white man was "standing with his feet on this black man's neck."[45] Referring to these cities as "Mississippi in disguise," Hamer acknowledged that though her state is the worst of the worst, her audience should acknowledge the similarities of their experiences.[46]

Accordingly, the MFDP congressional challenge she waged was not just about seeking justice in Mississippi; Hamer suggested that the challenge would reveal if the "Constitution is really going to be of any help in this American society." This revelation affects all Americans because "how can a man be in Washington elected by the people, when 95 percent of the [black] people cannot vote in Mississippi?"[47] Voter intimidation and discrimination in Mississippi, reasoned Hamer, is not just unfortunate for blacks in her state; it impacts all Americans because the officials sent from her state go on to make decisions with implications for all the nation's inhabitants. "Those people were illegally elected," Hamer argued. Jamie L. Whitten, the Second Congressional District representative she challenged in the state's primary, "has been in Washington thirteen years and he is not representing the people of Mississippi because not only do they discriminate against the poor Negroes, they discriminated . . . against the poor whites."[48] By stressing interconnection—the fact that all Americans' freedoms are weakened when the nation's Constitution is violated and as unrepresentative representatives sit in Washington making decisions on their behalf—Hamer urged her Harlem auditors to join her in fostering change.

Immediately following Hamer's speech, Malcolm, clad in a dark-blue suit with his signature black-rimmed spectacles, took his turn at the microphone. Assuredly pointing his forefinger as he spoke, Malcolm extemporaneously incorporated several of Hamer's central ideas into his own address.[49] He envisioned their two speeches working in tandem, claiming that the people of Harlem first "need to hear [Hamer's] story," that they "need to know more, first hand, about what's happening down there, especially to our women." After Hamer worked to make the audience aware of these injustices, Malcolm reasoned, "then they need[ed] some lessons in tactics and strategy on how to get even."[50] As he envisioned the rally functioning, therefore, Hamer would prompt awareness—the type of recognition that offers the basis for action—and *he* would prescribe the form of action that they should follow. What occurred in practice, however, was that both Hamer and Malcolm interpreted her experiences for the audience. Hamer provided an interpretation that urged all Americans to wake up and work together, within the system, to make America's professed values a reality for all its citizens, while Malcolm drew upon Hamer's experiences to justify retributive violence. Analyzing the ways in which Hamer and Malcolm made sense of the same narrative provides a unique opportunity to place Hamer's evolving Jeremiad within a comparative context of black freedom movement advocacy.

Like Hamer, Malcolm worked to invest the Harlem audience in her life story by emphasizing the interconnection of their struggles. Specifically, he urged the audience to acknowledge the connection between their self-conception as American citizens and the plight of poor black Mississippians. "What has Mississippi got to do with Harlem?" Malcolm asked his audience, "It isn't actually Mississippi; it's America," he quickly responded. Reasoning, that "There's no such thing as the Mason-Dixon Line," he claimed further, "There's no such thing as the South—it's America." Malcolm explained that the elected representatives coming out of Mississippi, "and any state where our people are deprived of the right to vote," are "in Washington, D.C., illegally."[51] What's worse, they serve the Congress and they chair powerful committees, like Eastland's post on the Senate Judiciary Committee, which issue decisions that affect all Americans.

Malcolm also made personal the white supremacist retaliation Hamer endured during her jail beating: "When I listen to Mrs. Hamer, a black woman—could be my mother, my sister, my daughter—describe what they had done to her," he confessed, "I ask myself how in the world can we ever expect to be respected as *men* when we will allow something like that to be done to our women, and we do nothing about it?"[52] Because Malcolm regarded Hamer's beating as a direct challenge from white supremacists to black masculinity, his response to the violence differed markedly from Hamer's use of her own testimony. Whereas Hamer demonstrated her strength and contributed to the fashioning of her warrior status by recounting the barriers she has overcome in her fight for justice, Malcolm championed retributive violence as a means for blacks to achieve self-recognition, and as a method of gaining recognition from whites.

Poignantly, Malcolm drew a parallel line between the struggle in America and African liberation movements. "When I was in Africa," he recalled, "I noticed some of the Africans got their freedom faster than others . . . I noticed that in areas where independence had been gotten, someone got angry." Extending the comparison, Malcolm advocated achieving liberation—to use his popular phrase—"by any means necessary":

> When they get angry, they bring about change . . . When they get angry, they realize the condition that they're in—that their suffering is unjust, immoral, illegal, and that anything they do to correct it or eliminate it, they're justified. When you and I develop that type of anger and speak in that voice, then we'll get some kind of respect and recognition . . .[53]

Whereas Hamer asked both her white and black auditors for "what support they can give" with regard to her congressional challenge, Malcolm dared the white audience members present, in particular, to prove their sincerity to the struggle by "recognizing the law of justice . . . 'as ye sow, so shall ye reap' . . . 'he who kills by the sword, shall be killed by the sword,'" and to help blacks achieve a type of recognition that would manifest itself in "evening the score."[54]

Malcolm's appeal to retributive justice not only targeted blacks and whites among his Harlem audience, he made direct advances to the SNCC activists present. He began his appeal to this particular subset of the audience with a compliment, "I couldn't help but be very impressed at the out start when the Freedom Singers were singing the song 'Oginga, Odinga,' because Oginga Odinga is one of the foremost freedom fighters on the African continent."[55] "The fact that" the Freedom Singers were singing about Kenya's newly appointed vice president, Malcolm remarked, "to me is quite significant." Noting the recent change in movement discourse, he suggested, "Two or three years ago, most of our people would choose to sing about someone who was, you know, passive and meek and humble and forgiving. Oginga Odinga is not passive. He's not meek. He's not humble. He's not nonviolent. But he's free."[56] Lifting up Odinga and the revolutionary Mau Mau freedom fighters with whom he worked as exemplars, Malcolm asked the SNCC activists plainly: "those of you who are singing—are you also willing to do some swinging?"[57]

Malcolm's message to the SNCC activists came at a crucial moment when the organization was reexamining its mission and strategies after what many perceived as a failed attempt to integrate the Democratic Party in Atlantic City. Recognizing their frustration, Malcolm conceded that "The head of the Democratic Party is sitting in the White House. He could have gotten Mrs. Hamer into Atlantic City. He could have opened up his mouth and had her seated. Hubert Humphrey could have opened up his mouth and had her seated."[58] The fact that these powerful leaders did not seat Hamer and the MFDP delegation she represented, posited Malcolm, suggests the need for a new approach. "We need a Mau Mau," he proposed. "If they don't want to deal with the Mississippi Freedom Democratic Party, then we'll give them something else to deal with. If they don't want to deal with the Student Nonviolent Committee, then we have to give them an alternative," Malcolm reasoned.[59]

Remarkably, he constructed this alternative by Signifyin(g) upon the same resources Hamer and SNCC activists used in appealing to blacks throughout the Delta: traditional biblical types and America's civil religion. The image of Jesus that Malcolm emphasized, however, was from the Book of Revelation wherein "Jesus [is] sitting on a horse with a sword in his hand, getting ready to go into action."[60] Similarly, he emphasized the revolutionary nature of Anglo America's struggle for freedom, speaking to SNCC activists *apostrophically*[61] by momentarily addressing whites in the audience: "Now if you are with us, all I say is, make the same kind of contribution with us in our struggle for freedom that all white people have always made when they were struggling for their own freedom."[62] Reminding the audience that the Revolutionary War was a freedom struggle, that Patrick Henry said "'liberty or death,'" and that "George Washington got the cannons out," Malcolm claimed that "all the rest of them that you taught me to worship as my heroes, they were fighters, they were warriors."[63] The alternative solution he proposed, therefore, was fundamentally rhetorical: Malcolm urged his audience to learn a new language. "[W]e will never communicate talking one language while he's talking another language. He's talking the language of violence while you and I are running around with this little chicken-picking type of language—and think that he's going to understand."[64]

As Malcolm suggested in reference to the Freedom Singers' marked ideological transformation in choosing to sing "Oginga Odinga," he perceived their previous emphasis on nonviolence as weak. And as his interpretation of the DNC challenge also intimated, this approach was ineffectual: "The language that you and I have been speaking to this man in the past hasn't reached him." So the change he proposed was rendered obvious: "Let's learn his language. If his language is with a shotgun, get a shotgun. Yes, I said if he only understands the language of a rifle, get a rifle."[65] By confronting the DNC disappointment head on, by couching the American struggle in an international context, and by offering justification for this approach in a reversal of the nonviolent movement's own rhetorical resources (the Bible and civil religion), Malcolm's alternative began to resonate with many SNCC activists who had been beaten down and disillusioned. "In defiant tones," Jeffries explains, "Malcolm gave voice to the young radicals' hopes and frustrations."[66]

Although Hamer admired Malcolm, telling one radio journalist shortly after his assassination that "Malcolm X was one of the best friends I ever had. A remarkable man," she gushed, "Oh, he was a great man!"[67] And while she unabashedly confessed that "I keep a shotgun in every corner of my bedroom and the first cracker even look like he wants to throw some dynamite on my porch won't write his mama again."[68] Hamer never advocated retributive justice as a strategy for social or political change and she continued to work within the Democratic Party for the next several years. Comparing Hamer's and Malcolm's Harlem addresses suggests that both advocates worked to incite an awakening in their audiences. They both emphasized the interconnection of all Americans' freedom struggles, and they even utilized similar narratives and modes of proof in their appeals. Hamer, unlike Malcolm, possessed an unyielding faith in the possibility of transforming even the staunchest white supremacist and in the ability for a fallen nation to make good on its founding promises. As she soldiered forward in her battle with the US Congress, however, this faith became severely tested.

THE 1965 CONGRESSIONAL CHALLENGE

No more than two weeks after Hamer asked audiences in Harlem to support her campaign to unseat the illegally elected congressmen from Mississippi, she was in Washington, DC, watching the MFDP's case unfold before the House of Representatives. On January 4, 1965, Fannie Lou Hamer, Annie Devine, and Victoria Gray attempted to enter the floor of the House of Representatives. The chief of the capitol police, Carl Schamp, and several other officers met the group at the door. The MFDP representatives were told they could not enter the floor of the House because they did not have privileges. To which Gray responded, "But we are attempting to enter as contestants"; Mrs. Hamer showed Schamp an affidavit, indicating that this was evidence of their challenge. Schamp nevertheless insisted that the challengers did not have floor privileges.[69] Barred from entering the chamber, the challengers, their lawyers, and as many MFDP supporters as space would allow, took seats in the gallery. But there were hundreds of MFDP supporters—too many to be seated—so the remainder lined the tunnel from the congressional representatives' offices to the chamber of the House. These supporters, "maids, farmers, a few teachers," stood silently, "one person every ten yards" without signs, just meeting the gaze of the representatives as they made their way to the opening session. Representatives describe their presence as "intimidating . . . in a moral sense."[70] Their silent demonstration was, indeed, persuasive. One congressman recalled that when he "started into the tunnel," he was planning on voting to "seat the [white] Mississippians," but after encountering so many disenfranchised Mississippi blacks, he was compelled to ask himself: "What kind of a person are you?" By the time he reached the chamber he had changed his mind on the vote.[71]

Hamer, Devine, and Gray watched from the balcony as the House Speaker, Representative John McCormack, called the new session to order. They looked on as Representative William Fitts Ryan, an early ally of the MFDP and third-term Democrat from Manhattan's Upper West Side, quickly got the Speaker's attention by objecting to the "oath being administered to the gentlemen from Mississippi." He informed the Speaker that his objection to the seating of Jamie Whitten, John Bell Williams, Thomas G. Abernathy, Prentiss Walker, and William Colmer was rooted in the rampant civil rights abuses in the representatives' home state—"facts and statements which [he] consider[ed] to be reliable." Before Ryan finished speaking, widespread support for the challenge became clear on the floor as nearly seventy members of Congress rose to their feet and stood with him.[72] The congressmen from Mississippi—four Democrats and one Republican—were asked to step aside while their colleagues were sworn in and the challenge brought by Ryan was considered. As debate over their seating drew to a close, Congresswoman Edith Green called for a roll-call vote to decide whether the representatives from Mississippi should be sworn in separately or not. This roll call resulted in a 276–149 vote. While the Mississippians won enough votes to be seated as the MFDP challenge was considered in greater depth, more than a third of the Congress had gone on record in support of the MFDP's challenge. "We did it," Gray proclaimed to her comrades, "even if just for this moment, we did it."[73]

The representatives who backed Ryan's objection had been persuaded by the tireless lobbying efforts of the Hamer, Devine, and Gray team. These three Mississippi women came from different backgrounds and each played complementary roles in garnering support for the challenge. As Gray explained it, she was the tactician of the group. A Palmer's Crossing native, mother of three, and a successful cosmetics business owner, Gray became active in the movement as a

SNCC fieldworker in 1962. She taught in the Freedom Schools during the summer of 1964, and helped found the MFDP. Hailing from Canton, Devine was a mother of four with experience working as an elementary school teacher, a life insurance agent, and an active member of her church. Devine was discerning and focused and, according to Gray, she "supplied the wisdom" for the challengers. Hamer "was the orator, the one who took the message to the people."[74]

Hamer also became the symbol of their collective struggle. In the weeks leading up to Congress's opening session, for instance, the MFDP ran an advertisement in the *New York Times* with a large picture of a stoic Mrs. Hamer seated sideways, gaze fixed ahead, holding an American flag in her lap. The text surrounding the warrior-like image read in bold, "NOW IS THE TIME . . . and we of Mississippi ask: WHERE ARE 'THE GOOD MEN'?" Under this eye-catching question, was an appeal from Hamer to "people of conscience and courage, who believe all Americans have a right to representation . . . to all of you good men." Hamer's missive to the people explained her background and acknowledged the small strides made in her state's struggle for civil rights. She was quite clear, however, that grave problems persisted—the most notable of which was lack of representation for blacks. "We are still denied a voice in our own government by complicated tests invented for just that, by the threat of losing our jobs, by terror. It's been that way for almost a hundred years, and still is." She clarified: "*And if you don't have a voice, you really don't have anything.*" Hamer called upon Americans of good conscience to support the congressional challenge by writing their representatives, by forming groups in support of the challenge in their own communities, and by donating to the cause.[75]

Through widely circulated appeals such as these, in addition to her national speaking tour that featured speeches like the address Hamer delivered with Malcolm in Harlem, Hamer came to visually and verbally represent the congressional challenge. Guyot recalls, nevertheless, that the women worked as a team, "the three of them travelled the country, advocated for the congressional challenge, defended it against all comers . . . nobody else could have done a better job than they did," remembers the MFDP chair.[76]

The challenge itself began after these three, and several other, MFDP candidates were defeated in the spring 1964 congressional primaries. Several of the defeated candidates attempted to run again as Independents in the general election. They were barred from doing so by a Mississippi law, which stipulated that if a candidate ran and lost in the primary that candidate could not run again in the general election. The MFDP knew that if blacks were free to register in Mississippi then their candidates would have had a fighting chance in the initial contests. To demonstrate what could have been, COFO orchestrated another "Freedom Vote" mock election. This election was a four-day event, running from October 30 to November 2, 1964. It was open to all, with polling places set up in churches and community centers to attract a broad base of voters. Given the accessibility of this mock election, it made sense that the results differed markedly from the state's official primaries. In COFO's mock election, for instance, Hamer received 33,009 votes to Whitten's 59—a stark contrast to the primary earlier that spring when Whitten beat Hamer handily—35,218 to 621 votes. This mock election, like the others before it, demonstrated that blacks would vote if given the chance and that their votes would yield different results.

In this manner, COFO's mock election dramatized the unjust voting conditions that resulted in the election of five unrepresentative Mississippi representatives. Motivated by these results, the MFDP launched the congressional challenge spearheaded by Hamer, Devine, and Gray. The central premise of their challenge was the fact that these women were barred from running against Whitten, Abernathy, and Colmer, respectively, in the general election.[77] Further, the widespread voter discrimination and intimidation in the state of Mississippi suggested that even if the women had been permitted to run as Independents in the general election, a minority of eligible voters would have elected their opponents. Not only did this voter discrimination violate the Fourteenth and Fifteenth Amendments by depriving black Mississippians of their constitutionally mandated rights, but it also defied the Compact of 1870, argued the MFDP. The Compact of 1870 was the agreement by which Mississippi was readmitted into the Union and it specified, as a condition of this readmission, that the state could not bar or intimidate black people from voting. Guyot felt that this strategy and the evidence backing their claims was strong; their case was "very clear," he contends.[78]

What was less clear than the discrimination black Mississippians faced, and the legal principles this discrimination violated, was what action the MFDP wanted Congress to take in response to their challenge. At times it seemed that the challenge was geared toward unseating the representatives, by ordering an investigation that would hopefully result in reelections. At other times, however, it seemed that the MFDP was suggesting Hamer, Devine, and Gray be seated in place of the illegally elected congressmen.

The suggestion that the three women be seated in the place of the three congressmen they challenged provoked opposition from otherwise sympathetic allies. The National Council of Churches' (NCC) Commission on Religion and Race issued an official statement in support of challenging the "five prospective Congressmen's" seats, but remarked that the appeal for Hamer, Devine, and Gray to replace the congressmen "clouds the clear issue of the legality of the present election system in that state."[79] The NAACP was also in favor of getting "rid of the Mississippi Congressmen," but did not "endorse the method proposed by the MFDP." The Americans for Democratic Action (ADA) warned of the "dangerous implications" of such replacement, given that the women were "not elected in any regularly-constituted state election." The *New York Times* went further in referring to the appeal for replacement as a "preposterous gesture."[80] The NCC, the NAACP, the ADA, and the *Times* all suggested that the MFDP's case for unseating the representatives had merit, but they firmly objected to the proposal of seating the challengers in their place. As the challenge wore on, perhaps in response to such criticism, the MFDP focused less on the argument for replacing the congressmen with Devine, Gray, and Hamer and emphasized their case for unseating the representatives, instead.

Hamer, Devine, and Gray brought this argument before members of Congress, sympathetic audiences across the country, and, ultimately, to the Speaker of the House. Congress referred the case to the House Subcommittee on Elections, chaired by Robert T. Ashmore (D-South Carolina). To gather evidence for their challenge, the MFDP recruited nearly one hundred lawyers who traveled the state taking depositions. In all, they interviewed over six hundred witnesses who were denied the opportunities to register and vote across the state of Mississippi. The lawyers also subpoenaed Mississippi election officials and state leaders who had carried out or who otherwise permitted this discrimination. The "legal peace corps," as the volunteers were dubbed, put the white segregationist power structure on the defensive, deposing the state's former governor, the present secretary of state, and the attorney general. The MFDP compiled their findings into three thousand single-spaced pages of testimony, which they delivered to House Speaker McCormack. The extensive report ensured the MFDP a hearing with the subcommittee, though it would be closed to the public and was scheduled eight months out.

As Hamer, Devine, and Gray prepared for the September hearing, SNCC activists were working for the cause of black suffrage in Selma, Alabama. In many ways, the MFDP's congressional challenge and the Selma campaign proceeded along parallel tracks and worked toward similar causes. Temporally, the two campaigns both gained momentum in January 1965. The two campaigns also reached relative resolution by the fall when Johnson signed the Voting Rights Act into law on August 6, and when Congress officially voted on the challenge on September 17. Not unlike the MFDP's three thousand pages of testimony detailing abhorrent and widespread voter-discrimination practices, the Selma campaign also vividly exposed the violence and brutality with which black suffrage was met by leading marches that tested local officials. In this regard, each campaign prompted Americans to recognize their own hypocrisy by illuminating the way in which constitutional principles were violated and violently prohibited by federal- and state-sanctioned authorities.

Given the similarities between these two battles for civil rights, it makes sense that the MFDP received backing from major civil rights groups such as SNCC, CORE, and the SCLC. Hamer's ambivalence toward the Selma campaign, however, is rather unexpected. Disregarding the tangible gains made by the Selma to Montgomery March, Hamer told one interviewer: "this voting bill that the President passed last week it doesn't mean anything. I'm not looking for a voting bill in 1965 when they're not enforcing . . . our voting rights with the 15th Amendment."[81] Part of her antipathy toward the Selma campaign's success stemmed from her conviction, informed by her lived experience, that rights on paper did not translate to rights in practice for many of the country's black citizens.

Another source of her hostility toward the Selma campaign was perhaps less principled, and more personal. Years later, Hamer remarked: "Dr. King is dead now, and I wouldn't want no strikes against him. But one of the things that diverted the attention from the challenge was his march, from Selma to Montgomery." She recalled being in "the middle of that challenge . . . drumming up all of this support" and King "turned their attention . . . away."[82] In these statements, Hamer voiced a common objection—shared by members of SNCC, who were ambivalent about King's participation in the Selma protests—to King's status as a media magnet. The fact that the press followed King was certainly an asset to the black freedom movement campaigns he supported, but the King-centered myopia of the press inevitably deflected attention from the nuances of particular mobilizing efforts, as well as from other forms of civil rights activism and other styles of leadership.

The critical statements Hamer advanced about the Selma campaign also reveal that she was human. She was sometimes jealous and her activism and advocacy was not without occasional contradictions. She would go on to champion the positive effects of the VRA in her official testimony before the House Subcommittee. But in August, when Johnson signed the bill into law, thereby suspending such discriminatory registration practices as the literacy test and providing long-awaited federal examiners, Hamer knew that many a detractor could now point to the VRA as the solution to Mississippi's discriminatory election machinery. The VRA did, in fact, make the MFDP challenge seem less pressing. Ashmore's decision to close the hearings to the press and protestors, allowing only the challenged and challenging parties, their lawyers, and the committee members in, also resulted in decreased national attention to the MFDP's argument for reparative justice.

On September 13, 1965, in a small room on the third floor of the capitol building the two sides talked past each other. The challengers held fast to their arguments about the specific ways in which voter discrimination violated constitutional principles, as well as the Compact of 1870, and thereby invalidated the election of the congressmen. The MFDP argued that the congressmen should be suspended while further investigation and potential reelections occurred.

The five congressmen responded to the MFDP in much the same way that the Mississippi Regulars countered their credentials committee challenge a year before. Represented principally by Colmer, dean of the Mississippi House delegation, the congressmen emphasized the unofficial and illegitimate nature of the challengers' mock election. Suggesting that the Freedom Vote was "held without any sanction of law."[83] The mock elections were, as the challenged went on to accuse, simply used to dramatize injustice. With regard to the challengers' arguments about such injustice, the congressmen's strategy ranged from denying that voter discrimination occurred in Mississippi to suggesting that the congressmen did not play any direct role in the injustices. Finally, in response to the MFDP's allegation that the widespread voter discrimination in Mississippi violated the Compact of 1870, the challenged reminded the Subcommittee on Elections that all of the Confederate states were readmitted to the Union under similar provisions. Siding with the MFDP would, therefore, encourage challenges across the South. This final argument smacked of the threat of a southern walkout made by the Regular Party during the credentials committee hearings a year earlier. And its appeal to fear was similarly persuasive.

Into this hostile setting, Hamer donned her warrior persona and carried forth her Jeremiadic appeal. Hamer's testimony conveys her uncompromising advocacy of meaningful recognition, which not only protects against future injustice, but also works to repair inequality based on past injustice. This speech also exhibits Hamer's ability to adapt her rhetorical signature to varied situations, while demonstrating her range as a rhetor. Friends recall that in addition to Hamer's extemporaneously delivered, impassioned, and moving speeches "she could also be quiet," calculated, and forceful.[84] In this address, Hamer was just that. From the hearing record, one can observe Hamer indicating in several places that she was reading from a script, which was quite unusual for her. Hamer once asked fellow challenger Gray if she could teach her to speak from a prearranged text—to which Gray responded: "My God! You don't need to. You tell what you understand, what you're feeling and why you think it's important," she instructed Hamer, "and don't you worry about notes or writing it out beforehand. *I* have to do some of that," Gray admitted, "but *you* don't."[85]

Though somewhat anomalous, the relatively quiet nature of this speech and its apparent scripted quality reflect Hamer's adaptability. These textual markers also strategically function to achieve Hamer's rhetorical purposes. Specifically, she used her testimony to factually demonstrate the illicit activity in her Second Congressional District so that the country would "wake up" and redress the grievances.[86]

The scripted quality of the text enabled Hamer to garner specific statistics and particular pieces of evidence in support of her claims. Her well-informed, factually based discourse, in turn, helped construct for her the persona of a capable congresswoman. Consistent with this persona, Hamer began her address by representing the concerns of her constituents. She offered three examples of would-be voters who were fraudulently barred from, and even arrested for, exercising their constitutional rights. Demonstrating that the concerns she presented before the committee were more than just hearsay, Hamer moved into a brief discussion of her own beating in the Winona jailhouse. She bolstered her congresswoman persona by reminding her audience that she possessed the strength and bravery of a wounded warrior: "I am standing here today suffering with a permanent kidney injury and a blood clot in the artery from the left eye from a beating I got inside of the jail in Winona, Mississippi, because I was participating in voter registration." The danger that politically assertive blacks in Mississippi face is ever present, Hamer made lucid: "When we go back home from this meeting here today, we stand a chance of being shot down, or either blown to bits in the state of Mississippi." "It is only when we speak what is right," she clarified, "that we stands a chance at night of being blown to bits in our homes."[87] These examples of white supremacist retaliation to black civic assertion ground Hamer's critical question, "Can we call this a free country," she asks, referencing her well-known DNC testimony, "where I am afraid to go to sleep in my own home in Mississippi?"[88]

As was characteristic of speeches from the middle period of her career, Hamer not only offered a representation of injustice, she worked to incite recognition regarding the implications of this injustice by both Signifyin(g) upon American maxims like "the land of the free" and also by interpreting the effects of injustice for her audience. Offering a series of facts that she claimed the representatives on the committee "should know," Hamer nevertheless informed them about the widespread disparity between black and white voters in her district. "Negroes make up 58% of the potential voters of the Second Congressional District," moving directly from fact to analysis, Hamer claimed: "This means that if Negroes were allowed to vote freely, I could be sitting up here with you right now as a congresswoman."[89] But blacks are not free to vote and, Hamer argued, the committee should know that "Negroes . . . have not been permitted [to vote] for almost ninety years" in her district and "any [other] congressional district in Mississippi." She illustrated the effects of this prohibition, using Humphreys County as a particularly vivid example of fraud within Hamer's larger district. In this particular county, Hamer explained, "Negroes outnumber whites two to one," and yet "not a single Negro out of 5,561 of voting age were on the rolls when this contested election took place." Deriving strength from apparent weakness, Hamer reminded her audience that her district was the worst of the worst when it came to civil rights. "It is significant that one of the first federal examiners sent into the South after signing out the voting rights bills in 1965 was Leflore County in the Second Congressional District."[90]

Acknowledging Mississippi's, and her district's, especially discriminatory status reinforced her bravery in battling such discrimination, even as it refuted the allegation that African American apathy explains low voter-registration figures. She even drew upon the success of the recent Voting Rights Act, using the presence of federal examiners in Humphreys County as evidence of black people's willingness to vote. "Since the arrival of the Federal examiner just a few weeks ago," Hamer pointed out, "more than 3,000 Negroes have managed to become registered voters." Making her point plain, Hamer again interpreted the data for her audience: "This reflects the eagerness of the Mississippi Negro to participate in the elective process."[91]

"This eagerness has so frightened officials in the state of Mississippi," she went on to explain, "that the State Attorney General has just started a lawsuit to keep the names of these newly . . . registered Negroes off the voting rolls." Hamer returned again to the violence and terror that accompanied black civic assertion, mentioning the murder of a man in her community who was seen around an MFDP worker. "This is the price we have to pay in the state of Mississippi for just wanting to have a chance, as American citizens, to exercise our constitutional right that we were insured by the Fifteenth Amendment." This bold statement grounded her central plea for recognition from the committee: "sweeping this challenge under the rug . . . would be wrong for the whole country because it is time for the American people to wake up."[92]

Just as she positioned the credentials committee members as agents of change during her Atlantic City testimony, here Hamer suggested that the Congressional Election Subcommittee members could incite this awakening by honoring, rather than dismissing, the MFDP's challenge. Signifyin(g) upon hallowed maxims like the "land of the free," and demonstrating her faith in the promise of American principles like the constitutional amendments she cited, Hamer held out a "flattering self-image" for the nation's empowered inhabitants.

In this case, she adapted America's civil religion to appeal to the committee members who take pride in their national identity and see themselves and their country as fundamentally moral.[93] Such a principled self-conception makes those in power especially vulnerable to Jeremiadic appeals. The myths, symbols, and rituals that perpetuate the nation's self-conception provide ready-made rhetorical resources for those who sit outside institutions of power to reveal the distance between the country's professed values and the nature of their oppressed existence. As she had in Atlantic City, Hamer was offering the committee members a chance to reaffirm their own morality and legitimate the nation's principles.

Illustrating the lesson she learned in Atlantic City, however, Hamer distinguished knowing something to be true from "waking up" and doing something about it. In fact, the structure of her address is organized around this movement from knowing to a form of recognition that acts upon that knowledge. In the beginning of her address, Hamer introduced the statistics she explicated with the phrases: "You gentlemen should know . . ." and "You also know that . . ." Toward the conclusion of her testimony, after she moved from the racially disparate voting figures, to the recent gains made by the VRA, to the violent retaliation with which the legislation was met, Hamer clarified—"I am not saying that Mr. Whitten or the other Congressmen helps in that, but I am saying that they know this is going on and . . . they have let it happen."[94]

The action she instructed the committee to take was an outgrowth of what they already knew to be true, but had permitted to occur through their inaction. Unseating the illegally elected representatives would, as her directional argument[95] went, signal an acknowledgment of the rampant constitutional violations in the state of Mississippi. It would also redress an indisputable wrong and, in so doing, help spark a national awakening. Hamer's appeal, thus, reached its culminating point when she combined her congresswoman persona with the Mississippi injustices she represented, "I might not live two hours after I get back home, but *I* want to be part of helping set the Negro free in Mississippi."[96] This declaration functioned as an argument by *a fortiori*[97]—if Hamer, the would-be congresswoman, could face death to accomplish this aim, surely the legitimate congressional representatives seated before her as committee members could risk political consequences to awaken the nation to its own hypocrisy, to reverse the effects of discrimination, and to help ensure freedom for all Americans.

Hamer's demand for recognition and redress, however, only further aggravated an already frayed nerve. One of the primary reasons given in opposition to the MFDP challenge was that it would touch off a series of challenges from similarly disenfranchised groups across the South. Just as the fear of a southern walkout prevented the seating of the MFDP delegates in Atlantic City, the possibility of "a Dixie rebellion on Capitol Hill" protected the congressmen's seats.[98] "We won't say that you nigras are not right," Hamer remembered the committee telling Devine, Gray, and her behind closed doors, "but if you get away with this type of challenge, they will be doing it all over the South."[99] The MFDP would likely have welcomed and supported additional challenges against officials from similarly discriminatory southern states. And this potential effect is at the heart of what distinguished their congressional challenge from the Selma campaign: Hamer, Devine, and Gray sought to contest an illegal election in a manner that would redress the past and alter the present, as well as protect against similar injustices in the future. The Selma campaign, however, sought to expose the illegal voting prohibitions so that these prohibitions would be lifted and the vote would become more accessible. The Selma protests were primarily oriented toward the future whereas the MFDP's challenge held implications for the past and present as well. This subtle, yet significant, difference might explain the contrasting outcomes of each campaign. Unlike Selma, which resulted in the passage of the VRA, members of the House Subcommittee on Elections voted against the MFDP challenge by a 19–5 margin. When it reached the floor of the House for a full debate, moreover, 228 members of Congress voted to dismiss it and only 143 voted to keep deliberating.[100]

If there was a silver lining to yet another national defeat, it could be found in the symbolic value of the MFDP challenge. When their challenge was considered on September 17, 1965, Speaker McCormack invited the three MFDP representatives into the House chamber. Upon accepting this invitation, Fannie Lou Hamer, Annie Devine, and Victoria Gray became the first African American women to be seated on the floor of the United States Congress and the first African Americans from Mississippi to be seated there since 1882. The symbolic significance of this gesture was not lost on MFDP onlookers. "That trio of women was just *awesome* in terms of people sitting looking at them. They represented all of us with our weaknesses, our strength, our future, our hope for the future of our children, and generations gone and generations to come," Dorsey recalls.[101] At the end of the day, this had always been Hamer's guiding purpose: to secure representation for all of the people in Mississippi.

The Hamer, Devine, Gray team may not have unseated the Mississippi congressmen, but the challenge itself humiliated the representatives, who were forced to step aside while their colleagues debated their legitimacy. It put Mississippi election officials on guard as the legal volunteers, through federal subpoena power, forced the white segregationists to account for their discriminatory actions. Perhaps most important, it sent a signal of strength back to black Mississippians, many of whom began referring to the three challengers as "their congresswomen."

The symbolic charge that the Devine, Gray, and Hamer team issued to their constituents back home, remembers Dorsey, was "that you have to get involved because this cycle that we were going through started with slavery and until we break it we're still slaves. Even if we think we're free, we're still slaves."[102]

THE RHETORICAL FORCE OF SYMBOLIC ACTION

Even as Hamer traveled the country drumming up support for the congressional challenge, she was waging several battles closer to home. Hamer and four other Sunflower County residents filed a lawsuit against the Sunflower County registrar, Cecil Campbell. The suit was filed immediately following the court decision in *US v. Campbell*, which the Justice Department had brought against Campbell in 1963 for routinely turning away black citizens. In his April 1965 ruling on the *US v. Campbell* suit, federal judge Claude Clayton "ordered the registrar to make it no harder for blacks to register than it was for whites."[103] In *Hamer v. Campbell*, the suit filed two weeks following the *US v. Campbell* ruling, the litigants urged the court to postpone the upcoming municipal elections so that blacks would have a chance to benefit from the court-ordered equality in registration practices. Clayton denied their request and the elections proceeded with approximately 80 percent of the white residents of Sunflower County registered and less than 10 percent of the county's black citizens on the rolls.[104]

Less than a year later, in March 1966, a federal appeals court overturned Judge Clayton's opinion in *Hamer v. Campbell* and ordered reelections. Though this reversal was indeed historic—"a federal appeals court for the first time threw out an election because black voters had not had fair opportunity to participate"—the US Court of Appeals for the Fifth Circuit clarified that the decision did not necessarily set a precedent for throwing out elections all over the South. In the particular case of *Hamer v. Campbell*, the appellants had tried to delay the election, and failed "where they should have succeeded," on the basis of the very discrimination that, in turn, invalidated the results.[105] Thus, the circuit court ordered Clayton to set a date for reelections in communities affected by his initial decision to allow the elections. The state of Mississippi appealed the circuit court's reversal, but the US Supreme Court denied their appeal and reelections in the small Sunflower County towns of Moorhead and Sunflower were ultimately scheduled for May 2, 1967.

At a time when civil rights activism in Mississippi no longer took center stage in national politics, these landmark reelections momentarily placed the Delta's enduring struggle back in the spotlight. The MFDP redoubled their voter-registration and civic-education efforts, holding mass meetings and workshops, even as they assembled a slate of candidates to run in the reelections. The Freedom Democrats also reached out to national figures like King, Belafonte, A. Philip Randolph, Eugene McCarthy, William Fitts Ryan, and Franklin D. Roosevelt Jr. Together movement veterans and their white allies formed the National Committee for Free Elections in Sunflower County, Mississippi, an organization that helped raise national awareness and funds for the reelections. Hamer stood at the helm of the fundraising effort. In her increasingly well-known role as a representative of black life in the Delta, Hamer headlined a fundraising campaign for the MFDP's candidates. Her ten-day tour throughout the Northeast in March of 1967 included radio and television appearances, house parties, and press conferences; the tour raised thousands of dollars and exposed northern audiences to the voting-rights struggle that persisted in the Mississippi Delta.[106]

To encourage such donations, Hamer stressed the convergence of interests between Americans in the Northeast and the Deep South. She professed her belief in the interconnection of all Americans and the need for collaborative effort to restore the nation's principles. Hamer explained that whatever her audiences could give would go to help "not only to free me in Mississippi, but it's also to help to free yourselves . . . until I'm free in Mississippi, let's not kid ourselves, you're not free in Connecticut," she insisted.[107] The part to the whole logic that Hamer relied upon here was central to the national campaign for reelection support, but it was also a pivotal aspect of Hamer's developing Jeremiad. As Hamer's congressional challenge testimony indicated, the effort to make democracy real for all the nation's inhabitants did not just entail future promises, but relied upon reparative efforts. The 1967 reelections provided both: a chance for the nation to indicate its recognition of discrimination in Mississippi and an opportunity to reverse its effects.

The symbolic significance of the 1967 reelections was tempered by the actual results. For as hard as the MFDP worked to register voters, support candidates, and publicize the Mississippi struggle before national audiences, the white establishment combined both old and new methods to hold fast to their power. Myriad explanations have been offered for why the MFDP-backed candidates faired so poorly against whites in this reelection. The simplest explanation was still disproportionate voting figures—even two years after the passage of the VRA and the 1965 court order to equalize the registration process, registration among Delta blacks only rose by 11 percent from 13 percent in 1965 to 24 percent in 1967. As Moye points out, however, "Black voters actually formed a majority in the town of Sunflower." They also turned out in large numbers, with 95 percent of eligible black voters in the Sunflower precinct casting ballots on May 2, and yet the six candidates the MFDP fielded there were unsuccessful. Moye largely chalks up their defeat to voter intimidation, noting that the "Sunflower chief of police greeted each voter at the door," as a "white man" took each black voters' picture. What's more, illiterate voters were given assistance by local whites rather than by Freedom Democrat supporters, as previously promised.[108]

Hamer biographer Kay Mills provides a different explanation for the MFDP-backed-candidates' defeat, suggesting that MFDP candidates lost because "whites cast their votes in a bloc while some blacks voted for whites." Mills indicates that this was a much broader phenomenon, reasoning that "[w]hat happened in Sunflower would happen in many other areas when black candidates first ran: Black voters did not reward civil rights activism at the polls and sometimes found black candidates' backgrounds wanting in comparison to those of whites." This reluctance can partially be attributed to that deeply engrained plantation mentality, which manifested itself in class-based judgments. "Accustomed" as blacks were to "whites running government," posits Mills, "they could not believe blacks could do it—unless they were flawlessly educated and impeccably dressed."[109]

The white establishment fed into these preconceptions with fliers and letters targeted at black voters. These circulars aligned the MFDP candidates with "paid racial agitators" and suggested that the black candidates were not "the kind of [people] you want as leaders of the Negro community." Tapping into the well-worn argument that civil rights supporters were outside (often allegedly communist) agitators who had come into Mississippi to stir up "division and mistrust," white Democrats planted suspicion in the minds of black voters and coupled this suspicion with an appeal to fear. "[T]hese agitators should not be trying to run your business. Your homes and property are at stake," one flier warned. By contrast, the establishment candidates cast themselves as "sensible leaders" who sought to "make this community a good place to live." Though Moye notes the marked contrast of what making their community "a good place to live" meant for MFDP candidates—safety, jobs, and help acquiring federal entitlements—versus white Democrats—keeping property taxes and city service budgets low—he nevertheless acknowledges that this was the first time "white politicians had to pander for black votes."[110] White pandering to black voters became a statewide trend seen first in the spring reelections in Sunflower and Moorhead and noticed later in the fall elections. Indeed, Dittmer refers to these later elections as a "turning point of sorts in Mississippi politics," because "race-baiting" had "all but disappeared" and white candidates now "sought black votes." They simply had to, as over half of the black electorate was registered to vote by the fall of 1967—over 180,000 voters, up from just over 28,000 voters two years before—blacks now constituted a majority in four counties, though they were only a quarter of the total registered voters in the state.[111]

Perhaps these figures gave Hamer hope as she pressed ahead following the disappointing results in the spring reelections, attempting to run for state senate in the general election held on November 7, 1967. She was barred from appearing on the ballot once again. This time it was because of a technicality, which stipulated that anyone who voted in a party's primary was automatically disqualified from running as an Independent in the general election. When Hamer registered to run on June 9, 1967, she was fairly certain that her name would not appear on the fall ballot. She specifically ran on a political platform that included reforming the "voter registration and election law" because, she reasoned, "voting in a party primary shouldn't disqualify an Independent Candidate," and yet she still referred to herself as a "Candidate for State Senator" in correspondence dated October 23, 1967.[112] In fact, Hamer was among nineteen black candidates barred from appearing on the ballot because of new qualifying requirements the state imposed on Independent candidates. The election law that Hamer sought to challenge with her candidacy was but one of thirty laws the 1966 Mississippi legislature passed to curtail the influence of newly registered black voters.[113] The new legislative efforts, combined with familiar tactics of intimidation and white pandering for black votes, resulted in the election of only six of the sixty candidates backed by the MFDP statewide.

The MFDP's most notable victory in the fall of 1967 was the election of Robert Clark. Clark, a schoolteacher from Holmes County, became the first black state legislator since Reconstruction when he beat his opponent James P. Love by 116 votes. Not surprisingly, his victory was hotly contested by both his opponent and by Mississippi officials. When it appeared that this contestation might preclude Clark from taking the seat he had rightfully won, Hamer launched a two-pronged attack, calling both the secretary of state and the press and threatening to "lead a march on the state capitol from the North" while Charles Evers moved into Jackson from the South. Years later, Clark recalled that without the attention garnered from Hamer's status as a "national figure," the state legislature "probably would have kept me out." Although Hamer worked hard for Clark, this particular gesture was not entirely selfless. After he was seated, she called to warn him that if he did not use his post to "do right," she would challenge him just as forcefully as she had challenged the state on his behalf.[114]

Clark's January 2, 1968, induction marked a much-needed victory for Hamer as it symbolized the influence she now had within her home state, while also offering a tangible result for the last five years of her devotion to registering black voters. Less immediate, but arguably no less significant, were the changes to the Mississippi electorate wrought by the legal challenges Hamer waged. Arthur Kinoy, who was on the MFDP's legal team for the congressional challenge, remembers Hamer teaching him about the mobilizing power of legal struggles; he suggests that "more than almost anyone else," Hamer "understood that the legal struggles were in essence organizing tools for the people's movement." She taught him that "the question was not whether or not you were going to win ultimately in the Supreme Court or any of the higher courts or whether the precedents were all against you—and most of the time they were—but whether this was an organizing tool."[115] In addition to the *Hamer v. Campbell* suit, which helped pave the way for the 1967 reelections, so much of Hamer's civic activity had functioned precisely this way. During the credentials committee challenge, the congressional challenge, and her 1967 candidacy for state senate, Hamer faced daunting odds and yet she persevered, armed with her conviction that she had a right to act and a mission to repair the broken nation. In the process, she was demonstrating what was possible if her neighbors stood up and acted likewise. But Hamer was human; even she grew weary of the slow pace of change wrought by symbolic victories and material defeats. In the wake of the Sunflower and Moorhead reelections, Hamer told one reporter: "There was nothing symbolic about this election . . . I'm sick of symbolic things. We are fighting for our lives."[116]

THE TURN TO TOUGH LOVE

Hamer's statement was far from hyperbolic. Within the first few years of her activist career, she had come to symbolize not just the struggle for suffrage in the state, Hamer, argues biographer Chana Kai Lee, also became "the personification of a kind of historical force that created conditions for the existence of the Mississippi Freedom Labor Union." The MFLU, formed in Bolivar County in 1965, was a fight for the lives of day laborers, domestic servants, and tractor drivers who banded together to secure a living wage. Hamer "became the union's adopted leader and figurehead," posits Lee; as the narrative of her life circulated throughout the Delta it carried with it an ideology that fostered "a lush environment of boldness and daring for the growth of independent alternative organizations such as unions." The circulation of "Hamer's courageous tale . . . throughout the Delta between 1962 and 1964" helped "establish an inspirational and institutional foundation for the MFLU."[117] Though the MFLU's success was curtailed by the massive restructuring in Delta's cotton economy which undermined the union's bargaining power, Hamer's symbolic position within the union and her advocacy on the organization's behalf convey both the influence of her warrior persona and her increasingly militant tone.

In a widely quoted speech, from which only excerpts recorded in a *Delta Democrat-Times* article survive, Hamer lambasted not only "bourgeoisie Negroes" and "chicken-eating preachers" who were not helping with the poor worker's plight; she also threatened the "nervous Nellies and the Toms" who undermined the union's efforts by working on the plantations in the striking workers' absence. "I don't believe in killing," Hamer clarified, "but a good whipping behind the bushes wouldn't hurt them."[118] Lee uses statements such as this one to ground her contention that Hamer "filled her speeches with calls for retributive violence, which characterized the Black Nationalist phase of the modern civil rights era."[119] In this sense, Lee characterizes Hamer as "a woman of her time," influenced by the movement trend away from moral suasion and toward the discourse of Black Power.[120] It is significant to note, however, that Hamer's advocacy of physical intimidation was not a call for the type of retributive violence that Malcolm X and some Black Power activists championed. Whereas their call for retribution was against whites who had used violence for centuries against blacks, Hamer's advocacy of physical intimidation was an extension of the harsh and direct challenges she had been issuing to Delta blacks since she began her activist career. As her Harlem address intimates and as speeches she delivered throughout the remainder of her career demonstrate, Hamer did not abandon her faith in moral suasion and she did not give up on her hope for an integrated solution to the nation's problems. This commitment differentiated Hamer's ideology from what Lee characterizes as a broader movement trend toward deeming "a waste of time" the "matter of appealing to the hearts and minds of the oppressors."[121] Instead, Hamer advocated her own version of a Black Power philosophy. Hamer's advocacy of Black Power and the increasingly confrontational quality of her discourse, combined with her evolving but everpresent promotion of an integrated solution to America's fallen state, created a distinctive tough love message that went against the grain of popular movement discourse and simultaneously fortified her warrior persona.

Even as Hamer held fast to her faith in an integrated solution, and as she continued to appeal to the hearts and minds of white Americans throughout the nation, SNCC became increasingly focused on third-party solutions. SNCC's ideological transformation was exacerbated in 1966 when Carmichael was elected chair. Payne suggests that Carmichael's election was a testament to his successful grassroots work in Lowndes County, but that it was also "a repudiation of the tradition of Christian nonviolence symbolized by John Lewis, who had been chair since 1963."[122] Cobb reasons, furthermore, that Carmichael's election "changed the character of the organization." Suggesting that, "For the first time, SNCC had a charismatic leader. It never had a charismatic leader before and that really, in my view, was detrimental to the community organizer." Not only did Carmichael's bold charismatic personality differ from the modest and understated quality SNCC fieldworkers had expressed in their effort to empower local people, Carmichael's star quality attracted "the interest of all sorts of people all over the country and outside of the country," Cobb remembers. "I think Mrs. Hamer felt left out of this. This was not the SNCC that she recognized, the SNCC that had pulled her in to the movement," he surmises. Though Hamer's disaffection from the organization is often attributed to SNCC's narrow decision to expel whites, Cobb's explanation suggests that "the expulsion of whites is a little bit overdone," in general, and in particular, Hamer's separation from SNCC can be more carefully attributed to a loss of connection. "I think a lot of the 'new people' in SNCC didn't know how to relate to Mrs. Hamer and people like that," and Hamer became "disappointed in SNCC" as an organization that once amplified the voices of local people and now included members who regarded these people as relics of an outgrown era of movement activism.[123]

While she retained close ties with activists she had met through SNCC—folks like McLaurin and Baker—Hamer grew increasingly distant from the organization responsible for her political awakening. And though her political philosophy was not seamlessly aligned with the shift to Black Power made by both SNCC and CORE, she nevertheless participated in both James Meredith's March Against Fear and she spoke at a CORE conference alongside Carmichael during the summer of 1966. Her public statements in connection with these two events help define her distinctive mid-decade ideology regarding race relations and social change, even as they challenge overly simplistic explanations of the Black Power concept.

Having integrated the University of Mississippi in 1962, Meredith now proposed walking from Memphis, Tennessee, to Jackson, Mississippi. The 220-mile hike, which began at the Peabody Hotel on Sunday, June 4, 1966, was intended to challenge blacks' fear and convince them that it was now safe to register and vote. Meredith's symbolic display of black strength and his assurance of safety were undermined on the second day of his journey. Shortly after Meredith crossed into the state of Mississippi, Aubrey James Norvell unloaded three rounds of shotgun shells, from which sixty to seventy pellets struck Meredith and sent him tumbling to the ground. Meredith was rushed to a Memphis hospital where black freedom movement leaders Whitney Young of the Urban League, King of the SCLC, Wilkins of the NAACP, Carmichael of SNCC, and Floyd McKissick of CORE sought and received Meredith's blessing to continue the march.

The movement leaders convened at the Lorraine Motel in Memphis to discuss strategy. Wilkins and Young pledged money and national political support for the march, on the condition that it was carried out in a respectable and responsible manner. SNCC was growing increasingly weary of nationally publicized marches that only momentarily drew in allies and temporarily brought attention to injustice. What Carmichael proposed, instead, was that the remainder of the Meredith March take on a decidedly local focus. He suggested: "We should do voter registration in every town with a courthouse. Urge local leaders to run for office. The local communities should be the entire focus. Local leaders should speak on every platform." Wilkins and Young interpreted this suggestion as an effort by SNCC to exclude whites from the march. Furthermore, Wilkins and Young strongly objected to Carmichael's insistence that the Louisiana-based Deacons of Defense provide security for the marchers. As Carmichael tells it, "[t]hose two were the sticking points," which engendered heated deliberation well into the night. McKissick and Carmichael promoted a locally focused march protected by the Deacons, while Young and Wilkins insisted that national leaders be invited to participate and opposed the Deacons' presence, maintaining they would erode political support and obfuscate the march's nonviolent message. In the end, King—who had "played a patient, conciliatory role, seeking . . . unity"—recognized "the logic of emphasizing local initiative" and was assured that the Deacons could both protect the marchers while respecting the march's commitment to nonviolence. Unable to budge on these sticking points, Wilkins and Young withdrew their organizations' support for the march.[124]

Two weeks into the trek, as marchers passed through Carmichael's old organizational territory of Greenwood, Mississippi, he was arrested and jailed for the twenty-seventh time during his activist career. Shortly after Carmichael was released on bail, he spoke before a crowd of six hundred marchers and movement supporters eagerly gathered to hear the SNCC fieldworker-turned-chair of the organization. "The spirit of self-assertion and defiance was palpable" among the "valiant, embattled community of old friends and fellow strugglers," recalls Carmichael, who "told them what they knew, that they could depend only on themselves, their own organized collective strength." "Register and vote," was the crux of Carmichael's message during which he proclaimed: "the only rights they were likely to get were the ones they took for themselves." And he "raised the call for Black Power," which he describes as "nothing new"—the phrase had been used long before in other contexts. In fact, Carmichael claims that the spirit of the slogan came out of the pride he and SNCC found stretching back through generations of black families carving out a life in the Delta. Black Power, as Carmichael used the slogan, meant "The power to affirm our black humanity; to defend the dignity, integrity, and institutions of our culture; and to collectively organize the political and economic power to begin to control and develop our communities." Carmichael's advocacy, defined this way, was not a radically militant departure from SNCC's organizing work, but rather an extension of it. Carmichael's promotion of Black Power during the Meredith March, however, launched both himself and the phrase into the center of the contemporary black freedom movement. The slogan caught on like wildfire among many marchers, but it was harshly criticized by more conservative civil rights organizations. And the slogan threatened and confused many whites, who understood it in zero sum terms: that being pro-black meant you were antiwhite. Though Carmichael repeatedly explained that Black Power "was patently not about either hating or loving white people . . . That it really had nothing to do with them was something they could not seem to grasp," he laments.[125]

Hamer, who joined the march as it crossed through the Delta and who addressed a crowd of supporters gathered at the Enid Dam campsite, readily reconciled her abiding faith in integration with Carmichael's call for Black Power.[126] In a historical moment when the media conflated the slogan with "reverse racism," "violent retaliation," and "separatism," Hamer explained the concept to reporters this way:

> What we mean by "Black Power" is we mean to have not only black political power, but black economic power, to have a voice in the educational system that our kids will know—not only the black kids, but the white kids should know—the kinds of contributions that have been made by black people throughout this country. We want to determine some of our destiny and this is what "Black Power" means.[127]

Unlike many Black Power advocates, Hamer was not formally educated, nor was she schooled in the literature of revolution and rebellion, but she had traveled to Africa, she had spent time with Malcolm X, and she was raised by a mother who taught her to respect herself and to take pride in her black identity. She understood the importance of self-determination, and she saw the connection between politics, economics, and education. To her, these objectives did not clash with an integrationist philosophy, nor did they conflict with an effort to work within existing structures to foster change. Hamer and the MFDP even capitalized on the attention and enthusiasm the march generated as it crossed through the Delta—just as Carmichael had hoped local leaders would—registering sixty-nine new voters during its three-week duration.[128]

Lest Hamer's vision of Black Power seem all too encompassing, it is important to note that she did emphasize for whom the philosophy would be most helpful and against whom the chants of empowerment were directed. On July 1, 1966, at the twenty-third annual CORE convention, held in Baltimore just one week after the Meredith March wrapped up in Jackson, Hamer and Carmichael addressed an enthusiastic crowd of two hundred convention attendees. Carmichael spoke about strategy—referring to integration as an irrelevant question, suggesting that discussing nonviolence with whites who supported government intervention in Vietnam was futile, and asserting that "we will define our own tactics whether they like it or not." Hamer fostered identification with the crowd by distinguishing their struggle from the fight waged by well-connected middle-class blacks. As she had for the last four years, Hamer criticized "chicken-[eating] black preachers," adding the "Negro bourgeoisie" and "the PhD's" to this group of blacks who "sold out" the "Negro people" to whites.[129] Claiming that in contrast to this group of sellouts: "The black people in the United States are starting to move for black power," Hamer suggested that Black Power is both a racial and a class-based form of empowerment.[130] Championed by the most oppressed within an oppressed race, the philosophy of Black Power was, in part, a reaction to the efforts made by middle- and upper-class blacks to strip the lower classes of gains they had made in the early stages of the movement. Although Hamer did not share Carmichael's view that the question of integration was irrelevant, she did recognize the urgent need for an emboldening philosophy in the struggle not only for rights in America, but also for voice within the movement. For Hamer, as for Carmichael, Black Power was about self-determination and black leadership among the most oppressed, which was a logical outgrowth of Hamer's view that Delta blacks' suffering imbued them with the superior perspective needed to right the nation's wrongs.

WAR ON POVERTY

In the years following Johnson's introduction of wide-ranging domestic initiatives like Medicaid, food stamps, and Operation Head Start—collectively

constituting his War on Poverty, a key plank in his Great Society initiative—
Hamer sent Johnson a telegram, quipping: "If this society of yours is a 'Great
Society,' God knows I'd hate to live in a bad one." And she would sardonically
joke that his War on Poverty was aptly named—"that's exactly what it is, a war
against poor people."[131] Her relationship to these programs did not start out
this cynical, however. Hamer was initially quite supportive of CDGM, an OEO-
funded Head Start program that began in the summer of 1965 and enlisted
the help of local COFO-affiliated movement activists. With "nearly 1.5 million dollars" granted by the OEO, the CDGM began serving "6,000 children
through eighty-four centers in twenty-four counties" across Mississippi.[132] This
initiative, the largest Head Start program the OEO funded in the summer of
1965, not only provided warm meals, medical care, and preschool education
for impoverished children across the state, it also brought badly needed jobs
to adults. Employing over one thousand workers, CDGM hired people who
had first become active in their communities through COFO initiatives. In this
sense, argues Dittmer, "CDGM was unique . . . it was led by people who did not
apologize for their civil rights movement involvement and who saw CDGM
as an opportunity to provide education and services while at the same time
advancing the movement agenda."[133] As an organization that cared for the state's
neediest children while employing their parents and enlisting them in understanding and enhancing their children's development, CDGM promoted the
type of self-determination Hamer called for when she advocated Black Power.
This type of self-determination, furthermore, dovetailed with what Sargent
Shriver, the OEO director, envisioned for Head Start programs when he called
for the "maximum feasible participation of the poor in the solutions of their
own problems."[134]

This type of self-determination and empowerment, however, posed a fundamental threat to the race- and class-based caste system that had benefited whites
and a few upper-class blacks in the state of Mississippi for centuries. The challenge did not go unnoticed by either group. Not long after its inception, CDGM
came under fire from Mississippi's political leaders who appealed to Shriver on
the grounds that the organization's funds were supporting civil rights activities.
Senators Eastland and John C. Stennis took this argument a step further invoking anticommunist hysteria when they alleged that OEO money flowing into
the state through CDGM was being used to fund "the extreme leftist civil rights
and beatnik groups in our state, some of which have definite connections with
Communist organizations."[135] The OEO ultimately conceded to white segregationist pressure by withholding funding from CDGM and opting to support
more moderate Community Action Programs. Unable to overlook the value of

federal aid flowing into their state, whites and more conservative blacks joined forces to form rival Head Start centers, which eventually replaced CDGM by December of 1967, when the organization's funding ran out.[136]

Hailing from the poorest state in the union's poorest region—an area that, once toured by members of the US Senate Subcommittee on Employment, Manpower, and Poverty in April of 1967, was deemed to be in a state of emergency due to the rampant illness, malnutrition, and starvation that existed there—Hamer grew especially disgusted by the political battle for control over poverty funds.[137] She made statements, reminiscent of her opposition to the Nervous Nellies and Uncle Toms who crossed the MFLU's picket lines, lambasting middle-class blacks, who she claimed sold out CDGM to the white power structure. "Sometimes I get so disgusted I feel like getting my gun after some of these school teachers and chicken-eatin' preachers."[138] Even in the midst of this anger and disgust, Hamer did not abandon the prospect of working together with whites and middle-class blacks to solve the problem of poverty in her state. "The Only Thing We Can Do Is to Work Together," a speech Hamer delivered in 1967 before a gathering of the NCNW in Jackson, Mississippi, offers a final instance for examining the way in which Hamer constructed her warrior persona while advancing her distinctive mid-decade argument for social and political change.

This particular address, given before a chapter meeting of the NCNW, was an appeal to the very whites and middle- to upper-class blacks who formed alliances which Hamer felt undermined the power of the poor to determine their own destiny. She urged this audience to recognize the vital role poor blacks must play in the struggle. To accomplish this, Hamer extended upon Jeremiadic themes she developed in her Harlem speech and her congressional challenge testimony. She emphasized the interconnection of the races and the convergence of their interests, while coupling the sacrifices poor blacks had made in their early commitment to the movement with biblical warrants, which established the special position of the most oppressed in the struggle for freedom.

Looking out into the interracial audience seated before her, Hamer began by declaring that she was "glad to see white and Negro working together for the cause of human dignity." Her tone quickly changed from one of congratulation to one of condemnation. After recounting the hardships faced by those blacks who risked their lives and livelihoods to become active early on in the movement—noting that they worked for racial advancement "without money, without food, and . . . [without] decent clothes"—Hamer emboldened her own warrior persona by drawing attention to her marked body. "I know some of you see me with this leg, where I'm suffering now from permanent kidney damage because of my experience in Montgomery County."[139] The story of her Winona beating was so well known that Hamer need only allude to its effects to establish her rhetorical strength through sacrifice. In a similar fashion, Hamer recounted the names of those black Mississippians who gave their life for the cause of freedom. She mentioned Herbert Lee, E. H. Hurst, and Medgar Evers among others—pausing briefly in response to the disinterest she perceived among some audience members. "I hope I don't hold you up too long," Hamer said, her voice dripping with sarcasm, "I just want to tell you some of the things . . . that you have failed to do in helping make this a better place for all of us."[140] She returned to her oration, mentioning the names of Goodman, Schwerner, and Chaney, "three young men that gave their lives for a cause," and she contrasted their sacrifice with the behavior of "professional people in the state of Mississippi—teachers and preachers," she specified, who "don't have the dignity—they have these degrees but they don't have the dignity and respect for their fellow man to stand up for a cause."[141] Hamer recounted the sacrifices made by local people in the early stages of the movement to establish their commitment to the struggle and hence their entitlement to lead. Furthermore, she contrasted this commitment with the meekness of professional people who activists "couldn't get to say a word" in the early stages of the movement.[142]

To further develop the contrast between those who "have gone through the suffering" and those who possess the traditional qualifications to lead, Hamer turned to scripture. "I strictly believe in Christianity," declared Hamer as she countered the conception that "you've got to have a PhD degree to live," with biblical assurances such as "my Holy Bible tell me that He was taking from the wise and revealing it to babies," "whether you got a degree or no degree, all wisdom and knowledge come from God," and her old stand-by, "'The spirit of the Lord is upon me because he has anointed me to preach the gospel to the poor.' Not to the rich," Hamer clarified.[143] Hamer garnered strength not only from suffering and the special position that experiential wisdom established for poor blacks, she also made it clear that God was on the side of the oppressed. She alluded to the gains CDGM made in her home county—"we have in Sunflower County fourteen hundred children what we were able to get out . . . of the country, and most of these children had never seen a commode in their lives. Some of these children had never had their faces washed in a bowl . . . we got these children and brought them in the little town and began to work with them as best as we could do"—but then "the professional Negro got with the power structure white," she explained, "and they have done everything to drag us down."[144] Never one to back away from a fight, Hamer made her resolve in the face of this oppression clear: "I am going to stand . . . I have a principle and not only do I have a principle, I have a charge."[145]

Casting the battle for leadership between poor blacks and black professionals in apocalyptic terms, Hamer told the NCNW that the conflict made her
"think about the sixth chapter of Ephesians and the eleventh and the twelfth
verse that say, 'Put on the whole armor of God that he may be able to stand
against the wiles of the devil. For we wrestle not against flesh and blood.'"
Adapting the scripture to the situation in Mississippi, Hamer designated the
specific roles in this epic confrontation, "We are not wrestling against flesh and
blood today, people, but against principalities—powers of darkness. The rulers
of darkness of this world, which is the power structure. Spiritual wickedness in
high places—that's the ministers." Though the fight is "long," Hamer gathered
strength from the assurance that "this fight is not mine alone." She insisted that
the fight for freedom was a national and an interracial struggle: "I'm not just
fighting for myself and for the black race, but I'm fighting for the white; I'm
fighting for the Indians; I'm fighting for the Mexicans; I'm fighting for the Chinese; I'm fighting for anybody because as long as they are human beings, they
need freedom."[146]

As was characteristic of the Jeremiad she advanced, Hamer emphasized
the interconnection of America's races and regions. Directly addressing those
seated before her, she informed them: "you are not free whether you white or
whether you black, until I am free. Because no man is an island to himself.
And until I'm free in Mississippi, you are not free in Washington; you are not
free in New York." Invoking John Donne's famous meditation, which Joan Baez
adapted into a movement anthem, she charged her audience "to work together."
In fact, she prophesied that if they could not find a way to utilize God's wisdom and respect one another as "our brother's keeper," then "I'm afraid we won't
make it."[147]

More so than the fiery one-liners and dramatic statements of frustration
excerpted from larger speeches and replicated in mass-mediated representations, "The Only Thing We Can Do Is to Work Together" provides a sustained
account of the ways in which Hamer's vision of social and political change
evolved within a tumultuous mid-decade context. Hamer's address before the
NCNW conveys her frustration and disappointment with both the white power
structure and the black middle class. It extends her argument about the special
role the most oppressed must play in the national struggle for freedom. And
it updates her perspective regarding the problems that continued to plague
the movement. No longer is Hamer railing against pitiful white supremacists
and urging her audience to overcome their plantation mentality by registering
to vote. In this speech, she indicts those whites and black professionals who
have banded together to push poor blacks aside. But she does not simply con-
vict this audience, rather Hamer encouraged them to recognize the rightful

position poor blacks ought to assume within the struggle—by virtue of the sacrifices they made and the suffering they endured—and she advanced an imperative for all races and classes to acknowledge their interconnection and to work together. What's more, the direct and often confrontational tone of the speech when considered alongside statements Hamer made regarding her own strength and sacrifices contributed to the evolution of her persona—from that of a simple sharecropper with an abiding faith in American principles to that of a warrior, a seasoned veteran in the battle for equality.

SPEAKING THROUGH SILENCE

Hamer's warrior persona, which was constructed through her speeches and was reinforced both by her symbolic activity as well as by representations and evocations of her image, kept Hamer relevant at a time when the nation's attention began shifting away from the struggle of poor southern blacks. Hamer's warrior persona, however, belied her physical weakness, her wavering resolve, and the substance of the personal struggles she faced. In a series of letters Hamer sent to Rose Fishman, a civil rights supporter from Waban, Massachusetts whom Hamer met during her fundraising tours of the Northeast, Hamer let down the guard of her public persona and revealed a more complex self. The depth of the women's bond was made clear by Hamer, who referred to Fishman as her "second mother" within the letters and also by the outpouring of support Fishman provided Hamer. Together, the Fishmans and the Sugarmans helped Hamer buy a decent home for her growing family. The Fishmans also sent bedding and furnishings for it, in addition to baby clothes for Hamer's granddaughters-turned-daughters and clothes and shoes for Hamer's teenage daughter Vergie, whom Hamer worried would be made fun of at the previously all-white school she integrated. Hamer thanked the Fishmans profusely for their ongoing assistance, but she also filled her letters with comments about the poor state of her own health. Over the three years (1965–1968) of their preserved correspondence, Hamer's physical weakness was a recurring theme. She asked Fishman, for example, "Rose, I wonder will I ever feel good?" Hamer also kept Fishman abreast of the lingering effects of the Winona beating she suffered, "my kidneys are giving me trouble and my head too," not to mention the blood clot in her eye, which continued to worsen to the point where Hamer told Mrs. Fishman that she "couldn't hardly see."[148]

Emotional struggles only compounded these physical maladies, as Hamer confessed: "we have to fight for everything. My God it is hard," and sought reassurance, "do you think that one day my troubles won't be so bad? I hope so." She admitted in the wake of the Meredith March, "Rose, I have marched until my body and soul is tired," adding in a later letter, "Rose, my soul is tired, but somehow God keeps me going," and later still, "Rose, I am so tired it seems like my soul needs a rest." Hamer was fatigued by her continued drive to effect change even after "everybody"—the majority of SNCC/COFO organizers—had "left the state" and by the white supremacist terror she still endured. Hamer told Fishman about crosses being burned throughout the state, about "dirty calls" she personally received, and even about the continued political support given to vitriolic segregationists like former governor Ross Barnett and Medgar Evers's assassin, Byron de la Beckwith. She often wavered between despair and hope. "Rose, I wonder when will people love each other as human beings and stop killing, hanging, hating and fighting?" Responding to her own query, Hamer continued: "I hope one day we can truthfully say, 'peace on earth goodwill toward men.' Until then my mission is to keep telling the world it is wrong to hate anybody."

Even as she publicly executed this mission, Hamer was also wearied by the personal hardships she faced. She was beat down by the daily effort of "keeping [her] babies clean and with what food and milk" she could provide, not to mention "keeping them warm" in the drafty house on East Lafayette Street, where she lived before moving into the house the Fishmans helped her obtain. Hamer mentioned to Fishman more than once that "these two little girls plus Virgie[149] . . . and campaigning at night . . . keep me very busy." Though wearied by both the circumstances surrounding, and the very act itself of, becoming a mother of an infant and a toddler when in her fifties, Hamer would not have traded the experience of raising Dorothy Jean's children, Jacqueline and Lenora, for the world. To Fishman she confided, "Although my daughter was taken, she left me two little darling girls to love and do for. I don't have everything, but one thing I know they are rich with love. I love them so very very much that make a part of my life beautiful." The joy the young girls brought Hamer helped ease the pain of Dorothy's loss, which Vergie remembers would overwhelm her mother at times.

Dorothy Jean "had been ill all her life," her younger sister Vergie remembers. By the spring of 1967, though, the situation became dire. Dorothy gave birth to the two girls within two years—Lenora was born in October 1965 and Jacqueline was born just eleven months later, in September 1966. Even for a healthy woman's body the nearness of these two births would have taken their toll, but for Dorothy, who "was a sick baby" herself and had long suffered from anemia related to malnutrition, the nearness of these births proved to be more than her body could bear. Early in the month of May, Dorothy got a nosebleed, which Vergie remembers as a common ailment for her older sister. But this time it was different; Vergie recalls with a tremble in her voice, "this time we couldn't get it to stop. . . . This particular time we had to take her to the doctor." Over forty years later you can still hear a trace of desperation as Vergie recounts the family's futile efforts. First, they took Dorothy "to this little place called Minter City to this doctor, his name was Dr. Creek and he worked with her and he worked with her. Finally he got her nose to stop bleeding." They brought her home, but she was weak and by that evening she started bleeding again. "So, mama took her to Mound Bayou hospital in Mound Bayou, Mississippi," where she stayed for over three weeks, "from the first of May to the twenty-third."

When it became clear that Dorothy needed more expert medical attention than the small hospital in Mound Bayou could provide, Fannie Lou Hamer made the decision to transport Dorothy to the nearest major hospital. They eventually gained admittance 119 miles away, in Memphis, Tennessee. Before they embarked on the lengthy drive, the Hamers took Dorothy to Vergie's school to say goodbye. Vergie remembers that encounter vividly: "my sister looked like she was nine months pregnant! She had a growth," an aggressive uterine tumor, also known as a fibroid, for which African American women are at an especially high risk. Even in her weakened state, Dorothy managed to joke with Vergie, telling her, "Girl, mama said she was going to take me up there to Memphis and leave me!" As Vergie and Dorothy shared a laugh outside the schoolyard, an eighteen-wheeler drove by the main road next to them— a picture of a stretched-out camel was emblazoned on the side of the truck. Dorothy pointed to it and said, "That's probably going to be me. I'm going to be straightened out like that humpback camel." She said, "I ain't got no hump in my back, I got a hump in my stomach!" To which Vergie quipped, "Girl, please!" With fondness in her voice, Vergie uses this anecdote to encapsulate her sister's personality, "she was so—oh honey, she was so much fun!"

But Dorothy did not get "straightened out" in Memphis. The growth, which doctors explained to the family as a "molecular myoma—growing and eating up her blood," might have been removed if the Hamers had brought Dorothy to Memphis much sooner. By the time she arrived, there was little doctors could do for her; Dorothy died soon after arriving at John Gadsden Hospital. Vergie believes that "mama prayed and the Lord brought Dorothy back" for one more day, but the family ultimately lost twenty-two-year-old Dorothy Jean on the twenty-fourth of May 1967. Dorothy's passing "took tolls on mama's little heart," Vergie contends, "mama never did get over it." More so than the death of Hamer's own mother, Lou Ella Townsend, the death of Dorothy sent Hamer into a deep depression. "She didn't even go that way . . . when grandmamma died," Vergie told me, remembering that from time to time Hamer would mistakenly refer to Vergie as Dorothy, even years after her sister's death. And when Vergie would correct her saying, "Mama, I'm Bebe," Hamer would reply simply, "Forgive me, I just can't get over it."[150]

Although the loss of her daughter deeply impacted her life, the experience of Dorothy's sickness and her eventual death did not become a staple in Hamer's rhetorical repertoire. Perhaps Hamer's relative silence surrounding Dorothy's death is a telling measure of just how devastating the experience was for her—so much so that she could barely bring herself to discuss it publicly. Unlike her own Winona tragedy, which Hamer referred to in nearly every one of her major public addresses throughout her activist career, she rarely mentioned Dorothy's death.[151] Even when the circumstances surrounding her passing—malnutrition, inadequate access to quality healthcare, and perhaps even race-based exclusion from medical facilities—would have been relevant to Hamer's various campaigns for social and economic justice.[152]

The fact that Hamer shied away from discussing Dorothy's death publicly offers a glimpse into the flip side of her warrior persona. Just as the warrior image of Hamer was constructed through discourses of strength, sacrifice, and commitment to her mission, it was also sustained through silences. Hamer's letters to Fishman are quite revealing in this respect. To Fishman, Hamer divulged her doubts, her personal loss and feelings of despair, as well as her most basic needs—food for her children, blankets to keep them warm, and shoes for Vergie to go to school—but these humanizing aspects of Hamer's life get overshadowed by representations of her as "the country's number one freedom fighting woman" and a "warrior of warriors." The flattening of Hamer's image, which is perpetuated through her symbolic warrior legacy, is unfortunate because it overlooks core aspects of who she was and what she struggled with during her lifetime. The Hamer-as-warrior symbol also risks placing her on an unattainable mythical plane from which her example might actually prove disempowering to future generations.

CONCLUSION

As Payne contends in the bibliographic essay following *I've Got the Light of Freedom,* "social analysis which does not somehow make it clear that ordinary, flawed, everyday sorts of human beings frequently manage to make extraordinary contributions to social change, social analysis which does not make it easier for people to see in themselves and in those around them the potential for controlling their own lives takes us in the wrong direction."[153] Rhetorical analysis of the ways in which Hamer's warrior persona was constructed through her own discourse, through symbolic representations of her, as well as by silences surrounding significant aspects of her personal struggle, goes beyond demonstrating the persuasive power of her symbolic stature to also consider what this status overlooks. Recovering the silences surrounding Hamer's ill health, her weary spirit, and the tragedy in her personal life adds a layer of complexity to her public struggles even as this recovery makes it possible for ordinary people to see themselves in Hamer's powerful example. Though she clearly had natural talents and while her life path intersected with movement trends at fortuitous moments, in her example one can imagine the possibility of balancing overwhelming personal hardships with at least some level of contribution to collective life.

Striving for this balance became even more difficult for Hamer over the next four years, which were the busiest period in her activist career. Chapter 5 delves into this demanding period of activism—1968–1972—by thematically analyzing Hamer's discourse as it related to the increasingly integrated realm of institutionalized politics, the burgeoning second-wave feminist movement(s), and the push for poverty programs on both local and national fronts. Carried along as Hamer was by these larger currents of change, she also remained committed to the values she espoused and the programs for social transformation she advocated. Hamer promoted an interracial, bi-gender, grassroots coalition for human rights and dignity, even as her means of articulation grew to a radically prophetic pitch.

CHAPTER 5

"To Tell It Like It Is," 1968–1972

HAMER PLACED HER WHITE-LAPELLED BLAZER ON THE CHAIR BEHIND HER and her purse on the table in front as she rose to speak at the Holmes County Courthouse in Lexington, Mississippi, on May 8, 1969. Her hair was pulled up and back into a beehive; the sleeveless white shell she wore underneath the blazer permitted her greater range of motion as she dove into her passionate address. As vice president of the MFDP, Hamer was in Lexington speaking on behalf of the candidates running for office in the May 13 election. Flanked by such notables as MFDP chair Lawrence Guyot, state NAACP president Aaron Henry, and state representative Robert Clark, Hamer offered words of encouragement to the MFDP candidates, even as she used the speech to address problems plaguing the nation. Hamer's Holmes County address, "To Tell It Like It Is," is emblematic of her fiery turn-of-the-decade oratorical style through which she transformed her prior ethos as a simple honest sharecropper and a warrior into the persona of an uncompromising truth teller. Her prophetic position as an outsider—excluded from mainstream political and educational institutions yet schooled in suffering through Mississippi's fiery furnace—was amended during this period. Hamer now argued that sick as the systems were, she was better off having been excluded from them; free from their taint, she now stood in a privileged position to "tell it like it is."[1]

The truth, according to Hamer, was bound to make her audiences "feel uncomfortable," but she proclaimed repeatedly, "I got to tell you where it's at."[2] In Hamer's assessment, "America is sick, and man is on the critical list."[3] The national ills she railed against in "To Tell It Like It Is" ranged from the specific problems facing black candidates in Mississippi—race-based "redistricting" and the "power structure" alleging that black candidates were "unqualified"—to problems targeting the poor blacks in her state, who were being "starved out" through agricultural policies that benefited the wealthy, and because whites feared blacks' growing political influence—and even to problems facing the nation, including the anger expressed by its youth, black and white alike. As Hamer's oration encircled these topics, she asserted her prophetic position as an outsider whose distance from the center provided a superior vantage point: "I can challenge any white man anywhere on the face of this earth because God knows he made a mistake when he put me behind. I watched him, now I know him; he doesn't know me. You know that, baby."[4] What she learned from this position is that "[t]hese people have been trying to trick us a long time. A few years ago, they were shooting at us," then "they redistricted us," and now "what they decided to do was starve us out of the state." Hamer interpreted white resistance to black assertion as she always had—"[t]his man is scared to death because of what *he* done done"; she explained: "They're frightened of what they think that we'll do back to them." But Hamer wasn't promoting retribution in Lexington or anywhere else during her turn-of-the-decade speaking engagements: "I wouldn't drag my moral and my dignity low enough to do all the things . . . to *you* that you've done to us," she made clear.[5]

Instead, Hamer was fighting for a "people's Mississippi," not "fighting to seat an all-black government in the state," but "it certainly ain't going to be an all-white one either."[6] Hamer located the solution to her state's and the nation's ills in a familiar source: scripture, and more specifically, the scriptural assurances that undergird her Jeremiad. Informing the audience seated in the courthouse gallery before her that "I'm going to tell you what we have to do at this time . . . We got to think about the Holy Bible."[7] She pulled through her rhetorical touchstones, including "Has made of one blood all nations," further emphasizing the interconnection of the races with aphorisms like Donne's "no man is an island to himself," and her more insistent proclamation, "I want you to know something black and white, especially to white America: you can't destroy me to save your life without destroying yourself" (Acts 17:26, NKJV).[8] She also utilized scripture, in much the same way as she had throughout her rhetorical career, to convince her audience that God was on the side of the oppressed. Urging those seated before her to "put on the whole armor of God that [they] may be able to stand against the wiles of the devil," Hamer reminded them, "'He said, 'Thy will be done on earth as it is in heaven.'"[9] And yet, she knew "some of the stuff that's going on down here. God don't want this stuff in heaven. That means, we're going to have to push these men and these women and put them in office." Promoting leadership among the oppressed as the solution to societal ills, Hamer encouraged the candidates: "baby, you're going to be beautiful."[10] And she allayed their insecurities: "Don't worry about what the world say about you, and don't worry about what the power structure going to say about you because right now, whatever you do, if it's anything, you going to beat what he's already done . . . you go on up there trusting God."[11]

Hamer's Holmes County address did not just extend her biblically rooted Jeremiad in support of the MFDP candidates, however. "To Tell It Like It Is" also revealed that by the end of the 1960s she was reaching a breaking point in her struggle to work within American institutions as an avenue for social change. Within her Holmes County address, she championed activists who took a militant approach, promoted an unabashedly uncompromising stance, and even showed signs of passing the torch to a younger generation. Twice during this speech Hamer acknowledged the growing militancy among the nation's youth, suggesting at one point: "I can see why these young mens are angry because they're going to make democracy work, or we ain't going to have nothing. And I'm grateful to them for it" and at another: "Young black men and young white men throughout the country and Mississippi, too, is angry because they found out what's been in the books hadn't been functioning like it's supposed to. And they found out that somebody has been lying. And that's why they're angry."[12] Although very few radicals in the late 1960s would label themselves as such, Hamer began characterizing America's angry youth as God's chosen people whom Jesus was referring to "when Christ said he would raise up a nation that would obey him."[13] She carried forth the militant spirit of the times in statements proclaiming, "I'm not compromising, and . . . we're not going to put up with it," as well as "I don't believe in compromising. Because if something supposed to be mine a hundred years ago, don't offer me a piece of it now. I want every bit of it yesterday."[14] Even as her tone grew more insistent, Hamer took a step aside. Commonly promoting the activism of black men, as in "To Tell It Like It Is," where she cast herself in a supporting role, "honey, I'm right there patting you on the shoulder saying, 'Go ahead, brother,' because a few years back these brothers couldn't do it." Now that women have paved the way, getting "it prepared," she urged black men to "come on and do your [thing]."[15]

Hamer's Holmes County address offers a glimpse into the ways in which her activist career transitioned and transformed from 1968 to 1972. Most notably, she began distancing herself from the National Democratic Party (NDP), and preferred to sit outside the official ranks of political organizations like second-wave feminist groups and the Poor People's Campaign. What's more, she no longer advocated piecemeal solutions to larger systemic problems. Instead, Hamer focused her activist efforts on Freedom Farm, a cooperative she spearheaded in Sunflower County that confronted the multifaceted causes of the Delta's endemic poverty. When raising funds for Freedom Farm, moreover, Hamer consistently combined the narrative of her life of exclusion and oppression with radical appeals to repair human dignity and American democracy. Her message was radical in the sense that she urged fundamental changes at the root of political structures and human relations. As she told her Holmes County audience, "this country . . . is upset, and the only way we going to have a change throughout this country is [to] upset it some more."[16]

As her tone grew more confrontational and as she grew more radical in her advocacy of social change, Hamer became an increasingly sought-after speaker. She received speaking requests from sororities across the country that looked to Hamer as a strong woman who could "help" their members "realistically" grapple with "the crucial issues which America faces today."[17] With similar admiration, a "chair-lady" from the Memorial Baptist Church in New York wrote to Hamer seven months before their congregation's annual Women's Day Celebration to secure her as their featured speaker.[18] In addition, representatives from private colleges and public universities across the nation invited Hamer to come and share her perspective with their student body. She was able to meet many of these requests, speaking at Harvard in November 1968 and Duke University and Mississippi Valley State University in February 1969. In addition, she spoke to the students at Tougaloo College in Mississippi, Carleton College in Minnesota, and Seattle University in March of that same year. In April 1969, Hamer participated in a three-week lecture series at Shaw University, teaching students at this historically black college in North Carolina about "The Black American in the 20th Century."[19] In 1970, she traveled to Indianola, Iowa, and was a featured speaker during a "one month in depth course on civil rights" at Simpson College. The following year, Hamer traveled to the East and Southeast, addressing the students of Wheelock College in Roxbury, Massachusetts, as well as those involved in the Black Student Educational and Cultural Center at Florida State University in Tallahassee. She also addressed several college organizations explicitly concerned with issues of hunger, speaking to Walk for Development groups in Madison and Milwaukee and to Walk Against Hunger participants from the University of North Carolina-Chapel Hill.[20] For her civil rights and educational endeavors, moreover, Hamer earned honorary degrees from several collegiate institutions including Tougaloo College, Shaw University, and Howard University.

Hamer's turn-of-the-decade rhetorical transition from discourse that represents injustice and fosters recognition of societal ills to rhetoric that deliberately sits outside the centers of power to preach redemption through radical social change can be most clearly discerned through analysis of her involvement in the increasingly racially integrated realm of electoral politics, the budding women's liberation movements, and poverty politics. This focus illuminates the various ways in which Hamer utilized her persona as an uncompromising truth teller to urge the type of introspection that exposes complacency and hypocrisy, all the while promoting an interracial coalition among the poor. Although Hamer confronted each political realm simultaneously in her own liberation struggle, this chapter will proceed thematically, accruing greater analytical depth by considering, in turn, the arenas of electoral, feminist, and poverty politics.

ELECTORAL POLITICS

The period between 1968 and 1972 was marked by an influx of radicalism in American politics. As Vietnam War protestors rallied in opposition to America's international policies, urban centers also became sites of opposition and evidence of the failure of domestic programs. Urban uprisings began as early as 1964, but grew in both frequency and intensity toward the end of the decade. The aftermath of the riots was devastating as, in all, they affected nearly three hundred US cities, took the lives of 250 people, left thousands of people seriously injured and homeless, and cost millions of dollars in property damage.[21] Upon investigation of the 1967 uprisings, the National Advisory Commission on Civil Disorders (the Kerner Commission) found the root cause to be white racism.[22] The social reformers who comprised the Kerner Commission advocated dramatic institutionalized change to bridge the gap between the nation's principles and its practices. While many black activists agreed with the commission's assessment concerning the cause of America's race problems, by the time the report was released in February 1968, few were persuaded to forge interracial collaborations with white liberals. Instead, a growing number of black activist groups such as CORE and the Black Panther Party (BPP) focused on black-led community empowerment.

For people like Hamer, who spoke out about the danger of hypocrisy and the importance of reconnecting with American values by matching principle with practice, the realm of institutionalized politics had never provided a comfortable home. While many black activists used this discomfort to ground their refusal to forge coalitions with whites and to abandon the pursuit of racial advancement through institutionalized avenues, Hamer never completely lost her faith in interracial coalitions or in the potential for American institutions to effect the change she desired. In 1969, she preached an assertive form of forgiveness before her Holmes County auditors, maintaining: "we going to forgive our white brother for what he done in the past, but I'll be doggoned if he going to do it to us again."[23] That same year, she reasoned before an audience of Vietnam protestors in Berkeley that although "a lot of people . . . said: 'well, forget about politics,'" this was a piece of instruction she found impossible to heed because, "Baby, what we eat is politic. And I'm not going to forget no politic. Because in 1972, when I go to Washington as Senator Hamer from Mississippi . . . it's going to be some changes made."[24] Although Hamer never made it to Washington as a senator, she did exemplify her faith in the American system of politics through her position as a delegate to the 1968 DNC and in her 1971 campaign for state senate.

In fact, Hamer's continued faith in the American political system is one of the few explanations for her participation in the 1968 DNC. Unlike the 1964 challenge waged by the MFDP, the 1968 challenge to the segregated delegation from Mississippi came from a coalition of rights groups who formed the Loyal Democrats of Mississippi, commonly known as the "Loyalists." Not long after the 1964 convention, an interracial coalition of Mississippi politicians including Charles Evers, Aaron Henry, Pat Derian, and Hodding Carter III came together to ensure that the 1968 convention challenge would not be "too radical to . . . prevail."[25] One way to interpret these politicians' motivations would be to reason that they were integration-oriented Mississippians who saw themselves as the most fitting representatives to spearhead the 1968 challenge because they were well connected, experienced, and less extreme in their ideology than most members of the MFDP. As such, they sought to ensure that the Freedom Democrats' radical appeals did not undermine this historic opportunity for an integrated delegation from Mississippi to be seated at the DNC.

Hamer, however, provided another interpretation. She suggested that middle- to upper-class Mississippi politicians—black and white alike—formed the Loyalist coalition because if the MFDP had succeeded in 1968 "it would be too much recognition for a bunch of niggers. So, why not step on the bandwagon and take it over?"[26] As Hamer saw it, the Loyal Democrats' action in 1968 was not unlike the way in which seasoned civil rights movement leaders sought to control the MFDP challenge in 1964 or the way in which upper-class blacks paired with the white establishment to commandeer poverty programs in Mississippi. Now, as then, Hamer objected to being pushed aside because of her lower-class status.

Incensed as they were by being supplanted, the Freedom Democrats did not fold into the Loyalist coalition without some fierce opposition. At issue was not just the displacement; there was also a fundamental clash of principles. Original members of the MFDP including Guyot, Hamer, and Unita Blackwell fought for more radical solutions to meet the needs of the rural poor as well as dramatic shifts in foreign policy, issues that they felt were being pushed aside in an effort to ensure the seating of the integrated delegation. "For political purposes," explains Guyot, "we needed to create a coalition with some people who had opposed our very existence and sought to destroy us." Nevertheless, Guyot remains "very proud of the fact that [he] was able to hammer out an agreement" with the Loyal Democrats' coalition, which encapsulated Mississippi branches of the NAACP, the American Federation of Labor-Congress of Industrial Organizations (AFL-CIO), the Young Democrats, the Black Prince Hall Masons, and the Black Mississippi Teachers Association. Members of the MFDP ultimately compromised aspects of their more radical platform, posits Guyot, because "somebody was going to be seated other than the Regulars," and the MFDP "wanted to be a part of that."[27]

Just as the MFDP eventually relied upon the broad base of support the Loyalist coalition held to guarantee that they too would be a part of this historic political victory, the Loyal Democrats benefited from the perceived authenticity that the Freedom Democrats' membership bestowed upon their challenge. Common membership, however, was a far cry from support on both sides. Hamer told an interviewer before she left to the Chicago convention that she really did not know what to think about the 1968 challenge, comprised as it was of "folks . . . that [she] knew would sell whoever is for sale." As a chosen delegate, she had made up her mind to go to the convention because she agreed "that we should have a challenge," but that did not mean that she would identify with the Loyalists wholeheartedly. "I definitely think that we as FDP people should keep our identity, to let the world know that we are still FDP . . . The basic principles that I believed in then, I believe in them now."[28] This statement was more than an affirmation of the consistency of her beliefs—it also functioned as a critique of those members of the original MFDP who had lost their ties to the organization. Dr. Aaron Henry was one such person whose principles Hamer questioned because of his support for the two-seat compromise that President Johnson offered the MFDP back in 1964, and because of his recent selection as a more moderate black leader of Mississippi poverty programs.[29]

Though the Loyalists acknowledged that Hamer was central to their legitimacy as a collective, they did not provide her the platform that SNCC and the MFDP had four years earlier. Her riveting 1964 testimony secured her position as "the member of the delegation whom others most wanted to meet."[30] Guyot recalls, furthermore, that he was slated "to escort Fannie Lou Hamer to the podium for the purpose of her nominating Ted Kennedy President of the United States." Though John Lewis stopped them on their way to the microphone, Guyot uses this example to illustrate Hamer's symbolic standing within the National Democratic Party.[31] With this notoriety came a high degree of influence, which made some members of the Loyalist coalition nervous. Dorsey casts this tense relationship in the context of Mississippi politics by describing the "socialization of place." Wealthier blacks became "threatened by the upstarts who sort of displace the middle class in terms of their negotiating ability with the white people who are really the power brokers," she explains.[32]

Earlier in the decade, SNCC had undermined the traditional hierarchy in the black community by empowering the poor and bypassing those middle-class black power brokers who were reluctant to become involved in the movement. Now that the most dangerous work of confronting the violently repressive system of white supremacy was over, many more middle-class blacks were becoming involved with Mississippi politics. The national attention Hamer garnered during the 1964 DNC gave her formidable political influence on a much larger stage, and the means by which she garnered that influence—principled straightforward speech—made her impossible for the more traditional leaders within the Mississippi black community to control. The concern shared both by power brokers in the Loyalist delegation and by "establishment politicians" running the DNC was "that she might transform an already volatile convention with an emotional speech."[33] As a result, several steps were taken to quell the power of Hamer's discourse, including the decision not to televise her address and to closely monitor her activity throughout the convention.[34]

The 1968 convention's volatility stemmed not so much from domestic racial politics as it did from the Vietnam protestors and the Chicago police officers' handling of their demonstrations. After three years of involvement in the Vietnam War, American military action abroad became increasingly unpopular at home. Newly formed student groups and well-established leaders alike virulently opposed the war's continuation. Members of the Youth International Party, in particular, drew attention toward their cause and away from the internal politics at the 1968 DNC through protests that led to rioting and police brutality. By the end of the convention, over 500 protestors were injured, 152 police officers were reportedly wounded, and nearly 100 civilians had been affected by the violence. Though Hamer was an early and ongoing opponent of the war, first speaking out against American involvement in Vietnam in 1965 and continually reiterating her position at rallies and in published statements throughout the decade, she did not join the protests outside the convention.[35] Hamer even warned others not to protest alongside the Vietnam demonstrators because she believed that the establishment "planned to kill a lot of us," so we "told our black brothers, said: 'Don't go out there, because they're planning to get us, man.'" "So they didn't go," she explained before the Vietnam War Moratorium rally in Berkeley the following year, "but they was so determined to do something, they beat you kids nearly to death."[36]

With this chaos in the streets, the three credentials committee hearings, initiated by civil rights activist groups in Georgia, Alabama, and Mississippi, received less national attention than had the Freedom Democrats' 1964 challenge. There was also less controversy surrounding the nature of the challenging groups' claims. The Loyal Democrats from Mississippi, for example, followed the NDP's rules for the formation of an integrated representative delegation whereas the Mississippi Regulars disregarded these provisions. The Regular Party did not have a single black delegate, not even from congressional districts where over 70 percent of the population was African American. The regular delegation's disregard for the NDP's pledge to never again seat a segregated delegation made the committee's verdict relatively easy: eighty-four members of the credentials committee voted to unseat the Regulars and ten voted against the measure. Similarly, eighty-five committee members voted to seat the Loyalists in place of the Regulars and only ten voted against this provision. When she took her hard-won seat as a delegate on the convention floor, with her official credentials badge strung across her chest, Hamer received a standing ovation.

Victory was not as swift for the integrated Alabama and Georgia delegations. The case was clearest in Mississippi because the NDP had been monitoring the segregated party there and also because the Loyalists were well organized and their allegations well researched. Led by the politically experienced Julian Bond, the Georgia challengers received half of their state's delegate seats for the convention. Alabama's delegation, however, needed all the help they could get when their case was brought to the convention floor. This challenge was brought by the National Democratic Party of Alabama (NDPA), which formed in 1967 and whom Jeffries characterizes as drawing "inspiration from the LCFO," but "more closely resembl[ing] the Freedom Democrats" given its interracial membership and support of the NDP's candidates.[37] On August 27, 1968, during the convention's second evening session, Hamer delivered a short speech on the NDPA's behalf. Though the speech is no more than four paragraphs in length, it goes a long way toward exemplifying the evolution of Hamer's persona from a simple honest sharecropper to an uncompromising truth teller.

Hamer's 1968 DNC speech on behalf of the Alabama delegation was much like the scripted 1965 testimony she delivered before the House Elections Subcommittee: convicting and incisive. She began the address by speaking about herself in the third person, thereby acknowledging her symbolic status. "In 1964," she reminded the convention participants who had recently risen to their feet in support of her, "Fannie Lou Hamer was on the outside trying to get in." Offering this exclusion as a source of experiential wisdom, she went on to recount the facts in support of seating the Alabama delegation, continuing to remind the audience of knowledge they shared in common. "We know the long pattern of discrimination not only in . . . Mississippi, but also in the State of Alabama," she reasoned logically, using the similarities between these two cases to argue from a successful outcome to a contingent instance. Extending this *parallel case*[38] logic into an argument by *a fortiori*, Hamer implied that aspects of Alabama's racist climate are even worse than Mississippi's and, thus, Alabama should be assured a victorious outcome. Hamer reminded her audience: "We also know that Governor Wallace is running today for President of the United States, and he is only pledged as a Democrat in the State of Alabama." In light of this shared knowledge, Hamer called her audience to action, urging: "It is time for us to wake up." Significantly, Hamer used plural pronouns such as "we" and "our" to transition from the persona of an outsider—speaking in the third person and "trying to get in"—to one who shared knowledge with her audience, and, ultimately, to a well-respected participant in the NDP who was invested in bringing an end to its hypocrisy.

Hamer's support for the delegation led by Dr. John Cashin, a black dentist from Huntsville, Alabama, was rooted not just in representing injustice, or in encouraging America to "wake up" and recognize its ubiquity. Rather, Hamer supported the Alabama delegation because, as she explained it, their challenge to be seated was a fundamental challenge to the identity of the NDP. "I support Dr. Cashin from Alabama," she informed the seated delegates, "because it's time for us to stop pretending that we are, but act in the manner that we are, and if we are the Democratic Party of this Country, we should stop tokenism." Here, Hamer echoed Bob Moses's opposition to the Atlantic City compromise; in 1964, Moses told reporters bluntly, "the people want to represent themselves. They don't want symbolic token votes. They want to vote themselves."[39] Instead of offering two seats here, or a half-seated delegation there, Hamer pushed the party to take a radical stance, in line with their fundamental duty to represent American citizens, and "seat the delegation . . . that represent all the people, not just a few, representing not only the whites, but the blacks as well."[40]

Although Hamer was intimately aware of how complicated the process of unseating a delegation could be, the crux of her plea rested on a profoundly simple form of definitional logic: The NDP believes in representation for all, Cashin's interracial delegation is the only truly representative delegation from Alabama, therefore the NDP should seat Cashin's delegation. Much like the three simple words Hamer used to capture the national imagination four years earlier—"Is this America?"—she now seemed to be asking: "Is this the Democratic Party?" More than raising a critical question here, however, the strength of her political persona enabled her to confront the national party's hypocrisy head-on.

Yet again, Hamer's appeal for justice from the Democratic Party was unsuccessful in bringing about the outcome she desired. The integrated Alabama delegation was not seated in Chicago. This disappointment, unfortunately, was one among many for Hamer and those who sought to bring radical change to the convention. She and members of the MFDP were not only concerned about securing seating for representative delegations, they also worked to infuse issues like comprehensive healthcare, free higher education, land grants, subsidies for co-ops, a guaranteed annual income, and foreign policy concerns such as the removal of troops from Vietnam and an arms embargo against South Africa into the party's platform. In Hamer's words, they went seeking "real change" and "true reform—for a true Democratic Party," but what they found when they arrived in Chicago was "the funeral of the Democratic Party."[41]

A little less than a year after the convention, Hamer told the Democratic Reform Committee that she felt "fenced in" and "left out" in Chicago, that the convention was "closed to the people," and that "grassroot people in Mississippi and nowhere else in this country—whether they're white, black, or polka-dot— hadn't been represented" there. Hamer referred to Nixon's election as a direct result of the Democratic Party's failure to live up to its principles. She expressed her hope that the disappointing loss of the election and the disturbing violence outside of the convention, which left the "party . . . naked for all to see," would help trigger the process of radical change. She implored: "now maybe . . . you will start talking about principles and not just how many votes that [Chicago] Mayor Daley or any man at the top can steal for the party."[42] Hamer's use of pronouns shifted yet again in this speech. Whereas she attached herself to the NDP before, urging its restoration in her 1968 DNC address, here she offered the Democratic Reform Committee suggestions as to how *they* ought to improve their party. Both the tenor of her message and the shift of her pronouns indicate a critical transition, signaling that though Hamer was willing to lend her perspective to the Democrats, she would pursue alternative avenues to effect the change she advocated.

In 1971, Hamer ran as an Independent candidate for one of the two Eleventh District seats to the Mississippi state senate. Her district covered the large northwestern stretch of the state between Bolivar and Sunflower Counties and so did her campaign. She enlisted the help of old SNCC allies, John Lewis and Julian Bond, as well as new feminist friends, Liz Carpenter and Betty Friedan. She also drew upon the local endorsement of Gussie Mae Love, the mother of Jo-Etha Collier, who had been gunned down on May 25, 1971, in front of a Drew, Mississippi, grocery store by three drunken white men. Collier was celebrating her high school graduation, which had taken place just hours earlier, when she was fatally shot in the back of the neck. The murder elicited statewide and even national attention to the racial injustice that persisted in the Delta; Hamer spoke out about the murder and helped raise money for the family. Collier's

mother often traveled with Hamer to campaign stops. The family so supported
Hamer's endeavors and was so thankful for the financial assistance she provided them that they gave her the original copy of the high school diploma that
Collier was holding when she died.[43] With the support of these well-known
local and national figures, Hamer traveled throughout her district in a rented
Winnebago motor home, meeting and talking with people face to face. She
bought airtime on radio and television stations to broadcast her message of
hope for the Delta and for the country's salvation.

Hamer's increased national notoriety enabled her to pull out all of the stops
for this campaign and the effort seemed well justified, considering that she had
a much stronger chance of being elected in 1971, than she had in either of her
1964 or 1967 runs for public office. The voting registration figures had changed
dramatically over the last seven years. The number of registered black voters
in the state of Mississippi increased from 7 percent to 34 percent; this marked
change was brought about by the incessant advocacy of suffrage by groups like
the MFDP, as well as by the removal of discriminatory obstacles like the literacy test, and by the federal registrars that the 1965 VRA brought into the state.
Similar to the aim of her 1964 campaign when she challenged Representative
Whitten, Hamer now took on Robert Crook in an effort to give these newly
registered voters a reason to cast their ballot, in this her final major campaign
for public office.

Undergirded by the principles of representation, service, and equality, Hamer's platform consisted of practical solutions to the problems that plagued the
Delta. Increased farm mechanization had left many sharecroppers and day laborers jobless. By the turn of the decade, chemical weed killers and mechanical
cotton pickers performed 90 percent of the labor involved in cotton production; plantation owners now needed only a few skilled workers who could run
the equipment. Because agricultural technology displaced thousands of workers whose families had chopped and picked cotton for generations, many blacks
were forced to leave Sunflower County in search of employment. The Delta
experienced a 25 percent dip in its population within a decade of the turn to
mechanization. Of those who stayed in the region, over 70 percent battled poverty—their median family income amounting to less than $500 a year.[44]

To combat this grave reality, Hamer advocated bringing more industry to
the Delta and making jobs equally available to all races. Welfare was also a key
plank of Hamer's platform. Through her national travels and her work with the
NCNW, Hamer learned that there were federally funded health initiatives, free
lunch programs, and food subsidies available to the poor in her district. From
her struggles to maintain federal funding for Head Start programs, however,

she was mindful of the state and local roadblocks that impeded federal entitlements. So she ran on the promise of securing health and welfare for impoverished members of her district—knowing this would be no easy feat.[45]

One speech manuscript, "If the Name of the Game Is Survive, Survive," from Hamer's 1971 bid for the state senate remains in its entirety. This speech was likely penned by Charles McLaurin, who was running for the other post in the state's Eleventh District. As a close friend and campaign manager for previous elections, McLaurin would often work with Hamer to construct her address before speaking engagements, and she would then use their preparation as a launching pad to deliver more extemporaneous remarks. As such, the manuscript offers an indication of Hamer's and McLaurin's philosophies for social change and a representation of the arguments made during their 1971 bids for public office, even if the prepared remarks do not provide a precise record of what Hamer actually said before an audience gathered in Ruleville on September 27, 1971.[46]

"I expect a drastic change to occur in this country, particularly in the Deep South," the speech began. The desperate need for this change, Hamer elucidated, was readily observable in the violence and riots pervading the nation, the hypocrisy of politicians and religious institutions, and the widespread poverty. These dire problems threatened the nation's survival, leading Hamer to the contention that "the salvation of this nation . . . rest in the hands of the Almighty God and the <u>black striving politicians</u> attempting to save his people and thus the free world."[47] Consistent with her Jeremiad, Hamer underscored the struggle of impoverished blacks claiming that "God has blessed the black man to endure more than three hundred years of suffering," and yet "today he stands at the crossroads of the greatest period in American history, not as a slave, but as a man claiming full rights to all privileges to which this nation has to offer." The oppressed black person's entitlement was born from "his contribution to every stage of development that this country has had" and also from the black person's "struggle to survive."[48] Declaring that her Christian principles formed the basis of her political action, Hamer maintained: "As a believer in God, I keep struggling with the belief that the situation in the South CAN and MUST be changed as more and more Blacks become registered voters."[49] As she explained it, political action was inextricably bound to economic empowerment: "Land . . . is important in the '70s and beyond, as we move toward our ultimate goal of total freedom." This assertion, in turn, laid the groundwork for a statement regarding her own attentive and principled leadership experience: "Because of my belief in land reform, I have taken steps of acquiring land through cooperative ownership."[50]

After Hamer outlined the nature of the problem and the source of the remedy, she expounded upon the types of solutions needed to combat threats against America's well-being. "If this nation is to survive," she declared boldly, "we must return to the concept of local self-government with everyone participating to the maximum degree possible." In an era when politics was tainted by the "'white racist politicians'" who sought to "to control the minds of blacks and poor communities," and during a time when Black Power organizations promoted alternative channels for reform and revolution, Hamer prescribed greater participation in mainstream politics as the cure to political ills.[51] She built upon SNCC's early vision of a representative and responsive government brought about by an interracial coalition of grassroots activists, participating at the community, state, and national level. Phrases such as "communication and race relations" and "total commitment to a true Democratic Process" are underlined in the manuscript version of the campaign speech, indicating the centrality of these ideas to Hamer's and McLaurin's philosophy of social change.[52] Though her address dangled promises that "the South will be a much better place to live than any place in the North" before her audience's eyes, Hamer was careful to remind her audience that "until communication and race relations improve and the total community become united then we will not see a real change in the South."[53]

If there is not a real change in the South, reasoned Hamer, more violent confrontations will ensue. She positioned her belief that "the key to real progress and the survival of all men, not just the black man, must begin at the local, county, and state levels of governments" between the poles of what she labeled "the late Dr. Martin Luther King's 'nonviolent approach'" and a "more militant approach" to social change. Suggesting that while she agreed with King's approach "in some cases . . . in other cases, one has to take a more militant approach and I am not referring to turning the other cheek." Hamer recognized the power of militancy as a tool to prompt awareness, reasoning that the "new militancy on the part of blacks and many young whites have caused [people], not only in the Deep South but the North as well, to realize that racism is an unnecessary evil which must be dealt with by 'men and governments' or by 'men and guns.'" Paraphrasing Malcolm X's well-known ultimatum (the ballot or the bullet) Hamer underscored the urgency of the change she advocated. "If survival is the name of the game," she put it plainly, "then men and governments must not just move to postpone violent confrontations, but seek ways and means of channeling legitimate discontentment into creative and progressive action for change."[54]

As Hamer's 1971 stump speech suggests, she saw a dire need for change in the Delta and in the nation. Oppressed blacks were best positioned to lead this process of change because of the wisdom gleaned from their struggle to survive. Their exclusion from the political process and the racism that continued to dominate their lives had reached a boiling point. Either the system would need to expand to include them and allow them to use their experiential wisdom to bring about constructive social change, or they would move to destroy the system that oppressed them. The nation's survival, Hamer's turn-of-the-decade Jeremiadic appeal reasoned, depended upon recognizing this critical crossroads and choosing the path candidates like she and McLaurin charted.

Unfortunately, staunch segregationists met the increase in black voter registration with increasingly sophisticated modes of intimidation, voter fraud, and racial gerrymandering. In addition to the mandatory federal examiners sent to the state to enforce the VRA, several groups allied with the Concerned Citizens of Sunflower County to Elect Black Officials predicted the segregationists' retaliation and also came to observe the elections. A team of students from Madison, Wisconsin, who served as observers in counties across Mississippi, returned to their own Dane County with an arsenal of incriminating stories to tell. One student journalist, Jonathon Wolman, wrote about the ways in which white poll workers manipulated the votes of blind and illiterate black voters.[55] A reporter for Madison's *Capital Times* echoed Wolman's observations with accounts of white poll workers throwing out black votes, deeming them "damaged" or "invalid."[56] Moreover, a *New York Times* piece reported the physical violence and arrests with which northern poll watchers were met in small Mississippi counties.[57] When the ballots were tallied, the results were characteristically disappointing: Hamer had lost to Crook by a margin of 11,770 to 7,201 votes. Results like these were common across the state as only 50 out of 309 black candidates were victorious. "And so it came to pass," Wolman told his fellow students at the University of Wisconsin, "that no major black candidate won any elected position in a state in which 25 counties out of 82 have a black majority."[58]

While Hamer firmly believed that the election was stolen, and though these northern observers would certainly concur, other explanations for her defeat have been offered. Some people reason that Hamer was the object of envy within her local community, that her nationally renowned symbolic status fostered resentment throughout Sunflower and Bolivar Counties.[59] Others suggest that black voters held candidates from their own race to different standards than their white counterparts and, thus, they may have found Hamer's ideology too radical or her educational credentials lacking.[60] Still, there are those who contend it was never Hamer's election to win, that though the VRA eliminated vestiges of Jim Crow such as the poll tax, literacy tests, and the widespread practice of publishing the names of black registrants in the newspaper, race-based gerrymandering still occurred. Frank R. Parker, the director of the Voting Rights Project and author of *Black Votes Count: Political Empowerment in Mississippi after 1965*, posits that after 1965, "the focus of voting discrimination shifted from preventing blacks from registering to vote to preventing them from winning elections," and one of the most popular modes of prevention was diluting the black vote.[61]

Unita Blackwell concurs with Parker's explanation. Blackwell, a member of the MFDP and the first female African American mayor in the state of Mississippi, remembers that during the 1971 election: "The vote wasn't out there in the first place. We couldn't win it," but Hamer ran anyway "because it was right to run, and it was a political showing that we needed as black people" to prove that "[we] could run for office, whether [we] win or not."[62] Blackwell's explanation is consistent with Hamer's prior political attempts—Whitten defeated Hamer handily in 1964, and she was disqualified on the very election rule she sought to challenge through her candidacy in 1967. So, it is plausible that Hamer ran again as a rhetorically symbolic gesture to prove it could be done and to demystify the political process, but this time her candidacy succeeded in reaching well beyond an audience of black Mississippians.

Hamer's run for the Mississippi state senate helped to bring the national spotlight back to the South, even if it shone just briefly. Her defeat was a microscope focusing the attention of the country on a sample of the sickness that still plagued its democratic body. Her campaign, and the vast increase of campaigns by black Mississippians, did exemplify small improvements in the patient's condition. Though a mere fifty successful elections was no political landslide, it brought the total number of black elected officials in Mississippi to 145, thereby making Mississippi the state with the most black elected officials in the South. This was no small achievement, especially considering that when SNCC began its work in the state blacks in Mississippi held the least amount of political power nationwide, and Mississippi was deemed the most fiercely segregated of any southern state.

Although Hamer lost yet another election and though she never managed to hold public office, she was instrumental to political progress. The contribution her campaign made to an audience of black Mississippians who were inspired by her action and who saw themselves represented by her platform, not to mention the attention her defeat brought back to the problems that remained in the state, demonstrate that many of Hamer's political successes are best captured in rhetorical terms. Terms like *consciousness-raising*, *dramatization*, and *exposure* move outside the realm of tangible institutionalized gains, offering a variety of ways to understand Hamer's contributions to history.

Within the political structure of the National Democratic Party, Hamer's rhetoric was feared and thus restricted. The experience of marginalization that accompanies poverty, moreover, was not one that Hamer chose to distance herself from. It was reflected in the image she conveyed, in the words she spoke, and in the political ideology she adhered to. This experience of marginality informed her radical approach to social change, which, in turn, led the middle-class power brokers within the Mississippi Loyalist and National Democratic Parties to fear and constrain her political expression. In a similar manner, Hamer's lower-class status may have led members of her own community— even people who shared her economic station—to resent her success, fear her radical ideology, or question her credentials.[63] So, even as electoral politics in Mississippi became increasingly integrated, thanks in no small part to Hamer's own activism, her lower-class standing kept her from working inside the system of governance to effect the type of radical social change she envisioned. Fortunately, the realm of electoral politics was not the only avenue of activism available to Hamer. There was another powerful social movement afoot, and this collective actively sought Hamer's prophetic insight and promoted her radical discourse.

FEMINIST POLITICS

As the 1960s drew to a close, black and white women were both inspired and disenchanted by the movements for social change that surrounded them. Their experiences within civil rights, Black Power, and newly formed student organizations reinvigorated the centuries-long struggle for gender equality. Turn-of-the-decade calls for female empowerment, economic opportunity, protection against discrimination, and reproductive rights were far from monolithic, however. Though the inceptions of both black and white women's movements for social change have been traced to late 1967 or early 1968, and while many of the movements' initial leaders worked alongside one another in the earlier part of the struggle for black freedom, black and white women's particular life experiences informed their respective demands and belied an unconditional unity.[64] Nevertheless, the radical way in which women of all races sought to reconfigure relations between the sexes as the basis of a more egalitarian society significantly contributed to the larger climate of social change surrounding Hamer's activism.

Ask just about anyone who knew her well and the response is the same: "Fannie Lou Hamer was not a feminist."[65] Core aspects of the women's liberation movements in their varied instantiations—black, white, middle to upper class, revolutionary, reform oriented, young and old—did not sit well with Hamer. Flowing from the civil rights movement of the 1950s and 1960s, as the second wave did, Hamer's movement experience could have secured her a prominent position of leadership among the ranks of the 1970s feminists. To assume such a post, though, would have meant making ideological compromises to fit within the confines of popular belief systems that did not comport with Hamer's lived experience. Instead of seeking a central position, therefore, she remained on the periphery of women's liberation movements as well as the realm of electoral politics. She held fast to her principles and let them echo through her prophetic speech. Just as she reasoned regarding the realm of institutionalized politics that "We must not allow our eagerness to participate lead us to accept second-class citizenship," she refused anything less than principled political action from her participation in the network of second-wave feminist organizations.[66] The principled objections that Hamer had to central spokes of feminist ideologies fell into three general categories. Specifically, Hamer objected to feminists' oppressive view of relations between the sexes. She took issue with feminist stances on birth control and other aspects of reproductive rights. And, she argued that the banner of "sisterhood" glossed over centuries of significant racial and class differences between women.

As a closer look at Hamer's discourse from this era makes clear, she was not antifeminist, nor was she against coalition building between women. "Fannie Lou Hamer supported women's empowerment," reasons Guyot, "but Fannie Lou Hamer was not a feminist. Fannie Lou Hamer was a humanist . . . she had a broader vision."[67] This broader vision, at times, came into conflict with the aims of the mainstream women's liberation movement. What Hamer fought especially hard against was an overeager and overly simplistic push for unity amid difference. To Hamer, difference had always mattered and now the differences she saw between herself and various strands of feminism functioned not as impediments to social change, but as necessary considerations for meaningful progress.

In 1971, Hamer underscored these differences through five speeches and one article that each broached the topic of feminism to greater and lesser degrees. During her speeches at the founding conference of the National Women's Political Caucus (NWPC) and the NAACP special meeting on the particular plight of black women, for instance, Hamer addressed feminism throughout, relating even seemingly divergent topics back to this central focus. Throughout her speeches at the University of Wisconsin-Madison and Tougaloo College, though, feminism was not the guiding topic, but her commentary on this aspect of the political scene was a salient feature of the addresses. In an article she wrote for *Essence* magazine, furthermore, Hamer targeted a younger generation of primarily black women with her message of both criticism and hope. Though the venues for and guiding focus of each of these six texts[68] differ markedly, reading them as a mosaic of Hamer's views regarding feminism helps guard against reducing her critique to a matter of identity politics. Hamer did not object to white feminists, black revolutionary freedom fighters, northern feminists, or feminists from a younger generation. Rather, as the consistency of her message across these varied texts indicates, Hamer's discourse dug deeper to uncover the principles that were violated through racism, classism, regionalism, or ageism, and she highlighted the effects of this exclusion on the lives of both women and men.

Hamer fundamentally objected to the second-wave feminist focus on seeking liberation from men. "My liberation is different from yours," she argued, "because the same thing that kept me from being liberated kept my black man from being liberated."[69] In this regard, Hamer was not unlike scores of black feminists who resisted prioritizing any one aspect above another in their simultaneous struggle for gender, race, and class equity.[70] For many black women, in fact, family was one of the most empowering sources in their lives.[71] This was certainly true in Hamer's case, as she distanced herself from the center of the feminist movements and moved herself closer to male influences in her family and in her community. Before her NAACP audience, Hamer proclaimed: "I'm not hung up on . . . liberating myself from the black man, I'm not going to try that thing." She informed them proudly, "I got a black husband, six feet three, two hundred and forty pounds, with a 14 shoe, that I don't *want* to be liberated from." Instead, she offered a counter-prescription: "we are here to work side by side with this black man in trying to bring liberation to all people."[72] It was counterintuitive for Hamer to seek distance from one of the most enabling forces in her life. While traveling in Wisconsin, Hamer told one reporter about how her husband cared for their home and their adopted daughters in her absence. "Without a husband like that," she reasoned, "I couldn't be around doing what I do."[73] Hamer routinely bestowed this type of recognition upon Perry "Pap" Hamer. McLemore recalls how supportive Pap was of her and that "she was so supportive of him. She gave him his props."

Not only did Hamer acknowledge Pap and appreciate his support, she also advanced a conservative view of gender relations between them, asserting that "he was the man of the house," McLemore remembers.[74] Wally Roberts, a Freedom Summer volunteer, shares a similar memory about enjoying a meal at the Hamer's home and then rising to wash the dishes as a demonstration of his gratitude. Witnessing this, Pap asked him "angrily, 'What you doin' women's work for?'" After Pap left the room, Mrs. Hamer told a confused Roberts not to worry about her husband's exclamation, reasoning: "Pap don't have many ways left of being a man." Roberts characterizes this brief encounter as an "epiphany," through which he realized both "the degradation that must be the inevitable consequence of racism" and also the way in which Fannie Lou Hamer "had triumphed over the anger and rage that surely had struggled to control her spirit and her life."[75]

In Pap, Roberts saw a man who had been prohibited from providing for his family by economic reprisals. A skilled tractor driver, Pap had difficulty finding employment because of his wife's civic engagement. This added economic woes to the racist emasculation he endured as a black man in the Mississippi Delta. In Fannie Lou's comment to Roberts during the summer of 1964, he also foresaw something of the woman who would later tell the NWPC:

> I'm not fighting to liberate myself from the black man in the South because, so help me, God, he's had as many and more, severer problems than I've had. Because not only has he been stripped of the right to be a politician but he has been stripped of the dignity and the heritage and all the things that any citizen of a country needs.[76]

Roberts characterized Hamer as a woman who recognized gender-based oppression, but more than this, he realized that she was able to replace frustration or offense with understanding. Accordingly, he interpreted her small expression as an indication of Hamer's nuanced comprehension of the interconnections between racism, classism, and sexism. She took no offense to Pap's remarks, reasons Roberts, because she knew the larger context in which they were given; she understood the many factors impinging upon his life over which he had no control.

Hamer's effort to understand Pap's behavior and her insistence on building him up was indicative of the profound respect she had for black men. "I really respect this black man," she told an audience of Tougaloo College students, "because we've been catching hell and he's caught more than we've caught."[77] Believing that racist oppression was worse for black men than black women, Hamer worked to "uplift male leadership in Sunflower County" and "to project male leadership [into the] struggle," recalls fellow activist Owen Brooks.[78] Hamer's effort to increase black male leadership was frequently conveyed in gender-conservative arguments that distinguish her from both black and white feminists of the era. "I am a woman, strong as any woman my age and size . . .

but I am no man," Hamer remarked. "I can carry the message but the burdens of the nation and the world must be shouldered by men." Outlining what she deemed as preferable relations between the sexes, Hamer continued: "Women can be strength for men, women can help with the decision-making, but men will ultimately take the action."[79] While she did propose collaboration between the sexes here, Hamer also unabashedly placed women in a subordinate position with regard to effecting social change. Not only did she suggest that the hierarchical configuration would be a preferable arrangement, but she implied that this is the natural order, a belief she made transparent in speaking with a young man from the Delta region. "The men are the leaders . . . you are born leaders," she informed him; "if you were made on earth to lead then you have to lead me. But don't wait until you get seventy-five to do it," she warned.[80] Many who heard this type of declaration from Hamer were surprised, even the young man who had come to Hamer for advice on a cooperative project, snickered at the thought of him leading her.[81]

Her rural southern upbringing in the black Baptist church, in addition to her class standing, provide partial explanations for the relatively conservative thrust of her remarks. Given the staunchly patriarchal nature of the black Baptist church, Hamer doubtlessly grew up seeing men in leadership positions. Although women certainly wielded influence within the church, formal positions of authority were reserved for men, and thus Hamer likely naturalized this arrangement as the proper order of things.[82] Observing the geographical difference between herself and the strands of feminism growing out of northern urban centers, moreover, Hamer told *Essence*'s primarily black female readership: "I see so many hang-ups in the North that I don't see in the South. In the South men don't expect their wives to be seen and not heard and not doing anything." More than just a regional divide, however, Hamer was expressing an economic difference that also crossed racial lines. She agreed with the feminist assertion that "it's ridiculous to say that a woman's place is in the house, not doing anything but just staying at home." That type of claim was nonsensical to Hamer not so much because of its oppressive tenor, but rather due to its infeasibility. She could not imagine what would happen "if my husband was making $15 a week" and "I didn't try to get out there and make another $15 . . . so them kids could eat." For practical reasons alone, Hamer maintained: "There's nothing wrong with a mother raising her children and there's nothing wrong with her working if it's necessary."[83]

At the same time she was promoting black male advancement, therefore, Hamer was also championing the independence of and the advances made by black women. Beyond their contribution to the household, Hamer acknowledged black women's political efforts in the South, arguing: "it was women that made what little progress we have had. It was women in Mississippi that really started the ball rolling."[84] Hamer's view of the role each sex should play in household affairs and in the broader political arena was multifaceted; she suggested that women were capable and effective leaders in both realms, but that men should assume a more prominent position.

In addition to her regional, religious, and class background, her relatively conservative ideology regarding gender relations can also be explained by contextual factors such as the 1965 release of *The Negro Family: The Case for National Action*, known more commonly as The Moynihan Report. In this report, Senator Daniel Patrick Moynihan argued that the destruction of the black family was the primary impediment to the black race's progress in both the economic and political arenas. Furthermore, he reasoned that the matriarchal structure of the black nuclear family was at the core of black men's inability to function as leaders in their communities.[85] Although Hamer virulently contested Senator Moynihan's assertions, writing: "you know that Moynihan who wrote about Black matriarchal society, knows as much about a Black family as a horse knows about New Year's," she also acknowledged the dearth of male leadership in black communities, and she sought to rectify that deficiency through her insistent promotion of black men.[86] So, while Hamer disagreed with Moynihan's assessment of the cause of black male inaction, she shared his concern for its effects. In fact, she offered her own diagnosis for the cause, explaining in a 1965 oral history interview that "As much as Negro womens are precious, men could be in much more danger. If my husband had gone through or attempted one-third of what I've gone through he would have already been dead."[87] Since black women "got the ball rolling" earlier in the decade—clearing a safer path for black men's involvement—Hamer tailored her turn-of-the-decade addresses to urging black men's participation. She concluded her address to the students at Tougaloo College, for example, by suggesting that the "salvation of this nation lies in the hands of black men," imploring them: "this nation needs you, mothers need you." The desperation evident in Hamer's plea for black men to "stand up with pride and dignity" demonstrates that Hamer regarded feminist calls for liberation from men as a further threat to the already fragile state of black men's civic involvement.[88]

Hamer was also quite wary of white feminists' advocacy of abortion rights, and she was not alone in her opposition. Sociologist Benita Roth contends, "Black feminists assailed white women's failure to acknowledge class and racial aspects of the abortion issue." Many black feminists argued that white women's insistent advocacy of "[a]bortion on demand" was short-sighted, maintaining that it overlooked "other reproductive concerns that were tied to class power: involuntary sterilization; life circumstances that compel poor women to abort; and the possibility that women on welfare would be forced by the state to have abortions."[89] The concerns were close to Hamer's heart, rooted as they were in her own lived experience. Having been involuntarily sterilized in 1961, Hamer had reason to fear this form of public policy. In the late 1960s, furthermore, the Mississippi legislature was debating two bills, one that proposed sterilization for "anybody convicted of a third felony, at the discretion of the Parchman Penitentiary Trustees," and the other would mandate the procedure for any "parent of a second illegitimate child." These measures were not even veiled attempts at racist repression, as state representative Ben Own was quoted in the *Delta Democratic Times* proclaiming: "'This is the only way I know of to stop this rising black tide that threatens to engulf us.'"[90] The sterilization of black women "was so common" in the state, notes historian Danielle L. McGuire, "that blacks often called it a Mississippi appendectomy."[91] Although voluntary abortion is quite different from forced sterilization, Hamer feared that championing one form of reproductive control might open the floodgates for abuse of the other.

In fact, Hamer objected to all forms of reproductive control and even criticized women who gave their children up for adoption. "The methods used to take human lives, such as abortion, the pill, the ring, etc. amounts to genocide," she declared before her Tougaloo audience. "I believe that legal abortion is legal murder and the use of pills and rings to prevent God's will is a great sin," she elaborated.[92] Although Hamer delivered this particular critique in 1971, two years before the Supreme Court decided *Roe v. Wade*, Norma L. McCorvey's (Jane Roe) initial case had already begun making its way through the courts and into the national headlines. Hamer was, thus, objecting to a national push, spearheaded by feminist organizations, to legalize abortion.

Hamer's objection was at once personal, principled, and political. On a personal plane, she informed her Wisconsin auditors that "if they had had [birth control] pills" in her mother's day then she "probably wouldn't be standing here today." Having made what she deemed "a narrow escape to be here," Hamer now took it upon herself to "fight for other kids too, to give them a chance."[93] According to her friend and confidante, Reverend Edwin King, Hamer's objection to abortion was also rooted in race-based political terms. King remembers Hamer tentatively broaching the subject of abortion with him, fairly confident that he shared her pro-life stance. In their discussions of the topic, he recalls, "she analyzed it in [race-based] civil rights terms"; she would say to King: "It's those Republicans. Those white Republicans . . . it is a new repression." Fearful of institutionalized retaliation to civil rights advances, Hamer interpreted the Supreme Court's decision to legalize abortion as a means, not unlike the sterilization proposals working their way through the Mississippi legislature, to repress the growing black population and the political influence their larger numbers now afforded them.[94]

Hamer also opposed abortion and contraception on moral grounds. King remembers Hamer casting her objection in biblical terms, as in her public statements when Hamer celebrated the sanctity of life, while championing God's love for all human beings. Mindful of her principles, in addition to her efforts to repair the structure of the black family, it is not altogether surprising that Hamer took a strong stance against an issue so central to many feminists. In light of the popularity of contraception, and the growing advocacy of abortion rights, however, Hamer was engaged in an uphill battle. Acknowledging this, she wrote in *Essence*: "Some of the hang-ups that the younger black women have today are kind of frustrating. Too many seem to have lost all sense of morals and integrity." Speaking about black women more broadly, Hamer contrasted the older and the younger generations, "That's one of the things that helped us, the moral integrity that we had even though we were poor. We had that."[95]

The younger generation's moral degradation, according to Hamer, is evidenced by their use of contraceptives, their promotion of abortion rights, and even their decision to let other people adopt their biological children. "I think it's a disgrace for people to put their babies up for adoption. There is no need to put this kid up for adoption," she argued. Hamer's bold contention did not stem from the naïveté for which some black activists critiqued middle- to upper-class white women.[96] Rather, Hamer reasoned from her own experience of living in poverty and still being able to care for children in her community: "As long as I can eat, them two grandbabies of mine are going to eat. I'm raising them because their mother's dead, but she loved them babies with all of her heart."[97] Having adopted Dorothy, Vergie, and Dorothy's two children, Hamer could not have been opposed to the practice itself, but she took issue with separating children from their community-based family. Essentially, she was a strong proponent of "othermothering," a community-oriented form of raising children that was prevalent in both urban northern and rural southern black communities.[98] At the same time, Hamer was a staunch opponent of preventing, aborting, or abandoning any form of life.

In every address Hamer delivered about or around the topic of feminism, she engaged the issue of experience in such a manner that highlighted difference and the importance of considering how different life experiences inform politics. Hamer's routine consideration of difference challenged the feminist tendency to emphasize the unifying experience of gendered oppression,

ostensibly shared by women across the boundaries of race, class, sexuality, ge-
ography, religion, and age. Toward audiences of northern white women, Hamer
contended: "baby, your liberation ain't never been like mine . . . 'cause, number
one, you ain't never had to suffer like I suffer . . . what happened to you is the
Man never told you what was going on, but we've been knowing he was a rat."[99]
Here, Hamer argued both that black women have experienced harsher forms of
oppression than white women and that black women were more aware of the
white male patriarchal system, which oppressed black men as well as black and
white women.

Not only did Hamer's objection to similitude challenge interracial sisterhood, but it also positioned black women in an experientially superior position.
In light of all the oppression they endured, black women's marginality provided
them with a superior vantage point. This position of difference, in turn, guarded
against a hasty coming-together before there had been a recognition of past injustice. Speaking before an interracial audience gathered by the NAACP, Hamer
reminded both black and white women of their shared history of exploitation.
"I really feel more sorrier for the white woman than I feel for ourselves," Hamer
explained, "because she been caught up [in]. . . feeling very special." Her address
then turned to confront white women, in particular. Hamer declared directly:
"you worked my grandmother, you worked my mother, and then finally you got
hold of me . . . You thought you was more because you was a . . . white woman." According to Hamer, white men had placed white women "on a pedestal,"
which made them feel superior to black women, and provided them with the
license to use black women "over and over and over."[100]

The tables, in Hamer's account, were now turning precisely because black
women were emboldened and simultaneously revitalized by the black freedom
movement. Essentially, black women, in Hamer's words, "busted the [white
women's] castle open and [were] whacking like hell for the pedestal." Assuming the more experienced and knowledgeable position, Hamer informed white
women: "when you hit the ground, you're [going to] have to fight like hell, like
we've been fighting all this time."[101] As the indicting narrative of oppression and
liberation that Hamer recounted suggests, she was unwilling to bury hundreds
of years of exploitative treatment between white and black women under a false
banner of unity. Nor was she willing to let white women assume a leading position in the struggle for human liberation, considering that black women already had a wealth of experience with this battle.

Hamer's critique of the historical disunion between women extended beyond a race-based objection and even beyond an objection to the class differences that were parasitic upon this racial distinction. Hamer also reminded

middle- to upper-class black women of how they had treated their lower-class sisters. At the same NAACP conference, Hamer raised the specter of intra-racial class tension. She began with a small dose of her derisive wit: "A few years ago throughout the country the middle-class black woman—I used to say not really black women, but the middle-class colored women, c-u-l-l-u-d," Hamer emphasized with an air of elitism, "didn't even respect the kinds of work that I was doing."[102] No doubt Hamer was referring to those blacks, with more formal education than she possessed, who took issue with her leadership in the movement and with the honorary degrees bestowed upon her.[103]

Continuing to temper her critique with humor, Hamer carried forth Ella Baker's assertion that she had never "been diploma conscious," reasoning similarly: "But you see now, baby, whether you have a Ph.D., a D.D., or no D, we're in this bag together. And whether you're from Morehouse or Nohouse, we're still in this bag together."[104] Considering the setting for this speech—an NAACP conference on the special plight of black women—Hamer's remarks can be read as more than a variation of her refrain that Americans from all walks of life need to band together to fight injustice. This statement touches on an issue even more germane to the black community. Specifically, Hamer confronted the type of racist oppression that lumps a diverse group of people together based upon the arbitrary factor of skin color. This is the type of racism that black club women at the turn of the nineteenth century organized to combat with their "lift as we climb" philosophy. And this is the type of racism, which breeds intra-racial classism.[105] By borrowing the same logic, middle- to upper-class black women have relied on for decades—that each member of the black race is only as strong as its weakest link—Hamer called this argument into question in such a manner that revealed its elitist underpinnings.

Through her discourse on feminism, Hamer distanced herself from young black women, from white women, and from middle- to upper-class black women. Her indicting words rejected the wide-ranging acceptance undergirding feminist calls for sisterhood. Yet, Hamer would commonly advocate unity on her own terms. The following quotation from the speech Hamer gave at the founding of the NWPC aptly conveys this balance: "[F]or so many [white women] it was a rude awakening a few years ago when they woke up and found out that not only were they not free but that they had a whole lot of problems not like mine but similar to mine. But somehow we're going to have to bridge this gap."[106] Although she was quick to assume a superior posture when it came to understanding the nation's history of oppression—remarking elsewhere in this speech, "honey, this hasn't just started"—and while she was careful to guard against conflating white and black women's experiences of oppression, Hamer also promoted unity. In fact, some of her statements reaffirming unity in the face of diversity were quite encouraging. "If you think about hooking up with all these women of all different colors and all the minority [groups] hooking on with the majority of women of voting strength in this country," Hamer prodded her audience, "we would become one hell of a majority." In other statements she espoused a similar faith in collaborative political action, declaring: "we're going to have to work together . . . because when women team up together we can do a whole lot of things."[107] Through statements like these, it becomes clear that Hamer "supported the advancement of the rights of as many different people as possible," as Guyot put it.[108] She was not averse to coming together to work with women across experiential divides. She recognized the political advantages of unity. Her principled prophetic position, however, guarded against becoming so tempted by this potential power that she overlooked the truth of her own experience and accepted a "second-class position"—one of compromise and sacrifice—within feminist movements for social change.

So, Hamer remained on the relative margins of feminist politics as well. From this position as an outsider, however, Hamer crafted a prophetic uncompromising truth-telling platform informed by her superior vantage point. While it seems a bit odd that feminist organizations invited Hamer to deliver speeches in which she criticized their objectives and exposed their hypocrisy, members of these organizations likely discerned her benevolent objectives, even shrouded as they were within her confrontational speech. Hamer was popular within feminist circles because she was a strong woman. She was part of the civil rights stream out of which the second-wave feminist collectives flowed. Her values clashed with segments of this larger movement, but as a humanist she was still invested in the success of their push for liberation.

POVERTY POLITICS

Although Hamer played symbolic roles in the increasingly integrated realm of electoral politics, and while she was a widely solicited speaker among feminist organizations, the bulk of her energy during the turn-of-the-decade portion of her activist career was expended in the ongoing fight against poverty. By the end of the 1960s, whether black activists urged communist or capitalist oriented solutions, the problem of economic inequality was central to programs for community development. King and the SCLC spearheaded a Poor People's Campaign (PPC) to demand an economic Bill of Rights. The actual demonstration, wherein an interracial coalition of the nation's dispossessed erected a tent city on the Washington Mall, occurred a month after King's assassination. Though Hamer did not participate in the encampment, she did express her personal disgust with federal policies for the poor in an address to marchers departing to the protest from Marks, Mississippi.[109]

A year later, former SNCC executive secretary James Forman issued a "Black Manifesto" to white religious organizations threatening violence and demanding $500 million dollars in reparations for the National Black Economic Development Conference (NBEDC).[110] Hamer, who attributed her political conversion in no small part to Forman's 1962 speech at her Ruleville church, was one of the initial signatories of Forman's "Black Manifesto." Her support for Forman's program was based on more than their friendship, however. Hamer not only signed the "Manifesto," she also served on the board of the NBEDC, and in her own speeches she actively encouraged churches to heed Forman's demand for the "seed money" that would foster black economic development.[111]

As the PPC emphasized, poverty was not only a problem for black Americans. The federal government acknowledged that poverty affected all races and it sought to bridge the nation's ever-widening economic gap through a variety of social welfare programs. Some of these programs were shortsighted and some long lasting, but all were met with unprecedented involvement. In fact, the "most dramatic increase" in families receiving public assistance occurred between 1968 and 1972, "when the welfare rolls grew [from 1.5] to three million."[112] While growing economic need in areas like the Mississippi Delta, where farm mechanization threatened to starve out unskilled sharecroppers, provides part of the explanation for this dramatic increase, historians also suggest that the black freedom movement succeeded in raising expectations among Americans. That is, the movement succeeded in making blacks more conscious of their rights and more assertive in their demands for basic entitlements like food, housing, education, and job opportunities.[113]

For Hamer, economic concerns had always been a central part of her struggle, which reached its culminating point with the formation of the Freedom Farm Cooperative in 1969. Freedom Farm was a response to Hamer's lifelong battle with poverty. It was an extension of the political career she had built over the last decade; and it was also a means to grapple with controversial poverty politics at the local, state, and national level. Efforts to combat poverty at the national level waxed and waned over the years, but in the mid-1960s the struggle became heartened when the OEO was formed to carry out the programs mandated by President Johnson's War on Poverty initiative. In 1966, Hamer attended an OEO conference in Madison, Wisconsin, to learn ways she could help people in her community benefit from these federal poverty programs.

As the programs were instated at the local level, however, several debilitating problems arose.

The first problem was access. For most people living in the Mississippi Delta in the mid- to late 1960s, life was difficult by any measure. In 1968, when the federal government launched its emergency food and medical program, 39 of the 256 counties it targeted were in the state of Mississippi, with Sunflower County near the top of its priority list.[114] Although federal money was coming into the Delta to combat rampant malnutrition, in Hamer's assessment, it was not reaching its intended beneficiaries. She told one interviewer that "when this white man handle this [poverty] program, it is rotten to the core, because you wouldn't believe it, and my little girl . . . wouldn't believe . . . a man going to bring me out of poverty, he forced me to be in it."[115] When speaking before northern audiences, she supported this assertion with stories about food stamps being withheld from mothers of infants by local welfare workers, and children in their teens dying of malnutrition.[116]

Moreover, Hamer posited that withholding federal aid at the local level was just another in a long line of efforts by the white power structure to drive black people out of Mississippi. She explained that local officials "don't want poor people to have anything to eat, so that they will go away, up North, maybe, to the ghettos and slums of Detroit and Chicago and Newark and New York City."[117] Fellow Mississippian Edwin King's memories from this era support Hamer's contention, as he recalls signs posted in Mississippi welfare agencies advertising how much more money recipients could get if they moved, for example, to Detroit.[118] Dittmer also suggests that white leaders in the state "adopted policies whose impact was to accelerate the black migration—particularly in the heavily black Delta counties—that had been underway since the 1940s."[119] The federal money intended to combat malnutrition was being withheld from its beneficiaries for reasons Hamer and others interpreted as politically motivated and racially based.

Although poor blacks had trouble receiving the economic aid that the federal government designated for them, according to Hamer, plantation owners had no problem receiving their subsidies. Senator Eastland, for instance, owned 5,800 acres of rich Delta soil and Hamer loved to point out that people in Sunflower County called him "Big Jim" because "he's the biggest welfare recipient in the state."[120] Under the auspices of the 1965 federal farm bill, which Eastland helped push through the Senate, the government paid him not to plant. Receiving nearly $170,000 in federal payments in 1967, Eastland was perhaps the biggest, but he was not the only landowning "welfare recipient" in the state. Asch documents that "seventy-seven Sunflower County planters received more than

$25,000 apiece in 1967" to let their land sit idle.[121] While this policy helped control agricultural prices and guarded against a surplus, Andrew Young pointed out that the governmental policy also made it so "the men had no jobs" in the Delta. So, while the landowners got subsidies, the farmworkers never saw this money.[122] To Hamer, who watched her own daughter grapple with the lifelong effects of malnutrition and who, herself, remembered being perpetually hungry as a child, this waste of fertile acreage was proof positive of America's sickness.

The corruption and counterintuitive practices signaled to her that solutions to the problems associated with poverty—hunger, powerlessness, poor education, sickness—would not come from the top down. Real change in the realm of poverty politics would need to be radical, beginning at the grassroots. "If what the politicians have done to the poverty program hasn't taught us anything else," she exclaimed, "it has taught us that we are not going to get much help from the politicians."[123] The reasons she gave for this fact were simple: "we are poor and we are black." An admittedly harsh reality, Hamer's experience in the realm of electoral politics, not to mention the battles waged over the control of Head Start money in the state, revealed to her the difficulties of working within racist and classist structures. Thus, the conclusion Hamer reached by 1968 "as hard as this may seem," was that "the time has come now when we are going to have to get what we need for ourselves. We may get a little bit of help, here and there, but in the main, we are going to have to do for ourselves."[124]

By the end of the 1960s, the civil rights organizations, volunteers, and ideologies that abounded throughout the Delta earlier in the decade were few and far between. But like her mother, who would use scraps of cloth and patches to dress her children, tie bags around their feet for shoes, and cut the tops off of beets to feed them, Fannie Lou Hamer was resourceful. So even in the absence of the organizational assistance on which she had relied earlier in her career, Hamer found new sources of experiential wisdom and financial backing. Her resolve to become self-reliant took the form of an interracial farming cooperative. Owen Brooks, of the Delta Ministry of the National Council of Churches—one of the few organizational strongholds that remained in the region—posits that the "cooperative ethic" was reinfused into the country's consciousness during and after the civil rights movement of the 1950s and 1960s. Cooperatives, explains Brooks, were "important to the struggle because [they] allowed . . . grassroots people to become involved in raising and producing and developing an economic alternative for themselves."[125] Hamer certainly saw this potential in Freedom Farm, as she repeatedly cast the project in terms of political leverage. "'For the first time we are not beholdin' to the power structure,'" she

told a student reporter in Madison, who reasoned, in turn, that "Hamer emphasizes . . . the leverage of owning land and the fact that the land supports people
[and has] given those people a wedge into the political machine—rich, white
and racist—that has always run Mississippi."[126] To challenge the "rich, white and
racist" members of the "political machine," Hamer encouraged poor black and
white people to form their own power structure based on their majority status and enabled by the relative protection that the cooperative afforded them
against retaliation.

Hamer was inspired not only by the cooperative ethic that the civil rights
movement reignited, but also by the more specific model of the North Bolivar
County Cooperative (NBCC) just northwest of Ruleville. Dorsey, an integral
member of that farming cooperative, remembers how Hamer adopted their
model and benefited from the NBCC's labor, equipment, and even the seeds
her co-op donated for Freedom Farm's first crop. In a pamphlet promoting the
NBCC, the founders explain the purpose and the function of such an organization while also promoting pride, strength, and unity among black people. The
NBCC ran a store with books, records, and "other educational material about
black people"; in this way, explained the pamphlet, the "co-op is helping us learn
about our history." The founders also connected the cooperative effort to electoral politics within the state suggesting that the jobs the co-op provided gave
its members strength, offering them freedom from the control of the white establishment: "When black people have a steady job, we don't need to worry
about what the white folks are thinking. We can vote for whom we want without having to fear anybody." And, above all else, the cooperative fostered unity
among black people so that they could "become a strong force," reasoning: "the
co-op can help bring us together. We own it. We run it. We benefit from it and
only we can make it grow."[127]

Hamer drew upon the NBCC's message of race pride, strength, and unity,
but she also distinguished her cooperative from existing models. "She was one
of the first people who really started" communicating a message to "poor *white*
people." Dorsey recalls that Hamer wanted whites to envision Freedom Farm
as "an opportunity . . . to put aside the difference in our colors." Hamer encouraged poor whites to understand that "if you can't feed your children, if you can't
protect your family, if you can't earn a living, then there's something wrong
with that picture. And that you need to cast your lot with us and try to make
it right."[128] Freedom Farm was, thus, fundamentally rhetorical in the sense that
it functioned as a symbol of unity and possibility. Hamer's effort to reach out
to poor whites also sent a message of forgiveness and understanding. Bridging

the gap between the races and banding together, furthermore, communicated strength and security to the white landowners, constituting the farm cooperative as a "power structure" for poor people.[129]

Members of the NBCC not only lent Hamer their founding principles and helped her get the first crop planted; they also put Hamer in contact with charitable organizations, which enabled her to purchase the initial acreage for Freedom Farm. On their trip to Madison for the OEO conference in 1966, Dorsey introduced Hamer to a Madison man named Jeff Goldstein, who served as the treasurer for Measure for Measure. Founded by John Colson in 1963, Measure for Measure took its name from the Shakespeare play by the same title, which was itself derived from the New Testament instruction attributed to Jesus Christ: "Take heed what you hear. With the same measure you use, it will be measured to you; and to you who hear, more will be given" (Mark 4:24, NKJV).[130] This biblical instruction informed Measure for Measure's charitable philosophy. It was not complicated, according to Goldstein, "we would simply support self-help projects that were either part of or alongside the civil rights movement." Rather than take the lead on these projects, the Madison-based organization was responsive to the needs and ideas of those they assisted. "We were dependent on the people down South," he jokes: "Of course, we had the weird idea that they knew best what their community needed."[131] The symbiotic relationship Measure for Measure formed with Hamer "worked like a charm." Goldstein offers countless examples of how Measure for Measure was able to meet Hamer's requests. Perhaps the most serendipitous was also the first. Hamer asked the organization for $10,000 to put toward Freedom Farm's first forty-acre plot of land. While the request seemed out of the small organization's league initially, it was not long before two English professors from the University of Wisconsin approached Goldstein. The professors informed him that their aunt had bequeathed them $10,000, which they wanted to donate to Measure for Measure.

That $10,000, combined with money raised from Hamer's connections at Harvard University, donations from Washington, DC's American Freedom from Hunger foundation, and from Hamer's longtime friend and ardent movement supporter Harry Belafonte, gave Freedom Farm its start. In 1969, the fledgling organization drafted by-laws and created a board. On their first forty acres of land, the Freedom Farm Cooperative planted cash crops like soybeans and cotton to sell and pay the taxes, the administrative staff, and the few hired hands, who cultivated food crops such as cucumbers, corn, peas, beans, squash, okra, and collard greens. The cost for membership was set at $1 per month, though only thirty families could afford to pay dues, so the other 1,500 belonged in name. Regardless of one's membership status, any family who needed food could work the land for a few hours and take home a bushel of produce.

In addition to produce, Hamer also partnered with the NCNW and undertook a Pig Project. The NCNW had been active in the Delta region, and well acquainted with Mrs. Hamer, since the summer of 1964 when they began the interracial and interregional support program dubbed "Wednesdays in Mississippi."[132] The Pig Project, or "pig bank" as it was commonly known, began four years later as an effort to provide protein to the many people in the Delta who could not afford to buy meat. The NCNW donated forty pigs, thirty-five gilts, and five boars. Once a gilt became impregnated by a boar, she would be given to a needy family, contingent upon the family's willingness to return her and two of her offspring to the bank after she birthed a litter. The family also had to agree to pass on several pigs from the sow's large litter (typically eighteen to twenty piglets) to other needy families in the area. The program took off; by 1972, the original forty pigs had multiplied to nearly three thousand, providing families across the Delta with food and relative security.

More than this, the pig bank and the vegetables grown in the Freedom Farm functioned rhetorically in the sense that they constituted a new sense of selfhood for the impoverished inhabitants of the Delta. Hamer referred to the NCNW-sponsored pig bank as a "beautiful program," expressing her gratitude to a representative from the organization: "Honey, I wouldn't take nothing for our golden pigs." She underscored their utility with pride, "Child, we cured our meat this year and then Pap brought it home and I wanted some of it hanging up so I could paint it [with seasoning] and then we painted it and put it in the freezer." Elaborating on her praise for the program, Hamer contended further: "There's nothing no better than get up in the morning and have . . . a huge slice of ham and a couple of biscuits and some butter." What's more, she bragged, "today, you know, we can have company anytime we get ready . . . We can have ham and we can have biscuit and you got a good meal and it's a good project." She even joked about their newfound plenty, "at one time it looked like pigs was coming out of our pockets!"[133] These remarks aptly convey the importance of the pig bank for Hamer and other poor inhabitants of the Delta. Those who sustained and benefited from the pig program, much like the Freedom Farm cooperative, were quite proud of its effects. Though having pork in the freezer, ham for breakfast, or cured meat for company may not seem like a notable conversation piece, it was for Mrs. Hamer and others like her who had suffered without such resources their whole lives. Having them now, and being able to share them, gave the pig bank participants a new sense of pride and security. Hamer commonly cast Freedom Farm in these terms. "If you give them the food, they'll eat for a few days; if you give them the tools, they'll produce for themselves," she would say. "The land has given us hope, dignity and self respect."[134] Thus, even as the interracial nature of Freedom Farm communicated a message of unity toward poor whites, and sent a message of strength to powerful whites who had taken advantage of the Delta poor for centuries, Freedom Farm's produce gave its participants security and pride, enabling them to see themselves as controllers of their own destiny.

As this message of self-empowerment spread, Freedom Farm and the poverty programs associated with it grew exponentially. By 1970, Hamer raised enough money from her grant applications and national travels to foot the down payment for 600 more acres of land, increasing Freedom Farm to 640 acres total. In light of this expanding acreage, it is not surprising that Freedom Farm had the third-largest payroll in Sunflower County, close behind the Head Start program with which Hamer was affiliated, and the garment factory she supported. In fact, Goldstein remarked that the "best we ever did" for Mrs. Hamer was when he discovered that there was "a huge supply . . . of treadle sewing machines" in Madison-area attics. So, he asked Hamer if she could use them and soon discovered that the sewing centers she was assisting had limited access to electricity, so the treadle machines were a highly desirable donation.[135]

Perhaps her longest-lasting triumph, though, was the money she raised for the construction of two hundred units of low-income houses, many of which still stand in Ruleville today. She helped her neighbors gain access to low-interest government loans, and Freedom Farm helped those who could not acquire these loans by purchasing their home and selling it back to them for a reasonable monthly payment. Though modest, these new homes were better insulated, more heartily constructed, and had indoor plumbing, all of which positively distinguished them from the "tar paper shacks" to which many of the Delta poor were previously consigned.[136] Through initiatives such as these, the poverty programs Hamer developed for Sunflower County met not only the physical needs of her impoverished neighbors, but the programs also accomplished a psychological transformation by offering a sense of self-reliance and human dignity.

Given the high cost of keeping alive these various projects—growing vegetables, breeding livestock, and securing decent homes, not to mention awarding scholarships to area youth—the cooperative constantly struggled financially. While its participants' dues and their labor, combined with help from the NCNW and some governmental assistance in the form of low-interest loans, accounted for a portion of the funds used to stay afloat, a great deal of the Freedom Farm programs were financed from money Hamer raised through her national travels. Never one to adequately care for herself, Hamer donated virtually all of the honoraria she received from her speaking engagements. But even this money, which ranged on average from $200 to $500 per event, would not have been enough to sustain her ambitious Freedom Farm.[137]

To accomplish this, Hamer undertook a series of fundraising tours speaking on television programs like the *David Frost Show*, to solicit funds for the farm. Her appearance on that particular program elicited a flood of responses to the station, many of which included financial donations. One such letter read: "Dear David, This is only a dollar but please give it to Mrs. Fannie Lou Hamer to buy land for our people and the cause she spoke so eloquently about on today's program." Another came from a viewer in New York who was similarly inspired by Hamer's "eloquent and moving description of" her poverty programs in Mississippi. This viewer admitted that "it is hard to believe that conditions such as you describe still exist in the United States," but that Hamer's "sincerity convinced" him that she was "telling the truth." The viewer went on to praise Hamer's "courage and devotion," likening her to Washington, Jefferson, "and other great American patriots."[138]

Hamer's fundraising speaking tours on behalf of Freedom Farm also brought her back to places like Seattle, Madison, and the Boston area, where she had previously fostered connections. The archived collection of her papers contain two boxes filled with at least one thousand donation envelopes sent from audience members to the NCNW's Freedom Farm Fund after hearing Hamer speak about the cooperative. The donations commonly range from ten to fifteen dollars and the envelopes bear return addresses from places as far reaching as Anchorage, Alaska, Sugarland, Texas, and Issaquah, Washington.[139] Through either Hamer's live or mediated speeches reaching into these various locales, Hamer solicited direct donations from individuals and she also tapped into larger networks of student projects aimed at raising funds for self-help organizations.

These projects commonly took the form of sponsored walks, hikes, or runs wherein the participants collected pledges from donors in their community. The Young World Development group orchestrated both "Hunger Hikes" and "Walks for Development" through which they raised nearly $200,000 for Freedom Farm in a four-year period.[140] Hamer had always been fond of young people, but in response to the contributions made by students across the country, she began touting them as the indisputable saviors of this sick nation. This sentiment was only further solidified as groups of students began not only donating money, but coming to Ruleville to watch the polls during the 1971 election and bringing books, clothing, water tanks, and even driving farming equipment down from Wisconsin to Mississippi.

Young people reciprocated the admiration and praise Hamer lavished upon them. After a speech Hamer delivered on the University of Wisconsin-Madison campus, for instance, the student newspaper ran an article about her that demonstrated the close attention youth still paid to Hamer's struggle. It read, in part, "The dignity of the people, reinforced by the Sunflower Farm Co-op is the strongest basis yet for viable political struggle . . . an example from which student radicals likely have a lot to learn."[141] Closer analysis of Hamer's national travels to raise money for Freedom Farm's many operations suggest that her speeches sought to do much more than fundraise. In fact, these speeches suggest that Freedom Farm, as a symbol, not only sent a message of unity toward poor whites, a message of strength to landowners, and messages of security, dignity, and pride to its participants, but that Freedom Farm also sent a message of interconnection to northern audiences. Hamer's speeches featured Freedom Farm as a symbol to demonstrate that northern audiences could help Deltans help themselves while also revealing their commitment to the maxim: "nobody's free until everybody's free."

Hamer's connection with activists in Madison, Wisconsin, was perhaps the strongest she fostered with any northern community. She referred to the charitable organizations in Madison as her "radical caucus," and Hamer achieved nothing short of iconic status through her frequent travels there. The *Washington Post* even took notice of this impenetrable bond, informing their national readership: "In Madison, Mrs. Hamer became something of a celebrity. One university student, who had met her in Mississippi, drove around the state capitol square with a sign on his car, announcing her arrival." On the same trip, Measure for Measure threw a sherry reception for her and raised over $4,000 for poverty programs in the Delta.[142] Each of the Measure for Measure veterans with whom I spoke had fond memories of Hamer's relationship to their city. For instance, Martha Fager remembered Hamer as "a much beloved member of the community" and Jeff Goldstein insisted that she got "barrels of love in Madison."[143] Like many relationships in Hamer's life, the "warmth and love" of this union was constituted, in large part, through her speech.[144] Yet, like most of Hamer's speeches from this era, the addresses she delivered in Madison were highly confrontational and utterly judgmental.

While newspaper articles, archival sources, and members of the Madison community all indicate that Hamer spoke in Madison quite often during the last ten years of her life, the recordings of four speeches—two delivered in 1971 and two in 1976—are the only complete accounts of Hamer's Madison addresses that have been recovered to date. Through an analysis of Hamer's two speeches delivered in January 1971, one at the Great Hall on the University of

Wisconsin-Madison campus and the other at a local church, a clear pattern of address emerges. In each speech, Hamer combined her representation of impoverished Mississippians' plight with a critique of northern individuals and national institutions. This combination was oriented toward inducing critical self-reflection that would yield responsive giving.

Attention to the finer aspects of the rhetorical pattern featured in her Madison addresses, moreover, reveals the larger program for radical social change Hamer was crafting. She began both of these addresses in her characteristic fashion, by recounting her story of growing up poor and black in the Mississippi Delta. This aspect of her address resonated with many Madison auditors, who—decades later—still recalled that Hamer's speeches "told us what it was like to live in Mississippi."[145] After describing a life of sharecropping, white supremacist retaliation to her attempts at civic engagement, and the current plight of Mississippians who are still "living in run-down dilapidated shacks," Hamer would target a specific source of institutionalized oppression.[146] She brought her audience into the speech by matching the oppression she targeted with the venue of her address.

Toward her university audience, for instance, Hamer lamented the miserable state of the country as evidenced by the college shootings at Kent State and Jackson State colleges. Altering her familiar refrain, she reasoned: "America is sick and man is on the critical list . . . when people can be shot down at a college . . . there's something very wrong." As she was wont to do, Hamer tempered her revulsion with resolve by probing at the root of the nation's problems. "We have to work to make this a better place and we have to deal with the politics and the history of this country that's not in the books," she instructed her college-educated audience. Providing examples such as the fact that "it was a black doctor that learned to give blood transfusions," and "the first man to die in the revolution was Christopher Attuck [Crispus Attucks] another black man," Hamer then indicted them, "you never taught us that, white America . . . you never taught that in the institution." Contrasting lessons like "Columbus discovered America" with the fact that her own congressional challenge was not taught, Hamer further proved that "[t]he education has got to be changed in these institutions."[147]

Similarly, in the speech she delivered at a Madison-area church, Hamer criticized institutionalized religion. "The church is really lagging," she maintained. Speaking to the hypocrites, whom Hamer described as those parishioners who go to church on Sunday and "then leave until next Sunday," Hamer informed them that their apathetic practices are "not serving God." And she reminded them, "We are our brother's keeper."[148] Hamer's criticism of both the hallowed institutions at which she spoke also persisted in the memories of her audience, as Goldstein recalled bluntly: "She told you what the shit was and told you how to get rid of it."[149] In a similar vein, other Measure for Measure members contend that she "opened people's eyes" and that Hamer's speeches "grabbed the audience to tell them what was right."[150]

Once she had essentially weeded the garden by tugging at the flaws of the broader American systems of oppression, Hamer planted the seeds for change. Consistent with her prophetic style of discourse, she showed the audience their hearts by inducing self-reflection. "Must I be carried to the sky on flowery beds of ease," she challenged both audiences to ask themselves, "while others fight to win the prize and sail through bloody seas?"[151] Using the words of an Isaac Watts hymn, Hamer conveyed the interconnection of the human struggle and she attached it to Measure for Measure's driving ideology: be compassionate toward those who seek assistance, for by the same standard you will also be treated. Through this oratorical pattern, furthermore, Hamer sought to provoke critical reflection among her audience in such a manner that would compel them to "search their hearts *and* their pocketbooks."[152]

Finally, Hamer paired the self-reflection she urged with a model for social change. The exemplar was the same in both the university and the church speech: Hamer championed the actions of America's youth. "The church is behind the young people" in terms of moral development "because the young people throughout the country is proven to us that they really care." In stark contrast to "people my age or older and a little younger than I am," she argued that, with young people's actions you "don't see all of the kind of hypocrisy and all of the kind of put on." In her estimation, the youth of this country "are the nation that I believe is going to obey God," she proclaimed in a Madison church.[153] Her message was consistent on the University of Wisconsin campus as well, identifying people her age as "hopeless cases" and praising instead young people's ability to "bridge the gap between the races." Like the marginalized person who gains a superior perspective by sitting outside the center of power, "the children know what's going on and you [are] not going to be able to fool them any longer," Hamer told her contemporaries. To the contrary, the youth should be leading the nation; "fighting" as they are "for justice for all human beings," they represent "the chosen people that's going to lead this country out if it's not too late."[154]

Considering Hamer's fervent praise for student activists, it is not difficult to see why they listened to and revered her prophetic style of speaking. In light of her critique of the hypocritical, ignorant, and apathetic ways of her contemporaries, however, Hamer's popularity among the older generation of audience members in Madison is not as easy to explain. Firsthand accounts from those who sat in packed venues to hear her speak do suggest that she was just as beloved among audience members in her age group as she was among the youth. Hamer's popularity was explained by one Measure for Measure couple as resulting from the fact that she was "preaching to the choir," telling white liberals what they already knew about the problems of this country.[155] While this explanation is partially illuminating, tapping into a shared recognition of the nation's malaise is not the same as compelling people to not only recognize their interconnected fate, but also to act in a specific manner to redirect it. Recall that Hamer did not just secure passive agreement from audiences on her fundraising tours; her speeches resulted in myriad forms of direct action. Adult members of the Madison community donated money, food, clothing, books, sewing machines, and farm equipment. In addition, Madisonians took trips to Ruleville to help with her projects and to see for themselves the pangs of poverty they had heard Hamer describe. Thus, these liberal people who might have already been prone to give, gave responsively, in line with the program for social change Hamer advocated and thereby according her a large measure of respect. So, while this symbiosis between Hamer and the Madison-area liberals can be explained, in part, by a previous state of ideological alignment, Hamer's choice to expend her activist energy cultivating a relationship there, and the Madison folks' willingness to follow Hamer's lead, are also testaments to her rhetorical acumen.

What Hamer advocated through her Madison speeches and in her poverty programs, more generally, was radical social change that went to the root of the problem, quite literally. She took a step back from the increasingly integrated realm of state and national politics and returned wholeheartedly to the land and the community that sustained her. Her shift in focus was not a 360-degree movement, however, because she assumed a community-based focus armed with national notoriety. Hamer utilized her talent as a speaker to raise much-needed money for the Delta. She used these funds to change the self-perceptions of both its impoverished inhabitants and of her northern audiences. Her poverty projects, thus, "spoke to" multiple audiences, offering an invitation of unity to poor whites, communicating the presence of strength to the oppressive white power structure, constituting a self-image of security, dignity, and pride for poor blacks, and even challenging northerners' relative life of ease in the midst of southerners' suffering. Hamer's poverty programs showed Americans their own hearts and called them back to principled solutions that would effect radical social change. Positioning America's youth as the model for activism, she advocated an interracial grassroots movement concerned with the fate of all people—a collective oriented toward promoting human dignity by maintaining people's well-being. Hamer reasoned plainly, "it's no way on earth that we can gain any kind of political power unless we have some kind of economic power."[156]

CONCLUSION

The period between 1968–1972 in Hamer's activist career was her most widely acclaimed. Although she was an incredibly humble person, being named the "First Lady of Civil Rights" by the League of Black Women, receiving the Noble Example of Womanhood and the Mary Church Terrell Awards, in addition to numerous honorary doctorate degrees, must have been validating experiences. Perhaps Hamer's most remarkable commendation came from a rather unlikely source. Charles M. Dorrough Sr., the mayor of Ruleville, had long opposed Mrs. Hamer's efforts to alter the segregated social fabric of the city he led. However, in 1970, in honor of Ruleville's first-ever "Fannie Lou Hamer Day," Dorrough sent Hamer a letter of praise. In this letter, he acknowledged not only that Hamer had "put up a valiant fight for those things [she] truly believed in," but that in the process she had been "exposed to the real dangers and wrath of the enemy." Beyond this, he surmised, "If more Americans gave of themselves as you have for the things they believe in, ours would be a better nation." Dorrough concluded his missive with a statement that reflected a surprisingly clear understanding of Hamer's battle: "The history books of tomorrow will record your efforts," he predicted, "but I am sure you are more interested in tangible things around your own community that speak of a better, more comfortable way of life for those you love."[157]

Just as Hamer finally succeeded in securing such a life, however, the Herculean effort she exerted to achieve it caught up with her. Nervous exhaustion, for which she had been hospitalized several months prior, kept her from delivering an address at the 1972 Democratic National Convention. Even without her renowned speaking ability, Hamer left a mark on the gathering held in Miami Beach, Florida. David Lopez, a delegate from Texas, read her short seconding speech for Frances "Sissy" Farenthold's vice presidential nomination. After Lopez read her statement, a sickly Hamer rose to momentarily address the crowd: "Madam Chairman, fellow Democrats, and sister Democrats, I am not here to make a speech," she made clear from the outset, I am "just giving support and seconding the nomination of Sissy Farenthold for Vice President. If she was good enough for Shirley Chisolm," Hamer reasoned, "she is good enough for

Fannie Lou Hamer."[158] This brief statement in which Hamer refers to herself in the third person, coupled with Hamer's greater effort to fulfill her duty as an elected delegate, indicate Hamer's recognition of her own political influence as well as her strong desire to remain involved with national politics, in some capacity.

Over the next four years, as the last chapter will detail, the many needs surrounding Hamer persisted. She continued to struggle with the tension between her compelling desire to provide for the Delta poor and the increasingly poor state of her own health. In a vain attempt to keep Freedom Farm financially solvent, Hamer would undertake a few more national trips, but after 1972, her poor health did not permit much travel. Thus, the period in Hamer's activist career between 1968 and 1972 is significant not only because of the wide acclaim she garnered, and the uncompromising truth-teller persona she assumed throughout the variety of battles she waged, but this period is also significant because these battles were among her last.

CHAPTER 6

The Problems and the Progress

ON A COLD JANUARY AFTERNOON IN A PACKED THIRD-FLOOR LECTURE HALL on the University of Wisconsin-Madison campus, Fannie Lou Hamer informed her audience of students, professors, and community members that "we haven't arrived yet. You know, you here and we there haven't arrived yet." In her characteristic confrontational candor, Hamer admitted that "some of you all ain't going to like it because . . . I am just telling the truth . . . so you can . . . respect the truth because if changes is not made in this sick country, it's not going to be me crumbling, we are going to crumble," she warned.[1] The strength of her truth-telling message once again belied the weakness of her body—she was not well. As Hamer described the challenge that remained before them, even the casual observer could see that her life of hard labor combined with the breakneck speed at which she traveled since becoming involved with the movement had taken its toll. Her hair, one of her rare vanities, had become too difficult to manage and was now tied up in a scarf with a decorative broach holding together the makeshift turban. The whites of her eyes, once gleaming with energy, were now yellowed and dull. Her body, once robust and forceful, now remained seated, weakened as it was by her childhood bout with polio, lingering ailments from her Winona beating, and newly found cancer cells.

The year was 1976. Four years had passed since Hamer limped her way to the podium at the DNC in Miami to offer words of support for Frances Farenthold. Like most other years in Hamer's life, the past four had been filled with both problems and progress. Increasingly, though, it seemed the problems she endured were far outweighing the progress she enjoyed. She had been in and out of the hospital since 1972, when she was first admitted for nervous exhaustion. Her list of illnesses multiplied; she was now suffering not only from exhaustion, but also from bouts of grave depression, breast cancer, hypertension, and diabetes. Her poor health precluded her from honoring the steady stream of speaking requests that poured into her home from sororities who wanted to honor her on their founders' day celebrations, black-owned banks that praised her work toward economic independence, and even from prisoners who were eager to experience her narrative of captivity and liberation firsthand.[2] When she did travel, she now required a companion and much more rest than on past trips.

Over the last several years, Hamer had focused primarily on human rights work in her home state. In January 1973, she was among a group of black leaders in Mississippi who visited the state penitentiary at Parchman to observe the prisoners' living conditions and to recommend much-needed reforms. She also sat on the board of the daycare center bearing her name in Ruleville and she continued to work for the cause of voter registration alongside John Lewis, who was now directing the Voter Education Project (VEP). What's more, Hamer testified in federal court on behalf of two female school employees who had been fired from their jobs with the Drew School District for having children out of wedlock. And she traveled to the state capitol in Jackson to join the three-hundred-person protest against Mississippi's new co-pay requirement for individuals receiving prescriptions through Medicaid. At the rally outside the capitol building, Hamer led the protestors in singing her signature movement anthems: "This Little Light of Mine" and "We Shall Overcome." In addition to hearing her sing, local Mississippians could still occasionally experience Hamer's moving narrative of the injustices she endured upon her first attempts at civic engagement. She shared her renowned testimonial, for instance, with parents and community leaders during the spring 1976 forum on the state's rising crime rates.[3]

As voter-registration figures for black Mississippians steadily improved, as schools and other public facilities became increasingly integrated, and as the overt climate of white supremacy began to subside, there were some who found aspects of Hamer's civil rights message passé. By 1972, Mississippi boasted a 60 percent registration rate among blacks of voting age. The state continued to battle white supremacist resistance to black voting power, now in the form of diluting the black vote through redistricting. And some blacks, influenced by centuries of the ubiquitous plantation mentality, remained convinced that whites were more qualified to lead. Nevertheless, the increase in black voters did increase the number of black elected officials. By 1972, Mississippi had 145 blacks in office and by 1976, the state led the South with 215 black elected officials. Lloyd Gray of the *Delta Democrat-Times* attributed both Hamer's fading star and the dearth of media attention that the Delta region now received to these gains. "No longer are circumstances so intense that they call forth simple uneducated farm folk like Fannie Lou Hamer and turn them into national—even international—figures," he wrote in the fall of 1976. "Now that the glitter of the old civil rights movement is gone—the TV cameras and foreign journalists no longer flock into the Rulevilles of the South—the emphasis has shifted," he explained.

During his October 1976 interview in preparation for his article-length tribute to Mrs. Hamer, though, Gray soon learned that she was never one to bow to national trends. She was sticking by her assessment of the nation's problems and holding fast to her advocacy of individual empowerment and interracial cooperation. Hamer even struggled to command attention back to the South by promoting the region as a model of improved race relations. When she referred to the mid-1970s busing debates, for instance, Hamer suggested, "Look at what is happening in Boston," by contrast, "our little kids go to school together right around the corner from here every day. You go to a PTA meeting, and there's black and white together . . . [the South] has a real chance to lead this country."[4] While public schools in Mississippi were certainly more integrated by 1976 than ever before, Hamer's statement glossed over her state's lingering problems—most notably, the large number of white students who flocked to private segregated academies and took precious resources with them.[5] Characterizing her "'black and white together' message" as "old-time civil rights talk," furthermore, Gray at once testified to the consistency of Hamer's rhetorical appeal over time, as he concomitantly echoed the national media's assumption that the country had somehow moved past Hamer's enduring refrain.[6]

During her last years, as the nation grappled with implementing integration policies and a faltering economy, as Nixon's Watergate scandal was unearthed and pending impeachment forced his resignation, and as the war in Vietnam brought foreign policy tensions to a breaking point, current events overshadowed Hamer's persistent struggles. Many notable organizations worked to keep her in the spotlight, but the honorary degrees she received from Tougaloo, Shaw, Howard, and Columbia, to say nothing of the Sojourner Truth and Mary Church Terrell Awards that hung from the walls of her modest Ruleville home, did little to ward off her heartbreak.[7] Described by family as a competitive person, these accolades surely filled Hamer with well-deserved pride in her accomplishments, but plaques could not save her beloved Freedom Farm from bankruptcy, certificates could not pay her mounting medical bills, and honors did nothing to ensure that old friends would stop by to visit an increasingly lonesome Hamer.[8]

This chapter considers the last four years of Hamer's life, focusing especially on the failure of her Freedom Farm and her futile attempts to save it. I analyze what about Hamer's rhetorical appeal remained consistent and what shifted over time as well as what about her arguments did and did not resonate with which audiences, before examining how her life story gets interpreted symbolically in postmortem remembrances.

"A DREAM DEFERRED"

The demise of Freedom Farm suggested that Hamer's message of interracial cooperation, self-help, and community empowerment not only failed to sustain national attention, but that it also failed to resonate with members of her own community.[9] There are a variety of explanations for how Freedom Farm went from a 640-acre enterprise that included a pig bank, supported a garment factory, and became the third-largest employer in Sunflower County, to a failed venture that lost everything but the first forty acres Hamer bought outright. Some suggest that programs like the pig bank, from which the NCNW eventually withdrew their support, were not feasible ideas to begin with. Dorsey, of the neighboring Bolivar County cooperative, refers to the pig bank as a "[Dorothy] Height problem," maintaining that "that was not a good project and we only stayed with it for a couple of years," suggesting "no real farmers would ever have come up with anything that crazy."[10] McLaurin concurs, remembering, more specifically, that few families who received the pregnant gilts ever fulfilled their contractual obligation to return two piglets from the litter to the bank and even fewer families shared the other piglets with needy families in their communities. The lack of commitment to the spirit of this particular enterprise was only compounded by the fact that the pigs themselves were expensive to maintain.[11]

Others suggest that Freedom Farm failed because of poor management. "The failure of Freedom Farm was because Hamer got bad advice and got bad people to help her run it," argues McLemore, who remembers that Hamer was surrounded by people who "either through intentional wrongdoing or the lack of knowledge" drove her dream into the ground.[12] Dorsey agrees, "Hamer surrounded herself with people that she liked and trusted . . . she had some good folks around and she had some people that were ill-suited for the tasks that she had."[13] Moye reasons that the mistakes that ultimately bankrupted Freedom Farm were "inevitable" because the project was run by "poor people who had been ill-educated by a state that regarded them as racially inferior in the first place and who had been denied jobs that would have taught them the skills of money management."[14] Freedom Farm deliberately sought to empower those who had been barred from determining their own destiny, but the cooperative did not have the necessary structures in place to provide the support and training that had been withheld from its previously oppressed members.

Not all the management's problems can be blamed on inexperience, however. While Measure for Measure treasurer Jeff Goldstein attributed some of Freedom Farm's troubles to circumstances beyond human control—"a dry season and practically no crop, and a wet season that practically drowned all their crops," he was also quite candid in blaming those ill-intentioned coopera- tive members to whom Dorsey and McLemore allude. He recalls administrative members of the cooperative, "who ripped the Farm off blind . . . filling up their own vehicles with gasoline," for example. "It went on for a couple three years," Goldstein contends, "if your own people steal you blind, you usually end up in shit."[15] So whether the farm's board lacked the necessary skills and experience or whether some members of the farm's leadership were blatantly corrupt, both scholars and activists suggest that Freedom Farm's management was primarily responsible for the enterprise's failure.

Still there are those who suggest that Freedom Farm failed because Hamer's message of interracial cooperation and self-help for the good of the community never fully resonated with its members. As the failure of the pig bank suggests, few cooperative participants viewed Freedom Farm like Hamer did—as an av- enue to protect the poor against retaliation from wealthier landowners. Few- er still conceptualized the cooperative as a chance for lower-class whites and blacks to band together against the oppressive power structure. Instead, most members considered picking cotton and tending to crops for little material gain to be an extension of the system of exploitation they and their ancestors had suffered under for centuries. "The mentality of black people in Ruleville was: going to Freedom Farm to work was too much like being a sharecropper or a slave on the plantation," Jean Sweet of Measure for Measure explains. "They didn't see it as a co-op," she reasons, "and they didn't see it as theirs."[16] After generations of associating poorly remunerated and grueling farm labor with oppression, people throughout the Delta wanted air-conditioned jobs in offices. In fact, Dorsey remembers a woman from her community marching into the office of the Bolivar cooperative and contending, "I want your job. I don't want to be out there picking cucumbers!" "They just weren't interested in the work," she explains, "because they weren't making a lot of money and it wasn't glamor- ous."[17] Given the economic climate of the Delta, there was really no way for the small cooperative farms to become profitable. Asch explains that by the time Freedom Farm was established, "small family farms were becoming a thing of the past." "Simply put," he reasons, "labor-intensive, hand-picked Freedom Farm cotton could not compete with its machine-harvested, chemically chopped cousin." So even if the participants had adhered to the cooperative ethic Hamer espoused, and even if Hamer had surrounded herself with knowledgeable and experienced staff, Asch surmises Freedom Farm would have had "difficulty" be- coming a "successful economic venture."[18]

This absence of investment in the cooperative ethic and paucity of knowledge regarding how to run such an enterprise combined with the presence of corruption among the administrative membership and the inability for small farms to compete with large mechanically run and federally incentivized plantations ultimately culminated in rusted machinery, crops that spoiled for lack of harvesting, and land that was returned to creditors when payments were no longer made. More important than the material loss suffered by Freedom Farm, however, was the formidable human cost that accompanied its demise. In January 1974, when Freedom Farm lost all but forty acres, Hamer suffered another nervous breakdown, and by August of that same year her devoted farm manager, Joe Harris, died of a heart attack.

Although Hamer's rhetoric may not have been able to overcome the stigma surrounding farmwork in order to instill a cooperative ethic in her local community, Hamer's message of interracial cooperation, self-help, and community empowerment—that refrain dismissed as passé by Gray—did resonate with certain audiences who worked tirelessly to save her cooperative and to mend her broken spirit. In particular, the strong connection Hamer made with Measure for Measure helped see her through trying times.

From 1973 onward, Hamer rarely fulfilled speaking engagements and when she did she poured every dime of her honoraria back into the failing Freedom Farm. She applied for disability income and was initially turned down.[19] Mr. Hamer was only employed as a Head Start bus driver nine months out of the year. He spent the remainder of his time struggling to salvage his wife's dream, and caring for the Hamers' school-aged children.[20] As a result, the couple was in desperate need of money to pay not only for her medical bills, but also to meet their family's basic needs. Members of the Measure for Measure organization, who were worried about their friend and also quite curious about the sorry state of the farm in which they had invested so much, made several trips from Madison to Ruleville in the mid-1970s. When they arrived on one such visit, they found the cupboards in Hamer's home as barren as the fields of her failed Freedom Farm. Upon finding nothing but frozen opossum carcasses in Hamer's freezer, Goldstein waited until Hamer left the house—knowing full well that she would resist accepting his charity outright—and stocked her shelves with hundreds of dollars in groceries.

When they returned to Madison, Jeff and his wife, Sarah, told their friends about the Hamers' deplorable state, that they did not have money to run their air conditioner, let alone feed themselves and clothe their children. Before long, Hamer's Madison supporters established a fund called "Friends of Fannie Lou

Hamer," for which Jeff gathered $100 a month to send to the Hamers in Ru-
leville.[21] Beyond this, the Goldsteins and the Sweets helped gather the $1,500
cashier's check gift presented to the Hamers on their thirtieth wedding anniversary. The Hamers' anniversary celebration took place on July 12, 1974, in Greenville, Mississippi, and included both a recitation of their vows and a reunion
of their friends and family. In spite of her ill health, Hamer enjoyed herself
immensely. And she did not soon forget her kind friends who organized this
special occasion.

"WE HAVEN'T ARRIVED YET"

As sometimes happens with terminal illness, Hamer experienced a period of
calm rejuvenation before the deep storm of sickness set in. The year 1976 was
marked by incrementally better health for Hamer. In January, she was able to
travel to Madison and join in the celebration of Measure for Measure's eleventh
anniversary. This would be Hamer's last trip to visit her radical caucus, and she
certainly made the most of it. Accompanied by her traveling companion, she
spoke in at least three locations in two days, receiving standing ovations, a key
to the city of Madison, and an outpouring of local media attention.[22] A handwritten poster with the small illustration of a farmer hoeing a row plastered the
University of Wisconsin campus and hailed Hamer not only as a "Renowned
Black Civil Rights Leader," but also as a "Dynamic Lecturer and Warm, Loving
Human Being." The poster implored members of the campus community to
"Hear and Meet Fannie Lou Hamer. You owe it to Yourself." By noon on Thurs-
day, January 29, the lecture hall on the third floor of the Humanities building was filled to capacity—students, faculty, Measure for Measure activists, and
the local press all gathered to hear Mrs. Hamer report on "black Mississippi to
date."[23] As cameras flashed and tape-recorders rolled, Hamer spoke at a slower
pace, but in a no less impassioned tone, about the problems that persisted, the
progress that had been made, and the power of interracial cooperation. In this
speech, "We Haven't Arrived Yet," Hamer combines elements of her signature
Jeremiad—warning of the nation's demise and prescribing interracial cooperation as the cure to the country's ills—with statements promoting the healing
power of steadfastness, love, and forgiveness.

She began her speech by thanking the crowd, then acknowledging the Goldsteins and the Sweets by name—"As I look out into the audience and look at
Sarah and Jeff and I saw . . . Mrs. Sweet . . . [I see] a lot of my friends who's done
a tremendous job in helping us in the state of Mississippi." Hamer's words of

praise and recognition, however, were notably brief and served more as a segue into her central contention. "Even though we've received, you know, quite a bit of assistance from the organization Measure for Measure . . . we have not arrived," she told her audience. As far as Hamer was concerned there was little time for celebration in the midst of urgent and persistent problems.

She characterized 1976 as a "crucial time," a claim she supported with a variety of evidence ranging from Alabama governor "George Wallace making his pitch [for state's rights] in Boston, Massachusetts," to "Central Intelligence Agents [killing] my people in Angola," and even onto the fact that "minority people in this country—not only Indians, Puerto Ricans, blacks, and poor whites—can't get jobs." These current symptoms of the nation's sickness, as Hamer explained it, were clear manifestations of America's fundamentally hypocritical nature. Aspects of the country's hypocrisy and deceit, she illustrated, stretch back to the time of Columbus's claim that he "discovered America" and to the slave trade that "destroyed twenty-five million of my people that was being brought here on the slave ships of Africa." Yet, in 1976, "everybody is running around talking about the bicentennial year of the 200 years of American progress . . . How do you think black people, Indian people, and any other oppressed folk feel," Hamer asked her audience to consider, "celebrating something that . . . wiped out our heritage?"[24]

Having alluded to just why "it's pretty hard to stand up and pledge allegiance to something we've never had," Hamer coupled her exposition of hypocrisy in principle with additional signs of the nation's sickness in practice. She referred to such disparate symptoms as the assassination of "Martin Luther King, Jr. [a man] that preached nothing but love and says it's wrong to kill," and the fact that Nixon brought us to the "peak of being in a dictatorship" before he was forced to resign and yet he "had the power to dictate who the next president would be."[25] Given the variety of evidence Hamer garnered in defense of her central contention, the abstracting archivist for the university found this speech "thematically inconsistent," but "representative" of speeches she gave before northern audiences.[26]

While some found her speech incoherent because of its vast array of evidence, other members of the audience might have expected a more commemorative address—an encomium of the progress Measure for Measure helped usher in. Hamer, though, was never one to miss an opportunity tell it like it is, fostering harsh awareness not only of the interconnectedness of the nation's problems, but also of their pressing nature. This harsh awareness was commonly followed by her trademark warning: "if changes is not made in this sick country it's not going to be *me* crumbling *we* are going to crumble because a house divided against itself cannot stand. A nation that's divided against itself is on its way out."[27]

Hamer's threat of demise, however, always held within it a pathway to her proposed solution. In keeping with the multifarious nature of the nation's problems, Hamer did not place the cause of those ills on any one individual or set of hypocritical practices. Instead, she blamed a sinful lust for power and control over others met by complacency among the masses of people as the primary sources of the country's pitiful state. Connecting biblical instruction from the Book of Ephesians—that her audience needed the armor of God to protect themselves from the wiles of the devil—to America's present political situation, Hamer expounded upon the scripture's message: "And people will go to any limit just for personal power. It doesn't really matter how the masses suffer, but just a few people, you know, controlling." The fact that the few in power commonly lack experiential knowledge of the problems that those they control suffer from is both the fundamental danger of such oligarchic systems and also what motivated Hamer's lifelong battle for representation. Put plainly, "there's no way in the world you can tell me how it feels to be hungry, if you've never been hungry yourself," which is why "you cannot say that you represent me when you don't know how I feel."

Beyond a lust for power, Hamer went after the ill of complacency, calling out those northern blacks who have turned their backs on the struggle. "Some of you get a few degrees, a pretty good house and a bill you can't hardly pay. Trying to live like somebody else and think you have arrived, but, honey," she put it to this particular audience bluntly, "we are in this bag together and there's nobody at the University of Wisconsin and no other place in this country is free until I am free in the South." Personal power waged against the collective good, misrepresentation that silences the voice of the masses, and callous individualism that finds contentment in personal success, Hamer charged, can only be overcome by people working "together to bring about a change." "So, what I am saying," she prescribed, "if there's going to be any survival for this country . . . we have to make democracy a reality for all people and not just a few."[28]

In this address, however, Hamer's signature Jeremiad was softened by her insistent promotion of love's healing power. Before this Madison audience in one of her final speeches on record, Hamer espoused the need for love to challenge power's corrupting influence: "the shame that we have before us today is whatever happened it have to be legislated. But you can't legislate love," she contended. "That's the one thing that you can't do. And what America and the rest of the world need today—some kids put out a song some time ago—is what the world need now is love."[29] If love cannot be legislated, but love is what is needed, then how is it fostered? How does Hamer advise her audience to administer this cure to the sick nation?

To address these pressing questions, Hamer altered the rhetorical approach that launched her activist career. Rather than coming before northern audiences to expose the southern evils she endured, Hamer now held up the South as the exemplar of love and reconciliation between the races. Hamer combined this 180-degree rhetorical turn with more consistent discursive progressions. Maintaining that racism knows no borders, Hamer posited, "it's up South and down South because it ain't no different." In fact, she argued that the disguised brand of racism in the North might be even worse than the overt racism in the South. "I used to just *love* to go North because I figured that people was, you know, kind of free," she explained to her audience. "But . . . blacks in the North is in the worse condition, most of them, than we are in the South because we know where we stand!" The racism in the South, reasoned Hamer, is easier to combat because it is apparent, overt, out there to be dealt with: "if I would have to take the chance I would take it in the South because if you can convince one that he is wrong you don't have a hypocrite; he's real. And we have made some changes." Southern race relations also differed from those in the North, she elucidated, "because we got more contact with each other than is here in the cities throughout this country. We can talk and we got more communication than you have in most of the places in the North." The races' proximity to one another, she explained, breeds more interaction and communication, which makes mutual respect—the basis for reconciliatory love—possible.[30]

"I am not fighting to be equal with you, but I am fighting for human dignity," Hamer stipulated. To hearten the struggle, in fact, she offered signs of progress. Admittedly, "our struggle has been very hard from the jailhouses to the graveyard, but we still have put 215 blacks in office in the state of Mississippi." And these black elected officials are "going to fight for the kinds of education that not only black folks should be aware of, but whites as well. Because you have been conditioned into the system, too." As Hamer envisioned change coming about, the black elected officials would work to challenge racist preconceptions while individual southerners stayed in the South to do the same. One audience member asked during the question and answer period if Hamer would advise black youth to go north to make a better life for themselves. Hamer responded swiftly that she would take her chances in the South; "I would tell them to stay in Ruleville . . . I say stay at home, let's make that better." Hamer not only espoused this instruction, she lived it. She endured years of oppression, followed by retaliation for standing up against systems of exploitation, but she always held fast to her mother's proverbial wisdom—"respect yourself and others will respect you too"—and now, *finally*, she could testify to the power of persistence. "You see I just kept staying there in Ruleville," she explained, "and I let them know that . . . I couldn't boss theirs, and they wasn't going to boss ours. And some of those same people [who exploited her] now call me *Mrs. Hamer.*"[31]

Though the country had not yet arrived, there had been progress bred by love, steadfastness, and forgiveness. This was the message Hamer was putting to her Madison audience, a thesis she aptly illustrated with a personal encounter that occurred just two weeks before her address. Hamer had flown to Rockville, Maryland, as an honored guest at a Martin Luther King Jr. Day commemoration.[32] On her return to Ruleville, she ran across Senator Eastland's son-in-law, Champ Terney, whom she described to the audience as her "arch nemesis." "We always go in nose to nose. Because if he [was] for it, I was always against it, even if I hadn't heard what it was. Just knowing who he was, I was against it." But all that animosity did not stand in the way of the two greeting each other at the airport in Rockville, and then interacting once again on the plane from Memphis to Greenville. As Hamer passed his first-class seat on her way to coach, Terney said to her, "you done fought to ride in the front. You ain't going to the back now; you going to set down here with me," which she did and the two talked for the duration of the hour-and-a-half flight. Terney even offered to take Hamer home from the airport if she needed a ride. "So, that's come a long way," Hamer shared with her Madison audience. If he was willing to respect her, then she was willing to forgive him.[33] That is the kind of progress Hamer described as happening throughout Mississippi and that is the kind of change that love, freely shared, among individuals of all races, can bring about. Hamer succeeded in shocking her northern audience by featuring the shining example of race relations in the South as a cure to the country's sickness. The solution itself, though, concocted as it was from her staple ingredients—interracial cooperation, individual empowerment, love for humanity, respect for oneself, forgiveness, and perseverance—was but a softer variation of her signature recipe.

After Hamer finished answering the university audiences' questions, she traveled ten miles west to Middleton, Wisconsin, where she spoke at an assembly of nearly eight hundred high school students. She shared her recipe for reconciliation with these listeners as well—arguing that kids learn to hate in the home and that a community of love is needed to overcome this learned behavior. She also reinforced her message of human dignity, informing the students that her activist career had been aimed toward, "'letting the world know that we are human beings and should be treated as such.'" Her message of love, perseverance, and human dignity was met by two separate standing ovations from the crowd assembled at Middleton High School.[34]

A little over twenty-four hours later, Hamer addressed a more intimate gathering of Measure for Measure activists and members of Madison's First Unitarian Society. She was the featured speaker at a potluck dinner the society held to celebrate Measure for Measure's anniversary. In this smaller setting, Hamer spoke for a shorter period of time, even more slowly, and with slightly less passion than she was able to muster the day before. A local reporter who was covering Hamer's visit noted that while "nobody sleeps in the back of the hall when Fannie Lou Hamer speaks . . . she tires more easily now than she once did."[35] Though relatively brief, Hamer's talk reconstructed the thrust of her previous day's lesson: that freedom "is a constant struggle," and that while problems persist, there has been some progress. And this progress has been wrought by those who "care enough to fight to make that piece of paper that was written a long time ago, which was the Constitution . . . a reality."[36]

Tailoring her message to the more expressly religious setting, Hamer added additional scripture. She emphasized the union between the races, as she had throughout her career, by invoking Acts 17:26: "'I have made of one blood all nations.' We are *no* different," she made plain for her audience. Although not all those gathered at the First Unitarian Society that evening necessarily adhered to her Christian faith, Hamer nevertheless used biblical proof and enlisted divine assistance to reach out to members of her audience. "We are sick and we had better work, to pray, that God will lead us out of the dilemma that we are in now." This prayer was an extension of the Ephesians verse she had been featuring over the last five years, which she paraphrased in this speech as well, telling her audience that the nation's sickness is not "really a *racist* thing, but it's a *power* thing . . . we are not dealing with men, but we are dealing with the devil himself," she contended. Illustrating the biblical contention with a concrete example, Hamer shared an extended story of Freedom Farm helping a poor white family with a sick child. The father of the family came to Hamer seeking help and she delivered. No sooner had Freedom Farm gotten this child to the hospital and set the family up in a small dwelling, however, than "the power-structure seen that there will be some kind of coalition with poor white and poor black as human beings," and "right away they throwed him out of Ruleville," she testified. Her example demonstrated both the potential of interracial cooperation and the way in which it still threatened those in power, vividly establishing the evil against which her audience must continue fighting.[37]

As the audiences' frequent "amens," laughter, and applause intimate, Hamer was essentially preaching to the choir. Members of her Madison audiences, after all, had raised nearly $250,000 for Hamer's causes over the past decade.[38] They created a "Friends of Fannie Lou Hamer" fund, compelling Mrs. Hamer to save a small bit of their charity for her family's own pressing needs. They sent clothing, food, books, tractor equipment, and vitamins to Ruleville, using Hamer's home as their central distribution center. They came to monitor Sunflower County elections, helped with Hamer's 1971 state senate campaign, and listened closely to the real lessons in political science she taught them on her frequent visits to their churches and lecture halls. The relationship Mrs. Hamer cultivated with the Madison community of activists—largely through her widely celebrated public speeches—embodied nothing short of her proposed solution to the country's problems.

In the bond Hamer forged between Sunflower and Dane Counties, one could find interracial love fueled by mutual respect and an awareness of the fundamental interconnectedness of each race's fate. One could also witness a working example of the cooperative ethic Hamer tried to promote in Ruleville. And, on this cold night in the dead of Madison's harsh winter, one could sense a spirit of endurance. Despite the fact that several Measure for Measure activists had traveled to Ruleville and seen the rusted tractors, the spoiled crops, and the confiscated land they helped her acquire, these activists still supported Hamer's message and her mission. As she attempted to adequately recognize this unconditional love, Hamer experienced a rare loss for words. "I am deeply grateful for being here tonight," Hamer told her friends. "A couple of years ago when I got very sick, I never thought that I would be able to see a lot of people here in Madison." Still trying to express the depth of her gratitude, she continued: "I really couldn't put into words what you has meant to the people of Sunflower County . . . And not only that, I would like to thank everybody for the role that you played in Pap and my anniversary a couple of years ago. I was very sick at that time." The ever-loquacious Hamer was uncharacteristically limited in her speech: "I could just never put into words what you have meant to a lot of people in Sunflower County." Try as she might in this final address before them, there were aspects of the profound love she shared with her radical caucus in Madison that remained ineffable.

COMING HOME

Hamer did not return to a community that gave her as much love and support as had her friends and fellow activists in Madison. Even many of Hamer's close personal friends did not realize how ill she was during the last year of her life. "Most of us thought she had so many pains and aches and assumed that people are supposed to have pains and aches," remembers Edwin King, who bemoans the fact that her cancer went untreated for so long. "I've heard medical people say that she could have been given another ten years or so, but she was so late in actually going" to get treatment. He remembers Hamer insisting that other movement participants see the doctor, but she did not want to give into pain herself and those around her did not force her hand, King theorizes, so she missed reporting her symptoms early enough to effectively treat the cancer.[40] Those around her certainly observed that she was much slower in those later years, but as McLemore decries, her friends failed her. "All of us, so many of us who knew her and loved her, we didn't do enough. We were not as proactive as we should have been . . . it appears to me on that level that was a failure by her friends."[41]

There were some friends and fellow activists who cared for her closely toward the end. June Johnson, who was jailed in Winona with Hamer, would regularly stop by her Ruleville home. On one of these visits, Johnson found Hamer in an agitated state. Hours before, Hamer had sent for a neighbor to help her with her hair, but the neighbor never showed up. So Johnson fixed Mrs. Hamer's hair. This simple act of kindness was all she needed to relax her and warm her spirit.[42] Surely Johnson wondered where all those people who once crowded Hamer's front porch had gone. Pap Hamer found their absence cruelly curious. He told Dorsey that there was a time when he would come home from work and there "would be so many people in here I couldn't hardly get in the door. They came to get clothes, food, money—everything," he recalled. "But when she fell sick . . . the only way I could get people to stay with her was when I paid them," confessed Pap.[43]

Just months following Hamer's final trip to Madison, she had a mastectomy—in a futile attempt to end her bout with cancer. The surgery bought her a few more months of activity. By May 1976, she was well enough to draft a letter to "Friends" of the VEP, urging them to continue their support of registration activity in Sunflower County. Her increasingly common rhetorical strategy of blending the progress that had been made with an assessment of the problems that remained found expression in this letter as well. "In 1964, only about 23,000 blacks were registered out of Mississippi's voting age population of over 450,000 black people," she reminded the VEP's supporters. By contrast "today, almost 300,000 black voters are registered." And these voters were changing the political landscape of the state, which could already boast eleven more black elected officials than when Hamer recently recited the figures in Madison, for a new total of 226 black elected officials in Mississippi. The political changes extended to the realm of interpersonal relations as well, Hamer contended, noting that "some white folks a few years ago would drive past your house in a pickup truck with guns hanging up in the back and give you hate stares." Now, "these same people call me Mrs. Hamer, because they respect people that respect themselves." Connecting self-respect with voting rights and representation, Hamer reiterated: "It's time now for people to do their own thinking—we have to think and act for ourselves . . . these are the things that we are working towards."[44] Her bold message of persistence and self-empowerment immediately resonated, as two days after Hamer sent the letter a response came back from Columbia, Missouri, pledging support and thanking "God for the wonderful work [Hamer] and others are doing."[45]

By the fall of 1976, furthermore, Hamer was even well enough to travel outside of Mississippi. In late September, she visited Washington, DC, where the Congressional Black Caucus presented her with the George W. Collins Memorial Award for Community Service. Hamer was chosen as the recipient of this honor because of her success in establishing "housing, jobs, and a new security and dignity for many people in Mississippi."[46] After her trip to DC, she also made her way to Evanston, Illinois, where she spoke on the topic "Action Oriented Ministry: Confronting the Power Structure" at Garrett-Evangelical Theological Seminary. Because Hamer was dubbed "one of the top 'Models' for young black women in Seminary," the Ecumenical Women's Center and the National Institute for Campus Ministries worked hard to bring her to Illinois. Yet, in pooling their resources, these two nonprofit organizations managed to pay Mrs. Hamer only a $200 honorarium for her talk. Apologizing for the meager compensation, they nevertheless profusely thanked Mrs. Hamer for her willingness to participate in their conference.[47]

Back in the Delta, she got a bit more financial assistance to put toward her mounting medical bills. Funds were raised for her debt at the annual Fannie Lou Hamer Day, held on an October afternoon in Ruleville. The festivities included the presentation of additional honors for Hamer: the Alpha Phi Alpha fraternity presented her with the Paul Robeson award for humanitarian service and a local Parent Teacher Association honored her with a certificate of appreciation. The celebration also featured remarks by Amzie Moore and Charles Evers, demonstrating that by the mid-1970s tensions between Hamer and those middle- to upper-class "power brokers" within the black community had faded.[48] Evers helped raise nearly $2,100 for Hamer's medical expenses, publicly donating $500 of his own money. The money raised and the people gathered around her succeeded in lifting Hamer's spirits for a short time.[49]

By the beginning of the New Year, however, the merriment had all but disappeared. Hamer was once again penniless, depressed, and in ill health. She was eventually admitted to the Mound Bayou Community Hospital. Some of her movement friends suggested that she be taken to a hospital in Memphis instead; they worried that Hamer would not get the best treatment in what they characterized as a small, understaffed hospital without many resources.[50] But it was her will to stay at Mound Bayou—just twenty miles from her Ruleville home—and there she remained until the cancer, the hypertension, and the diabetes finally caught up with her. Hamer's heart failed on March 14, 1977; she was fifty-nine years old.

OUT OF THE SEEDS SHE PLANTED

All but abandoned during the last months of her life, by contrast, Fannie Lou Hamer's death drew the largest funeral crowd Ruleville, Mississippi, had ever seen.[51] Sunday, March 20, 1977, was a bright spring day in this rural Delta town.[52] The afternoon sun beat down on the field surrounding the small white church where Hamer first heard James Bevel and James Forman speak about voter registration. Fifteen years after that fateful mass meeting, William Chapel Baptist Church was now overflowing with Hamer's family, her fellow community members, and activists from all over the nation—and even the world—who had come to pay their respects. If Hamer had never attended that mass meeting in the summer of 1962, odds are her funeral service would still have been held at this modest local church. If Hamer had never attended that mass meeting, however, the funeral service would have proceeded much differently. Because Hamer did come to that fateful mass meeting, and because Hamer did embrace the message of freedom Bevel and Forman preached there, her life inspired more people than the rural church house could hold. So many of the people Hamer touched came to honor her, in fact, that two services were held on this mid-March afternoon—a funeral at the William Chapel and a memorial at Ruleville Central High School. The funeral service included such honored guests as Ella Baker, Dorothy Height of the NCNW, Michigan congressman Charles Diggs, executive director of the National Urban League Vernon Jordan, as well as former SNCC members Stokely Carmichael and H. Rap Brown. Ambassador to the United Nations Andrew Young, Assistant Secretary of State Hodding Carter III, and the associate general secretary of the National Council of Churches, Lucius Walker, also participated in Hamer's last rites. The second memorial service, which was open to all, featured special tributes by the mayor of Ruleville, Mississippi representative Robert Clark, L. C. Dorsey, Amzie Moore, Annie Devine, and Leslie McLemore, among other Mississippi natives.

Although Owen Brooks and his fellow funeral coordinators packed the small chapel to well beyond a comfortable capacity, only 350 of the nearly 2,000 mourners were able to file past Mrs. Hamer's white casket with intricate silver ornamentation. Only 350 of Hamer's family members and fellow freedom fighters witnessed the uncharacteristically frail nature of her body, clothed in a soft white dress that elegantly contrasted her carefully combed black hair. Only 350 people could smell the fragrant yellow roses surrounding the church altar or notice how much the white carnations that lay on top of Hamer's casket resembled cotton bolls waiting to be plucked. Only 350 people could experience these sights and smells, but all who came to pay their respects could hear the Jackson State University and Tougaloo College choirs and all could enjoy the words of comfort and inspiration shared about this woman. Half a dozen microphones were mounted to the church lectern and they carried the words that began immediately crafting Hamer's symbolic legacy over loudspeakers and into the crowd of people left to mourn outside.

Between renditions of Hamer's favorite hymns, all who gathered—whether seated or standing, inside or outside the chapel—could hear Vernon Jordan celebrate the meaning of her life's contributions. "Mrs. Hamer truly, truly lived and leaves to us today an irrevocable legacy of service, of commitment, of sacrifice, and of love," he began. To demonstrate these principles, Jordan shared the memory of hearing Hamer sing the movement anthem, "Ain't Gonna Let Nobody Turn Us Around," at an MFDP meeting in the summer of 1964. He testified to the strength of Hamer's spirit conveyed through that song—a spirit so brave and so contagious that Jordan no longer feared the long night drive from Jackson to Memphis that he was to make alone that evening. The strength and commitment in Hamer's voice conquered even the terror that white segregationists had unleashed on movement activists by killing three civil rights workers in Neshoba County, just months before Jordan first heard Hamer sing that powerful anthem. "As life is action and passion," Jordan concluded his brief tribute, "it is required of men and women to share the action and passion of their times . . . Mrs. Hamer truly, truly lived and we celebrate that living today."[53]

All who gathered that day also enjoyed a special tribute from Dorothy Height, who spoke about the Wednesdays in Mississippi program, which supported Freedom Summer efforts.[54] Ella Baker spoke that day as well, delivering an address which Guyot remembers as "the best speech given" during the service. Unfortunately, the commemorative addresses these two women delivered were not fully preserved. Guyot remembers, though, that Baker's speech was convicting—she called out high-profile members of the audience who had worked against Hamer's objectives and concluded by suggesting that Hamer would be watching over the individuals gathered there to ensure they engaged in the extensive work that remained.[55]

Several of the lengthier eulogies delivered by prominent men were preserved on the videotaped footage of Hamer's last rites and, among those, three stand out as particularly significant in their attempts to craft Hamer's symbolic legacy. Although Ambassador Young offered the official funeral oration of the day, the addresses delivered by Stokely Carmichael and Hodding Carter III also fulfilled core functions of this rhetorical genre. Taken together, the words of Young, Carmichael, and Carter each marked Hamer's passing, paid tribute to her life, comforted the living, and inspired them to carry on their lives in the way Hamer's example directed.[56]

Carter, who grew up in Greenville, wrote for the *Delta Democrat-Times*— the paper his family owned and operated—was a driving force within the 1968 Loyal Democratic Party, and had been recently appointed by President Jimmy Carter as the assistant secretary of state for public affairs, delivered an address which still stands out in the minds of those who heard it. In fact, when we met thirty years later to discuss the funeral he coordinated, Brooks quoted specific passages from Carter's oration.[57] What made the words of this white Mississippian so memorable was that they so adeptly amplified Hamer's message of interracial love and her later-in-life promotion of Mississippi as an exemplar of racial reconciliation.

Carter told the audience that he "felt excited" as he flew from Washington, DC, to Mississippi that day. Admitting that excitement may be a "rather strange emotion" to feel when coming to a funeral, Carter stood by his instinct. "As a Mississippian," he reasoned, "I was coming back to a state that I could be far prouder to live in because of the life of Mrs. Fannie Lou Hamer." He characterized the memorials of this day as "a reunion of many . . . who are responsible, with her and because of her, for what has become one of the great changes of this nation's history." Echoing the contention Hamer made during her final years—that Mississippi was no longer the most viciously segregated state in the union, but now an exemplar of racial reconciliation—Carter suggested that the state "still can become one of the great places in the nation." And he elaborated on his strange emotional condition, claiming that he "felt excited at this homecoming because [he] knew that what Mrs. Hamer had done with her life was to ensure that her death did not end a process, but could give it another impetus." Reasoning that Hamer's death gathered her fellow activists together and reminded them "of what was not here when she started," as well as "how many of you are now here *because* of what she started."

Up to this point, Carter remained composed. When his address unearthed what Hamer's life struggle had meant for white Mississippians, however, he could no longer maintain his poise. Carter's voice quivered and his gaze turned downward as he gripped the lectern, maintaining: "Mrs. Hamer did a lot of freeing in her lifetime and I think that history will say that among those who were freed more totally and earlier by her were white Mississippians." Carter's address stood out from the speeches that came before and after it because he focused on her ability to spark renewed humanity for whites. Hamer freed white Mississippians—"if they had the will to be free—from themselves, from their history, from their racism, from their past." Switching from third- to first-person plural pronouns, Carter set himself apart from the majority of mourners and returned to the main purpose of his tribute. "I know that there's no way for us, who have been free, to adequately thank those who freed us," he contended, "except to try also to continue the work that Mrs. Hamer and so many of you began, are continuing, and will continue in the future."

Though Carter and Mrs. Hamer had their differences—he was part of the biracial middle- to upper-class contingent of "power brokers" who displaced poorer blacks working on both poverty projects in the state and on the 1968 DNC challenge—Carter's address is significant in crafting Hamer's symbolic legacy. Despite their well-known tensions, Carter's oration reveals that he clearly understood how central interracial love and cooperation was to Hamer's vision of social change and through his own example he bore witness to its transformative power.[58] What's more, Carter represented Hamer as a rhetorical symbol with the capacity to constitute community among a widely diverse contingent of people, to call them back to a set of fundamental values, and to breathe new life into the movement for social change.

Carter's address was not the only speech that featured Hamer's symbolic capacity. "We come to honor Mrs. Hamer because Mrs. Hamer represents something," Stokely Carmichael's oration began, "Mrs. Hamer represents the best not only in us—African Americans who suffer here in America—but she represents the best of all humanity, who is constantly struggling against unjust systems." Carmichael offered a tribute to Hamer that simultaneously displayed his distinctive oratorical style, connected Hamer's life and death to the worldwide human struggle for freedom, and worked to inspire her friends to carry out the legacy of consciousness that she left behind.

Though few who knew Carmichael would have expected anything different, the way his fists pounded the pulpit, the surging cadence of his speech, and the rising volume at which he conveyed his tribute differentiated his remarks from the relatively calmer carriage of the remaining speakers. Beyond his startling

delivery, Carmichael appropriated the voice of white segregationists like Senator Eastland when he posed the question: "Who is Mrs. Hamer?" Responding
derisively, "Mrs. Hamer is just a woman just like anybody else . . . This is Mrs.
Hamer who can't read or write . . . This is Mrs. Hamer who is not intelligent," he
continued, "this is Mrs. Hamer who sweats and sweats . . . and everything she
produces goes into the pockets of Mr. Eastland." Carmichael continued to in-
voke Eastland's opinion of Hamer: "certainly Mr. Eastland never thought much
of Mrs. Hamer, no, Mr. Eastland didn't think that Mrs. Hamer could come and
disturb and shake and rock and smash his entire system." Though at times the
connection between the two strands of argument was disjointed, upon closer
examination one can discern Carmichael used Eastland's derogatory impres-
sion of Hamer to support his contention that the potential for change lies within everybody—even the presumably least among us.[60]

The realization of this potential, posited Carmichael, hinges upon consciousness. Building upon Hamer's plainspoken sharecropper persona, Carmichael reminded the audience of Hamer's ordinary roots and her extraordinary
example:

> Here among us, from the sharecropping plantations of racism—someone
> suffering, someone struggling without education, someone exploited, some-
> one pushed out . . . Here this one can rise up and this one can gain con-
> sciousness. What we must get from Mrs. Hamer is consciousness.

Hamer's ability—with limited education and against a forcefully oppressive system—to "see and understand things outside and know the truth," reasoned Carmichael, provides hope that anybody can rise up against systems of oppression.
"Hamer is no different from any of us. Truth is not inside any of us; truth is outside all of us. Thus, any of us can see it and any of us can do what Mrs. Hamer
did." Throughout his tribute, Carmichael reiterated this trajectory from igno-
rance and exploitation to the recognition of truth and the empowering force it
yields, suggesting "like any and all of us" Hamer "can see and understand things
outside and know the truth. And once we find the truth," he shouted, pounding the lectern for emphasis, we "live by the truth!" Yet again he proclaimed
that Hamer is worthy of praise because she was "someone who once seeing the
truth, grabs the truth and would never let go of truth, and would die for the
truth." She had a willingness to learn and to work, insisted Carmichael: "Mrs.
Hamer came and said, 'I don't know, but show me.'" Then she saw "the truth"
and she understood "exploitation" and she "said that our purpose on earth is to
end exploitation . . . Mrs. Hamer knew that . . . she must do something about it."

So, "she got up and she worked. Mrs. Hamer represents the best in us," Carmichael insisted.[59]

Carmichael echoed this line of praise for Hamer nearly thirty years later in his autobiography. Hamer embodied all that he loved about "local people," whom he regarded as "heroes. Humble folk, of slight formal education and modest income, who managed to be both generous and wise. Simple, home-spun, unlettered, hardworking, self-respecting men and women." Of Hamer, in particular, Carmichael shared SNCC's sentiments, when he wrote:

> We knew and loved this stout, earthy, kindhearted lady. . . . Yes, she repre-sented something important to us. . . . [S]he did not merely represent an *idea*, some SNCC theory of grassroots leadership . . . Mrs. Hamer *was* the grassroots . . . I'm talking here about Mrs. Hamer's spirit. Her warmth. Her values. A fundamental decency and generosity . . . She simply embodied in her jes'-plain-folks way all the qualities and values we were coming to ad-mire in local peoples. She was smart and really funny, and by virtue of her history and experience, politically very astute.[60]

In fact, Carmichael attributed Hamer—among other movement mentors like Baker and King—with having "formed" him in such a way that he remained consistently mindful of how to represent "the best of our people" and the seri-ousness of the "struggle" throughout his life.[61]

As he sought to live in a manner that did justice to Hamer's example, Carmi-chael encouraged the audience of mourners gathered inside and outside William Chapel to do the same. Hamer's perseverance in the face of harassment and persecution proves that she represents the best of all humanity, he rea-soned. She is both ordinary and an extraordinary exemplar whose "blood was spilt in Winona, Mississippi" and whose house was "shot into . . . so many times," and yet "the more they tried to stop her, the stronger she became." Riffing on Hamer's symbolic warrior persona, Carmichael likened her life struggles to the "blood of our brothers and sisters in Soweto," to the "blood of the sweating people in South America," and to the "blood of the Palestinian people," sug-gesting that "like Mrs. Hamer, the more they shoot at them, the stronger they will become." Carmichael's speech built to a climax through these comparisons and he concluded his address by imploring the audience to draw strength and confidence from Hamer's example. "Mrs. Hamer's death today is not a death for us to be sad about," he attempted to console the bereaved, "but for us to be very happy about. . . . We can be happy today. We know with Mrs. Hamer there is inevitable victory in our course."[62] Though his address built in rate and volume to this climactic conclusion, and while his delivery was impassioned through-out, Carmichael's funeral oration received no applause and very limited verbal feedback from the audience of mourners.[63]

In marked contrast, Ambassador Young—the trained minister—managed an impressive call-and-response cadence throughout his address. Phrases like "yes" and "tell the story" were common reactions to his sermon, as were less verbal forms of agreement, sounds such as "mmm hmm," laughter, and clapping filled the chapel while he spoke. Respectfully, Young proclaimed: "everything I learned about preaching, politics, life and death, I learned in your midst." This was indeed a bold contention, considering that since his movement days in the South, Young served multiple terms as a member of the United States Congress and President Carter had recently appointed him ambassador to the United Nations. Young repeatedly connected these accomplishments back to the Delta soil that nurtured him. Urging the audience to recognize their own roots, Young surmised: "When I see people gathered in this room, knowing where you are now, knowing that none of us would be where we are now, had we not been here then, that when we stood up," he returned to his own testimony, "it never dawned on me that I would run for congress one day, much less be an Ambassador."

The audience urged him on, "tell the story, tell it," they pleaded. Young responded by reminding the mourners that Jimmy Carter's recent election had been so close supporters watched the results roll in with bated breath. "And when I first heard that the election might turn on how things went in Mississippi, I said: 'Oh Lord, have mercy! We came so close, why did we miss again.'" But, "when they said that Mississippi went our way," Young continued, "I knew the hands that had been picking cotton had finally picked a President." Considering that over a decade of concentrated voter-registration advocacy, dramatic protest, and court challenges had increased black civic participation—by as much as 59 percent in some counties—it is not mere hyperbole to attribute the surprising election results in Mississippi to the hard work of the people there to mourn Hamer and, in part, to the valiant efforts of Hamer herself.

Young drew several more lines of influence between the Delta region, Mrs. Hamer's activism, and the success of this nation. Arguing that seeds planted in the Delta soil made it possible for "the newspaper writers [to] have written some beautiful editorials for the *Washington Post* [and] the *New York Times*," not to mention that "many people who are now elected officials" have their movement years in Mississippi to thank. Those "who are working on poverty programs," posited Young, "wouldn't have [even] had a poverty program had it not been for those early summers from '60 right on through to '64." Similarly, he contended that "young white men and women" who were inspired by the spirit of the Delta during the Freedom Summer of 1964 and were later told to "go back to [their] own homes and deal with the problems" in their own communities, followed this instruction. Armed as they were with the lessons they learned in Mississippi, these young white men and women "started teach-ins on Vietnam" and they also "put in place a movement to . . . bring about the liberation of the women of this nation." Even more specifically, Young pointed to Hodding Carter's position as assistant secretary of state, Pat Derian, "who learned about human rights in this community [and who] is now the State Department Commissioner for Human Rights," in addition to "the Volunteer Operation Action . . . deputy director, Mary King, who got her lessons here from you." As Young's address made manifest, there was no shortage of examples to illustrate just how many people and programs grew out of the Mississippi movement and were "influenced by the spirit of this one woman," who illustrated just "how far we can come simply on the power and faith of the human spirit."

This spirit will endure even after Hamer's death, contended Young, and her spirit is the gift that those gathered should be thankful for. Young characterized Hamer's life on earth as a true blessing from God. "Once in a while in the course of human events," he explained, "there comes a person who by the sheer force of the human spirit is able to change that course of events." Extending upon Hamer's own Jeremiadic reasoning, Young referred to her as one of "God's chosen," someone sent to "change the lives of us all." He recounted her initial activist struggles, reminding the audience that she was kicked off the plantation for trying to register and that there were very few black people, even in Ruleville, who would help her after that. He reminded them that she "had no great wealth, no lawyers . . . no formal education," she—like many of those huddled around speakers outside—"simply had the power of her own soul," which made Hamer both ordinary and extraordinary. What she managed to cultivate from the seeds planted in the Delta is remarkable, but not out of the reach of any audience member gathered to remember her. What she had already inspired and enabled others to accomplish warrants the type of sincere gratitude that elicits action to carry her mission forward.

Young concluded his eulogy by blending comfort and conviction. "To memorialize Fannie Lou Hamer abroad and not carry on her work at home," he warned, "is to betray everything she lived and stood for." Prescribing the appropriate attitude for his audience to leave the chapel with, he specified:

We are here not to mourn, but we are here to gather strength from each other. Get our marching orders, going back to our various places of calling and in the differing ways to which we've been called, saying to Mrs. Hamer: Thank you for the inspiration. Thank you for the example. Thank you for so strengthening our lives that we might live so God can use us. Anytime. Anywhere.

After words of consolation had been offered—the "marching orders" delivered—Hamer's three-and-a-half-hour funeral service came to a close in the most fitting of ways: Young led the congregation in a spirited rendition of "This Little Light of Mine."[64]

The sheer number and broad ideological range of people who participated in Hamer's last rites suggest that her life story spoke to and inspired many who heard it. Moreover, her activist message—the Jeremiad she constructed over the course of her career, the tough yet abiding love she held for all people, and her firm belief that reconciliation and cooperation between the races was not only possible, but the only way for the country to repair itself—resonated broadly.

The telegrams that poured into her Ruleville home, offering words of comfort and condolence to her bereaved family, echo the funeral orations in offering a sense of her immediate symbolic significance. For instance, Representative Walter E. Fauntroy wrote on behalf of the Congressional Black Caucus that "Fannie Lou Hamer will live as a symbol of courage and dedication to the principles of human rights for all people . . . she was indeed one of God's good people." Gloster Current and Roy Wilkins of the NAACP offered a similar depiction of Hamer as a "great freedom fighter" and a "vigorous defender of the rights of all people." Representative John Conyers also referred to Hamer as a "dedicated fighter in the struggle for equality," additionally noting her "strong sense of duty to speak out on the issues of vital importance to us all." The Reverend Jesse Jackson Sr. characterized her as a "soldier in the army who would not except [sic] excuses but pursued excellence while she sought a just entitlement for all its citizens." Harry and Julie Belafonte remembered her as a "giant in her time," and the "Democratic National Committee Family" praised Hamer as a "model champion for the causes of political reform, human and civil rights, and humanitarian ideals."[65]

The Democratic National Committee, as had Young, attributed tangible social and political change to Hamer's activism. In their message to her family, the committee suggested that Hamer's insistence on "full participation of all segments of the party membership" created an "atmosphere" which contributed to the party's recent success in electing a "new presidential administration . . . an administration committed to the principle Mrs. Hamer worked so hard to see realized." Others suggested more abstractly that Hamer "plowed furrows in the conscience of the nation," that she "paved the way for the New South," and that she "changed history."[66] Even in the midst of brave characterizations and grand attributions, most telegrams also included a recognition that Hamer was, in Diane Nash Bevel's words: "a warm and for real person." Others wrote similarly of Hamer's "compassion for others," her "love and generosity," and the way in which she taught northern audiences about love's "healing power."[67]

In the immediate aftermath of Hamer's death, as the funeral tributes and telegrams suggest, there was a fullness to what was becoming Hamer's symbolic legacy. Aspects of her simple honest sharecropper persona were remembered alongside her strong warrior status and her truth-telling, tough-loving nature. What's more, organizations like the NAACP's Legal Defense Fund, the Democratic National Committee, and the Civil Rights Division of the Department of Justice all recognized that Hamer stood for total participation and full acknowledgment of the rights of all people.

CONTEMPORARY REMEMBRANCES

Over the last thirty-five years, Hamer's symbolic legacy has deflated. On the national and international level, popular memory about Hamer is now typically limited to her participation in the 1964 credentials committee challenge at the DNC. Within that frame, her transformation from sharecropper to civil rights activist is emphasized—earning her larger-than-life attributions that overshadow the details of her activism and the destitute state in which she died. A review of widely adopted United States history textbooks, for instance, reveals that if Hamer is mentioned within their pages, she is represented in the context of Freedom Summer and its culmination in the 1964 DNC challenge.[68] Within this narrow context—three months of Hamer's fifteen-year career as an activist—the narrative of her life is limited to her identity as a "poor sharecropper," who "lost her job" for attempting to register and then was "severely beaten by police while in jail" for "attending a voter registration workshop" and for "urging African Americans to register."[69] The majority of textbooks that mention Hamer also include a quotation from her 1964 DNC testimony, which "shocked the convention and viewers nationwide," as she recounted her experiences and questioned America.[70]

Like the brief mentions of her in textbooks, her plainspoken sharecropper persona is emphasized in a children's book, which features a picture of Hamer with her hands on her hips standing knee-deep in a field of cotton stalks on the back cover.[71] The Juvenile reader entitled *Fannie Lou Hamer: From*

Sharecropping to Politics also amplifies her plainspoken sharecropper persona.[72] The US Postal Service's Civil Rights Pioneers stamp collection, issued in commemoration of the NAACP's 100th Anniversary, focused on Hamer's sharecropping past and her role in the MFDP's fight for representation at the DNC as well. The image of Hamer on the stamp dedicated to her and Medgar Evers displays Hamer bearing a weary smile at the 1964 convention. On the back of the sheet of stamps, the description of Hamer reads: "She was a Mississippi sharecropper who fought for black voting rights and spoke for many when she said, 'I'm sick and tired of being sick and tired.'"[73] Moreover, the image of Hamer chosen by the International Slavery Museum to remain on permanent display is a picture of her delivering her credentials committee testimony at the 1964 DNC.

During the fortieth-anniversary celebration of the MFDP's credentials committee challenge, which took place at the 2004 DNC, slightly more robust memorial tributes were paid to Hamer. Speakers praised her plainspoken sharecropper persona while also heralding her bravery and attributing legendary status to Hamer as a guiding symbol of strength. Ruby Dee and Ossie Davis, renowned actors and civil rights activists, recalled how Hamer was born in rural Mississippi and how she "toiled under the injustices of Jim Crow" before the "movement came to her town and stirred in her the desire for something greater." Dee and Davis, in their address delivered antiphonally, also recounted the "harassment and physical threats" Hamer received upon becoming active in the movement. Davis emphasized that Hamer "helped others register to vote. And for that, she was arrested and nearly beaten to death on the jailhouse cell floor." Dee and Davis referred to Hamer as a "leader of the MFDP" and emphasized the significance of her credentials committee testimony, declaring:

[B]efore millions watching on television, she spoke of her ordeal. What she did, she gave voice to all of us who wanted more. Who dreamed of a possibility of better days. She reminded us of our basic values and our purpose. And she helped this nation find its way again.

Even more boldly, Davis proclaimed: "Fannie Lou Hamer's single decision to stand up and be counted brought us here!" Dee concurred; through cheers she invoked Hamer's prophetic persona, linking her to the Moses generation of mid-twentieth-century activists.[74] "Yes. She guided us," riffing on the Exodus narrative Dee continued, Hamer "guided us out of the wilderness of death threats and disenfranchisement, of lynching and literacy tests of segregation and second-class status. One woman from Mississippi did this. One voice lifted so many. All of us."[75] Dee clearly overstates and oversimplifies Hamer's relationship to the movement for dramatic effect.

Like Dee and Davis, Dr. Maya Angelou's tribute to Hamer at the 2004 DNC highlighted the importance of Hamer's 1964 testimony, although Angelou was more careful to ground Hamer's activist contributions in the nation's centuries-long struggle for freedom. Angelou began her address just as Hamer had concluded her remarks, quoting:

I question America. Is this America? The land of the free and the home of the brave where we have to sleep with our telephones off the hooks because our lives be threatened daily? Because we want to live as decent human beings in America?

Suggesting that it was "fitting tonight that the delegates—you and I—hear the questions raised by Fannie Lou Hamer 40 years ago," Angelou summed up Hamer's importance as one who asked fundamental questions with enduring relevance. She tethered Hamer to the historical struggle for freedom in America, comparing her to such mythical figures from America's civic religion as Patrick Henry, Harriet Tubman, and Frederick Douglass. Angelou contended: "Fannie Lou Hamer and the Mississippi Freedom Democratic Party were standing on the shoulders of history when they sought to unseat evil from its presumed safe perch."[76]

Two years after the 2004 DNC tributes, Congress named the Voting Rights Act Reauthorization in honor of Hamer, Rosa Parks, and Coretta Scott King. Like Dee, Davis, and Angelou, then senator Barack Obama addressed the inspirational quality of Hamer's symbolic legacy as he expressed his support for the act. From the Senate floor, Obama invoked the famous words that Martin Luther King Jr. spoke during the Selma protests: "he told a gathering of organizers and activists and community members that they should not despair," Obama informed the Senate, "the arc of the moral universe is long, but it bends toward justice." Extrapolating upon King's words, Obama reasoned:

That is because of the work that each of us does that it bends toward justice. It is because of people such as John Lewis and Fannie Lou Hamer and Coretta Scott King and Rosa Parks—all the giants upon whose shoulders we stand—that we are beneficiaries of that arc bending toward justice.

Obama featured activists from the Moses generation, the "giants upon whose shoulders we stand," to inspire his contemporaries to follow in their footsteps.

His address balanced praise for the strides made by these "giants," with specific instances of ongoing voter discrimination—language barriers, fraud, and intimidation—to underscore the work that remains.[77]

While some of Hamer's compatriots are quite pleased with these types of contemporary invocations—Guyot, for one, maintains that "Fannie Lou Hamer is often mentioned by various political speakers who are moving forward and empowering others because that's what she stood for"—others, like Cobb, find little value in "speeches people make about this brave sharecropper."[78] Characterizing references like the one made during Bill Clinton's 1992 acceptance speech at the DNC, in which the presidential nominee adopted Hamer's "I'm sick and tired of being sick and tired" refrain, as "variations of the Noble Savage" trope. Cobb argues, instead, the real issues Hamer's memory should evoke are "who gets to be a full citizen? Who gets to make decisions in the political apparatus of the Democratic Party?" Critical questions like these, radically raised by Hamer during her lifetime, are what Cobb and others suggest are often overlooked in popular evocations of her symbolic legacy.[79]

Although speeches like Angelou's and Obama's raised critical questions, core aspects of Hamer's activist struggle and her message are commonly overlooked and their omission enables advocates all across the political spectrum to adapt public memory of Hamer to their rhetorical purposes. In the White House press release announcing the passage of the 2006 VRA Reauthorization, in Bush's remarks upon signing the act into law, even in Obama's speech regarding the act on the Senate floor, the history of the act is traced to the Selma campaign with no mention of the MFDP's concurrent congressional challenge. MFDP member Dorie Ladner is not surprised by this oversight. "You never see that," Ladner explains,

> because we challenged the government of the United States head on . . . this goes straight to the heart of government. They don't mind showing the horses that's going over John Lewis and others but they don't show you going straight and asking for those seats.

Ladner makes clear that the struggle for voting rights did not begin in Selma: "the congressional challenge, the democratic challenge of '64, and plus SNCC had filed suits . . . we had been fighting for a long time before then," she insists.[80] Ladner's objection to the popular conception of how the VRA passed is rooted not only in the incomplete history that fuels the narrative, but also in the way the story is told. By emphasizing the violence in Selma, the injustices in the nation's capitol are overshadowed.

Perhaps this shift in emphasis is what enables speakers like Bush to fold Hamer's activism into the myth of the American meritocracy. In his remarks upon reauthorizing the VRA, for instance, Bush promised:

> The Administration will continue to build on the legacy of the civil rights movement to help ensure that every child enjoys the opportunities America offers. These opportunities include the right to a decent education in a good school, the chance to own a home or small business, and the hope that comes from knowing you can rise in our society through hard work and using your talents.

Although the president referred to Hamer, Parks, and Scott King as "three heroes of American history who devoted their lives to the struggle for civil rights," and while he pledged his signature in "honor of their memory and their contributions to the cause of freedom," Bush failed to acknowledge that the MFDP was shut down by the Democratic Party in 1964 and by the US Congress in 1965. In attaching the legacy of the civil rights movement to the myth of the American meritocracy—the equal opportunity all citizens have to "rise in our society through hard work and using your talents"—moreover, Bush overlooks the struggles Hamer had with middle-class power brokers throughout her career, the failure of her beloved Freedom Farm, and the depressed and penniless state in which she died, despite her "hard work" and her many "talents."[81] Because aspects of the past are evoked by contemporary advocates to advance present purposes and because the details of Hamer's life have faded over time, Hamer-as-symbol now risks being folded into the very mythologies she challenged throughout her activist career.[82]

Thankfully, just as public memory is selective, agenda driven, sometimes contradictory, and often thin, it is also cocreated through symbolic interactions and is, therefore, fundamentally contestable. The book's Afterword, "We Ain't Free Yet. The Kids Need to Know Their Mission," examines the ways in which Hamer's life story and her symbolicity are rendered during the 2012 statue and museum dedication in her honor. As friends, family members, activists, politicians, and educators from both near and far converged upon Hamer's hometown of Ruleville, a thicker, more complex legacy of Hamer and her activist contributions was crafted.

"We Ain't Free Yet. The Kids Need to Know Their Mission," 2012

HAMER SPOKE THESE WORDS OF CONVICTION TO HER LONGTIME FRIEND, fellow activist, and confidante, Charles McLaurin, shortly before her death.[1] As she lay in a hospital bed in Mound Bayou, Hamer also insisted: "Mac, I don't want to be buried on a plantation . . . I want you to promise me that I will not be buried on a plantation. Promise me," she implored. "Ok, I promise," was McLaurin's simple reply. Fairly certain that the legendary Mrs. Hamer would "live forever," McLaurin did not think too much of the agreement he made with his friend that winter day in 1977. But it was not too long after he gave his word that Hamer passed away and the family put McLaurin in charge of her burial. He contemplated gravesites; "I thought about Mount Galilee, but that's on a plantation. Then I thought about out here east of Ruleville, it's on a plantation. See, she knew something I did not know," he explains, "she knew the only places to be buried were on a plantation!" "Why'd she do this to me?" McLaurin lamented, "God damn, there's nowhere else to bury her!"[2]

After some contemplation, McLaurin realized that the faltering Freedom Farm still owned the first forty acres of land they bought outright. McLaurin encountered strong resistance to his proposal to bury Hamer on this land from the remaining members of the board and from the City of Ruleville, which had a zoning stipulation that the deceased could not be buried on private property within the city's limits. Cleve McDowell, the first black student to attend the University of Mississippi Law School, a tireless crusader for justice in the Emmett Till lynching, and a friend of McLaurin and Hamer, came up with the plan to donate the Freedom Farm land to the city. McDowell reasoned that once the city held the property it would become public land, upon which Hamer could be buried. Thinking this was the only viable solution to honor the deathbed promise he had made, McLaurin went forward with the McDowell plan, hoping it would buy him some time to find a more appropriate resting place for her.

Over the last thirty-five years, the forty acres that McLaurin donated to the city grew to become the most fitting of resting spots for both Mrs. Hamer and her husband, Perry, who passed away in 1992. In 2008, a bright red gazebo emblazoned with the names of local freedom fighters like Joe McDonald, Ruby Davis, and Hattie and Herman Sisson was built near the couple's graves. The gazebo honors the Delta's rich history of black empowerment even as it provides shade and a place to reflect for those who come to pay their respects. A cement pathway, wrought-iron fence, brick lampposts, a fountain, and an archway announcing, "The Fannie Lou Hamer Memorial Garden," have also been installed, thanks to the fundraising efforts of the local Memorial Garden Committee, spearheaded by Mrs. Hattie Robinson Jordan. In 2011, the Mississippi State Department of Tourism placed a civil rights marker, designating the garden a destination along the state's freedom trail. And on October 5, 2012, the National Fannie Lou Hamer Statue Committee—comprised of activists, intellectuals, and members of the Hamer family—unveiled a nine-foot bronze sculpture of Hamer, built by artist Brian Hanlon.

The statue portrays Hamer in an active speaking pose, her left hand clasping the receiver of a megaphone and her right hand raised to the sky. Hanlon placed the sculpture atop a square marble base, replete with images of Hamer picketing alongside marchers in her home state, speaking at the 1964 DNC, and standing next to Gray and Devine in front of the nation's capitol during their 1965 congressional challenge. These images are surrounded by Hamer's widely revered quotations including, "This little light of mine, I'm gonna let it shine"; "If I fall, I'll fall 5'4" forward for freedom"; and "nobody's free until everybody's free"—her most famous quotation, "I'm sick and tired of being sick and tired" is etched into her nearby gravestone. Two marble plinths bearing the names of those who donated to the project stand in front of and to the side of the statue.[3] The statue itself faces the gazebo, behind it stand two large oak trees, and further back still is the Fannie Lou Hamer Recreation Center, now filled with memorabilia from her lifetime.

On a sunny fall morning in 2012, I drove past acres and acres of cotton fields awaiting harvest—white fluffy fiber stood stark between the blue sky and brown stalks. I made my way into Ruleville and turned onto Byron Street, parking my rental car in the open field between the memorial garden and the recreation center. Walking briskly toward the tarp-covered statue, I spotted McLaurin and I thought back to the last time I'd seen him here. A little over two years ago, we congregated here along with Hamer's daughter, Vergie, and my fellow Hamer researcher, Davis W. Houck, listening to "Mr. Mac" share memories about his dear friend and explain his vision for the monument. And now here we were again—an hour before the big unveiling, trying to get the CD of songs and speech clips I'd put together for the occasion to play from the old stereo he borrowed from his granddaughter.

Over the weekend of October 5–6, 2012, as crowds of people poured into this small Delta town, state senator Willie Simmons was reminded of Mrs. Hamer's last rites. Then, as now, hundreds of people gathered to remember her and to celebrate her contributions. Then, as now, there were songs of tribute, prayers offered, and words of praise spoken in appreciation of her life. Then, as now, the audience ranged from local and national politicians, educators, and fellow activists to family members, neighbors, and children bussed in from local schools. Simmons drew a contrast in comparison, however. If her funeral had been "Good Friday," he reasoned, then "today is Easter . . . she has risen!"[4] The mood was certainly more jubilant on this eighty-degree day, as young children marched through the gates into the garden donning Fannie Lou Hamer t-shirts and bearing signs that read: "I'm Sick and Tired of Being Unhealthy." Some high school students wore football jerseys, promoting games to be played that evening. While other community members sported straw hats or scrubs, suggesting that they had taken a break from their workday to mark this momentous occasion. In all, the roughly six hundred people who gathered to witness the statue unveiling and dedication listened as the Ruleville High School Band played the "Star Spangled Banner" and sang along to the black national anthem, "Lift Every Voice and Sing." Those gathered spilled out from the shade of the gazebo onto the lawn in front of Mrs. Hamer's grave, and they even spread over to the small circle of shade offered by the nearest oak tree.

The attendants were welcomed by local organizers like Mrs. Bobbie Allen and Mrs. Jordan, informed about the statue project by the national coordinator, Ms. Patricia Thompson and the national chairwoman of the Statue Fund Committee, Dr. Patricia Reid-Merritt. Those gathered listened on as Dr. Molefi Asante offered the libation and Reverend Johnny Hill provided the invocation. Simmons, McLaurin, and Dr. Julianne Malveaux each spoke about Hamer's memory, her legacy, and the value of the statue. All who filled the memorial garden that day were treated to a solo by Vergie Hamer Faulkner; she sang "I'm On My Way" in a voice that bore such a strong resemblance to her mother's that it brought tears to many who surrounded me. After the mayor of Ruleville accepted the gift of the statue, the crowd engaged in a joyful rendition of "This Little Light of Mine," concluding the service in the same way Ambassador Andrew Young had brought Hamer's funeral to a close over three decades ago.

The next morning was an overcast day in Ruleville. Far fewer people showed up to celebrate what would have been Hamer's ninety-fifth birthday and to witness the ceremonial ribbon cutting for the grand opening of the Fannie Lou Hamer Museum. Those fifty or so people who did gather in the Fannie Lou Hamer Recreation Center that early October morning sat at white folding tables decorated in a combined birthday and fall harvest theme. Orange-felt leaves and green and red gourds topped the tables, while balloons flanked the podium and banners reading "Her Light Still Shines" and "Celebrating the Legacy of Mrs. Hamer" hung from the front of the room. The educators, activists, politicians, and local Deltans gathered that morning heard more from state and local representatives and family and community members than from national figures. Saturday's crowd also enjoyed listening to two essays read by Ruleville Middle School students responding to the prompt: "How does the legacy of Mrs. Fannie Lou Hamer inspire you?" And Mrs. Ruby White engaged the more intimate group in a host of spirited movement anthems. After the service, both the ceremonial ribbon and Mrs. Hamer's birthday cake were cut.

The crowd was then led through the modest museum, which fills half of the recreation center and is divided into several sections including those labeled "Plantation," "MFDP/Freedom Summer," "Library," and "Freedom Farm." Within these rooms, relics from Hamer's agrarian and activist past sit alongside local and national news clippings, honors, and pictures. Toward the back corner of the museum, Tracy Sugarman's Freedom Summer illustrations are juxtaposed by Hamer's memorable quotations—including the words that surround the base of her statue and are etched onto her headstone, in addition to "All of this is on account of we want to register," and "We ain't free yet, the kids need to know their mission." Over the chatter of the museum visitors, you could faintly hear the recording of clips from her speeches and verses from her inspiring take on traditional spirituals-turned-movement anthems.

As I left the museum that morning, walking through the dewy grass toward the memorial garden, I reflected on the range of the tributes paid to Hamer over the weekend's course. I felt heartened by the range of memories offered and the richness with which her life story was told. Her humble beginnings were commonly recounted. Hamer was referred to as a "woman of the soil," and McLaurin remarked that she was a "sharecropper who was honored on a postage stamp."[5] Jordan connected Hamer's early life experience to her own, sharing with the audience that she grew up on Eastland's plantation and remembered her father wearing "patches upon patches."[6]

Throughout the tributes, Hamer's ordinary roots were often contrasted with her extraordinary traits and life accomplishments—intimating what Mississippi state representative Sarah Richardson-Thomas made explicit: "coming from poverty and facing adversity should not limit one's potential."[7] McLaurin recounted the story of Hamer's first mass meeting, noting the retaliation she suffered, being kicked off the plantation and stalked by night-riders, but proclaiming: "she was always ready to leave the plantation; Fannie Lou Hamer was always ready for freedom."[8] Rulevillean Willie Burton also emphasized Hamer's persistence in the face of the white supremacists who brandished guns and shouted, "Go back to the plantation!" at the bus carrying blacks back from their failed registration attempt in Indianola. Burton referred to Hamer as a "survivor," suggesting she had the "tenacity of a bull dog."[9] And her cousin, Nina Townsend, illustrated the range of Hamer's gifts when she contended Hamer had the "heart of a lamb, the courage of a lion, and the voice of a giant."[10]

Mention of Hamer's extraordinary traits often evoked her symbolic status as a warrior. Borrowing a popular chant from the 2012 DNC, Malveaux echoed McLaurin's characterization of Hamer as one who was always ready for freedom, contending that Hamer was "fired up and ready to go!" She reminded the audience not only of Hamer's bravery in "speaking truth to power," challenging the likes of Hubert Humphrey at the 1964 DNC, but also of Hamer's resilience in living through Mississippi terror, national political defeats, and even breast cancer. "Every time she was beaten down, she got back up," insisted Malveaux.[11] Simmons rounded out his Christ-like comparison of Hamer as having "risen" by referring to her, like her cousin had, as a "giant."[12] In his tribute to Hamer, Asante characterized her as a "giant" as well, even as he compared Hamer to "civil rights movement greats" like James Forman, James Bevel, Stokely Carmichael, and Amzie Moore.[13] Representative Richardson-Thomas extended the giant characterization into the realm of America's civic religion as she likened Mrs. Hamer to stalwarts of the Republic such as George Washington, Abraham Lincoln, and Theodore Roosevelt.[14]

Even in the midst of these lofty comparisons and larger-than-life attributions, the Hamer accolades were grounded by recognition of the family that supported her, the community that nurtured her, and the organizations that empowered her. McLaurin alluded to the strong tradition of black resistance in the Delta, mentioning that SNCC was invited into Ruleville by local people with national movement ties—singling out Joe McDonald and Mary Tucker, who had been previously trained by the SCLC Citizenship Education Program. These local leaders, McLaurin made clear, are the ones who initially convinced Hamer to attend the mass meeting at William Chapel. Community member Mrs. Aretha Tiggs, Ruleville mayor Shirley Edwards, and Hattie Jordan all praised the Townsend and Hamer families, acknowledging the sacrifices they made so that Hamer could serve the broader public. Hamer's daughter led into her solo by declaring: "I give thanks to God for making this day possible. But second of all, I give thanks to Ella and Jim Townsend that gave birth to this woman. I also give thanks to Perry 'Pap' Hamer who married this woman and this woman made *his* name famous: Hamer."[15] With a tear in his eye and a tremble in his voice, McLaurin pointed toward the statue and proclaimed: "this statue is about the movement." He supported this contention in his remarks by repeatedly acknowledging SNCC's role in projecting Hamer into the center of the struggle.[16]

Furthermore, local and national representatives alike tethered their success and the success of others to the sacrifices Hamer made. Senator Simmons underscored the fact that he is serving the very district that Hamer lost to Robert Crook over forty years ago; Simmons also attributed President Barack Obama's political victory to the advances in the Democratic Party wrought by the MFDP's 1964 DNC challenge.[17] Jordan could not resist acknowledging what the audience plainly saw: the mayor of Ruleville was "not only black, but a woman."[18] Tyler Price and Jaelyn Childs, the two Ruleville middle school students who read the award-winning essays they had written about Hamer, praised the sacrifices she had made so that they could have greater opportunity. Ruleville supervisor Edgar Donahoe, an elderly white man, echoed Hodding Carter III's funeral tribute to Hamer as he spoke of her legacy in the context of interracial love. He told a story of growing up in such close proximity to blacks that their families became affectionately interlaced. And yet, Donahoe's mother warned him about standing up against the unjust treatment he saw his black friends suffer: "Son, we don't believe that way but we can't say anything about it because we're scared," he remembered his mother instructing. Donahoe attributed his twenty-nine-year career as supervisor, which he characterized as "Heaven on earth," to the strides made by Hamer's activism and the activism of countless brave Deltans who overcame their fear and "said something" about the injustice in their state. Because of them, Donahoe now speaks openly about his beliefs and "works together" with blacks in Ruleville "to help each other" and "to serve mankind."[19]

Donahoe was not the only Deltan to emphasize the broad swath of contributions Hamer made to citizens of all races. Jordan mentioned Freedom Farm's "interracial initiatives," informing the crowd that programs like the garment factory, the daycare center, and the affordable houses Hamer secured were "not just for blacks." Making her point lucid, Jordan contended that through her "life of courage and commitment to human rights, Hamer fought for the political advancement of *all* individuals."[20] Richardson-Thomas praised the "difference Hamer made in the political, economic, educational, and social realms of our society."[21] Simmons extended this remembrance by suggesting that through the Fannie Lou Hamer Memorial Garden, the Statue, and now the museum "Fannie Lou Hamer just keeps adding value to the region." Positing that, just as she had during her lifetime, Hamer continues to serve as a "beacon, a light of hope, drawing people from both far and near to the Delta." Once there, Simmons suggested that visitors will learn more about Hamer's inspirational life and that their tourism will boost the area economy.[22] Moreover, both Malveaux and Richardson-Thomas featured "get out the vote" appeals within their tributes. Many of the speakers including Burton, Malveaux, and Richardson-Thomas suggested that the audience should draw inspiration from Hamer and that those gathered "ought to incorporate her example from the tips of our toes to the tops of our heads," or, put differently, that the audience should "look back at her life and glean traits so that we may all be better people on both sides of the Jordan."[23]

By the time I had walked from the museum to the memorial garden, my reflections on the weekend's tributes had left me feeling less heartened and a bit troubled. I wasn't disturbed by the occasional tensions and contradictions that inevitably arise in the collective effort of remembering. I acknowledged that the speakers often sent mixed messages to the audience when they proclaimed at once that Hamer was just an ordinary sharecropper, suggesting that if she could rise up then anybody in attendance could ascend to similar heights. While insisting, simultaneously, that Hamer was a giant, "a phenomenal woman," with gifts and talents that distinguished her as someone especially worthy of praise.[24] Nor was I overly concerned with the triumphalist overtones resulting from attaching Hamer's life story to the ubiquitous Horatio Alger-type narratives that permeate our collective consciousness. And I wasn't too bothered by the message of uncomplicated interracial cooperation advanced by the few white speakers who addressed the crowd. These tensions and overly simplistic renderings of Hamer's life story didn't trouble me because I had been paying close attention to national Hamer tributes and I anticipated them. I came into the weekend knowing full well that the black freedom movement and its iconic figures are often folded into larger cultural narratives such as the "pull yourself up by your bootstraps" mythology, the comforting understanding that the civil rights movement succeeded in mending relations between the races and that it left the doors of opportunity wide open for future generations to prosper.[25] I expected both local and national speakers to subscribe to these widespread ideologies, which we are all inundated with, and to craft Hamer's legacy within their common frames of reference.

What I initially found to be heartening about the weekend's tributes was that the speakers did not just propagate well-worn mythology about the movement and about Mrs. Hamer, but that they also demonstrated the significant role her family, her community, and organizations like SNCC played in her prominence. What's more, the speakers and the museum itself emphasized both the national battles Hamer waged and the contributions she made to her local community. And yet, as I stood alone in front of the towering bronze symbol, I couldn't shake the feeling that there was something missing from the weekend of accolades. As I tried to place the source of my unease, I was joined by others who made the short trek over from the museum to the statue. Soon visitors snapping pictures of Mrs. Hamer's gravestone and her newly unveiled statue surrounded me. I watched as they stood and smiled up at Mrs. Hamer, some patting each other on the back for a job well done in raising the funds for this monument.

Then it occurred to me what was overlooked, ignored, and ultimately lost from the weekend of tributes. I realized that Hamer's symbolic status as a plainspoken sharecropper and a warrior were consistently evoked, but that her radical truth-telling prophetic persona was overshadowed. I was reminded of the concluding reflection in *Local People*, wherein Dittmer mused: "In death Fannie Lou Hamer had become a person for all seasons, her name invoked by politicians and self-proclaimed leaders across the ideological spectrum. She is remembered for her deep religious faith, her ability to move an audience, and her refusal to hate those who oppressed her." And yet, Dittmer insists, "the Fannie Lou Hamer who speaks the loudest and with the greatest sense of urgency today is the angry crusader for social justice who relentlessly attacked power and privilege and believed that progress depended on continual struggle."[33] Dittmer's words aptly captured what was amiss about this occasion, and they made me think, even more specifically, of Hamer's consistent refrains: "I'm not here to make you feel comfortable," "I'm going to tell it like it is," and "I've got to tell you where it's at!"

As I watched young girls and boys encircle the monument, looking expectantly up at this icon, I remembered that Hamer did not just "speak truth to power"—she spoke truth to everybody, regardless of occasion. She called out chicken-eating preachers and members of the black middle to upper class who shied away from activism or who sought to control their lower-class brothers and sisters; she compelled northern white liberals to search their hearts and examine the precarious nature of their own freedom. She charged black men to take the lead in improving their communities and she told poor Delta sharecroppers that if they didn't "launch out in to the deep" that "God wasn't going to put [freedom] in their lap!" What was missing from the weekend's tributes, I realized, was a strong dose of Hamer's tough love—her habit of indicting all people and binding both the powerful and the powerless to the problems that persist.

People were feeling too good about themselves this weekend, I thought, only somewhat sarcastically. If this statue could speak, Hamer would doubtlessly be railing against enduring local, state, and national problems—voter suppression, redistricting, unequal educational systems, disparate poverty and unemployment rates among the races, housing discrimination, the racist criminal justice system, the obesity epidemic, and limited access to affordable healthcare. If this statue could speak, Hamer would not be placing the blame for these pressing social, political, economic, and educational issues solely on the shoulders of those in Washington or even on the backs of elected representatives and other self-proclaimed leaders among the crowd. If this statue could speak, she would compel each member of the audience to become a part of the solution. She would certainly urge the audience to vote, as some speakers had, but she would also feature specific marching orders within her convicting Jeremiad. The sense of urgency, conviction, and individual responsibility that so saturated Hamer's rhetoric during her lifetime is precisely what got lost by focusing on what she stood for to the exclusion of what she said, how she said it, and to whom it was addressed.

After participating in this weekend-long tribute, I became convinced of the value rhetorical biographies hold to teach the substance behind the symbol. For those participants like Malveaux, who admitted that she had never met Hamer and "everything she knew about her she learned from reading her biographies," or like Barry W. Bryant, of the Sunflower County Board of Supervisors, who confessed that he spent the evening before the statue unveiling learning more about Hamer by searching youtube, a rhetorical biography such as this provides a sense not just of what Hamer did, but of how she did it.[26] A rhetorical biography can reveal what is specifically compelling and persuasive about a historical figure's life, while also affording that figure a measure of agency by focusing on the way he or she used symbols to construct personae, advance objectives, and navigate her historical context.

In the case of Hamer and the context of the black freedom movement, *A Voice That Could Stir an Army* contributes to the ongoing construction of Hamer's symbolic legacy by recovering her agency and intellect as well as by demonstrating how she became iconic, of what, and how this status worked toward and against her activist purposes. What's more, it provides specificity, substance, and context to undergird her oft-cited quotations and one-dimensional symbolic representations. As it intersects with the robust literature on bottom-up localized approaches to studying the black freedom movement, moreover, the form of the rhetorical biography provides one possible antidote to the shortcoming Hogan exposes in movement scholarship. She observes, "almost no historians have been able to clearly explain how civil rights or Black Power activists accomplished their feats, except through highly generalized abstractions about people transforming the social and political landscape of the nation. The specifics have remained beyond reach."[27] This rhetorical biography locates these specifics, for one particular activist, at the level of the symbol. By analyzing the ways in which Hamer gets represented symbolically as well as the way she used images, words, and material objects to influence others, *A Voice That Could Stir an Army* suggests that taking movement discourse seriously is one way to learn more about how particular activists and the broader movement accomplished what it did. These lessons, in turn, offer more nuanced instruction about how we might all participate in the work that remains.

Acknowledgments

IT IS OFTEN SAID THAT THE LIFE OF AN ACADEMIC IS A LONELY ONE—LONG hours reading, writing, and researching permit little human contact. For some the solitude is an attractive aspect of the profession; the very thought of it terrified the unabashedly extroverted me. Fortunately, I chose to write a book about Fannie Lou Hamer—a person so deeply loved and so highly revered that those who remember her and those who write scholarship about her are moved by her generous spirit to welcome strangers into their community. It is thanks to Mrs. Hamer, to the community of activists and scholars who keep her memory alive, and to my own growing family that there were few lonely moments in crafting this book.

When I began researching Hamer's speeches, there was only a small handful of published texts. So, I knew from the outset that this would be a project rooted in an extensive recovery effort. The extraordinary lengths archivists and librarians like Clarence Hunter, Celia Tisdale, Wendy Shay, Kenneth Chandler, and Jessie Carney Smith went to help me find recordings of interviews and speeches Hamer gave was truly remarkable.

There were, however, precious few such recordings. In hopes of recovering more texts and filling out the project, I took a leap of faith and moved from the archives to small towns and big cities across the country in search of the people who knew her best. The people I met were gracious beyond my wildest expectations. I could have never imagined, for instance, that along the road to recovering more Hamer speeches, I would get to have lunch with Reverend Jesse Jackson Sr. in Chicago, with Reverend Edwin King in Jackson, and with Charles McLaurin in Ruleville. I never dreamed that I would sip a Coca-Cola in an Atlanta skyscraper while talking to Ambassador Andrew Young about his dear friend Mrs. Hamer. Nor did I imagine that Rita Schwerner Bender would so willingly agree to meet me for coffee in Seattle. I certainly did not expect Hamer's daughter, Vergie, to invite me into her home and to let me spend the day with her and Hamer's three-year-old great-grandson when I visited Memphis. Nor did I think that L. C. Dorsey would patiently sit down with me in her kitchen and explain the social mores of mid-twentieth-century rural Mississippi. I count myself blessed to have spoken to Lawrence Guyot over the phone, as he lay in a hospital bed, just weeks before his death. I'm also thankful that I had the chance to talk to Tracy Sugarman and Charles Sweet before they passed.

The Madison members of Measure for Measure—particularly Jean and Charlie Sweet and Jeff and Sarah Goldstein—were incredibly generous with their time, their memories, and their recordings of Hamer speaking.

Hattie Robinson Jordan gave me a tour of Ruleville that I'll never forget and only gently chided me for trying to take pictures of the Fannie Lou Hamer museum she helped curate. I am thankful to Patricia M. Thompson and the Repaying Our Ancestors Respectfully (ROAR) organization she spearheads for putting me in touch with Mrs. Jordan, for inviting me to be on the board of the Fannie Lou Hamer Statue and Education Fund Committee, and for supporting my project from the outset. Charles McLaurin's keen insight into Hamer's activism, not to mention his vivid movement memories, made the effort of winning his support for my project well worth the struggle. Dr. Leslie McLemore and the Fannie Lou Hamer National Institute on Citizenship and Democracy provided early assistance that was invaluable in getting my project off the ground, putting me in touch with Hamer's friends and fellow activists and even providing a space for me to conduct interviews. I would also like to thank Dr. McLemore, Keith McMillian, and the Institute for agreeing to host a site for the Hamer recordings that Davis W. Houck and I gathered. Dorie Ladner and Charles Cobb are both informative and dedicated to keeping the movement alive in public memory—their wisdom and charm came through the phone line; I only wish to meet them both in person someday. And I truly never imagined that a book project would bring such close friends as I have found in Monica Land, Mrs. Hamer's niece, and Houck, my fellow Hamer researcher.

In true Hamer spirit, Houck has been generous with his resources, constructive with his advice, and big hearted with his friendship. Kay Mills also shared interviews she conducted, Hamer speeches she found, and contact information for additional sources with me. Aram G. Goudsouzian was gracious enough to let me have a sneak peek at his forthcoming book on the Meredith March and to send me a recording of a Hamer speech he acquired through his research. I am thankful to him and to Emilye Crosby for putting us in touch. Moreover, Crosby's incisive read of my book proposal and manuscript gave the project clear direction and purpose. She went above and beyond the role of reviewer, as she put me in touch with movement activists and historians, shared archival sources, and provided much-needed encouragement. I am thankful to the University Press of Mississippi—particularly Craig Gill, Walter Biggins, Steven Yates, and Katie Keene—for supporting this project.

I was fortunate to have several opportunities to present and workshop the ideas in this book. I appreciate the kind invitations to give talks at the University of Wisconsin, Willamette University, University of Minnesota, and

University of Puget Sound—thanks to Erik Doxtader, Cindy Koenig Richards, David Beard, James Jasinski, and Dexter Gordon for their support of this project. Bruce Gronbeck, Gerard A. Hauser, and the members of the Rhetoric Workshop at the University of Colorado, Boulder, as well as David Zarefsky and the members of the 2010 Rhetoric Society of America workshop provided valuable feedback on aspects of this project. I also appreciate Liza Shaw's assistance, quickly and expertly transcribing many of the interviews I conducted. And Debbie Upton's careful copyediting of the manuscript is greatly appreciated as well.

As an independent scholar, I struggled at times with resources and guidance; I am thankful for the advice and support provided by Jacqueline Bacon, Louise W. Knight, and Lisa Corrigan. I feel compelled to thank the many rhetorical scholars whose friendship and scholarship inspire me—particularly Karlyn Kohrs Campbell, James Jasinski, Vanessa B. Beasley, Robert E. Terrill, Keith D. Miller, Angela G. Ray, Sarah Meinen Jedd, Wendy K. Z. Anderson, Michelle LaVigne, Belinda A. Stillion Southard, Marilyn Bordwell DeLaure, Robin E. Moore Jensen, Kristy Maddux, Kirt H. Wilson, John M. Murphy, Mary E. Stuckey, Brandon Inabinet, Bonnie J. Dow, Jeff Drury, Cara Finnegan, Paul Stob, Kristen McCauliff, Morgan Ginther, and Charles E. Morris—among so many others who kept me feeling connected to the discipline even without an institutional home. I appreciate the patience exhibited by Cindy Griffin, John Louis Lucaites, Martin J. Medhurst, and Shawn Parry-Giles, each of whom worked with me as editors on previous article-length projects and played invaluable roles in shaping and sharpening my writing. More specifically, I appreciate Terra Mahmondi's assistance gathering historical newspaper accounts of Hamer. Christina Greene provided early inspiration for this project. The support and feedback offered by Robert Asen, Robert Glenn Howard, Stephen E. Lucas, Erik Doxtader, and Christine Garlough was invaluable. Susan Zaeske's friendship and wisdom empowered me to write this book.

I have been working on this project for nearly a decade. During this time, I relocated to four different cities, married my best friend, and gave birth to two children. I could not have done any of this without the support of my family and friends. Thanks, especially, to my grandparents, my parents, my sisters, my aunts, my godmother, and my in-laws. Between my dear graduate school friends and the new mama friends I have made, I received ongoing support and humor that both humbled and sustained me. Since the day we met at the Civil Rights Museum in Memphis, Cindy Koenig Richards has been like a sister to me—whether I needed a smiling face to focus on during a nervous presentation, a friendly phone call in the midst of drafting an impossible chapter, or a weekend visit. I love that we have had each other to rejoice with and to lean on during life's many transitions. Thanks to Justine Sullivan for taking my little guy to the pool two mornings a week so I could finish revising the manuscript. Thank you to my sweet Sawyer for taking good naps and trying to understand when mama had to work on her book. Thank you to my dear Evalyn for sleeping soundly in my lap while I put the finishing touches on the manuscript.

I owe my most substantial debt of gratitude to my husband, David W. Brooks. Thank you for listening to me talk about this project with rapt attention, for providing technical support free of charge or derision, for caring for Sawyer and Evie with joyful silliness, for encouraging me to work on the book even when I was tired, and for helping me carve out the time and the resources to live the life I've always dreamed of—thank you, I love you, I can't imagine having completed this project without you.

Listen to the "Voice That Could Stir an Army"

"YOU'VE NEVER HEARD A ROOM FLYING [LIKE ONE] FANNIE LOU HAMER SET afire," recalls Eleanor Holmes Norton. Hamer's "speeches had themes. They had lessons. They had principles," Norton insists, when Hamer spoke "in this extraordinary ringing style . . .[y]ou never needed to hear anybody else speak again."[1] Norton's observations about Hamer's extraordinary speaking style were echoed in the dozens of interviews I conducted. Many of the people I met performed for me their own impressions of Hamer's matter-of-fact delivery and her robust speaking voice. Others shared their personal recordings of her speeches—cassette tapes they had kept safely stowed for the last forty years. And everyone I interviewed agreed that the words Hamer spoke were powerful, purposeful, and important, but her delivery was an *experience* not to be missed. It is thanks to those audience members who recognized the significance of preserving Hamer's voice, and to the researchers who have helped gather these recordings, that I can now share her speeches with you. The Fannie Lou Hamer National Institute on Citizenship and Democracy has graciously agreed to host a site featuring clips of the speeches analyzed within *A Voice That Could Stir an Army* and transcribed with annotation, in *The Speeches of Fannie Lou Hamer: "To Tell It Like It Is."*[2] To listen to these recorded clips, visit http://www.jsums .edu/hamerinstitute/.

Notes

INTRODUCTION

Taken from the title of Fannie Lou Hamer's first recorded speech, which references the quotation within the speech: "I don't mind my light shining; I don't hide that I'm fighting for freedom because Christ died to set us free." See Fannie Lou Hamer, "I Don't Mind My Light Shining," Speech Delivered at a Freedom Vote Rally in Greenwood, Mississippi, Fall 1963, in *The Speeches of Fannie Lou Hamer: "To Tell It Like It Is,"* ed. Maegan Parker Brooks and Davis W. Houck (Jackson: University Press of Mississippi, 2011), 6.

1. Interview with Vergie Hamer Faulkner by Maegan Parker Brooks, July 14 and July 17, 2009, in *The Speeches of Fannie Lou Hamer*, 205.
2. The plaques honoring Fannie Lou Hamer, President Barack Obama, and Dr. Mae Jemison were revealed on February 17, 2009, in a program celebrating Black History Month at the International Slavery Museum in Liverpool.
3. See, for example, Melissa Harris-Lacewell, "Obama and the Sisters," *Nation*, September 1, 2008; Farah Jasmine Griffin, "DNC Day 4: Remembering Fannie Lou Hamer," from *Conventional Wisdom*, National Public Radio Transcript, August 29, 2008. Available online, accessed January 7, 2009, http://www.npr.org/blogs/news andviews/2008/08/dnc_day_4_remembering_fannie_l.html; and "Key Historic Moments Set the Stage for Obama," National Public Radio Transcript, August 25, 2008. Available online, accessed August 30, 2012, http://www.npr.org/templates/story/story .php?storyId=93954228.
4. "Acceptance Speech to the Democratic National Convention by Governor Bill Clinton from Arkansas," July 16, 1992. Available Online, accessed August 30, 2012, http:// www.4president.org/speeches/billclinton1992acceptance.htm.
5. During its 1976 legislative session, this resolution passed the Mississippi State Legislature by unanimous vote, 116–0.
6. The Hamer Institute's mission statement can be found on its website. Accessed January 14, 2009, http://www.jsums.edu/hamer.institute/.
7. Interview with Harry Belafonte by Kay Mills, January 28, 1991, Los Angeles, California.
8. Interview by Maegan Parker Brooks, Dr. Leslie McLemore, Jackson, Mississippi, June 13, 2007.
9. J. Todd Moye, *Let the People Decide: Black Freedom and White Resistance Movements in Sunflower County, Mississippi, 1945–1986* (Chapel Hill: University of North Carolina Press, 2004), 99.
10. John Dittmer, *Local People: The Struggle for Civil Rights in Mississippi* (Chicago: University of Illinois Press, 1995), 433.
11. The book's title is a quotation taken from an Associated Press wire that read in full: "RULEVILLE—They gather here Sunday to bury Fannie Lou Hamer—a short woman with a lusty sense of humor, the courage of a lion and a voice that could stir an

army." Cited in "Hamer Rites: Civil Rights Leaders to Attend," *Jackson Daily News*, March 20, 1977.

12. For more background on rhetoric's rich history, see Patricia Bizzell and Bruce Herzberg, eds., *The Rhetorical Tradition: Readings from Classical Times to the Present*, 2nd ed. (Boston: Bedford, 2001).

13. Hamer often quoted from Luke 4:18, "The Spirit of the Lord is upon me, because he has anointed me to preach the gospel to the poor; he hath sent me to heal the brokenhearted, to preach deliverance to the captives, and recovering sight to the blind to set at liberty them that are bruised." New King James Version (NKJV).

14. Kay Mills, *This Little Light of Mine: The Life of Fannie Lou Hamer* (New York: Penguin Books, 1993); Chana Kai Lee, *For Freedom's Sake: The Life of Fannie Lou Hamer* (Urbana: University of Illinois Press, 1999).

15. In chronological order, additional studies of Fannie Lou Hamer include June Jordan, *Fannie Lou Hamer* (New York: Thomas Y. Crowell Company, 1972); Susan Kling, *Fannie Lou Hamer: A Biography* (Women for Racial and Economic Equality, 1979); David Rubel, *Fannie Lou Hamer: From Sharecropping to Politics* (Englewood Cliffs, NJ: Silver Burdett Press, 1990); Kay Griffin-Jeuchter, "Fannie Lou Hamer: From Sharecropper to Freedom Fighter" (Master's thesis, Sarah Lawrence College, 1990); Ernest R. Bracey, *Fannie Lou Hamer: The Life of a Civil Rights Icon* (Jefferson, NC: McFarland, 2011).

16. Such a focus, in fact, responds to the historiographical call Charles W. Eagles issued for enriching movement studies by approaching this commonly studied period through different lenses, such as paying more attention to the language of the movement. See Eagles, "Toward New Histories of the Civil Rights Era," *Journal of Southern History* 66, no. 4 (November 2000): 815–848.

17. The few analytical accounts of Hamer's rhetoric that existed prior to 2011 were not found in rhetoric journals. For example, Bernice Johnson Reagon incorporates elements of interpretive analysis into her scholarship; see Reagon, "Let the Church Sing 'Freedom,'" *Black Music Research Journal* 7 (1987): 105–118. See also Janice D. Hamlet, "Fannie Lou Hamer: The Unquenchable Spirit of the Civil Rights Movement," *Journal of Black Studies* 26 (1996): 560–576.

The editors of *The Speeches of Fannie Lou Hamer: "To Tell It Like It Is"* have followed the publication of the anthology with two rhetorical analyses of Hamer's rhetoric and Davis W. Houck is working on a third. See Maegan Parker Brooks, "Oppositional Ethos: Fannie Lou Hamer and the Vernacular Persona," *Rhetoric & Public Affairs* 14 (2011): 511–548; Davis W. Houck and Maegan Parker Brooks, "We're On Our Way," *Voices of Democracy* 6 (2011): 21–43. Available online, accessed September 2, 2012, http://www.voicesofdemocracy.umd.edu/vod-journal/vod-journal-volume-6/; and Davis W. Houck, "Fannie Lou Hamer on Winona: Memory, Trauma, and Recovery," in *The Rhetorical History of the United States: Social Controversy and Public Address in the 1960s and Early 1970s*, ed. Richard Jensen and David Henry (forthcoming 2013).

18. Bernice Price and Annie Pearle Markham, "Fannie Lou Townsend Hamer (1917–1977), Champion of the Poor, Civil Rights Warrior, Visionary," in *Women Public Speakers in the United States, 1925–1993*, ed. Karlyn Kohrs Campbell (Westport, CT: Greenwood Press, 1994), 424–435.

19. Price and Markham, "Fannie Lou Townsend Hamer," 431.

20. Interview by Maegan Parker Brooks with Reverend Edwin King, Jackson, Mississippi, June 17, 2007.

21. Interview by author with King; and Interview by Davis W. Houck and Maegan Parker Brooks with Charles McLaurin, Ruleville, Mississippi, April 10, 2010.

22.   Prior to the 2011 publication of *The Speeches of Fannie Lou Hamer*, only four of Fannie Lou Hamer's speeches had been published. For anthologies featuring Hamer's speeches (in chronological order), see Fannie Lou Hamer, "It's In Your Hands," in *Black Women in White America: A Documentary History*, ed. Gerda Lerner (New York: Vintage, 1972), 609–614; Fannie Lou Hamer, "Testimony of Fannie Lou Hamer," in *We Want Our Freedom: Rhetoric of the Civil Rights Movement*, ed. W. Stuart Towns (Westport, CT: Praeger, 2002), 167–172; Fannie Lou Hamer, "Untitled Speech 1964," in *Rhetoric, Religion, and the Civil Rights Movement, 1954–1965*, ed. Davis W. Houck and David E. Dixon (Waco, TX: Baylor University Press, 2006), 789–793; and Fannie Lou Hamer, "Untitled Speech," in *Women and the Civil Rights Movement, 1954–1965*, ed. Davis W. Houck and David E. Dixon (Jackson: University Press of Mississippi, 2009), 280–287.

23. The close reading approach to studying public address, which has become increasingly popular in rhetorical studies over the last thirty years, can be likened to the "new criticism" movement in literary studies. Like new criticism, close reading places the text at the center of analysis and seeks to better understand how a piece of discourse operates by moving beyond its surface-level features and unpacking core elements such as its syntactical construction, stylistic devices, and argument patterns, et cetera. This approach to rhetorical analysis is not without its detractors, however. Critics point to the danger of close analysis becoming an end in itself—occurring in a vacuum with little to no connection to the social/historical dimension of rhetorical practice. Mindful of these concerns, I couple the close textual analysis of Hamer's discourse with both oral history interviews and historical/contextual consideration. When woven together, this approach does more than eschew critiques of formalism, it provides a nuanced account of Hamer's public address and points to myriad ways in which texts both shape and are shaped by historical context. For more on close textual analysis, new criticism, and its detractors, see Celeste Condit, "Rhetorical Criticism and Audiences: The Extremes of McGee and Leff," *Western Journal of Speech Communication* 54 (1990): 330–345; Stanley Fish, *Self-consuming Artifacts* (Berkeley: University of California Press, 1972); Michael C. Leff, "Interpretation and the Art of the Rhetorical Critic," *Western Journal of Speech Communication* 44 (1980): 337–349; James Jasinski, "Close Reading," in *Sourcebook on Rhetoric: Key Concepts in Contemporary Rhetorical Studies* (Thousand Oaks, CA: Sage, 2001), 91–97; Stephen E. Lucas, "The Renaissance of American Public Address: Text and Context in Rhetorical Criticism," *Quarterly Journal of Speech* 74 (1988): 241–260; Martin J. Medhurst, "The Academic Study of Public Address: A Tradition in Transition," in *Landmark Essays on American Public Address*, ed. Martin J. Medhurst (Davis, CA: Hermagoras Press, 1993); Barbara Warnick, "Leff in Context: What Is the Critic's Role?," *Quarterly Journal of Speech* 78 (1992): 232–237.

24. In the introduction to her edited collection, *Civil Rights History from the Ground Up: Local Struggles, A National Movement*, Emilye Crosby offers a valuable review of historiographical literature constituting the shift to a "bottom-up," in contrast to "top-down," approach to movement studies. See "Introduction: The Politics of Writing

and Teaching Movement History," in *Civil Rights History from the Ground Up: Local Struggles, A National Movement*, ed. Emilye Crosby (Athens: University of Georgia Press, 2011), 1–39.

25. The "conservative master narrative" emphasizes a singular sanitized "movement" popularized by the media and top-down historical accounts, which focus "heavily on Martin Luther King Jr., nonviolence, national organizations, and the legal and legislative victories that serve as movement milestones." Crosby, "Introduction," *Civil Rights History from the Ground Up*, 5.

26. The historiographical shift to bottom-up studies of black freedom struggles ushered in a longer view of "the movement." It is quite common for bottom-up studies to recover traditions of resistance within the communities they study stretching back to WWII, or even to Popular Front–era activism. Similarly, these community studies follow the consequences of the mid-century surge in movement activity by considering how struggles continued into the 1970s and 1980s. J. Todd Moye's study of Sunflower County, for example, stretches well beyond the traditional 1954–1968 time frame, considering the period between 1945 and 1986. See Moye, *Let the People Decide*, 2004. For more on the "long view," see Jacquelyn Dowd Hall, "The Long Civil Rights Movement and the Political Uses of the Past," *Journal of American History* 91 (March 2005): 1233–1263. See also Steven F. Lawson's defense of the traditional time frame in "Long Origins of the Short Civil Rights Movement, 1954–1968," *Freedom Rights: New Perspectives on the Civil Rights Movement and the Struggle for Black Equality in the Twentieth Century* (Lexington: University of Kentucky Press, 2011), 9–37.

27. Clayborne Carson suggested that "black freedom struggle" would be a more accurate and encompassing label than "civil rights movement," in "Civil Rights Reform and the Black Freedom Struggle," in *The Civil Rights Movement in America*, ed. Charles W. Eagles (Jackson: University Press of Mississippi, 1986), 19–32.

28.   See, for example, Christina Greene, *Our Separate Ways: Women and the Black Freedom Movement in Durham, North Carolina* (Chapel Hill: University of North Carolina Press, 2005); Hasan Kwame Jeffries, *Bloody Lowndes: Civil Rights and Black Power in Alabama's Black Belt* (New York: New York University Press, 2009); and Moye, *Let the People Decide*, 2004.

29.   See, for example, Emilye Crosby, *A Little Taste of Freedom: The Black Freedom Struggle in Claiborne County, Mississippi* (Chapel Hill: University of North Carolina Press, 2005); and Chris Myers Asch, *The Senator and the Sharecropper: The Freedom Struggles of James O. Eastland and Fannie Lou Hamer* (Chapel Hill: University of North Carolina Press, 2008).

30. For example, Crosby concludes her edited collection with a detailed consideration of "Teaching Movement History." Insisting that "[we] must reclaim our symbols," Crosby explains that by "centering ordinary people who did extraordinary things" we are forced to "reconsider what this movement was about, how it worked, what it accomplished, and what remains to be done." See "Conclusion: 'Doesn't Everybody Want to Grow Up to Be Ella Baker?': Teaching Movement History," *Civil Rights History from the Ground Up*, 472.

31. Movement activist and historian Bernice Johnson Reagon defines a speaker's "signature" as that which is delivered in his or her "distinctive voice," and argues "[w]ithin African-American culture, there is a very high standard placed on the moment when

one not only makes a solid statement of the song or the sermon, but the offering is given in one's own signature." See Bernice Johnson Reagon, "'Nobody Knows the Trouble I See'; or 'By and By I'm Gonna Lay Down my Heavy Load,'" *Journal of American History* 78, no. 1 (June 1991): 118.

32. Dittmer concludes *Local People* with this memory from Charles McLaurin, SNCC activist, Hamer's campaign manager and close personal friend: "when I talked with Mrs. Hamer for the last time shortly before her death, she said, 'Mac, we ain't free yet. The kids need to know their mission,'" 434.

CHAPTER 1

1. Quotation for epigraph taken from *Freedom Is a Constant Struggle: Songs of the Freedom Movement*, ed. Guy Carawan and Candie Carawan (New York: Oak Publications, 1968), 109.

2. Chris Myers Asch, *The Senator and the Sharecropper: The Freedom Struggles of James O. Eastland and Fannie Lou Hamer* (Chapel Hill: University of North Carolina Press, 2008), 50.

3. Asch, *The Senator and the Sharecropper*, 67.

4. Hortense Powdermaker's findings from her study *After Freedom* (New York: Atheneum, 1968), as analyzed in Charles M. Payne, *I've Got the Light of Freedom: The Organizing Tradition and the Mississippi Freedom Struggle* (Berkeley: University of California Press, 1995), 23.

5. Maulana Karenga, "Nommo, Kawaida, and Communicative Practice: Bringing Good into the World," in *Understanding African American Rhetoric: Classical Origins to Contemporary Innovations*, ed. Ronald L. Jackson and Elaine B. Richardson (New York: Routledge, 2003), 14–15. Karenga draws heavily upon the groundbreaking work of Molefi K. Asante, *Afrocentricity* (Trenton, NJ: Africa World Press, 1988).

6. J. Todd Moye, *Let the People Decide: Black Freedom and White Resistance Movements in Sunflower County, 1945–1986* (Chapel Hill: University of North Carolina Press, 2004), 109.

7. Dr. L. C. Dorsey cited in Moye, *Let the People Decide*, 109.

8. Powdermaker, *After Freedom*, 88.

9. Asch, *The Senator and the Sharecropper*, 72.

10. The *Chicago Tribune* and the Tuskegee Institute each kept statistics about lynching in the United States. See also Neil R. McMillen, *Dark Journey: Black Mississippians in the Age of Jim Crow* (Urbana: University of Illinois Press, 1989), 306–307.

11. See, for example, J. H. O'Dell, "Life in Mississippi: An Interview with Fannie Lou Hamer," *Freedomways* 5 (1965): 231.

12. Fannie Lou Hamer, *To Praise Our Bridges*, in *Mississippi Writers: Reflections of Childhood and Youth*, vol. 2, ed. Dorothy Abbott (Jackson: University Press of Mississippi, 1986), 5.

13. O'Dell, "Life in Mississippi," 231.

14. Interview with Jean and Charlie Sweet by Maegan Parker Brooks, April 24, 2007, Madison, Wisconsin.

15. Hamer, *To Praise Our Bridges*, 17.

16. "Fannie Lou Hamer Speaks Out," *Essence* 1, no. 6 (1971): 54.

17. Interview with Fannie Lou Hamer by Robert Wright, August 6, 1968, Oral History Collection, Civil Rights Documentation Project, Moorland-Springarn Research Center, Howard University.

18. Interview with Hamer by Wright.

19. Hamer, *To Praise Our Bridges*, 6.

20. Interview with Hamer by Wright; Fannie Lou Hamer, "Songs My Mother Taught Me," audio-recording accompanying papers, Amistad Research Center, Tulane University, New Orleans. Tape produced by Bernice Johnson Reagon, financed by the We Shall Overcome Fund and the National Endowment for the Humanities, 1980. Songs taped by Worth Long and Julius Lester.

21. Hamer, "Fannie Lou Hamer Speaks Out," 54.

22.   Hamer, "Fannie Lou Hamer Speaks Out," 54.

23. Stokely Carmichael's memory cited in Moye, *Let the People Decide*, 103.

24. Hamer, "Songs My Mother Taught Me."

25. June Jordan, *Fannie Lou Hamer* (New York: Thomas Y. Crowell Company, 1972), 12.

26. Hamer, "Fannie Lou Hamer Speaks Out," 54.

27. See, for example, Fannie Lou Hamer, "Until I Am Free, You Are Not Free Either," Speech Delivered at the University of Wisconsin, Madison, January 1971, in *The Speeches of Fannie Lou Hamer: To Tell It Like It Is*, ed. Maegan Parker Brooks and Davis W. Houck (Jackson: University Press of Mississippi, 2011), 123.

28.   Hamer, *To Praise Our Bridges*, 11.

29.   Hamer, *To Praise Our Bridges*, 6.

30. John Dittmer notes that as late as 1950, "70 percent of blacks twenty-five years of age or older had less than a seventh-grade education." See *Local People: The Struggle for Civil Rights in Mississippi* (Urbana: University of Illinois Press, 1995), 34.

31. Asch, *The Senator and the Sharecropper*, 56. John Dittmer also cites the statistic that as late as 1950, Mississippi "spent $122.93 per pupil for the education of whites and $32.55 for blacks." See *Local People*, 34.

32. Asch, *The Senator and the Sharecropper*, 56.

33. Hamer, *To Praise Our Bridges*, 9.

34.   Jordan, *Fannie Lou Hamer*, 15.

35. Interview with Fannie Lou Hamer by Dr. Neil McMillen, April 14, 1972, and January 25, 1973, Ruleville, Mississippi. Oral History Program, University of Southern Mississippi, in *The Speeches of Fannie Lou Hamer*, 148.

36.   Interview with Dr. L. C. Dorsey by Maegan Parker Brooks, June 10, 2007, Jackson, Mississippi.

37. Interview with Jean and Charlie Sweet by Maegan Parker Brooks. Interview with Greg Bell by Maegan Parker Brooks, May 7, 2007 (phone).

38. Hamer, *To Praise Our Bridges*, 11.

39.   Interview with Dr. Leslie McLemore by Maegan Parker Brooks, June 13, 2007, Jackson, Mississippi.

40. Interview with Hamer by Wright.

41. Hamer, "Until I am Free," in *The Speeches of Fannie Lou Hamer*, 124.

42. Hamer uses this same characterization of her behavior in both the Wright interview and "Until I Am Free," in *The Speeches of Fannie Lou Hamer*, 124.

43.   In "The Prosegregation Argument," historian Neil R. McMillen explicates the Citizens' Council's arguments for segregation, including the assertion that "blacks were

more prone to disease." See *The Citizens' Council: Organized Resistance to the Second Reconstruction, 1954–1964* (Urbana: University of Illinois Press, 1994), 187.

44. Interview with Hamer by Wright.

45. Interview with Vergie Hamer Faulkner by Maegan Parker Brooks, April 9, 2010, Memphis, Tennessee.

46. I say "reportedly" here because Asch claims, "Fannie Lou gave birth to two stillborn children," but he does not cite a source for this information and I have not encountered it elsewhere. See Asch, *The Senator and the Sharecropper*, 58.

47. Interview with Faulkner by author.

48. O'Dell, "Life in Mississippi," 232.

49. Interview with Vergie Hamer Faulkner by Maegan Parker Brooks, July 14 and July 17, 2009, in *The Speeches of Fannie Lou Hamer*, 198.

50.   Interview with Faulkner by author.

51. O'Dell, "Life in Mississippi," 232.

52. Quotation adapted from W. E. B. DuBois, "We return. We return from fighting. We return fighting" in "Returning Soldiers," *Crisis* (May 1919): 13.

53. Asch, *The Senator and the Sharecropper*, 141.

54.   Charles Payne cites an interview with Mrs. Hamer by Anne Romaine in which he claims she is "vague" about the time of her NAACP memberships—he interprets this to suggest it was possible she was involved during the 1950s. Further, he borrows from Kay Mills's biography, noting that Hamer "regularly attended the annual Mound Bayou Days organized by TRM Howard," which, he reasons, "would have brought her into contact with the NAACP and RCNL networks." Finally, he mentions an interview he conducted with Hollis Watkins wherein Watkins remembers Amzie Moore introducing him to Mrs. Hamer on a tour of the Delta that took place months before the mass meeting on August 27, 1962, which Hamer usually marks as the moment of her political awakening. See Payne, *I've Got the Light of Freedom*, 155, and accompanying note 27.

55. Asch, *The Senator and the Sharecropper*, 141.

56.   The widely circulated "Black Monday" reference was coined by Mississippi judge Tom Brady, whose attack against the Supreme Court decision and "diatribe against the Negro race" was so titled. During the 1956 legislative session, the Mississippi House "passed a bill requiring the State Library Commission to buy books promoting white supremacy." Dittmer, *Local People*, 60.

57. Dittmer, *Local People*, 47.

58. Dittmer, *Local People*, 45.

59.   McMillen, *The Citizens' Council*, 159.

60. McMillen, *The Citizens' Council*, 161.

61. These genetic differences were frequently discussed on their weekly radio program. See, for example, Dr. Robert Gayre, n.d., "Racial Differences," Citizens' Council Radio Forum, Tape #6249, Mississippi State University, Starkville, MS; See also Carleton Putnam, n.d., "Race and Reason: A Yankee View," Citizens' Council Radio Forum, Tape #6219R.

62.   McMillen, *The Citizens' Council*, 185.

63.   Moye separates these movements in Sunflower County into "waves"—the first consisting of a "tiny group of black professionals and farm owners materialized in the years surrounding *Brown* and this was beaten back by white segregationists" and the

second "revolved around the charismatic personality of a farm worker named Fannie Lou Hamer. This was a poor people's movement, and its participants defined it as a human rights struggle as much as a civil rights movement." Moye, *Let the People Decide*, 25.

64. Hamer, "Songs My Mother Taught Me."

65. Hamer, *To Praise Our Bridges*, 18.

66. Henry H. Mitchell, *Black Preaching: The Recovery of a Powerful Art* (Nashville, TN: Abingdon Press, 1990), 20.

67. Mitchell, *Black Preaching*, 20 and 105, respectively.

68. Michael Walzer describes the functions of this narrative in *Exodus and Revolution* (New York: Basic Books, 1985), 7–8.

69. Interview with Dorsey by author.

70. Leroy Fitts, *A History of Black Baptists* (Nashville, TN: Broadman, 1985), 222.

71. Interview with Owen Brooks by Maegan Parker Brooks, June 14, 2007, Jackson, Mississippi.

72.   Fannie Lou Hamer, "We're On Our Way," Speech Delivered at a Mass Meeting in Indianola, Mississippi, September 1964, in *The Speeches of Fannie Lou Hamer*, 49.

73. Biblical typology is a form of symbolism with a predictive capacity. In this case, Bob Moses's presence in Mississippi functions as a sign or a symbol of eventual freedom.

74. William Harrison Pipes, "Old-Time Negro Preaching: An Interpretive Study," *Quarterly Journal of Speech* 33 (February 1948): 15–21.

75. See Mitchell's discussion of "The Bible as Oral Tradition," in *Black Preaching*, especially 56–62.

76. Interview with Brooks by author.

77. See Mitchell, *Black Preaching*, 20.

78.   Robert Glenn Howard, "A Theory of Vernacular Rhetoric: The Case of the 'Sinner's Prayer' Online," *Folklore* 116 (2005): 174.

79.   "Raising Cain" is a phrase used by Hamer most famously in her 1964 Testimony before the DNC. It also appears in other speeches that tell the story of her being fired from Marlow's plantation. See Fannie Lou Hamer, "Testimony Before the Credentials Committee at the Democratic National Convention," Atlantic City, New Jersey, August 22, 1964, in *The Speeches of Fannie Lou Hamer*, 43.

80. For more on common grammatical and syntactical patterns, as well as stylistic features of AAVE, see Geneva Smitherman, *Talkin and Testifyin: The Language of Black America* (Detroit, MI: Wayne State University Press, 1977).

81. The hypotactic style is characteristically complex, featuring "numerous subordinate or dependent clauses along with prepositional phrases." For a summary of hypotaxis and its opposite, parataxis, see James Jasinski, *Sourcebook on Rhetoric: Key Concepts in Contemporary Rhetorical Studies* (Thousand Oaks, CA: Sage, 2001), 540.

82. See Geneva Smitherman, *Talkin and Testifyin*; Smitherman, *Talkin That Talk: Language, Culture, and Education in America* (New York: Routledge, 2000); Smitherman, *Word from the Mother: Language and African Americans* (New York: Routledge, 2006).

83. Howard, "A Theory of Vernacular Rhetoric," 175.

84. Robert Glenn Howard makes this observation in "The Vernacular Web of Participatory Media," *Critical Studies in Media Communication* 25 (2008): 493.

85. Interview with King by author.

86. Interview with Dr. L. C. Dorsey by author.

87. Interview with Dr. Leslie McLemore by author.

88. Interview with Dr. L. C. Dorsey by author.

89. Franklyn Peterson, "Sunflowers Don't Grow in Sunflower County," *Sepia* 19 (1970): 17.

90. Quoted in Kay Mills, *This Little Light of Mine: The Life of Fannie Lou Hamer* (New York: Plume, 1993), 19.

91. Quoted in Mills, *This Little Light of Mine*, 20.

92. Bernice Johnson Reagon, "Let the Church Sing 'Freedom,'" *Black Music Research Journal* 7 (1987): 111. See also Bernice Johnson Reagon, *The Songs Are Free with Bill Moyers* (New York: Mystic Fire Video, 1991).

93.   Reagon, "Let the Church Sing 'Freedom,'" 112.

94. Reagon, "Let the Church Sing 'Freedom,'" 112.

95.   Molly McGehee, "'You Do Not Own What You Cannot Control': An Interview with Activist and Folklorist Worth Long," *Mississippi Folklife* 31, no. 1 (Fall 1998): 15.

96. Reagon, "Let the Church Sing 'Freedom,'" 109.

97. Interview with Reverend Edwin King by Maegan Parker Brooks, June 15, 2007, Jackson, Mississippi.

98. Both her campaign manager Charles McLaurin and friend Edwin King attest to how seriously Hamer took her role as an orator. Both McLaurin and King told me how she would strive to understand her rhetorical purpose and the best way to convey her message, revising her speeches continually over time. Interview with Charles McLaurin by Davis W. Houck and Maegan Parker Brooks, April 10, 2010, Ruleville, Mississippi. Interview with King by author.

99. See Mitchell's discussion of "The Sermon as a Creative Partnership," in *Black Preaching*, 123–127; see also Hamer, "We're On Our Way," in *The Speeches of Fannie Lou Hamer*; in this speech, for example, Hamer informs her audience: "You can pray until you faint, but if you don't get up and try to do something, God is not going to put it in your lap" (53).

100. For an in-depth look at nineteenth-century African American women's activism in the northern United States, see Carla L. Peterson, *"Doers of the Word": African-American Women Speakers & Writers in the North* (New Brunswick, NJ: Rutgers University Press, 1998).

101. McMillen details the "God was a segregationist" argument; see McMillen, *Citizens' Council*, 177.

102. The house divided refrain was very common in Hamer's public discourse. See, for example, *The Speeches of Fannie Lou Hamer*, 50, 52, 102, 120, 129, 137, and 182.

103. Interview with Fannie Lou Hamer by Anne and Howard Romaine, 1966, Wisconsin Historical Society, Madison, Wisconsin (WHS).

104. Hamer, "Until I Am Free," 125.

105. Quoted in Edwin King, "Go Tell It on the Mountain: A Prophet from the Delta," *Sojourner* (December 1982).

106. The characterization "chicken-eatin'" preachers or ministers was commonly used by Hamer. See, for example, *The Speeches of Fannie Lou Hamer*, 71, 91, and 118.

107. Moye, *Let the People Decide*, 36.

108. Hamer, "We're On Our Way," 49.

109. Asch, *The Senator and the Sharecropper*, 60.

110. Observations like this one are made by anthropologists Hortense Powdermaker and John Dollard as well as by historians Charles M. Payne, John Dittmer, and Chris Myers Asch. See, for example, Asch's discussion of Dollard's observations in *The Senator and the Sharecropper*, 60.

111. See also Asch's discussion of Powdermaker's observations in *The Senator and the Sharecropper*, 60, and accompanying note 50.

112. Dittmer, *Local People*, 76.

113. Dittmer, *Local People*, 77.

114. Fannie Lou Hamer, "Go Tell It on the Mountain," in *Voices of the Civil Rights Movement: Black American Freedom Songs, 1960–1966* (Washington, DC: Smithsonian Folkways, 1997).

115. Dittmer, *Local People*, 104.

116. Interview with Charles Cobb by Maegan Parker Brooks, September 25, 2012 (phone).

117. Dittmer, *Local People*, 136.

118. Wesley C. Hogan, *Many Minds, One Heart: SNCC's Dream for a New America* (Chapel Hill: University of North Carolina Press, 2007), 65.

119. Payne, *I've Got the Light of Freedom*, 141.

120. Interview with Hamer by McMillen, 180.

121. Barbara Ransby, *Ella Baker and the Black Freedom Movement: A Radical Democratic Vision* (Chapel Hill: University of North Carolina Press, 2003), 365.

122. Ransby, *Ella Baker and the Black Freedom Movement*, 364.

123. Joanne Grant, "Mississippi Politics: A Day in the Life of Ella J. Baker," in *The Black Woman: An Anthology*, ed. Toni Cade Bambara and Eleanor W. Traylor (New York: Washington Square Press, 2005), 67.

124. Interview with McLaurin by author.

125. Quoted in Dittmer, *Local People*, 129.

126. Dittmer, *Local People*, 109.

127. Interview with McLaurin by author.

128. Vergie Hamer Faulkner remembers her mother's initial reluctance and Mrs. Mary Tucker's encouragement and explanation. Faulkner, "Address at Southern States Communication Association," Memphis, Tennessee, April 9, 2010. Recording and transcript in author's possession. Hamer biographer Chana Kai Lee also notes that Hamer was not interested in the initial planning meeting held at her friend Mary Tucker's house, but later reconsidered Tucker's invitation to learn about voting rights and attended the service at William Chapel. See Chana Kai Lee, *For Freedom's Sake* (Urbana: University of Illinois Press, 1999), 24.

129. Interview with Hamer by Wright.

130. Interview with Hamer by Wright.

131. Bevel was born in Itta Bena, Mississippi, in 1936 and received his bachelor of arts degree from the American Baptist Theology Seminary in 1961.

132. Interview with Hamer by Wright.

133. At least two different accounts exist regarding the inception of Fannie Lou Hamer's civil rights activism. One account, promulgated principally by Charles Evers and passed along by several scholars (see note 54 above), suggests that Hamer was an early participant in the Regional Council of Negro Leadership (RCNL), a progressive civil rights organization founded in Cleveland, Mississippi, by the legendary

physician Dr. T. R. M. Howard in 1951. The second account, which I've privileged here is that Hamer's activism dates to August 1962 when she attended a meeting at William Chapel Church and heard SNCC's James Bevel and James Forman encourage local Ruleville blacks to attempt to register to vote. The plausibility of this second account is accentuated by the fact that Hamer never mentions the RCNL in her autobiography nor does she attribute her activist awakening to an RCNL meeting in any oral history or speech of which I am aware. Thanks to Davis W. Houck for bringing this biographical discrepancy to my attention.

134. Interview with Charles McLaurin by author.
135. Asch, *The Senator and the Sharecropper*, 170.
136. Quoted in Danny Collum, "Stepping Out into Freedom" *Sojourners* 11 (1982).
137. Interview with Fannie Lou Hamer by Project South, 1965, MFDP Chapter 55, Box 6, Folder 160, Department of Special Collections, Stanford University Libraries, Stanford, California.
138. Asch, *The Senator and the Sharecropper*, 16.
139. Asch, *The Senator and the Sharecropper*, 14.
140. Interview with Hamer by Wright.
141. Interview with Hamer by Project South.
142. Interview with Hamer by Project South.
143. Quoted in Mills, *This Little Light of Mine*, 37.
144. As remembered by Charles Cobb, "Fannie Lou Hamer 1917–1977," *Veterans of the Civil Rights Movement*. Available online, accessed February 8, 2007, http://www.crmvet.org/mem/hamer.htm.
145. Interview with Hamer by Wright.
146. Hamer, "Testimony before the Credentials Committee," *The Speeches of Fannie Lou Hamer*, 44.
147. Interview with Hamer by McMillen, 152.
148. Hamer, "Songs My Mother Taught Me."
149. Interview with Ambassador Andrew Young by Maegan Parker Brooks, June 25, 2007, Atlanta, Georgia.
150. Interview with Young by author.
151. "I train the people to do their own talking": Septima Clark and Women in the Civil Rights Movement from Interviews by Jacquelyn Dowd Hall and Eugene P. Walker, Compiled by Katherine Mellen Charron and David P. Cline in *Southern Cultures* 16, no. 2 (2010): 48.
152. Interview with McLaurin by author.

CHAPTER 2

1. Fannie Lou Hamer, "I Don't Mind My Light Shining," Speech Delivered at a Freedom Vote Rally in Greenwood, Mississippi, Fall 1963, in *The Speeches of Fannie Lou Hamer: "To Tell It Like It Is,"* ed. Maegan Parker Brooks and Davis W. Houck (Jackson: University Press of Mississippi, 2011), 4–6.
2. J. Todd Moye, *Let the People Decide: Black Freedom and White Resistance Movements in Sunflower County, 1945–1986* (Chapel Hill: University of North Carolina Press, 2004), 38.

3. David Howard-Pitney explores this tradition in African American appeals for so-cial justice, defining the Jeremiad as "a lamentation or doleful complaint," a term "derive[d] from the Old Testament prophet, Jeremiah, who warned of Israel's fall and the destruction of the Jerusalem temple . . . as punishment for the people's failure to keep the Mosaic covenant." See Howard-Pitney, *The Afro-American Jeremiad: Appeals for Justice in America* (Philadelphia: Temple University Press, 1990), 6.

4. In particular, see Howard-Pitney's discussion of "The Black Jeremiad and the Jackson Phenomenon," in *The Afro-American Jeremiad*, 185–194.

5. Hamer subscribed to what Walzer labels the "optimistic view of the effects of oppression on ordinary men and women," in his second chapter, "The Murmurings: Slaves in the Wilderness." See Walzer, *Exodus and Revolution*, 41–45.

6. John Dittmer, *Local People: The Struggle for Civil Rights in Mississippi* (Urbana: University of Illinois Press, 1995), 425.

7. Charles M. Payne, *I've Got the Light of Freedom: The Organizing Tradition and the Mississippi Freedom Struggle* (Berkeley: University of California Press, 1995), 70.

8. Wesley C. Hogan, *Many Minds, One Heart: SNCC's Dream for a New America* (Chapel Hill: University of North Carolina Press, 2007), 147.

9. Hogan, *Many Minds*, 2

10. Thomas B. Farrell, *Norms of Rhetorical Culture* (New Haven, CT: Yale University Press, 1993), 103.

11. Chris Myers Asch, *The Senator and the Sharecropper: The Freedom Struggles of James O. Eastland and Fannie Lou Hamer* (Chapel Hill: University of North Carolina Press, 2008), 180–181.

12. Interview with Charles Cobb by Maegan Parker Brooks, September 25, 2012 (phone), and Asch, *The Senator and the Sharecropper*, 181, respectively.

13. This phrase is taken from a SNCC fieldworker's characterization of the region. See Charles Cobb, "Special Report: Deprivation and Dissatisfaction in the Mississippi Delta," July 1964, Box 50, Mississippi Project Folder (SNCC Papers), Martin Luther King Jr. Library and Archives, Dr. Martin Luther King Jr. Center for Nonviolent Social Change, Atlanta.

14. Karlyn Kohrs Campbell, "Agency: Promiscuous and Protean," *Communication and Critical/Cultural Studies* 2, no. 1 (2005): 4, 2, 4–5.

15. See, for example, Aristotle, *Rhetoric*, translated by W. R. Roberts (New York: Modern Library, 1954); Wayne C. Booth, *The Rhetoric of Fiction*, 2nd. ed. (Chicago: University of Chicago Press, 1983), 73 and 83; and Eugene Garver, *Aristotle's Rhetoric: An Art of Character* (Chicago: University of Chicago Press, 1994).

16. Interview with Dorie Ladner by Maegan Parker Brooks, September 15, 2012 (phone).

17. This insight is taken from biographer Chana Kai Lee's interview with Perry Hamer. See Lee, *For Freedom's Sake: The Life of Fannie Lou Hamer* (Urbana: University of Illinois Press, 1999), 35, note 48.

18. Hamer, "Testimony Before the Credentials Committee," 44.

19. Dittmer, *Local People*, 138.

20. Payne, *I've Got the Light of Freedom*, 156.

21. Interview with Charles McLaurin by Davis W. Houck and Maegan Parker Brooks, April 10, 2010, Ruleville, Mississippi.

22.   Interview with Vergie Hamer Faulkner by Maegan Parker Brooks in *The Speeches of Fannie Lou Hamer*, 199.

23. Kay Griffin-Jeuchter, "Fannie Lou Hamer: From Sharecropper to Freedom Fighter" (Master's thesis, Sarah Lawrence College, 1990), 34.

24. Lee, *For Freedom's Sake*, 57.

25. Hamer, "I Don't Mind My Light Shining," 5.

26. Interview with Fannie Lou Hamer by Dr. Neil McMillen, April 14, 1972, and January 25, 1973, Ruleville, Mississippi. Oral History Program, University of Southern Mississippi, in *The Speeches of Fannie Lou Hamer*, 153.

27. Interview with Hamer by McMillen.

28.   Jerry DeMuth, "'Tired of Being Sick and Tired,'" *Nation*, June 1, 1964, 550.

29.   Moye, *Let the People Decide*, 108.

30. Interview with Hamer by McMillen, 155.

31. Interview with Hamer by McMillen, 155.

32. See Dittmer, *Local People*, 171–173.

33. Cotton refers to Hamer in several places as a "star Citizenship Education Program graduate" and a "star worker and participant" in their program. See Dorothy F. Cotton, *"If Your Back's Not Bent": The Role of the Citizenship Education Program in the Civil Rights Movement* (New York: Atria Books, 2012), ebook edition, Loc 2463 and 2995, respectively.

34.   Cotton, *"If Your Back's Not Bent,"* Loc 486.

35. Cotton, *"If Your Back's Not Bent,"* Loc 1929.

36.   The author wishes to thank Davis W. Houck, whose account of the events that transpired in Winona between June 9 and June 12, 1963, is unparalleled. Houck's explanation is carefully constructed from Hamer's FBI files, a transcript of the federal trial held on December 2–6 in Oxford, Mississippi, newspaper reports, reports filed with the Mississippi State Sovereignty Commission, speech texts, autobiographies, oral histories, and personal interviews with Lawrence Guyot, Rosemary Freeman Massey, John Rosenberg, Vergie Hamer Faulkner, Tracy Sugarman, and John Frazier. Houck's thorough and painstakingly researched narrative of these events makes an invaluable contribution not only to Hamer-related studies, but also to the history of police brutality in the American South.

37. For more on Winona's connection to the Citizens' Council, see Davis W. Houck, "Fannie Lou Hamer on Winona: Memory, Trauma, and Recovery," in *The Rhetorical History of the United States: Social Controversy and Public Address in the 1960s and Early 1970s*, ed. Richard Jensen and David Henry (forthcoming 2013).

38. Quoted in Annell Ponder, "Notarized Statement of Abuse in Winona," July 29, 1964. Access No: Z/1867.000/S Folder 15. B1-R74-B1-53 Box 4. Manuscript Collection, Special Collections Section, Mississippi Department of Archives and History, Jackson (MDAH).

39.   Herod cited in Houck, "Fannie Lou Hamer on Winona."

40. Hamer, "Testimony Before a Select Panel on Mississippi and Civil Rights," in *The Speeches of Fannie Lou Hamer*, 38.

41. Herod cited in Houck, "Fannie Lou Hamer on Winona."

42. Dittmer discusses the circumstances surrounding Reverend C. T. Vivian's arrest and beating, see *Local People*, 94–96. Payne cites Hollis Watkins's refusal to use the courtesy title "sir" during his interrogation upon arrest, see *I've Got the Light of Freedom*, 12.

43.   Ponder cited in Hamer, "We're On Our Way," in *The Speeches of Fannie Lou Hamer: "To Tell It Like It Is,"* 51.

44. The details of West's beating are most thoroughly recounted in Houck, "Fannie Lou Hamer on Winona."

45.   Hamer, "Testimony Before a Select Panel on Mississippi and Civil Rights," 38.

46. Basinger's insult is cited in Houck, "Fannie Lou Hamer on Winona."

47. Interview with Fannie Lou Hamer by Robert Wright, August 6, 1968, Oral History Collection, Civil Rights Documentation Project, Moorland-Springarn Research Center, Howard University.

48. "The Winona Incident, An Interview with Annell Ponder and Fannie Lou Hamer, June 1963," reprinted in Pat Watters and Reese Cleghorn, *Climbing Jacob's Ladder: The Arrival of Negroes in Southern Politics* (New York: Harcourt, Brace and World, 1967), Appendix I, 364.

49. "The Winona Incident," 364.

50.   Contrary to historian Danielle L. McGuire's assertion that "Hamer did not shy away from detailing the sexual aspects of her beating," it is worth noting that though Hamer mentioned the Winona beating in nearly every one of her public speeches on record, she did not frequently feature its sexual aspects. Hamer would commonly only allude to her dress being lifted above her head and would only occasionally mention that Surrell got "hot and worked up" during her beating. In only one public address of which I am aware does Hamer go into any greater detail than this about the specifically sexual nature of her abuse. In "America Is a Sick Place, and Man Is on the Critical List," Hamer mentioned: "And during the time my dress worked up and I smoothed my dress down, one of the white men walked over and pulled my dress up, and in the process from the prisoner beating me, one of the white men was trying to feel under my clothes." See Danielle L. McGuire, *At the Dark End of the Street: Black Women, Rape, and Resistance—a New History of the Civil Rights Movement from Rosa Parks to the Rise of Black Power* (New York: Vintage, 2010), 195; Surrell's abuse is cited in "The Winona Incident," in *Climbing Jacob's Ladder*, 371; Hamer, "America Is a Sick Place, and Man Is on the Critical List," Speech Delivered at Loop College, Chicago, Illinois, May 27, 1970, in *The Speeches of Fannie Lou Hamer*, 113.

51. Hamer, "America Is a Sick Place," 113.

52. Interview with Ladner by author.

53. Hamer, "Federal Trial Testimony," Oxford, Mississippi, December 2, 1963, in *The Speeches of Fannie Lou Hamer*, 15.

54.   Interview with Lawrence Guyot by Maegan Parker Brooks, September 20, 2012 (phone).

55. Cotton, *"If Your Back's Not Bent,"* Loc 2998.

56.   Young describes the delicate task of securing the prisoners' release without winding up in the Winona jailhouse himself: "We used to say we grew up with white people, we weren't afraid of white people, and we realized that they were afraid of us. So we did everything we could to put them at ease . . . We stopped to get gas because you don't ever go into a Mississippi town with an empty tank. You fill up before you get there. But that also gives them a chance to check you out, call ahead and let the sheriff know you're coming . . . When we got to the jail, we said, 'Yes, sir'—the reason that Mrs. Hamer and Annell Ponder had been beaten was that they wouldn't say, 'Yes, sir'—that was not a big deal, see. And people say, 'Yes, sir.' I mean I grew up saying that in New Orleans. Bevel grew up saying, 'Yes, sir' in Mississippi. Even Dorothy [Cotton] is from Virginia. It wasn't any strain. We got them out of jail and got them

out of town quickly." Interview with Ambassador Andrew Young by Maegan Parker Brooks, June 25, 2007, Atlanta, Georgia.

57. Cotton, *"If Your Back's Not Bent,"* Loc 3026.

58. Linguist Geneva Smitherman defines "testifyin" as a "concept referring to a ritualized form of black communication in which the speaker gives verbal witness to the efficacy, truth, and power of some experience in which all blacks have shared" (58). The practice of image making, furthermore, imbues testimony with salience by fostering connections with the audience and enabling them to visualize the shared tribulation (97). See *Talkin and Testifyin: The Language of Black America* (Detroit, MI: Wayne State University Press, 1977).

59.   Bernice Johnson Reagon, "Nobody Knows the Trouble I See"; or, "By and By I'm Gonna Lay Down My Heavy Load," *Journal of American History* 78, no. 1 (June 1991): 119.

60. Houck cites the cases of Johnny Frazier's August 27, 1960, beating, in addition to the November 1961 torture of Jake Daniels and Freddie and Nathaniel Moore. See Houck, "Fannie Lou Hamer on Winona."

61. See, for example, McGuire's description of the treatment endured by both male and female prisoners at Parchman following the 1961 Freedom Rides in Jackson, Mississippi. McGuire, *At the Dark End of the Street*, 196.

62.   The verbal feedback is expressed in the Smithsonian recording of Hamer's "Greenwood Mass Meeting Speech 1963," available in the Moses Moon Collection, Archives Center, National Museum of American History, Smithsonian Institution, Washington, DC.

63.   Smitherman, *Talkin and Testifyin*, 97. Robert Terrill also notes the use of sentient description in African American discourse; see Robert E. Terrill, "Irony, Silence, and Time: Frederick Douglass on the Fifth of July," *Quarterly Journal of Speech* 89, no. 3 (2003): 224–225.

64. "Interview with Fannie Lou Hamer by Colin Edwards, 1965, Berkeley, California," on *Collected Speeches of Fannie Lou Hamer*, Tarabu Betserai, prod. (North Hollywood, CA: Pacifica Radio Archives, 1989).

65. Fannie Lou Hamer, "Affidavit," May 24, 1964. Access No: Z/1867.000/S Folder 15. B1-R74-B1-53 Box 4 Mississippi Department of Archives and History, Jackson (MDAH).

66. Hamer, "Affidavit," (MDAH).

67. Interview with Fannie Lou Hamer by Jack Minnis, March, 17, 1964, Winona, Mississippi (SNCC Papers), Martin Luther King Jr. Library and Archives, Martin Luther King Jr. Center for Nonviolent Social Change, Atlanta.

68. Hamer, "Federal Trial Testimony," 34.

69. Interview with Hamer by Edwards.

70. Hamer, "Federal Trial Testimony," 13.

71. Hamer, "Federal Trial Testimony," 20.

72.   Hamer, "We're On Our Way," Speech Delivered at a Mass Meeting in Indianola, Mississippi, September 1964, in *The Speeches of Fannie Lou Hamer*, 50.

73. Hamer alludes here to the biblical Book of Daniel, chapters 1–3.

74. Hamer, "I Don't Mind My Light Shining," 5.

75. Ponder's prayer cited in Hamer, "We're On Our Way," 51.

76. Fannie Lou Hamer, *To Praise Our Bridges* (Jackson, KIPCO, 1967), 17.

77. Interview with Ladner by author.
78.   Interview with McLaurin by author.
79.   Interview with McLaurin by author.
80. Moye, *Let the People Decide*, 168.
81. Moye, *Let the People Decide*, 168.
82.   "Voter Registration Figures: 1962 Registration," 1963 Report of the United States Civil Rights Commission in Box 20, File 25 (SNCC Papers).
83. 1964 Second Congressional District Campaign Press Release, n.d., in Box 52 (SNCC Papers).
84. "Mrs. Hamer and Charles McLaurin—Campaign Mgr.," Campaign Schedule, Friday, March 20–Tuesday, June 2, in Box 52 (SNCC Papers).
85. Budget," n.d., in 1964 Second Congressional District Campaign Folder in Box 52 (SNCC Papers).
86. Quotation taken from untitled document within 1964 Second Congressional District Campaign folder in Box 52 (SNCC Papers).
87. Interview with McLaurin by author.
88. Interview with McLaurin by author.
89. Interview with Hamer by McMillen, 180.
90. Interview with McLaurin by author.
91. Interview with McLaurin by author. The author wishes to thank Emilye Crosby for bringing it to my attention that SNCC activist Gwen Gillon wrote speeches for Mrs. Hamer during this period of Hamer's career. Crosby located a transcript from a SNCC staff meeting wherein Jesse Morris speaks on Gillon's behalf for her nomination to chairperson. Morris notes that Gillon "wrote speeches for Mrs. Hamer" among other contributions she made to the movement. "SNCC Staff Meeting," February 13, 1965, in Box 36, File 2, James Forman Papers, Manuscript Division, Library of Congress, Washington, DC.
92. "Candidate Biography: Mrs. Fannie Lou Hamer, Candidate for U.S. Congress Second District," Mississippi Freedom Democratic Party Folder in Box 52 (SNCC papers).
93.   Asch, *The Senator and the Sharecropper*, 130.
94. Moye, *Let the People Decide*, 31.
95.   See Henry Louis Gates Jr., *The Signifying Monkey: A Theory of African American Literary Criticism* (New York: Oxford University Press, 1988), especially 44–51.
96. Quotation taken from untitled document within 1964 Second Congressional District Campaign folder in Box 52 (SNCC Papers).
97. Smitherman suggests that "mimicry"—"a deliberate imitation of the speech and mannerisms of someone else"—"may be used for authenticity, ridicule, or rhetorical effect." *Talkin and Testifyin*, 94.
98. Smitherman describes this trope's function as one that pulls on the "threads of . . . experience common to all." *Talkin and Testifyin*, 95.
99. Quotation taken from untitled document within 1964 Second Congressional District Campaign folder in Box 52 (SNCC Papers).
100. Fannie Lou Hamer, "Testimony Before the Subcommittee on Elections of the Committee on House Administration," House of Representatives, Washington, DC, September 13, 1965, in *The Speeches of Fannie Lou Hamer*, 69.
101. Testimony of Fannie Lou Hamer in United States Congress, "Hearing Before a Select Panel on Mississippi and Civil Rights, Testimony of Fannie Lou Hamer,"

Congressional Record, 88th Cong., 2nd sess., June 4, 1964 to June 16, 1964, vol. 110, pt. 10, 14001–14002. Cited in Hamer, "Testimony Before a Select Panel on Mississippi and Civil Rights," 37.

102. Hamer, "Testimony Before a Select Panel on Mississippi and Civil Rights," 41.

103. As cited in Perry Deane Young, "A Surfeit of Surgery," *Washington Post*, May 30, 1976, 549. The fact that during these early years in her activist career Hamer rarely discussed her forced sterilization and yet she chose to do so during a public hearing recalls key tensions in historiographical accounts of black women's activism. The tension between dissemblance and public testimony is discussed in detail in the following foundational essays: See Darlene Clark Hine, "Rape and the Inner Lives of Black Women in the Middle West: Preliminary Thoughts on the Culture of Dissemblance," *Signs* 14 (Summer 1989): 912–920; See also Danielle L. McGuire, "'It Was Like All of Us Had Been Raped': Sexual Violence, Community Mobilization, and the African American Freedom Struggle," *Journal of American History* 91, no. 3 (December 2004): 906–931.

104. Hamer, "Testimony Before a Select Panel on Mississippi and Civil Rights," 40.

105. Interview with Cobb by author.

106. Dittmer, *Local People*, 108.

107. Dittmer, *Local People*, 264.

108. Charlie Cobb Jr. quoted in Jerry Mitchell, "Freedom Schools for another generation," *Clarion-Ledger Online*, July 30, 2010, http://blogs.clarionledger.com/jmitchell/tag/charles-cobb-jr/.

109. Interview with Ladner by author.

110. Interview with Vergie Hamer Faulkner by Maegan Parker Brooks, April 10, 2010, Ruleville, Mississippi.

111. Interview with McLaurin by author.

112. Endesha Ida Mae Holland, a Greenwood native, quoted in *Freedom on My Mind*. DVD. Directed by Connie Field and Marilyn Mulford. South Burlington, VT: California Newsreel, 1994.

113. As explained in *Freedom on My Mind*.

114. Clayborne Carson, *In Struggle: SNCC and the Black Awakening of the 1960s* (Cambridge, MA: Harvard University Press, 1981), 112.

115. As quoted in Carson, *In Struggle*, 112.

116. Interview with Rita Schwerner Bender by Maegan Parker Brooks, July 15, 2010, Seattle, Washington.

117. Interview with Cobb by author.

118. Hogan, *Many Minds, One Heart*, 153.

119. Interview with Cobb by author.

120. Interview with Cobb by author.

121. Interview with Cobb by author.

122. J. Todd Moye, "Focusing Our Eyes on the Prize: How Community Studies Are Reframing and Rewriting the History of the Civil Rights Movement" in *Civil Rights History from the Ground Up: Local Struggles, A National Movement*, ed. Emilye Crosby (Athens: University of Georgia Press, 2011), 153; Interview with Cobb by author.

123. Incident recounted in *Freedom on My Mind*. See also Dittmer, *Local People*, 358.

124. Interview with Bender by author.

125. Interview with Bender by author.
126. Fannie Lou Hamer, "Foreword" to Tracy Sugarman, *Stranger at the Gates: A Summer in Mississippi* (New York: Hill and Wang, 1966), vii–viii.
127. Sugarman, *Stranger at the Gates*, 114.
128. Interview with Tracy Sugarman by Maegan Parker Brooks July 13, 2010 (phone).
129. Interview with Sugarman by author.
130. Quoted in *Freedom on My Mind*.
131. Karen Brodkin Sacks later dubs this vital organizing role a "centerwoman"; see *Caring by the Hour: Women, Work, and Organizing at Duke Medical Center* (Urbana: University of Illinois Press, 1988).
132. Lee, *For Freedom's Sake*, 63 note 7.
133. Quoted in Sugarman, *Stranger at the Gates*, 114.
134. Quoted in Sugarman, *Stranger at the Gates*, 117–119.
135. Moses's approach to canvassing as described by Payne, *I've Got the Light of Freedom*, 115.
136. Hamer, *To Praise Our Bridges*, 12.
137. Interview with Fannie Lou Hamer by Anne and Howard Romaine, 1966, Wisconsin Historical Society, Madison, Wisconsin (WHS).
138. Interview with Sugarman by author.
139. Pat Watters, *Down to Now: Reflections on the Southern Civil Rights Movement* (New York: Pantheon, 1971), 30.

CHAPTER 3

Epigraph taken from interview with Reverend Jesse Jackson Sr. by Maegan Parker Brooks, March 11, 2012, Chicago, Illinois.

1. James Forman, "Freedom Push in Mississippi: Civil Rights Leader Tells Aim of Ambitious Summer Project," *Los Angeles Times*, June 14, 1964, L3.
2. John Dittmer, *Local People: The Struggle for Civil Rights in Mississippi* (Urbana: University of Illinois Press, 1995), 273.
3. Senator James O. Eastland quoted in Chris Myers Asch, *The Senator and the Sharecropper: The Freedom Struggles of James O. Eastland and Fannie Lou Hamer* (Chapel Hill: University of North Carolina Press, 2008), 206–207.
4. Dittmer, *Local People*, 273.
5. Morgan Louise Ginther, "From the Closed Society to the Realization of Freedom: Mississippi Delegation Debate at the 1964 Democratic National Convention" (Ph.D. diss., University of Memphis, 2011).
6. Quoted in Dittmer, *Local People*, 272.
7. Quoted in Dittmer, *Local People*, 283.
8. Quoted in Barbara Ransby, *Ella Baker and the Black Freedom Movement: A Radical Democratic Vision* (Chapel Hill: University of North Carolina Press, 2003), 335.
9. Freedom Summer Volunteer, Marshall Ganz quoted in *Freedom on My Mind*. DVD. Directed by Connie Field and Marilyn Mulford. South Burlington, VT: California Newsreel, 1994.
10. Dittmer, *Local People*, 286.
11. Interview with Dorie Ladner by Maegan Parker Brooks, September 15, 2012 (phone).

12. Quoted in Dittmer, *Local People*, 283.
13. Dittmer discusses the "Atlantic City operation," *Local People*, 292.
14. Interview with Dr. Leslie McLemore by Maegan Parker Brooks, June 13, 2007, Jackson, Mississippi.
15. Interview with Rita Schwerner Bender by Maegan Parker Brooks, July 15, 2010, Seattle, Washington.
16. Ginther sets the stage for the convention and the debates in her dissertation. Information on these settings is also derived from news footage used in *Freedom On My Mind* and from my interviews with MFDP members who attended the convention.
17. Interview with Bender by author.
18. Ginther, "From the Closed Society to the Realization of Freedom."
19. Joseph Rauh, Democratic National Convention. *Credentials Committee Transcript from Hearing on August 22, 1964*, Austin, Texas, Lyndon B. Johnson Presidential Library (LBJ).
20. Bernice Johnson Reagon, *The Songs Are Free with Bill Moyers* (New York: Mystic Fire Video, 1991).
21. Interview with Ladner by author.
22.   Interview with Bender by author.
23. Interview with Dr. L. C. Dorsey by Maegan Parker Brooks, June 10, 2007, Jackson, Mississippi.
24. Interview with Dorsey by author.
25. Interview with Dorsey by author.
26. Interview with Tracy Sugarman by Maegan Parker Brooks July 13, 2010 (phone).
27. Both Jackson and Young use "ungrammatical profundity," interview with Jackson, by author; Interview with Ambassador Andrew Young by Maegan Parker Brooks, June 25, 2007, Atlanta, Georgia; Dorsey refers to Hamer's speaking style as "grammatically incorrect honesty," interview with Dorsey by author.
28.   Fannie Lou Hamer, "Testimony Before the Credentials Committee at the Democratic National Convention," Atlantic City, New Jersey, August 22, 1964, in *The Speeches of Fannie Lou Hamer: To Tell It Like It Is*, ed. Maegan Parker Brooks and Davis W. Houck (Jackson: University Press of Mississippi, 2011), 43.
29. Geneva Smitherman, *Talkin and Testifyin: The Language of Black America* (Detroit, MI: Wayne State University Press, 1977), 21.
30. Hamer, "Testimony Before the Credentials Committee," 45.
31. Interview with Jackson by author.
32. Smitherman, *Talkin and Testifyin*, 20.
33. Hamer, "Testimony Before the Credentials Committee," 43–45.
34.   Interview with Jackson by author.
35. Interview with Young by author.
36.   Interview with Ladner by author.
37. Freedom Summer Volunteer Heather Booth quoted in *Freedom On My Mind*; and the Los Angeles police motto, "to protect and serve," associated with forces nationwide.
38. Hamer, "Testimony Before the Credentials Committee," 43–45.
39.   Hamer, "Testimony Before the Credentials Committee," 43–44.
40. Hamer does not mention Annell Ponder by name in this DNC address.
41. Hamer, "Testimony Before the Credentials Committee," 44.
42. Hamer, "Testimony Before the Credentials Committee," 45.

43.   Nan Robertson, "Mississippian Relates Struggle of Negro in Voter Registration," *New York Times*, August 24, 1964, 17.

44. Quoted in Chana Kai Lee, *For Freedom's Sake: The Life of Fannie Lou Hamer* (Urbana: University of Illinois Press, 1999), 90.

45.   Interview with Senator Walter Mondale by Morgan L. Ginther.

46. Bender remembers that Hamer's testimony brought many committee members to tears that afternoon. Interview with Bender by author.

47. Interview with Reverend Edwin King by author, June 15, 2007, Jackson, Mississippi.

48. Interview with Ladner by author.

49. Interview with Sugarman by author.

50.   Interview with Sugarman by author.

51. Interview with Dorsey by author.

52. Interview with Dorsey by author.

53. Interview with McLemore by author.

54.   Interview with King by author.

55. Wilkins's quotation as remembered by Hamer. See interview with Fannie Lou Hamer by Anne and Howard Romaine, 1966, Wisconsin Historical Society, Madison, Wisconsin (WHS).

56. Interview with King by author.

57. Dittmer, *Local People*, 275.

58. For more on Rustin's lecture, see Dittmer, *Local People*, 300.

59.   Interview with Young by author.

60. See Ginther, "From the Closed Society to the Realization of Freedom."

61. Justice Tom Brady, "6435R—Freedom Democratic Delegation," n.d. Transcript of Citizen's Council Radio Forums, audiotape available from the Stephanie Rolph Transcripts Addition within the Special Collections Department, Manuscripts Division at the Mississippi Department of Archives and History (MDAH), Jackson, Mississippi.

62. Brady, "6435R—Freedom Democratic Delegation," Citizen's Council Radio Forum.

63.   E. K. Collins and Ruble Griffin, testimonies within Democratic National Convention. *Credentials Committee Transcript from Hearing in August 24, 1964* (LBJ).

64. The author wishes to thank rhetorical scholar Davis W. Houck for bringing to light this significant discrepancy in the mythology surrounding Hamer's DNC testimony. As Houck discovered, there is no press conference listed in Johnson's inventory of press conferences for August 22, 1964. He also notes that the *New York Times* did not report on any such conference. Secondly, in a recorded conversation with Senator Eastland, Johnson mentions leaving for a speech shortly after Rauh's opening remarks. And third, the speech Johnson delivered in the East Room of the White House was clearly scripted and tailored to an audience of thirty governors already assembled there. So while Johnson's speech did, in fact, interrupt Hamer's testimony, it does not appear that he surreptitiously called a spurious press conference to divert the media's attention away from her address. E-mail correspondence with Davis W. Houck, January 3, 2013; see also Recording of Conversation between Senator Eastland and President Lyndon B. Johnson, August 22, 1964. Available online, accessed January 3, 2013, http://millercenter.org/scripps/archive/presidentialrecordings/johnson/1964/08_1964.

See also President Lyndon B. Johnson, "536—Remarks to a Group of Democratic Governors, August 22, 1964." available online, accessed January 3, 2013, http://www.presidency.ucsb.edu/ws/index.php?pid=26461.

Moses's biographer, Eric Burner, notes that 416 telegrams came in support of the Freedom Democrats, while one telegram supporting the Regulars was received. See Eric Burner, *And Gently He Shall Lead Them: Robert Parris Moses and Civil Rights in Mississippi* (New York: New York University Press, 1994), 175.

65.   Johnson's offensive remarks as remembered in an interview with King by author.

66. Interview with Hamer by Romaine.

67. Interview with Hamer by Romaine.

68. Memories of this closed-door meeting are recounted in Anne Romaine interviews with Hamer and Reverend Edwin King, respectively (WHS). Kay Mills also has a great description of the meeting with excerpts of the memories in *This Little Light of Mine: The Life of Fannie Lou Hamer* (New York: Plume, 1993), 124–125.

69. Interview with Ladner by author.

70. Hogan discusses the Green proposal and SNCC's inclination to accept the compromise she proposed. See Wesley C. Hogan, *Many Minds, One Heart: SNCC's Dream for a New America* (Chapel Hill: University of North Carolina Press, 2007), 195. King discusses his more complex proposal in our interview.

71. Interview with Hamer by Romaine.

72.   Hamer, "Testimony Before the Credentials Committee," 45.

73. Brady, "6435R—Freedom Democratic Delegation," Citizen's Council Radio Forum.

74. Brady, "6435R—Freedom Democratic Delegation," Citizen's Council Radio Forum.

75. This encounter was included in footage from the convention featured on Reagon, *The Songs Are Free* (video).

76. The encounter with Moses and Chancellor was recounted by Dittmer, *Local People*, 299.

77. Hogan, *Many Minds, One Heart*, 195.

78.   Interview with Jackson by author.

79.   Dittmer, *Local People*, 301–302.

80. Interview with Sugarman by author.

81. Joyce Ladner, Bob Moses, and Cleveland Sellers all quoted in Dittmer, *Local People*, 302.

82.   Interview with Ladner by author.

83. Interview with Lawrence Guyot by Maegan Parker Brooks, September 20, 2012 (phone).

84. Interview with Guyot by author.

85. Interview with Jackson by author.

86. Given the significance of Hamer's Indianola speech—the enthusiasm this speech yielded, and in light of the fact that it represents one of the lengthiest extant recordings in Hamer's corpus—it is somewhat surprising that the speech has been routinely mis-cited from even those scholars who do pay careful attention to her discourse. Janice D. Hamlet includes at least two lengthy excerpts from a speech she cites as Hamer, F. L. (1963b) "Speech delivered at mass meeting in Hattisburg [*sic*]" belonging to the Smithsonian archives' Moses Moon Collection, but according to the chief archivist of the Moses Moon Collection no such speech exists. Correspondence by author with Wendy Shay, June 4, 2008 (e-mail). Interestingly, the excerpts from the speech match my transcription of another recording within the collection—the mass meeting speech Hamer delivered in Indianola in 1964. See excerpts on pp. 567–568, as well as 569–570 in Janice D. Hamlet, "Fannie Lou Hamer: The Unquenchable Spirit of the Civil Rights Movement," *Journal of Black Studies*, 26, no. 5 (May 1996): 560–576.

Furthermore, Reagon has a book chapter exploring what seems to be the Indianola speech. Reagon's book chapter came out before Hamlet's article. Hamlet cites Reagon's chapter heavily, so the citation confusion can be traced to Reagon. However, it is thanks to Reagon's efforts that the Smithsonian has the rare Moses Moon Collection in the first place. She was the first person to secure and work with these recordings so it is entirely possible that they were miscataloged to begin with and have since been revised. I am, however, confident that the recording now labeled "N 77: Indianola, Miss. Summer 1964" was actually delivered in Indianola in 1964 and not in Hattiesburg in 1963 because Hamer makes reference to both the location and the year within her speech.

Unlike Reagon and Hamlet, Davis W. Houck and David E. Dixon, editors of the anthology *Rhetoric, Religion, and the Civil Rights Movement*, do correctly cite the Indianola Address. Houck and Dixon cite the speech as occurring in September 1964, whereas the Smithsonian refers to it as taking place in the "Summer of 1964." Houck contends that September was an educated guess for the timing of the speech based in part on the content which speaks to her newly won celebrity and in part on information received from Charles McLaurin, Hamer's campaign manager who introduced her that day, Correspondence by author with Davis Houck, June 6, 2008 (e-mail). See Davis W. Houck and David E. Dixon, "Fannie Lou Hamer," in *Rhetoric, Religion, and the Civil Rights Movement: 1954–1965* (Waco, TX: Baylor University Press, 2006), 785. See also Bernice Johnson Reagon, "Women as Culture Carriers in the Civil Rights Movement: Fannie Lou Hamer," in *Freedom is a Constant Struggle: An Anthology of the Mississippi Civil Rights Movement*, ed. Susie Erenrich (Montgomery, AL: Black Belt Press, 1999), 402. First published in V. Crawford, J. Rouse, and B. Woods, eds., *Women in the Civil Rights Movement: Trailblazers and Torchbearers, 1941–1965* (New York: Carlson, 1990), 203–217.

87. Bernice Johnson Reagon, "Nobody Knows the Trouble I See"; or, "By and By I'm Gonna Lay Down My Heavy Load," *Journal of American History* 78, no. 1 (June 1991): 117.

88. Fannie Lou Hamer, "We're On Our Way," Speech Delivered at a Mass Meeting in Indianola, Mississippi, September 1964, in *The Speeches of Fannie Lou Hamer: To Tell It Like It Is*, ed. Maegan Parker Brooks and Davis W. Houck (Jackson: University Press of Mississippi, 2011), 47 and 54, respectively.

89. Charles M. Payne, *I've Got the Light of Freedom: The Organizing Tradition and the Mississippi Freedom Struggle* (Berkeley: University of California Press, 1995), 261.

90. Dittmer, *Local People*, 131.

91. Moses quoted in Dittmer, *Local People*, 131.

92. Emilye Crosby, *A Little Taste of Freedom: The Black Freedom Struggle in Claiborne County, Mississippi* (Chapel Hill: University of North Carolina Press, 2005), 106.

93. Interview with Charles Cobb by Maegan Parker Brooks, September 25, 2012 (phone).

94. Interview with McLemore by author.

95. Interview with Young by author.

96. Alan Ribback later changed his name to Moses Moon. His remarkable collection of audio from the movement is available at the Archives Center of the Smithsonian Institution's National Museum of American History in Washington, DC.

97. Interview with Ladner by author.

98. In their analysis of Hamer's rhetoric, Bernice Price and Annie Pearle Markham note that she would often "don the mantle of the prophet" in her mass meeting orations.

See "Fannie Lou Townsend Hamer (1917–1977), Champion of the Poor, Civil Rights Warrior, Visionary," in *Women Public Speakers in the United States, 1925–1993*, ed. Karlyn Kohrs Campbell (Westport, CT: Greenwood Press, 1994), 429.

99. Hamer, "We're On Our Way," 47.
100. David Howard-Pitney, *The Afro-American Jeremiad: Appeals for Justice in America* (Philadelphia: Temple University Press, 1990), 6.
101. Howard-Pitney, *The Afro-American Jeremiad*, 15 and 12, respectively.
102. Hamer, "We're On Our Way," 53.
103. Hamer, "We're On Our Way," 52.
104. Hamer, "We're On Our Way," 48.
105. Hamer, "We're On Our Way," 52.
106. Proverbs 14:34 (NKJV) cited in Hamer, "We're On Our Way," 49 and 53.
107. Hamer, "We're On Our Way," 52.
108. Howard-Pitney, *The Afro-American Jeremiad*, 6.
109. Howard-Pitney, *The Afro-American Jeremiad*, 7
110. Howard-Pitney, *The Afro-American Jeremiad*, 6.
111. Henry Louis Gates Jr., *The Signifying Monkey: A Theory of African American Literary Criticism* (New York: Oxford University Press, 1988), 44.
112. Burke explores this concept most fully in *Permanence and Change* (Berkeley: University of California Press, 1984), 89–96. See also Kenneth Burke, *Attitudes Toward History* (Berkeley: University of California Press, 1984), 308–314.
113. Hamer, "We're On Our Way," 50.
114. Hamer, "We're On Our Way," 49.
115. Hamer, "We're On Our Way," 53.
116. Hamer, "We're On Our Way," 50.
117. Hamer, "We're On Our Way," 54.
118. Hamer, "We're On Our Way," 54.
119. Hamer, "We're On Our Way," 53.
120. Hamer, "We're On Our Way," 50.
121. Hamer, "We're On Our Way," 50.
122. Hamer, "We're On Our Way," 50.
123. Hamer, "We're On Our Way," 55.
124. Howard-Pitney, *The Afro-American Jeremiad*, 12.
125. Hamer, "We're On Our Way," 54.
126. Hamer, "We're On Our Way," 49.
127. Hamer, "We're On Our Way," 49.
128. Hamer, "We're On Our Way," 54.
129. Molly McGehee, "'You Do Not Own What You Cannot Control': An Interview with Activist and Folklorist Worth Long," *Mississippi Folklife* 31, no. 1 (Fall 1998): 15.
130. Interview with Bender by author.
131. Reagon, *The Songs Are Free* (video).
132. Payne, *I've Got the Light of Freedom*, 261.
133. Interview with Guyot by author.
134. McGehee, "'You Do Not Own What You Cannot Control,'" 20.
135. Interview with McLemore by author.
136. Reagon, "Nobody Knows the Trouble I See," 114.

CHAPTER 4

1. When they spoke together in Harlem in December 1964, Malcolm X referred to Fannie Lou Hamer as "the country's number one freedom fighting woman." Malcolm X, "With Fannie Lou Hamer," in *Malcolm X Speaks*, ed. George Breitman (New York: Grove Press, 1966).
2. Interview with Reverend Edwin King by author, June 15, 2007, Jackson, Mississippi.
3. Interview with Tracy Sugarman by Maegan Parker Brooks July 13, 2010 (phone).
4. Interview with Lawrence Guyot by Maegan Parker Brooks, September 20, 2012 (phone).
5. Bernice Johnson Reagon, *The Songs Are Free with Bill Moyers* (New York: Mystic Fire Video, 1991).
6. The title of Bob Dylan's 1964 song is quite fitting for conceptualizing Hamer's role in the greater context of upheaval. His third stanza speaks to her situation, especially: "Come senators, congressmen, please heed the call / Don't stand in the doorway. Don't block up the hall / For he that gets hurt will be he who has stalled / There's a battle outside and it is ragin' / It'll soon shake your windows and rattle your walls / For the times they are a-changin'." For the rest of the song lyrics and information about the album that bears its name, visit http://www.bobdylan.com/albums/times.html.
7. Bob Moses quoted in John Dittmer, *Local People: The Struggle for Civil Rights in Mississippi* (Urbana: University of Illinois Press, 1995), 325.
8. Hasan Kwame Jeffries, "SNCC, Black Power, and Independent Political Party Organizing in Alabama, 1964–1966," *Journal of American History* 91, no. 2 (Spring 2006): 188.
9. Jeffries, "SNCC, Black Power, and Independent Political Party," 175.
10. Jeffries, "SNCC, Black Power, and Independent Political Party Organizing," 175 and 172, respectively.
11. Jeffries, "SNCC, Black Power, and Independent Political Party Organizing," 173.
12. Chris Myers Asch, *The Senator and the Sharecropper: The Freedom Struggles of James O. Eastland and Fannie Lou Hamer* (Chapel Hill: University of North Carolina Press, 2008), 237.
13. Dittmer, *Local People*, 317.
14. See, for example, Asch's extensive discussion of Eastland's anticommunist efforts in *The Senator and the Sharecropper*. See also Governor Ross Barnett, "6417R—Concern Over CRA," Transcript of Citizens' Council Radio Forums, audiotape available from the Stephanie Rolph Transcripts Addition within the Special Collections Department, Manuscripts Division at the Mississippi Department of Archives and History (MDAH), Jackson, Mississippi.
15. Jeffries, "SNCC, Black Power, and Independent Political Party Organizing," 187.
16. Charles Morgan Jr. quoted in Asch, *The Senator and the Sharecropper*, 237.
17. Gloster Current quoted in Dittmer, *Local People*, 317.
18. Asch, *The Senator and the Sharecropper*, 224.
19. Dittmer, *Local People*, 369.
20. Interview with Harry Belafonte by Kay Mills, January 28, 1991, Los Angeles, California.
21. Julian Bond's memory of Guinea is paraphrased here from a comment Kay Mills made to Harry Belafonte during their interview. The anecdote is discussed in the interview with Belafonte by Mills.

22. Clayborne Carson, *In Struggle: SNCC and the Black Awakening of the 1960s* (Cambridge, MA: Harvard University Press, 1981), 135.

23. Fannie Lou Hamer, *To Praise Our Bridges* (Jackson, MS: KIPCO, 1967), 21.

24. Interview with Fannie Lou Hamer by Dr. Neil McMillen, January 25, 1973, Ruleville, Mississippi, in *The Speeches of Fannie Lou Hamer: To Tell It Like It Is*, ed. Maegan Parker Brooks and Davis W. Houck (Jackson: University Press of Mississippi, 2011), 159.

25. Interview with Hamer by McMillen, 158.

26. Interview with Belafonte by Mills.

27. Hamer, *To Praise Our Bridges*, 21.

28.   Carleton Putnam, "6219R—Race and Reason: A Yankee View," n.d. Transcript of Citizens' Council Radio Forums (MDAH).

29. Dr. Robert Gayre, "6249—Racial Differences," n.d. Transcript of Citizens' Council Radio Forums (MDAH).

30. Hamer, *To Praise Our Bridges*, 21.

31. Interview with Hamer by McMillen, 159.

32. Hamer, *To Praise Our Bridges*, 23.

33. Staughton Lynd, "A Radical Speaks in Defense of SNCC," *New York Times*, September 10, 1967, 271.

34.   Fannie Lou Hamer, "I'm Sick and Tired of Being Sick and Tired," Speech Delivered with Malcolm X at the Williams Institutional CME Church, Harlem, New York, December 20, 1964, in *The Speeches of Fannie Lou Hamer*, 62.

35. Carson, *In Struggle*, 135.

36.   Jeffries, "SNCC, Black Power, and Independent Political Party Organizing," 177.

37. Hamer and Malcolm actually spoke together twice on December 20, 1964, but because Malcolm's remarks following Hamer's first address offer additional insight into what he deemed the most central aspects of her speech to be, this chapter focuses on the first of Hamer's two Harlem addresses. The second address was a meeting of the OOAU held later the same evening and at the Audubon ballroom. See "With Fannie Lou Hamer," 105.

38. Hamer commonly used the phrase "make democracy a reality"; it is adapted here from a question she posed to her Harlem audience: "we want to see, is democracy real?" Hamer, "I'm Sick and Tired of Being Sick and Tired," 63.

39.   Arnold H. Lubasch, "Malcolm Favors a Mau Mau in US," *New York Times*, December 21, 1964, 20.

40. Hamer, "I'm Sick and Tired of Being Sick and Tired," 62.

41. Hamer, "I'm Sick and Tired of Being Sick and Tired," 62.

42. Hamer, "I'm Sick and Tired of Being Sick and Tired," 62 and 63, respectively.

43.   Hamer, "I'm Sick and Tired of Being Sick and Tired," 58.

44. Hamer, "I'm Sick and Tired of Being Sick and Tired," 62.

45. Hamer, "I'm Sick and Tired of Being Sick and Tired," 62.

46. Hamer, "I'm Sick and Tired of Being Sick and Tired," 62.

47. Hamer, "I'm Sick and Tired of Being Sick and Tired," 62.

48. Hamer, "I'm Sick and Tired of Being Sick and Tired," 63.

49. Lubasch, "Malcolm Favors a Mau Mau in US," 20.

50. See Malcolm X, "With Fannie Lou Hamer," 113.

51. Malcolm X, "With Fannie Lou Hamer," 109.

52. Malcolm X, "With Fannie Lou Hamer," 107.
53. Malcolm X, "With Fannie Lou Hamer," 107–108.
54.   Malcolm X, "With Fannie Lou Hamer," 112.
55. Malcolm X, "With Fannie Lou Hamer," 105.
56.   Malcolm X, "With Fannie Lou Hamer," 106.
57. Malcolm X, "With Fannie Lou Hamer," 112.
58. Malcolm X, "With Fannie Lou Hamer," 110.
59.   Malcolm X, "With Fannie Lou Hamer," 107.
60. Malcolm X, "With Fannie Lou Hamer," 112.
61. Apostrophe is a figure of speech in which the "speaker begins to address an audience other than the one to which he or she is speaking." For additional examples of this device, see James Jasinski, "Apostrophe," in *Sourcebook on Rhetoric: Key Concepts in Contemporary Rhetorical Studies* (Thousand Oaks, CA: Sage, 2001), 545.
62. Malcolm X, "With Fannie Lou Hamer," 112.
63. Malcolm X, "With Fannie Lou Hamer," 112–113.
64. Malcolm X, "With Fannie Lou Hamer," 108.
65. Malcolm X, "With Fannie Lou Hamer," 108.
66. Jeffries, "SNCC, Black Power, and Independent Political Party Organizing," 177.
67. "Interview with Fannie Lou Hamer by Colin Edwards, 1965, Berkeley, California," on *Collected Speeches of Fannie Lou Hamer* CD, Tarabu Betserai, prod. (North Hollywood: Pacifica Radio Archives, 1989).
68. Hamer, *To Praise Our Bridges*, 12, in draft version available (MDAH).
69. Kay Mills, *This Little Light of Mine: The Life of Fannie Lou Hamer* (New York: Plume, 1993), 152, and Joseph A. Loftus, "5 Mississippians Seated By House: But Liberals Muster 148 Votes Against Them," *New York Times*, January 5, 1965, 17.
70. Mills, *This Little Light of Mine*, 153.
71. Mills, *This Little Light of Mine*, 153.
72.   Mills, *This Little Light of Mine*, 153.
73. Victoria Gray Adams quoted in Asch, *The Senator and the Sharecropper*, 219.
74. Victoria Gray Adams quoted in Mills, *This Little Light of Mine*, 155. See also Dittmer's description of Gray's and Devine's backgrounds, *Local People*, 181–182 and 189–190, respectively.
75. Display Ad—48 No Title, *New York Times*, December 9, 1964, 50.
76. Interview with Lawrence Guyot by Maegan Parker Brooks, September 20, 2012 (phone).
77. Early on, Dr. Aaron Henry was reportedly challenging Prentiss Walker, and Harold Ruby was also challenging John Bell Williams. As the MFDP congressional challenge persisted, however, Hamer, Devine, and Gray became the three main opponents to the five illegally elected congressmen.
78.   Interview with Guyot by author.
79.   "CORE to Urge House to Block Seating of Five Mississippians," *New York Times*, December 29, 1964, 14.
80. Dittmer, *Local People*, 339.
81. Interview with Hamer by Edwards.
82. Interview with Fannie Lou Hamer by Robert Wright, August 6, 1968, Oral History Collection, Civil Rights Documentation Project, Moorland-Springarn Research Center, Howard University.

83. "Subcommittee on Elections of the Committee on House Administration," House of Representatives, Washington, DC, *Congressional Record*, September 13, 1965.

84. Interview with King by author.

85. Gray instruction as remembered by King in interview with King by author.

86. The scripted nature of the address also permits the possibility that it was a collaboratively crafted text. Since her testimony followed Gray's and Devine's, it is entirely likely that the three women, along with the MFDP leaders and their legal team, worked out the specific arguments for each woman to emphasize in her speech. Textual markers such as adherence to her signature Jeremiad and the presence of Hamer's southern black vernacular sentence construction, however, demonstrate that whether or not the testimony was collaboratively constructed, she made it her own. Perhaps the most notable creative license she took was promoting the unpopular appeal of being seated in Congressman Whitten's place.

87. Fannie Lou Hamer, "Testimony Before the Subcommittee on Elections of the Committee on House Administrations, House of Representatives, Washington, DC, September 13, 1965," in *The Speeches of Fannie Lou Hamer*, 67–68.

88. Hamer, "Testimony Before the Subcommittee on Elections," 67.

89. Hamer, "Testimony Before the Subcommittee on Elections," 67.

90. Hamer, "Testimony Before the Subcommittee on Elections," 67.

91. Hamer, "Testimony Before the Subcommittee on Elections," 68.

92.   Hamer, "Testimony Before the Subcommittee on Elections," 68.

93.   David Howard-Pitney explains this rhetorical strategy, characteristic of the Jeremiad in *The Afro-American Jeremiad: Appeals for Justice in America* (Philadelphia: Temple University Press, 1990), 6.

94. Hamer, "Testimony Before the Subcommittee on Elections," 68.

95. Directional arguments are those that proceed in stages, premised upon the logic that if X occurs, it will lead to Y, and on to Z. If properly supported with evidence, these arguments can be quite compelling as they reveal the links between events and consequences. If, instead, they are built upon conjecture, they devolve into "slippery slope" fallacies. For more on this form of argument, see Chaim Perelman and Lucie Olbrechts-Tyteca, *The New Rhetoric: A Treatise on Argumentation* (Notre Dame, IN: University of Notre Dame Press, 1969).

96. Hamer, "Testimony Before the Subcommittee on Elections," 68.

97. The term *a fortiori* is taken from the Latin and literally means with stronger force. So, when a rhetor uses an argument by *a fortiori*, he or she is reasoning from a case of relative certainty to one of even greater strength.

98. This was President Johnson's argument, writes Dittmer, *Local People*, 340.

99. Interview with Hamer by Wright.

100. Mills also notes that "Ten people voted present, including the five Mississippians" and "fifty-one members did not vote." As cited in Mills, *This Little Light of Mine*, 169.

101. Interview with Dr. L. C. Dorsey by Maegan Parker Brooks, June 10, 2007, Jackson, Mississippi.

102. Interview with Dorsey by author.

103. Mills, *This Little Light of Mine*, 173.

104. Figures are estimates; see J. Todd Moye, *Let the People Decide: Black Freedom and White Resistance Movements in Sunflower County, Mississippi, 1945–1986* (Chapel

Hill: University of North Carolina Press, 2004), 164, and Mills, *This Little Light of Mine*, 173.

105. Mills, *This Little Light of Mine*, 176.

106. For more on the fundraising campaign, see Mills, *This Little Light of Mine*, 180.

107. Hamer quoted in Mills, *This Little Light of Mine*, 180.

108. Moye, *Let the People Decide*, 164.

109. Mills, *This Little Light of Mine*, 185.

110. Moye, *Let the People Decide*, 163.

111. Dittmer, *Local People*, 415.

112. Fannie Lou Hamer, "Letter to Friends of the Mississippi Freedom Democratic Party," October 23, 1967, in Fannie Lou Hamer file within the MFDP Papers, Wisconsin Historical Society (WHS), Madison, Wisconsin; Fannie Lou Hamer, "Platform," 1967 State Senate Race Materials in Fannie Lou Hamer Papers: Party Platform and Materials, Reel 3, Folders 16 and 17; Fannie Lou Hamer, "Registration Certificate for State Senate," June 9, 1967, in Fannie Lou Hamer Papers: Party Platform and Materials, Reel 3, Folders 16 and 17. Accessed via microfilm (WHS).

113. According to Frank R. Parker, the director of the Voting Rights Project and author of *Black Votes Count: Political Empowerment in Mississippi after 1965*, the 1966 election law changes that had the "most significant impact" on the outcome of the 1967 elections were "the increased qualifying requirements for independent candidates, the changes from district to at-large county supervisor elections, multimember legislative districts, and the primary runoff requirement" (Chapel Hill: University of North Carolina Press, 1990), 73.

114. Robert Clark quoted in Mills, *This Little Light of Mine*, 190.

115. Arthur Kinoy quoted in Mills, *This Little Light of Mine*, 148.

116. Robert Analavage, "Negroes Not Represented," *Southern Patriot*, May 1967.

117. Chana Kai Lee, *For Freedom's Sake: The Life of Fannie Lou Hamer* (Urbana: University of Illinois Press, 1999), 126.

118. John Childs and Noel Workman, "More Choppers Join Farm Labor Strike," *Delta Democrat-Times*, June 4, 1965.

119. Lee, *For Freedom's Sake*, 130.

120. Lee, *For Freedom's Sake*, 132.

121. Lee, *For Freedom's Sake*, 132.

122. Charles M. Payne, *I've Got the Light of Freedom: The Organizing Tradition and the Mississippi Freedom Struggle* (Berkeley: University of California Press, 1995), 376.

123. Interview with Charles Cobb by Maegan Parker Brooks, September 25, 2012 (phone); see also Payne, *I've Got the Light of Freedom*, 372.

124. Carmichael recounts his memory of the meeting's details in Stokely Carmichael with Ekwueme Michael Thelwell, *Ready for Revolution: The Life and Struggles of Stokely Carmichael {Kwame Ture}* (New York: Scribner, 2003), 488–500.

125. Carmichael reiterates the explanation of Black Power he has advanced throughout the years in *Ready for Revolution*, 531–532.

126. Aram G. Goudsouzian notes in his forthcoming monograph on the Meredith March, Fannie Lou Hamer addressed a crowd of marchers gathered at the Enid Dam campsite in northern Mississippi on June 12, 1966. Goudsouzian has a brief description of the speech in *Down to the Crossroads: Civil Rights, Black Power, and the Meredith March Against Fear* (New York: Farrar, Straus, and Giroux, 2014).

127. Hamer's comments on Black Power are excerpted in Fannie Lou Hamer, "Ole Freedom" audio-recording accompanying Fannie Lou Hamer Papers, Amistad Research Center, Tulane University, New Orleans (FLH). Goudsouzian surmises that Hamer's first public reflections on the Black Power concept likely came shortly after the Meredith March during one of the "mini marches" that followed. For instance, Martin Luther King Jr. came to Sunflower County on June 21, 1966—Hamer was there too—and members of the press were asking both movement leaders about the Black Power philosophy. E-mail correspondence between Maegan Parker Brooks and Aram G. Goudsouzian, May 20, 2013.

128. Hamer boasted about these registration figures to her confidante; see Letters to Mrs. Rose Fishman, dated October 13, 1965, and January 8, 1966. Box 1, Folder 1 (FLH).

129. The newspaper account misquotes Hamer as saying "chickeny preachers," rather than her well-known "chicken-eating preachers" characterization. For more coverage of the CORE convention, see M. S. Handler, "CORE Hears Cries of 'Black Power,'" *New York Times*, July 2, 1966, 18.

130. Handler, "CORE Hears Cries of 'Black Power,'" 18.

131. See, for example, Interview with Fannie Lou Hamer by Anne Romaine, 1966 (WHS). See also Fannie Lou Hamer, "What Have We to Hail?," Speech Delivered in Kentucky, Summer 1968, 80; and Fannie Lou Hamer, "To Make Democracy a Reality," Speech Delivered at the Vietnam War Moratorium Rally in Berkeley, October 15, 1969, 99—both speeches appear in *The Speeches of Fannie Lou Hamer*.

132. Dittmer, *Local People*, 369.

133. Dittmer, *Local People*, 370.

134. Sargent Shriver quoted in Dittmer, *Local People*, 370.

135. Quoted in Dittmer, *Local People*, 375.

136. Dittmer, *Local People*, 382.

137. Dittmer, *Local People*, 382.

138. Hamer, *To Praise Our Bridges*, 18, in draft version available (MDAH).

139. Fannie Lou Hamer, "The Only Thing We Can Do Is Work Together," Speech Delivered at a Chapter Meeting of the National Council of Negro Women in Mississippi, 1967, in *The Speeches of Fannie Lou Hamer*, 71.

140. Hamer, "The Only Thing We Can Do Is Work Together," 72.

141. Hamer, "The Only Thing We Can Do Is Work Together," 72.

142. Hamer, "The Only Thing We Can Do Is Work Together," 71.

143. Hamer, "The Only Thing We Can Do Is Work Together," 71–72.

144. Hamer, "The Only Thing We Can Do Is Work Together," 72–73.

145. Hamer, "The Only Thing We Can Do Is Work Together," 73.

146. Hamer, "The Only Thing We Can Do Is Work Together," 73.

147. Hamer, "The Only Thing We Can Do Is Work Together," 73.

148. Letters to Mrs. Rose Fishman (FLH).

149. It is not entirely clear from the handwritten letters, but it appears that Hamer spelled her daughter Vergie's name "Virgie." In my own correspondence with Vergie Hamer Faulkner, she spells her name "Vergie," so that is the spelling I have featured in this book.

150. Interview with Vergie Hamer Faulkner by Maegan Parker Brooks, July 14 and July 17, 2009, in *The Speeches of Fannie Lou Hamer*, 202–204.

151. The few examples of Hamer discussing the death of her daughter Dorothy that I have found include Fannie Lou Hamer, "America Is a Sick Place, and Man Is on the Critical List," Speech Delivered at Loop College, Chicago, Illinois, May 27, 1970, in *The Speeches of Fannie Lou Hamer*; and Edward H. Blackwell, "Taste of Hunger Menu," *Milwaukee Journal*, February 23, 1971.

152. Because Hamer rarely discussed Dorothy's death in public, the details surrounding this tragedy remain unclear. For example, citing Mills's and Lee's biographies, Chris Myers Asch engages in a questionable retelling of Dorothy's death, claiming, for instance, that she passed in September 1966. Furthermore, he questions (in a footnote) why Dorothy was never taken to Mound Bayou Hospital, which she did stay at for several weeks in the spring of 1967. Mills and Lee both correctly date Dorothy's death as occurring several weeks after the reelections in Sunflower and Moorhead, though Mills—who only cites Hamer's quotation in the *Milwaukee Journal* article above as evidence for her retelling of Dorothy's death—does not provide a clear picture of the cause of death or the details surrounding Hamer's experiences being turned away from hospitals with her dying daughter. Lee also relies on secondary sources in her retelling, but draws on several from which she offers the most detailed account of Dorothy's death. Lee suggests that Dorothy died of a cerebral hemorrhage in Memphis after Hamer drove her to several hospitals along the way. Though Vergie's account conflicts with Lee's retelling in several places, and while friends and relatives assure me that they had never seen Hamer drive, for example, it is quite plausible that Dorothy was turned away from some hospitals between Ruleville and Memphis. Denying medical care to blacks was one method by which white supremacists hoped to drive the black population out of the state once they were no longer needed for cotton production in the Delta and once the Voting Rights Act had passed. Dittmer discusses the refusal of medical care and other policies aimed at pushing blacks out of the state, see Dittmer, *Local People*, 388. For accounts of Dorothy's death, see Asch, *The Senator and the Sharecropper*, 249, note 49; Lee, *For Freedom's Sake*, 143, note 15; Mills, *This Little Light*, 191, note 60.

153. Payne, *I've Got the Light of Freedom*, 440.

CHAPTER 5

1. Fannie Lou Hamer, "To Tell It Like It Is," Speech Delivered at the Holmes County, Mississippi, Freedom Democratic Party Municipal Elections Rally in Lexington, Mississippi, May 8, 1969, in *The Speeches of Fannie Lou Hamer: To Tell It Like It Is*, ed. Maegan Parker Brooks and Davis W. Houck (Jackson: University Press of Mississippi, 2011), 87. The visual account of Hamer's address was made possible by photographs comprising Sue (Lorenzi) Sojourner's *Mrs. Hamer Speaks* photography exhibit within the touring show: "THE SOME PEOPLE OF THAT PLACE—1960, Holmes, Co.: The People and Their Movement," for more information see: www.crmvet.org/vet/sojourne.htm.

2. Hamer, "To Tell It Like It Is," 88.

3. Hamer, "To Tell It Like It Is," 90.

4. Hamer, "To Tell It Like It Is," 88.

5. Hamer, "To Tell It Like It Is," 89.

6. Hamer, "To Tell It Like It Is," 89.

7. Hamer, "To Tell It Like It Is," 87.

8. Hamer, "To Tell It Like It Is," 87–93.

9. Ephesians 6:11–12 and Matthew 6:10, respectively quoted in Hamer, "To Tell It Like It Is," 92.

10. Hamer, "To Tell It Like It Is," 92.

11. Hamer, "To Tell It Like It Is," 93.

12. Hamer, "To Tell It Like It Is," 88 and 90, respectively.

13. Hamer, "To Tell It Like It Is," 87.

14. Hamer, "To Tell It Like It Is," 93 and 91, respectively.

15. Hamer, "To Tell It Like It Is," 93.

16. Hamer, "To Tell It Like It Is," 88.

17. Ruby S. Couche, Letter to "Soror" from the National Sorority of Phi Delta Kappa, October 18, 1968, in Fannie Lou Hamer Papers: Speaking Engagements File (1968–1977). Accessed via microfilm at the Wisconsin Historical Society, Madison, Wisconsin (WHS).

18. Betty Neal, Letter to Mrs. Hamer from the Memorial Baptist Church, October 22, 1968, in Fannie Lou Hamer Papers (WHS).

19. Phaon Goldman, Letter to "Dr. Fannie Lou" from Shaw University, February 25, 1969, in Fannie Lou Hamer Papers (WHS).

20. Speaking Engagements File (1968–1977), Fannie Lou Hamer Papers (WHS).

21. See Vincent Harding, Robin D. G. Kelley, and Earl Lewis, "We Changed the World 1945–1970," in *To Make Our World Anew*, ed. Robin D. G. Kelley and Earl Lewis (Oxford: Oxford University Press, 2000), 245.

22.   Given the nature of the cause, the commission reasoned that "Only a greatly enlarged commitment to national action, compassionate, massive and sustained, backed by the will and resources of the most powerful and the richest nation on this earth, can shape a future that is compatible with the historical ideals of American society." Kerner Commission Report as cited in Harding et al., "We Changed the World," 252.

23. Hamer, "To Tell It Like It Is," 93.

24. Fannie Lou Hamer, "To Make Democracy a Reality," Speech Delivered at the Vietnam War Moratorium Rally, Berkeley, California, October 15, 1969, in *The Speeches of Fannie Lou Hamer*, 101.

25. Kay Mills, *This Little Light of Mine: The Life of Fannie Lou Hamer* (New York: Plume, 1993), 223.

26. Interview with Fannie Lou Hamer by Dr. Neil McMillen, April 14, 1972, Ruleville, Mississippi, in *The Speeches of Fannie Lou Hamer*, 166.

27. Interview with Lawrence Guyot by Maegan Parker Brooks, September 20, 2012 (phone).

28. Interview with Fannie Lou Hamer by Robert Wright, August 6, 1968, Oral History Collection, Civil Rights Documentation Project, Moorland-Springarn Research Center, Howard University.

29. Hamer describes this tension in the interview with Fannie Lou Hamer by Anne Romaine, 1966, Social Action Collection (WHS). See also Dittmer's discussion of Henry's role in the poverty program politics; see John Dittmer, *Local People: The Struggle for Civil Rights in Mississippi* (Urbana: University of Illinois Press, 1995), 377–378.

30. Mills, *This Little Light of Mine*, 217.

31. Interview with Guyot by author.

32. Interview with Dr. L. C. Dorsey by Maegan Parker Brooks, June 10, 2007, Jackson, Mississippi.

33. Mills, *This Little Light of Mine*, 217.

34. In "To Make Democracy a Reality," for instance, Hamer describes being trailed throughout the convention by a federal agent and also having her bags searched, with items from within confiscated. See Hamer, "To Make Democracy a Reality," in *The Speeches of Fannie Lou Hamer*, 102–103.

35. See Doug Archer, "'Send Troops to Mississippi, Not Vietnam,' Says Mrs. Hamer," *Worker*, July 13, 1965, and "We Support Oct. 15—Display Ad 12," *New York Times*, October 8, 1969, 12; See, for example, Hamer, "What Have We to Hail"; "To Make Democracy a Reality"; "America Is a Sick Place and Man Is on the Critical List," 119; "Until I Am Free, You Are Not Free Either," 129; and "Is It Too Late?," 133, all in *The Speeches of Fannie Lou Hamer*.

36.   Hamer, "To Make Democracy a Reality," 103.

37. Hasan Kwame Jeffries, *Bloody Lowndes: Civil Rights and Black Power in Alabama's Black Belt* (New York: New York University Press, 2009), 217–218.

38. Parallel case arguments rely upon a comparative logic in which two instances from the same general class are likened to each other. Oftentimes, advocates will use the successful outcome in one case to argue for the adoption of a particular policy with an unknown outcome. If the comparative logic holds, then the success in one case should lead to success in the other. See James Jasinski, "Parallel Case," *Sourcebook on Rhetoric: Key Concepts in Contemporary Rhetorical Studies* (Thousand Oaks, CA: Sage, 2001). See pp. 32–34 for further explanation of the concept and references for additional reading.

39.   Bob Moses quoted in Dittmer, *Local People*, 299.

40. Fannie Lou Hamer, "Speech on Behalf of the Alabama Delegation at the 1968 Democratic National Convention, Chicago, Illinois," August 27, 1968, in *The Speeches of Fannie Lou Hamer*, 85.

41. Fannie Lou Hamer, "Testimony Before the Democratic Reform Committee," Jackson, Mississippi, May 22, 1969, in *The Speeches of Fannie Lou Hamer*, 95–97.

42. Hamer, "Testimony Before the Democratic Reform Committee," 95–97.

43.   Jo-Etha Collier's original diploma is filed within Fannie Lou Hamer's papers at the Amistad Research Center, Tulane University, New Orleans, Louisiana (FLH Papers).

44. Chris Myers Asch, *The Senator and the Sharecropper: The Freedom Struggles of James O. Eastland and Fannie Lou Hamer* (Chapel Hill: University of North Carolina Press, 2008), 256; See also J. Todd Moye, *Let the People Decide: Black Freedom and White Resistance Movements in Sunflower County, Mississippi, 1945–1986* (Chapel Hill: University of North Carolina Press, 2004), 157.

45.   Fannie Lou Hamer, "Platform," 1967 State Senate Race Materials in Party Platform and Materials, Reel 3, Folders 16 and 17 in Fannie Lou Hamer Papers (WHS); "Elect Mrs. Fannie Lou Hamer," 1971 Campaign Card, courtesy of Jeff and Sarah Goldstein.

46. The original manuscript of the speech, which can be found in the Special Collections Section at Tougaloo, College, TO12, Box 1, Folder 6:1, Mississippi Department of Archives and History, Jackson, Mississippi (MDAH), bears Mrs. Hamer's signature. Upon discussing the speech with Charles McLaurin, he claims to have written it for her. Her signature, however, indicates her approval of the text. Furthermore, the

content within the speech is remarkably similar to commentary Hamer was making throughout this period in her activist career. One of the few aspects of the address that seems to distinguish it from others she delivered is the consistent use of male pronouns throughout the speech and the use of "man" to represent all humankind. While Hamer would use male pronouns universally on occasion, her pronoun use and her representation of humankind typically varied to more explicitly include women within her speeches. E-mail correspondence between Davis W. Houck and Charles McLaurin, January 13, 2010.

47. Emphasis in original. See Fannie Lou Hamer, "If the Name of the Game Is Survive, Survive," campaign speech delivered in Ruleville, Mississippi, on September 27, 1971 (MDAH).

48. Fannie Lou Hamer, "If the Name of the Game Is Survive, Survive," Speech Delivered in Ruleville, Mississippi, September 27, 1971, in *The Speeches of Fannie Lou Hamer*, 144.

49. Emphasis in original. Hamer, "If the Name of the Game Is Survive, Survive," 1971 (MDAH).

50. Hamer, "If the Name of the Game Is Survive, Survive," 142.

51. Hamer, "If the Name of the Game Is Survive, Survive," 143.

52. Emphasis in original. Hamer, "If the Name of the Game Is Survive, Survive," 1971 (MDAH).

53. Hamer, "If the Name of the Game Is Survive, Survive," 144.

54.   Hamer, "If the Name of the Game Is Survive, Survive," 142.

55. Jonathon Wolman, "Mississippi Elections: By Hook or Crook," *Daily Cardinal*, November 5, 1971, 1.

56.   Tom Hibbard, "Local Students Tell Why Blacks Didn't Get Vote," *Capital Times*, November 12, 1971, 9.

57. Thomas A. Johnson, "Mississippi Poll Watchers Say Harassment Barred Fair Tally," *New York Times*, November 6, 1971.

58. Jon Wolman, "Mississippi Elections: Facing an Old Political Reality," *Daily Cardinal*, November 11, 1971.

59.   Jason Berry posited: "In a land where no one has great power ... a person who suddenly obtains some of it, no matter how little, becomes the object of envy." Kay Mills extrapolated upon this resentment thesis, maintaining simply: "people are reluctant to vote for those they envy." See Mills, *This Little Light of Mine*, 289.

60. Related to the idea that local people resented Hamer's celebrity status was the explanation that Hamer's 1965 dispute with a group of Sunflower County women over Head Start programs in their area led to lingering resentments and may have cost her the 1971 election. In this case, it was also power, influence, and resources that were at the core of the dispute, which was only exacerbated by the paucity of all three. See Mills, *This Little Light of Mine*, 203–215, for more in-depth coverage of the Head Start dispute.

61. Frank R. Parker, *Black Votes Count: Political Empowerment in Mississippi after 1965* (Chapel Hill: University of North Carolina Press, 1990), 3.

62.   Blackwell cited in Mills, *This Little Light of Mine*, 289.

63.   Reverend Edwin King remembers: "there were people who were appalled that this person didn't have education and why should she be a leader?" Interview with Reverend Edwin King by Maegan Parker Brooks, June 15, 2007, Jackson, Mississippi.

64. See Roth's book chapter for the relationship between the beginnings of both. Benita Roth, "The Making of the Vanguard Center: Black Feminist Emergence in the 1960s and 1970s," in *Still Lifting, Still Climbing: African American Women's Contemporary Activism*, ed. Kimberly Springer (New York: New York University Press, 1999), 72–73.

65. Quotation is from Interview with Guyot by author; similar sentiments were expressed by nearly everyone I asked about Hamer's relationship to feminism.

66. Hamer, "Is It Too Late?," 133.

67. Interview with Guyot by author.

68. The six texts analyzed are Fannie Lou Hamer, "Speech to Tougaloo Students," January 11, 1971, Special Collections, Audio-Visual Records, MP 80.01 Newsfilm Collection, Reel D-0321, Item 1102, Stennis/Hamer/Legislature/Police (MDAH); Hamer, "Until I Am Free, You Are Not Free Either," Speech Delivered at the University of Wisconsin, Madison, January 1971; Hamer "Is It Too Late?," Speech Delivered at Tougaloo College, Tougaloo, Mississippi, Summer 1971; Hamer, "Nobody's Free Until Everybody's Free," Speech Delivered at the Founding of the National Women's Political Caucus, Washington, DC, July 10, 1971; Hamer, "It's in Your Hands," in *Black Women in White America*, ed. Gerda Lerner (New York: Vintage, 1972), 609–614; "Fannie Lou Hamer Speaks Out," *Essence* 1, no. 6 (1971): 75.

69. Hamer, "Speech to Tougaloo Students" (MDAH).

70. For more on poor black women's insistence that they should not have to prioritize one particular aspect of their struggle at a time, see Roth, "The Making of the Vanguard Center," 83.

71. Roth explains in her chapter exploring the emergence and influence of black feminism that "family was the least oppressive institution in [black women's] lives and constituted a refuge from white domination." Roth, "The Making of the Vanguard Center," 77.

72.   Hamer, "It's in Your Hands," 612.

73. Gay Leslie, "Rights Matriarch Pleads for Action Now," *Wisconsin State Journal*, July 19, 1969.

74. Interview with Dr. Leslie McLemore by Maegan Parker Brooks, June 13, 2007, Jackson, Mississippi.

75. As remembered by Wally Roberts, "Fannie Lou Hamer 1917–1977," *Veterans of the Civil Rights Movement*. Available online, accessed February 8, 2007, http://www.crm vet.org/mem/hamer.htm.

76. Hamer, "Nobody's Free Until Everybody's Free," 136.

77. Hamer, "Speech to Tougaloo Students" (MDAH).

78. Interview with Owen Brooks by Maegan Parker Brooks, June 14, 2007, Jackson, Mississippi.

79. Hamer, "Is It Too Late?" McLaurin claims to have penned this speech for Hamer as well. Like "If the Name of the Game Is Survive, Survive," the manuscript of this speech also bears Mrs. Hamer's signature. And it also is consistent with her turn-of-the-decade ideology, when compared to other recordings of speeches, statements, and writings from this period.

80. National Council of Negro Women Records, MAMC_001 Series 15 Sub-series 6, Folder 1, Fannie Lou Hamer, n.d. 1973. Mary McCleod Bethune Archives, Washington, DC (NCNW).

81. This laughter was recorded on a NCNW archive tape along with the young man's statement "you've been fumbling around pretty good for quite sometime," made in response to Hamer's modest declaration that she was fumbling around until men could come and take the lead (NCNW).

82.   For more on sexism within the black Baptist church and its effect on rhetorical leadership, see "Introduction," *Women and the Civil Rights Movement, 1954–1965*, ed. Davis W. Houck and David E. Dixon (Jackson: University Press of Mississippi, 2009).

83. "Fannie Lou Hamer Speaks Out," 75.

84. Hamer, "Nobody's Free Until Everybody's Free," 138.

85. Daniel Patrick Moynihan, *The Negro Family: The Case for National Action* (Washington, DC: US Department of Labor, 1965).

86. "Fannie Lou Hamer Speaks Out," 75.

87. Interview with Fannie Lou Hamer by Project South, 1965, MFDP Chapter 55, Box 6, Folder 160, Department of Special Collections, Stanford University Libraries, Stanford, California.

88. Hamer, "Is It Too Late?," 133.

89. Roth, "The Making of the Vanguard Center," 77.

90. Ben Own quoted in Franklyn Peterson, "Sunflowers Don't Grow in Sunflower County," *Sepia* 19 (1970): 17.

91. Danielle L. McGuire, *At the Dark End of the Street: Black Women, Rape, and Resistance—a New History of the Civil Rights Movement from Rosa Parks to the Rise of Black Power* (New York: Vintage, 2010), 192.

92.   Hamer, "Is It Too Late?" 133.

93.   Hamer, "Until I Am Free, You Are Not Free Either," 122.

94. Interview with King by author.

95.   "Fannie Lou Hamer Speaks Out," 75.

96. See, for example, Toni Morrison's discussion of the difficulty black women have respecting white women as a result of their historical relationship with one another in "What the Black Woman Thinks About Women's Lib," *New York Times*, August 22, 1971, SM14.

97. "Fannie Lou Hamer Speaks Out," 76.

98. For more on "othermothering," see Roth, "The Making of the Vanguard Center," 78.

99. During her speech to students at Tougaloo College, Hamer paraphrased earlier comments she made to a group of white women in New York City. See Hamer, "Speech to Tougaloo Students" (MDAH).

100. Hamer, "It's in Your Hands," 610.

101. Hamer, "It's in Your Hands," 610.

102. Hamer, "It's in Your Hands," 613.

103. Edwin King, Lawrence Guyot, and L. C. Dorsey all acknowledge the intra-racial class tension that arose as Hamer became better known and widely celebrated. For instance, King recalled that when Hamer received her honorary doctorate from Tougaloo College, alumni objected to the accolade because she was unlettered. Interviews with King, Guyot, and Dorsey by author.

104. Ella Baker quoted in Barbara Ransby, *Ella Baker and the Black Freedom Movement: A Radical Democratic Vision* (Chapel Hill: University of North Carolina Press, 2003), 363; and Hamer, "It's in Your Hands," 613, respectively.

105. For more on the "lift as we climb" ideology, see Deborah Gray White, *Too Heavy a Load: Black Women in Defense of Themselves, 1894–1994* (New York: W. W. Norton & Company, 1999).
106. Hamer, "Nobody's Free Until Everybody's Free," 136.
107. Hamer, "Nobody's Free Until Everybody's Free," 135–139.
108. Interview with Guyot by author.
109. Mills, *This Little Light of Mine*, 211.
110. For an in-depth analysis of Forman's appeal, see Maegan Parker, "Ironic Openings: The Interpretive Challenge of the 'Black Manifesto,'" *Quarterly Journal of Speech* 94, no. 3 (August 2008): 320–342.
111. See, for example, Hamer, "If the Name of the Game Is Survive, Survive," 143, and Dan L. Thrapp, "Forman Supplanted as Manifesto Spokesman," *Los Angeles Times*, August 17, 1969, 8—Hamer is listed as an NBEDC board member within this piece.
112. Harding et al., "We Changed the World," 246.
113. Harding et al. explain the phenomenon of "rights consciousness" and "rising expectations" in "We Changed the World," 246.
114. Office of Economic Opportunity, "Federal Government Launches Emergency Food and Medical Program," March 23, 1968, Press Release in Fannie Lou Hamer Papers, Reel 15, "Collected Newsletters and Articles" (WHS).
115. Interview with Hamer by Wright.
116. Hamer, "Until I Am Free, You're Not Free Either"; Fannie Lou Hamer, "Speech in Madison-area Church," Madison, Wisconsin, 1971. Transcribed by Maegan Parker Brooks from audio recording, courtesy of Jean Sweet.
117. Fannie Lou Hamer, draft of "Sick and Tired of Being Sick and Tired," in n.d. (1968) Box 5, FLH Folder, *Katallagete!*/James Y. Holloway Collection, 1945–1992, in Civil Rights and Race Relations Collection at the University of Mississippi Archives and Special Collections, Oxford, Mississippi.
118. Interview with King by author.
119. Dittmer, *Local People*, 388.
120. Megan Landauer and Jonathan Wolman, "Fannie Lou Hamer '. . . Forcing a New Political Reality,'" *Daily Cardinal*, October 8, 1971.
121. Asch, *The Senator and the Sharecropper*, 227.
122. Interview with Ambassador Andrew Young by Maegan Parker Brooks, June 25, 2007, Atlanta, Georgia.
123. In the draft of this article, there is a typographical error, which I have corrected in the text of the chapter. The draft actually reads: "If what the politicians have done to the proverty program . . ." See Hamer, draft of "Sick and Tired of Being Sick and Tired," in *Katallagete!*/James Y. Holloway Collection.
124. Hamer, draft of "Sick and Tired of Being Sick and Tired," in *Katallagete!*/James Y. Holloway Collection.
125. Interview with Brooks by author.
126. Landauer and Wolman, "Fannie Lou Hamer '. . . Forcing a New Political Reality,'" *Daily Cardinal*, 1971.
127. "North Bolivar County Cooperative Membership Booklet," in Box 11, Fannie Lou Hamer Papers at the Amistad Research Center, Tulane University, New Orleans, Louisiana (FLH Papers).
128. Interview with Dorsey by author.

129. Landauer and Wolman, "Fannie Lou Hamer '. . . Forcing a New Political Reality,'" *Daily Cardinal*, 1971.
130. Martha Fager, a founding member of the organization, remembers Alicia Cathwell suggesting the name. Interview with Martha Fager by Maegan Parker Brooks, July 6, 2007 (phone).
131. Interview with Jeff and Sarah Goldstein by Maegan Parker Brooks, July 2, 2007, Madison, Wisconsin.
132. For more information about the NCNW's Wednesdays in Mississippi program, see http://wimsfilmproject.com/.
134. National Council of Negro Women Records, MAMC_001 Series 15, Sub-series 6, Folder 1, Fannie Lou Hamer, n.d. 1973 (NCNW).
134. Landauer and Wolman, "Fannie Lou Hamer '. . . Forcing a New Political Reality,'" *Daily Cardinal*, 1971.
135. Interview with Goldsteins by author.
136. Jeff Goldstein's son briefly commented on his experience in Mississippi traveling with his parents as a child, and he remembers the distended bellies of the children and the "tar paper shacks" they lived in. Interview with Goldsteins by author.
137. Correspondence regarding requests for Hamer to speak indicate the range of her honoraria, which typically included the cost of travel and an additional $200–$300. See Fannie Lou Hamer Papers: Speaking Engagements File (1968–1977) (WHS).
138. Letters from Marion Loundsbury, October 1, 1969, and David Elliot January 14, 1968, respectively, Boxes 24 and 25 (FLH).
139. Boxes 24 and 25 (FLH).
140. Interview with Goldsteins by author.
141. Landauer and Wolman, "Fannie Lou Hamer '. . . Forcing a New Political Reality,'" *Daily Cardinal*, 1971.
142. Marian McBride, "Fannie Lou Hamer: Nobody Knows the Trouble She's Seen," *Washington Post*, July 14, 1968, H12.
143. Phone interview with Fager by author; interview with Goldsteins by author.
144. Interview with Goldsteins by author.
145. Sarah Goldstein offered this particular statement.
146. Hamer, "Madison-area Church," 1971.
147. Hamer, "Until I Am Free, You Are Not Free Either," 129.
148. Hamer, "Madison-area Church," 1971.
149. Interview with Goldsteins by author.
150. Interview with Fager by author; Interview with Greg Bell by Maegan Parker Brooks, May 7, 2007 (phone).
151. Hamer, "Madison-area Church," 1971; Hamer, "Until I Am Free, You Are Not Free Either," 130.
152. This particular statement was captured in the recording of her question-and-answer period following the more formal address she delivered: Hamer, "Madison-area Church," 1971.
153. Hamer, "Madison-area Church," 1971.
154. Hamer, "Until I Am Free, You Are Not Free Either," 130.
155. Interview with Jean and Charlie Sweet by Maegan Parker Brooks, April 24, 2007, Madison, Wisconsin.
156. Hamer, "Until I Am Free, You Are Not Free Either," 127.

157. I corrected a spelling error made in the original letter—changing "rath" to "wrath" in my representation of Dorrough's remarks. Letter from Ruleville mayor C. M. Dorrough Sr. to Mrs. Fannie Lou Hamer, March 26, 1970, in Correspondence-Tougaloo, 1976–1977, Box 1, Folder 1, FLH Files, Coleman Library, Tougaloo College, Jackson, Mississippi.

158. Fannie Lou Hamer, "Seconding Speech for the Nomination of Frances Farenthold," Delivered at the 1972 Democratic National Convention, Miami Beach, Florida, July 13, 1972, in *The Speeches of Fannie Lou Hamer*, 146.

CHAPTER 6

1. Fannie Lou Hamer, "We Haven't Arrived Yet," Presentation and Responses to Questions at the University of Wisconsin, Madison, Wisconsin, January 29, 1976, in *The Speeches of Fannie Lou Hamer: To Tell It Like It Is*, ed. Maegan Parker Brooks and Davis W. Houck (Jackson: University Press of Mississippi, 2011), 182.

2. See, respectively, Annie T. Moore, "Dear Mrs. Hamer: Letter requesting Hamer's participation in the Mississippi Gulf Coast Alumnae chapter of the Delta Sigma Theta Sorority's Founder's Day Program," November 22, 1976; Soror Staria Garth, "Dear Soror: Letter Requesting Hamer's participation in the Memphis State University chapter of the Delta Sigma Theta Sorority's Founder's Day Program," November 16, 1976, Speaking Engagements File (1968–1977); Mrs. M. A. Phelps, "Dear Fannie Lou Hammer [*sic*]: Letter requesting Hamer speak to the Educational Club of the Warren County Business Professional Credit Union," August 26, 1976, in "Correspondence 1976–1977" file of the Tougaloo Collection, Box 1, Folder 1, at the Mississippi Department of Archives and History, Jackson, Mississippi (MDAH); Leroy Mobley, "Dear Mrs. Hamer: Letter requesting that Hamer come speak to the first prison branch of the NAACP," November 1976 within Speaking Engagements File (1968–1977). Fannie Lou Hamer Papers, Accessed via Microfilm at the Wisconsin Historical Society, Madison, Wisconsin (WHS).

3. Bill Sierichs, "'Sin-Sickness' Probed at Crime Meet," *Jackson Daily News*, March 24, 1976, B.

4. Lloyd Gray, "The glitter is gone, but the fight goes on," *Delta Democrat-Times*, October 3, 1976, A12.

5. Chris Myers Asch discusses the impact of white flight from public schools as the federal courts bore down on southern states in the late 1960s and 1970s. See *The Senator and the Sharecropper: The Freedom Struggles of James O. Eastland and Fannie Lou Hamer* (Chapel Hill: University of North Carolina Press, 2008), 273–278.

6. Gray, "The glitter is gone."

7. As Jean Sweet contends, the failure of Freedom Farm "hurt her, yeah. She really died with a broken heart." Interview with Jean and Charlie Sweet by Maegan Parker Brooks, April 24, 2007, Madison, Wisconsin.

8. In e-mail correspondence between the author and Fannie Lou Hamer's great-niece, Monica Land, Land describes the way Hamer is remembered by her family in the following manner: "As a very funny person. Always had a good story. Always had a funny story. And a hard worker almost to a fault. Competitive. A religious person and a wonderful singer. She was very good natured and good hearted." Interview with Monica Land by Maegan Parker Brooks, January 6, 2009 (e-mail).

9. Section subheading is taken from the title of Langston Hughes's famous poem. For full text, see http://www.poetryfoundation.org/poem/175884.

10. Interview with Dr. L. C. Dorsey by author, June 10, 2007, Jackson, Mississippi.

11. Interview with Charles McLaurin by Maegan Parker Brooks and Davis W. Houck, April 10, 2010, Ruleville, Mississippi.

12. Interview with Dr. Leslie McLemore by author, June 13, 2007, Jackson, Mississippi.

13. Interview with Dorsey by author.

14. J. Todd Moye, *Let the People Decide: Black Freedom and White Resistance Movements in Sunflower County, Mississippi, 1945–1986* (Chapel Hill: University of North Carolina Press, 2004), 158.

15. Interview with Jeff and Sarah Goldstein by Maegan Parker Brooks, July 2, 2007, Madison, Wisconsin.

16. Interview with Jean and Charlie Sweet by author.

17. Interview with Dorsey by author.

18. Asch, *The Senator and the Sharecropper*, 260.

19. The initial refusal was ultimately reversed when Dr. Robert Smith—an ally of the movement—reviewed her case and determined that it was rejected without basis.

20. Jacqueline and Lenora, Dorothy's daughters, remained with the Hamers who raised them after their mother's death. The Hamers other adopted daughter, Vergie, had moved to Memphis by this point.

21. Interview with Goldsteins by author.

22.   Madison's two major newspapers took an avid interest, both printing feature articles with pictures of Mrs. Hamer. See Marvin Cook, "Despite Atrocities Fannie Lou Hamer Brings a Message of Love," *Capital Times*, January 29, 1976; Robert Pfefferkorn, "From one who pursued equality, a plea for love," *Wisconsin State Journal*, January 30, 1976.

23. Fannie Lou Hamer Lecture Flyer, available in the images collection (WHS).

24. Hamer, "We Haven't Arrived Yet," 182–193.

25. Hamer, "We Haven't Arrived Yet," 184 and 183, respectively.

26. See Thomas S. Flory, "Abstracter's Introduction" to "Presentation and Responses to Questions by FANNIE LOU HAMER," January 29, 1976, at the University of Wisconsin-Madison, Measure for Measure files, Tape 782 A (WHS).

27. Hamer, "We Haven't Arrived Yet," 182.

28.   Hamer, "We Haven't Arrived Yet," 182–193.

29. Hamer, "We Haven't Arrived Yet," 184. "What the World Needs Now" is a popular song, first recorded in 1965 by Jackie DeShannon. Hal David wrote the lyrics and the music was composed by Burt Bacharach. Since its initial recording, the song has been performed by over a hundred different artists. Perhaps most memorably, the Beatles performed the song as an anthem in protest of the Vietnam War.

30. Hamer, "We Haven't Arrived Yet," 182–193.

31. Hamer, "We Haven't Arrived Yet," 182–193.

32. See Nina Glover, "Dear Mrs. Hamer: Letter Explaining Mrs. Hamer's Sponsored Expenses to the Martin Luther King, Jr. Day Commemoration," dated December 30, 1975. In Speaking Engagements File (1968–1977), Fannie Lou Hamer Papers (WHS).

33. Hamer, "We Haven't Arrived Yet," 187–188.

34.   Cook, "Despite Atrocities Fannie Lou Brings a Message of Love," *Capital Times*.

35. Pfefferkorn, "From one who pursued equality, a plea for love," *Wisconsin State Journal*.

36.   Fannie Lou Hamer, "It's Later Than You Think: Speech at the First Unitarian Society," January 30, 1976, Madison, Wisconsin. Transcribed by Maegan Parker Brooks from audio recording. Speech available in the Measure for Measure Collection (WHS).

37. Hamer, "It's Later Than You Think."

38. Pfefferkorn, "From one who pursued equality, a plea for love," *Wisconsin State Journal.*

39.   Hamer, "It's Later Than You Think."

40. Interview with Reverend Edwin King by author, June 15, 2007, Jackson, Mississippi.

41. Interview with McLemore by author.

42. Kay Mills, *This Little Light of Mine: The Life of Fannie Lou Hamer* (New York: Plume, 1993), 303.

43.   L. C. Dorsey, "Epilogue," Fannie Lou Hamer files, "Tributes" Folder (WHS).

44. Fannie Lou Hamer, "Letter to 'Friends' of the Voter Education Project," reel 1, folder 9. Fannie Lou Hamer Papers (WHS).

45.   I have corrected a typographical error within my representation of the text—the original document read, "thw wonderful work." Minister Ralph Loomia, "Letter to 'Mrs. Hamer,'" in "FLH/pw Enclosures" folder, reel 1, folder 9, Fannie Lou Hamer Papers (WHS).

46. As cited in Gray, "The glitter is gone."

47. Although no recording or transcript remains from this mid-October speaking engagement, a letter sent in November from the NICM coordinating reimbursement confirms that she was healthy enough to participate in the conference; and secondary sources suggest that this was Hamer's last national speaking engagement. See the Reverend Marion Elaine Myles, "Dear Mrs. Hamer, Letter from the Ecumenical Women's Center," July 12, 1976, in Fannie Lou Hamer Papers: Speaking Engagements File (1968–1977); Rose M. Hicks, "Dear Mrs. Hamer, Letter from the National Institute for Campus Ministries," November 16, 1976. In Speaking Engagements File (1968–1977), Fannie Lou Hamer Papers (WHS); See also Susan Kling, *Fannie Lou Hamer: A Biography* (Chicago: Women for Racial and Economic Equality, 1979), 48.

48. In fact, tensions between Hamer and middle-class civil rights activists and organizations seem to have disappeared by this point in her career. In 1976, Hamer chartered an NAACP chapter in Ruleville. Although it seems surprising that Hamer would ever overcome her harsh criticism of class tensions within the movement, Edwin King suggests that by the turn of the decade, she could hardly afford to be so critical—there were just too few people and organizations still committed to the struggle in Mississippi. Beyond this logic, both Evers and the NAACP made clear commitments to helping the poor. Hamer began singing Charles Evers's praises on her national travels after he helped her secure funds for the low-income houses. Similarly, the NAACP developed a rural land program, which must have caught the interest of Hamer as a pamphlet for it remains among her papers. Over time, it seems both the NAACP and more moderate leaders like Evers had proven their devotion to many of the causes Hamer held so dear. Interview with Reverend Edwin King by author; Hamer, "Black Mississippi to Date," NAACP Correspondence, Box 1, Folder 8, Tougaloo Collection, Mississippi Department of Archives and History, Jackson, Mississippi (MDAH).

49. June Johnson remembered that Hamer invited everyone to her house after the festivities. State senator Robert Clark recalled, however, that there were fewer than one hundred people there to celebrate the last Fannie Lou Hamer day she ever witnessed. These recollections are cited in Mills, *This Little Light of Mine*, 304–305.

50.   Brooks, for example, expressed these reservations. Interview with Owen Brooks by Maegan Parker Brooks, June 14, 2007, Jackson, Mississippi.

51.   "Census" from "Funeral Program File," dated March 20, 1977, Special Collection—Fannie Lou Hamer, Box 1, Folder 2 (MDAH).

52.   As shown in the tape of Fannie Lou Hamer funeral, March 20, 1977, by Jane Petty and Patti Carr Black, Trans Video, Ltd., Recording available from (MDAH), MP81.2, Tape 1 and 2, Jackson, Mississippi.

53.   Vernon Jordan, "Tribute to Fannie Lou Hamer," March 20, 1977, Transcribed by Maegan Parker Brooks from video recording of funeral.

54.   Height's tribute is summarized in Mills, *This Little Light of Mine*, 310. The funeral tape available at the MDAH records a few seconds of Dorothy Height's address. It also shows Ella Baker approaching the podium and then cuts out. Yet Kay Mills has this to say about Baker's address: "Ella Baker, who had been the behind-the-scenes intellectual to Mrs. Hamer's out-front galvanizer, talked about how Mrs. Hamer not only spoke about the movement's ideas and ideals but lived them." See Mills, *This Little Light of Mine*, 310. Interestingly, Mills also cites the funeral tape recording from MDAH as her source for this information. So, perhaps the footage has degenerated over the years—to the point where their participation is no longer accessible—or possibly, she is relying upon an un-cited source for this information.

55.   Interview with Lawrence Guyot by Maegan Parker Brooks, September 20, 2012 (phone).

56.   These core functions are the generic elements of a eulogy, a subgenre of the epideictic form of discourse. For more in-depth scholarly considerations of this form, see Karlyn K. Campbell and Kathleen H. Jamieson, "Form and Genre in Rhetorical Criticism: An Introduction," in *Form and Genre: Shaping Rhetorical Action* (Falls Church, VA: Speech Communication Association, 1978); Celeste M. Condit, "The Functions of Epideictic: The Boston Massacre Orations as Exemplar," *Communication Quarterly* 33 (1985): 284–299; Adrianne D. Kunkel and Michael R. Dennis, "Grief Consolation in Eulogy Rhetoric: An Integrative Framework," *Death Studies* 27 (2003): 10–17.

57.   In particular, Brooks recalled the refrain about Hamer saving white Mississippians from themselves. Interview with Brooks by author.

58.   Hodding Carter III, "Tribute to Fannie Lou Hamer," March 20, 1977. Transcribed by author from video recording of funeral (MDAH).

59.   Stokely Carmichael, "Special* Tribute to Fannie Lou Hamer," (*as specified by the funeral program), March 20, 1977. Transcribed by author from video recording of funeral (MDAH).

60. Stokely Carmichael and Ekwueme Michael Thelwell, *Ready for Revolution: The Life and Struggles of Stokely Carmichael {Kwame Ture}* (New York: Scribner, 2003), 315–316.

61.   Carmichael and Thelwell, *Ready for Revolution*, 547.

62.   Carmichael, "Special Tribute to Fannie Lou Hamer."

63.   The videotaped recording of Carmichael's address indicates that he tries (unsuccessfully) to initiate a call-and-response cadence or to elicit at least some form of feedback at several points throughout his address. Initially, I assumed the audience was unresponsive because they were either offended by Carmichael's appropriation of white supremacists' impressions of Hamer or that his fiery delivery was off-putting, given the setting. When I asked funeral coordinator Owen Brooks about this,

however, he assured me that "Everybody likes Stokely. . . . And they understood he spoke what he believed in the manner in which he comported himself. . . . they didn't have a problem." Perhaps the lack of audience engagement, thus, stemmed from a sense of propriety—this was a funeral not a protest rally. And perhaps the contrast between the responses to his speech and Young's tribute was merely a matter of order. Carmichael spoke first and might have loosened up the audience—priming them to be more responsive during Young's oration. Interview with Brooks by author.

64. Ambassador Andrew Young, "Eulogy at Fannie Lou Hamer's funeral," March 20, 1977. Transcribed by author from video recording of funeral (MDAH).

65.   Mailgrams and Telegrams, Box 2, Folders 5, 6, and 7, in Fannie Lou Hamer's papers at the Amistad Research Center, Tulane University, New Orleans, Louisiana (FLH).

66. See, respectively, telegrams sent by Reverend Jesse Jackson Sr. and Staff and Board Family from Operation Rainbow PUSH headquarters, March 17, 1977; Jack Greenberg and the Legal Defense Fund of the NAACP, March 16, 1977; and Diane Nash Bevel and Children, March 17, 1977 in (FLH).

67. See, respectively, telegrams sent by Representative John Conyers, March 17, 1977; and Measure for Measure, March 15, 1977, in (FLH).

68. The following textbooks have no mention of Hamer within their pages: Daniel J. Boorstin and Brooks Mather Kelley with Ruth Frankel Boorstin, *A History of the United States* (Needham, MA: Pearson/Prentice Hall, 2005); Joyce Appleby, Alan Brinkley, and James McPherson, *The American Journey* (New York: Glencoe/McGraw-Hill, 2000); Sterling Stuckey, Linda Kerrigan Salvucci with Judith Irvin, *A Call to Freedom* (Austin, TX: Holt, Rinehart, and Winston/Harcourt, 2003).

The textbooks listed below do mention Hamer and frame her within the 1964 Freedom Summer/DNC challenge context: Joyce Appleby, Alan Brinkley, Albert S. Broussard, James M. McPherson, and Donald A. Ritchie, *The American Vision* (New York: Glencoe McGraw-Hill, 2003); Edward L. Ayers, Robert D. Schulzinger, Jesus F. de la Teja, and Deborah Gray White with Sam Wineburg, *American Anthem: Modern American History* (Orlando, FL: Holt, Rinehart, and Winston/Harcourt, 2007); Andrew Cayton, Elisabeth Israels Perry, Linda Reed, and Allan M. Winkler, *America: Pathways to the Present* (Needham, MS: Pearson/Prentice Hall, 2005); Gerald A. Danzer, J. Jorge Klor de Alva, Nancy Woloch, and Louis E. Wilson, *The Americans: Reconstruction to the 21st Century* (Evanston, IL: McDougal Littell, 2009).

69. See, respectively, Ayers, et al., *American Anthem*, 577; Cayton et al., *America: Pathways to the Present*, 720; and Appleby et al., *The American Vision*, 874.

70. Direct quotation from Danzer et al. *The Americans*, 715. See also Ayers et al., *American Anthem*, 577; Cayton et al., *America: Pathways to the Present*, 720.

71. June Jordan, *Fannie Lou Hamer* (New York: Thomas Y. Crowell Company, 1972).

72.   David Rubel, *Fannie Lou Hamer: From Sharecropping to Politics* (Englewood Cliffs, NJ: Silver Burdett Press, 1990).

73. United States Postal Service, "Fannie Lou Hamer (1917–1977)," within the Civil Rights Pioneers Postage Stamp collection, released 2009.

74. John M. Murphy discusses these generational attributions in Barack Obama's rhetoric—referring to the King generation as the Moses generation and the contemporary generation as the Joshua generation. See "Barack Obama, the Exodus Tradition, and the Joshua Generation," *Quarterly Journal of Speech* 97, no. 4 (November 2011): 387–410.

75. "Maya Angelou, Ossie Davis & Ruby Dee Pay Tribute to Fannie Lou Hamer and the Mississippi Freedom Democratic Party," *Democracy Now!* Aired on July 28, 2004. Transcript available online, accessed June 20, 2013, http://www.democracynow .org/2004/7/28/maya_angelou_ossie_davis_ruby_dee.

76. "Maya Angelou, Ossie Davis & Ruby Dee Pay Tribute to Fannie Lou Hamer and the Mississippi Freedom Democratic Party," *Democracy Now!*

77. Barack Obama, "Senate Floor Speech on Renewing the Voting Rights Act," Delivered July 20, 2006. Transcript and Audio available online, accessed June 16, 2013, http:// www.americanrhetoric.com/speeches/barackobama/barackobamasenatespeechon votingrightsactrenewal.htm.

78.   Interview with Guyot by author.

79.   "Acceptance Speech to the Democratic National Convention by Governor Bill Clinton from Arkansas," July 16, 1992. Available online, accessed August 30, 2012, http:// www.4president.org/speeches/billclinton1992acceptance.htm and Interview with Charles Cobb by Maegan Parker Brooks, September 25, 2012 (phone).

80. Interview with Dorie Ladner by Maegan Parker Brooks, September 15, 2012 (phone).

81. George W. Bush, "President Bush Signs Voting Rights Act Reauthorization and Amendments Act of 2008," July 27, 2008. Transcript Available online, accessed June 17, 2013: http://georgewbushwhitehouse.archives.gov/news/releases/2006/07/20060727 .html.

82.   My examination of public memory about Hamer is informed, in a theoretical sense, by the growing body of scholarship about the struggle and how it is collectively remembered. See, for example, Houston A. Baker Jr., "Critical Memory and the Black Public Sphere," in *The Black Public Sphere: a Public Culture Book*, ed. The Black Public Sphere Collective (Chicago: University of Chicago Press, 1995), 7–37; *The Civil Rights Movement in American Memory*, ed. Renee C. Romano and Leigh Raiford (Athens: University of Georgia Press, 2006); Davis W. Houck and Matthew A. Grindy, "Retrospective Prospects," in *Emmett Till and the Mississippi Press* (Jackson: University Press of Mississippi, 2008), 153–165.

AFTERWORD

1. Charles McLaurin quoted in John Dittmer, *Local People: The Struggle for Civil Rights in Mississippi* (Chicago: University of Illinois Press, 1995), 434.

2. Interview with Charles McLaurin by Davis W. Houck and Maegan Parker Brooks, April 10, 2010, Ruleville, Mississippi.

3. Over four hundred people, organizations, and businesses donated to the statue. The donations ranged in amount from one dollar to thousands of dollars. Those who donated five hundred dollars or more are recognized on the marble plinths. For a complete list of donors, see www.fannielouhamer.info.

4. Willie Simmons, "Reflections," Speech Delivered at the Dedication and Unveiling of the Fannie Lou Hamer Memorial Statue on October 5, 2012. Available online, accessed January 13, 2013, www.youtube.com/watch?v=LNjPgqjggSU.

5. Leslie McLemore was in attendance and distributed programs from the 29th Annual Fannie Lou Hamer Memorial Symposium held at Jackson State University from October 3–4, 2012. The brief biography of Hamer printed on the program refers to her as a "woman of the soil," program in author's possession. Charles McLaurin,

"Acknowledgments," Speech Delivered at the Dedication and Unveiling of the Fannie Lou Hamer Memorial Statue on October 5, 2012.

6. Hattie Robinson Jordan, "Expression of Appreciation," Speech Delivered at the Grand Opening of Fannie Lou Hamer Museum, October 6, 2012, recording in author's possession.

7. Sarah Richardson-Thomas, "Keynote Address," Speech Delivered at the Grand Opening of Fannie Lou Hamer Museum, October 6, 2012.

8. Charles McLaurin, "Tribute to Mrs. Hamer," Speech Delivered at the Grand Opening of Fannie Lou Hamer Museum, October 6, 2012.

9. Willie Burton, "Occasion/Welcome," Speech Delivered at the Grand Opening of Fannie Lou Hamer Museum, October 6, 2012.

10. Nina Townsend, "Reflections," Speech Delivered at the Grand Opening of Fannie Lou Hamer Museum, October 6, 2012.

11. Julianne Malveaux, "Remembering Fannie Lou Hamer" and "Reflections," Speeches Delivered at the Dedication and Unveiling of the Fannie Lou Hamer Memorial Statue on October 5, 2012, and at the Grand Opening of Fannie Lou Hamer Museum, October 6, 2012.

12. Simmons, "Reflections."

13. Molefi Asante, "Libation," Speech Delivered at the Dedication and Unveiling of the Fannie Lou Hamer Memorial Statue on October 5, 2012.

14. Richardson-Thomas, "Keynote."

15. Vergie Hamer Faulkner, "Solo," Speech Delivered at the Dedication and Unveiling of the Fannie Lou Hamer Memorial Statue on October 5, 2012.

16. McLaurin, "Acknowledgments" and "Tribute."

17. Simmons, "Reflections."

18. Jordan, "Welcome," Speech Delivered at the Dedication and Unveiling of the Fannie Lou Hamer Memorial Statue on October 5, 2012.

19. Edgar Donahoe, "Reflections," Speech Delivered at the Grand Opening of Fannie Lou Hamer Museum, October 6, 2012.

20. Jordan, "Welcome."

21. Richardson-Thomas, "Keynote."

22. Simmons, "Reflections."

23. Malveaux, "Reflections," and Burton, "Occasion/Welcome," respectively.

24. Malveaux included the characterization of Hamer as a "phenomenal woman"—riffing on the Maya Angelou poem by the same title—in both her addresses.

25. For an excellent account of the role symbolic representations of historical figures play in our public memory, see Nell Irvin Painter, *Sojourner Truth, A Life, A Symbol* (New York: W. W. Norton & Company, 1996), especially "The Life of a Symbol" and "Coda: The Triumph of a Symbol." For more on how the movement is popularly rendered, see Houston A. Baker Jr., "Critical Memory and the Black Public Sphere," in *The Black Public Sphere: a Public Culture Book*, ed. The Black Public Sphere Collective (Chicago: University of Chicago Press, 1995), 7–37; *The Civil Rights Movement in American Memory*, ed. Renee C. Romano and Leigh Raiford (Athens: University of Georgia Press, 2006); Davis W. Houck and Matthew A. Grindy, "Retrospective Prospects," in *Emmett Till and the Mississippi Press* (Jackson: University Press of Mississippi, 2008), 153–165.

26. Malveaux, "Reflections," and Barry W. Bryant, "Presentation of Sunflower County Resolution," Speech Delivered at the Dedication and Unveiling of the Fannie Lou Hamer Memorial Statue on October 5, 2012.

27. Wesley C. Hogan, *Many Minds, One Heart: SNCC's Dream for a New America* (Chapel Hill: University of North Carolina Press, 2007), 230.

CODA

1. Eleanor Holmes Norton quoted in Kay Mills, *This Little Light of Mine: The Life of Fannie Lou Hamer* (New York: Penguin, 1993), 85.

2. Maegan Parker Brooks and Davis W. Houck, eds., *The Speeches of Fannie Lou Hamer: "To Tell It Like It Is"* (Jackson: University Press of Mississippi, 2011).

Bibliography

MANUSCRIPT AND ARCHIVAL MATERIAL

Amistad Research Center, Tulane University, New Orleans
Fannie Lou Hamer Papers and accompanying audiotapes
Howard University, Washington, DC, Oral History Collection, Civil Rights Documenta-
tion Project, Moorland-Springarn Research Center
Lyndon B. Johnson Presidential Library, Austin, Texas
Martin Luther King Jr. Center for Nonviolent Social Change, Archives Department, At-
lanta, Georgia
Student Non-Violent Coordinating Committee Papers
Mary McLeod-Bethune Museum and Archives, Washington, DC
Fannie Lou Hamer File
Mississippi Department of Archives and History, Jackson, Mississippi
Fannie Lou Hamer Vertical File
Fannie Lou Hamer Funeral Videotape
Tougaloo College, *Zenobia* Coleman Library, Tougaloo, Mississippi
Fannie Lou Hamer Collection
Mississippi State University, Archives and Special Collections, Starksville, Mississippi
Citizens' Council Radio Forums
New York University, Tamiment Library/Robert F. Wagner Labor Archives, New York
George Breitman Papers
Smithsonian Institution, Washington, DC, National Museum of American History
Program in African American Culture, Moses Moon Collection
Stanford University, Department of Special Collections, Stanford, California
Project South Papers
University of Mississippi Archives and Special Collections, Oxford, Mississippi
Civil Rights and Race Relations Collection
University of Southern Mississippi McCain Library, Hattiesburg, Mississippi, Sue So-
journer Lorenzi Papers
Wisconsin Historical Society, Madison, Wisconsin
Civil Rights Collection
Measure for Measure File
Mississippi Freedom Democratic Party File
Social Action Vertical File
Sweet Papers

INTERVIEWS AND ORAL HISTORIES

By Author

Greg Bell, May 7, 2007 (phone)
Rita Schwerner Bender, July 15, 2010, Seattle, Washington
Owen Brooks, June 14, 2007, Jackson, Mississippi
Charles Cobb, September 25, 2012 (phone)
Dr. L. C. Dorsey, June 11, 2007, Jackson, Mississippi
Martha Fager, July 6, 2007 (phone)
Vergie Hamer Faulkner, June 14 and 17, 2009 (phone); April 9, 2010, Memphis, Tennessee; April 10, 2010, Ruleville, Mississippi
Jeff Goldstein, July 2, 2007, Madison, Wisconsin
Sarah Goldstein, July 2, 2007, Madison, Wisconsin
Lawrence Guyot, September 20, 2012 (phone)
Reverend Jesse Jackson Sr., March 11, 2012, Chicago, Illinois
Reverend Edwin King, June 15, 2007, Jackson, Mississippi
Dorie Ladner, September 15, 2012 (phone)
Monica Land, January 6, 2009; December 15, 2012 (e-mail)
Charles McLaurin with Davis W. Houck, Ruleville, Mississippi, April 10, 2010
Dr. Leslie McLemore, June 13, 2007, Jackson, Mississippi
Mary Moore, June 15, 2007, Ruleville, Mississippi
Hattie Robinson Jordan, June 16, 2007, Ruleville, Mississippi
Tracy Sugarman, July 13, 2012 (phone)
Charlie Sweet, April 24, 2007, Madison, Wisconsin
Jean Sweet, April 24, 2007, Madison, Wisconsin
Ambassador Andrew Young, June 25, 2007, Atlanta, Georgia

Secondary Interviews

Interview with Fannie Lou Hamer by Jack Minnis, March 17, 1964, Winona, Mississippi, Martin Luther King Jr. Center for Nonviolent Social Change, Archives Department, Atlanta, Georgia.
Excerpts of Interview with Fannie Lou Hamer by Colin Edwards, 1965, Collected Speeches of Fannie Lou Hamer, Pacifica Archives, North Hollywood, California.
Interview with Fannie Lou Hamer by Project South, 1965, MFDP Chapter 55, Box 6, Folder 160, Department of Special Collections, Stanford University Libraries, Stanford, California.
Interview with Fannie Lou Hamer by Anne Romaine, 1966, MFDP Papers, Wisconsin Historical Society, Madison, Wisconsin.
Interview with Fannie Lou Hamer by Robert Wright, August 9, 1968, Oral History Collection, Civil Rights Documentation Project, Moorland-Springarn Research Center, Howard University.
Interview with Fannie Lou Hamer by Neil R. McMillen, April 14, 1972. Part II of McMillen Interview, January 25, 1973, for the Mississippi Oral History Program of the University of Southern Mississippi.

Interview with Harry Belafonte by Kay Mills, January 28, 1991, Los Angeles, California. Courtesy of Kay Mills.

Interview with Senator Walter Mondale by Morgan Ginther, January 6, 2011, Minneapolis, Minnesota. Courtesy of Morgan Ginther.

ARTICLES AND BOOKS

Amossy, Ruth. "Ethos at the Crossroads of Disciplines: Rhetoric, Pragmatics, Sociology." *Poetics Today* 22, no. 1 (2001): 1–23.

Analavage, Robert. "Negroes Not Represented." *Southern Patriot*, May 1967.

Andrews, James R. "History and Theory in the Study of the Rhetoric of Social Movements." *Central States Speech Journal* 31 (Winter 1980): 274–281.

Appleby, Joyce, Alan Brinkley, and James McPherson. *The American Journey*. New York: Glencoe/McGraw-Hill, 2000.

Appleby, Joyce, Alan Brinkley, Albert S. Broussard, James M. McPherson, and Donald A. Ritchie. *The American Vision*. New York: Glencoe/McGraw-Hill, 2003.

Aristotle. *Rhetoric*. Translated by W. R. Roberts. New York: Modern Library, 1954.

Asante, Molefi K. *Afrocentricity*. Trenton, NJ: Africa World Press, 1988.

Asch, Chris Myers. *The Senator and the Sharecropper: The Freedom Struggles of James O. Eastland and Fannie Lou Hamer*. Chapel Hill: University of North Carolina Press, 2008.

Ayers, Edward L., Robert D. Schulzinger, Jesus F. de la Teja, and Deborah Gray White with Sam Wineburg. *American Anthem: Modern American History*. Orlando, FL: Holt, Rinehart, and Winston/Harcourt, 2007.

Bambara, Toni Cade, and Eleanor W. Traylor, eds. *The Black Woman: An Anthology*. New York: Washington Square Press, 2005.

Belfrage, Sally. *Freedom Summer*. New York: Viking, 1965.

Blackwell, Edward H. "Taste of Hunger Menu." *Milwaukee Journal*, February 23, 1971.

Booth, M. W. "The Art of Words in Songs." *Quarterly Journal of Speech* 62 (October 1976): 242–249.

Boorstin, Daniel J., and Brooks Mather Kelley with Ruth Frankel Boorstin. *A History of the United States*. Needham, MA: Pearson/Prentice Hall, 2005.

Booth, Wayne C. *The Rhetoric of Fiction*, 2nd ed. Chicago: University of Chicago Press, 1983.

Bosmajian, Haig A., and Hamida Bosmajian. *The Rhetoric of the Civil Rights Movement*. New York: Random House, 1969.

Bramlett-Solomon, Sharon. "Civil Rights Vanguard in the Deep South: Newspaper Portrayal of Fannie Lou Hamer, 1964–1977." *Journalism Quarterly* (Fall 1991): 515–521.

Breitman, George, ed. *Malcolm X Speaks*. New York: Grove Weidenfeld, 1965.

Brevard, Lisa Pertillar. "'Will the Circle be Unbroken': African-American Women's Spirituality in Sacred Song Traditions." In *My Soul is a Witness: African-American Women's Spirituality*. Edited by Gloria Wade-Gayles. Boston: Beacon Press, 1995.

Brockriede, Wayne E., and Robert L. Scott. "Stokely Carmichael: Two Speeches on Black Power." *Central States Speech Journal* 9 (Spring 1968): 3–13.

Brodkin, Karen Sacks. *Caring by the Hour: Women, Work, and Organizing at Duke Medical Center*. Urbana: University of Illinois Press, 1988.

Brooks, Maegan Parker. "Oppositional Ethos: Fannie Lou Hamer and the Vernacular Persona." *Rhetoric & Public Affairs* 14 (Fall 2011): 511–548.

———, and Davis W. Houck, eds. *The Speeches of Fannie Lou Hamer: "To Tell It Like It Is."* Jackson: University Press of Mississippi, 2011.

Burke, Kenneth. *Attitudes Toward History.* Berkeley: University of California Press, 1984.

———. *Permanence and Change.* Berkeley: University of California Press, 1984.

Burner, Eric. *And Gently He Shall Lead Them: Robert Parris Moses and Civil Rights in Mississippi.* New York: New York University Press, 1994.

Burns, Stewart. *Social Movements of the 1960s: Searching for Democracy.* Boston: Twayne Publishers, 1990.

Butler, Judith. *Giving an Account of Oneself.* New York: Fordham University Press, 2005.

Campbell, Karlyn Kohrs. "The Rhetoric of Black Nationalism: A Case Study of Self-Conscious Criticism." *Central States Speech Journal* 22 (1971): 151–160.

———, and Kathleen H. Jamieson, eds. *Form and Genre: Shaping Rhetorical Action.* Falls Church, VA: Speech Communication Association, 1978.

———. *Man Cannot Speak for Her, Volume I: A Critical Study of Early Feminist Rhetoric.* Westport, CT: Praeger, 1989.

———, ed. *Women Public Speakers in the United States, 1925–1993.* Westport, CT: Greenwood Press, 1994.

———. "Agency: Promiscuous and Protean." *Communication and Critical/Cultural Studies* 2, no. 1 (2005): 1–19.

Carawan, Guy, and Candie Carawan. *We Shall Overcome!: Songs of the Southern Freedom Movement.* New York: Oak Press, 1963.

———. *Freedom Is a Constant Struggle: Songs of the Freedom Movement.* New York: Oak Press, 1968.

Carmichael, Stokely, with Ekwueme Michael Thelwell. *Ready for Revolution: The Life and Struggles of Stokely Carmichael {Kwame Ture}.* New York: Scribner, 2003.

Carney Smith, Jessie, ed. *Epic Lives: One Hundred Black Women Who Made a Difference.* Detroit, MI: Visible Ink Press, 1993.

Carson, Clayborne. *In Struggle: SNCC and the Black Awakening of the 1960s.* Cambridge, MA: Harvard University Press, 1981.

———. "1965: A Decisive Turning Point in the Long Struggle for Voting Rights." *Crisis* 112, no. 4 (July–August 2005): 16–20.

Cayton, Andrew, Elisabeth Israels Perry, Linda Reed, and Allan M. Winkler. *America: Pathways to the Present.* Needham, MS: Pearson/Prentice Hall, 2005.

Childs, John, and Noel Workman. "More Choppers Join Farm Labor Strike." *Delta Democrat Times,* June 4, 1965.

Collier-Thomas, Bettye, and V. P. Franklin, eds. *Sisters in the Struggle.* New York: New York University Press, 2001.

Condit, Celeste. "Rhetorical Criticism and Audiences: The Extremes of McGee and Leff." *Western Journal of Speech Communication* 54 (1990): 330–345.

"CORE to Urge House to Block Seating of Five Mississippians." *New York Times,* December 29, 1964, 14.

Cortez, Jayne. "Big Fine Woman from Ruleville (for Fannie Lou Hamer)." *Black Collegian* 9, no. 5 (May/June 1979): 90.

Crosby, Emilye. *A Little Taste of Freedom: The Black Freedom Struggle in Claiborne County, Mississippi.* Chapel Hill: University of North Carolina Press, 2005.

————, ed. *Civil Rights History from the Ground Up: Local Struggles, A National Movement*. Athens: University of Georgia Press, 2011.

Dalek, Robert. *Flawed Giant: Lyndon Johnson and His Times, 1961–1973*. New York: Oxford University Press, 1998.

Danzer, Gerald A., J. Jorge Klor de Alva, Nancy Woloch, and Louis E. Wilson. *The Americans: Reconstruction to the 21st Century*. Evanston, IL: McDougal Littell, 2009.

DeLaure, Marilyn Bordwell. "Planting Seeds of Change: Ella Baker's Radical Rhetoric." *Women's Studies in Communication* 31 (2008): 1–28.

Demuth, Jerry. "'Tired of Being Sick and Tired.'" *Nation*, June 1, 1964, 548–551.

Dittmer, John. *Local People: The Struggle for Civil Rights in Mississippi*. Chicago: University of Illinois Press, 1995.

Dollard, John. *Caste and Class in a Southern Town*, 3rd ed. New York: Doubleday, 1957.

DuBois, W. E. B. "Returning Soldiers." *Crisis* (May 1919): 13–14.

Eagles, Charles W. "Toward New Histories of the Civil Rights Era." *Journal of Southern History* 66 (November 2000): 815–848.

————, ed. *The Civil Rights Movement in America*. Jackson: University of Mississippi Press, 1986.

Edgerton, John. *A Mind to Stay Here: Profiles from the South*. New York: MacMillan, 1970.

Erenrich, Susie, ed. *Freedom Is a Constant Struggle: An Anthology of the Mississippi Civil Rights Movement*. Montgomery, AL: Black Belt Press, 1999.

"Fannie Lou 'Tell it Like it Is.'" *Harvard Crimson*, November 23, 1968, 1.

Farrell, Thomas B. *Norms of Rhetorical Culture*. New Haven, CT: Yale University Press, 1993.

Fish, Stanley. *Self-consuming Artifacts*. Berkeley: University of California Press, 1972.

Fitts, Leroy. *A History of Black Baptists*. Nashville, TN: Broadman, 1985.

Forman, James. "Freedom Push in Mississippi: Civil Rights Leader Tells Aim of Ambitious Summer Project." *Los Angeles Times*, June 14, 1964, L3.

————. *The Making of Black Revolutionaries*. Seattle, WA: Open Hand Publishing, 1985.

Garver, Eugene. *Aristotle's Rhetoric: An Art of Character*. Chicago: University of Chicago Press, 1994.

Gates, Henry Louis, Jr. *The Signifying Monkey: A Theory of African American Literary Criticism*. New York: Oxford University Press, 1988.

Glaude, Eddie S., Jr. *Exodus! Religion, Race, and Nation in Early Nineteenth-Century Black America*. Chicago: University of Chicago Press, 2000.

Gray, Lloyd. "The glitter is gone, but the fight goes on." *Delta Democrat-Times*, October 3, 1976, 1 and 12.

Greene, Christina. *Our Separate Ways: Women and the Black Freedom Movement in Durham, North Carolina*. Chapel Hill: University of North Carolina Press, 2005.

Hall, Jacquelyn Dowd. "The Long Civil Rights Movement and the Political Uses of the Past." *Journal of American History* 91 (March 2005): 1233–1263.

————,Eugene P. Walker, Katherine Mellen Charron, and David P. Cline. "'I train the people to do their own talking': Septima Clark and Women in the Civil Rights Movement." *Southern Cultures* 16, no. 2 (2010): 31–52.

Hamer, Fannie Lou. "'Sick and Tired of Being Sick and Tired.'" *Katallagete!: The Journal of the Committee of Southern Churchmen* (Fall 1968): 26.

————. "Fannie Lou Hamer Speaks Out." *Essence* 1, no. 6 (October 1971): 53–75.

———. "To Praise Our Bridges." In *Mississippi Writers: Reflections of Childhood and Youth*. Edited by Dorothy Abbott, vol. 2. Jackson: University Press of Mississippi, 1986.

"Hamer Rites: Civil Rights Leaders To Attend." *Jackson Daily News*, March 20, 1977.

Hamlet, Janice D. "Fannie Lou Hamer: The Unquenchable Spirit of the Civil Rights Movement." *Journal of Black Studies* 26, no. 5 (May 1996): 560–576.

Handler, M. S. "CORE Hears Cries of 'Black Power.'" *New York Times*, July 2, 1966, 18.

Harris-Lacewell, Melissa. "Obama and the Sisters." *Nation*, September 1, 2008.

Hibbard, Tom. "Local Students Tell Why Blacks Didn't Get Vote." *Capital Times*, November 12, 1971, 9.

Hine, Darlene Clark. "Rape and the Inner Lives of Black Women in the Middle West: Preliminary Thoughts on the Culture of Dissemblance." *Signs* 14 (Summer 1989): 912–920.

Hogan, Wesley C. *Many Minds, One Heart: SNCC's Dream for a New America*. Chapel Hill: University of North Carolina Press, 2007.

Houck, Davis W., and David E. Dixon, eds. *Rhetoric, Religion, and the Civil Rights Movement: 1954–1965*. Waco, TX: Baylor University Press, 2006.

———, and David E. Dixon, eds. *Women and the Civil Rights Movement, 1954–1965*. Jackson: University Press of Mississippi, 2009.

———, and Maegan Parker Brooks. "We're On Our Way." *Voices of Democracy* 6 (2011): 21–43.

———. "Fannie Lou Hamer on Winona: Memory, Trauma, and Recovery." In *The Rhetorical History of the United States: Social Controversy and Public Address in the 1960s and Early 1970s*. Edited by Richard Jensen and David Henry (forthcoming 2013).

Howard, Robert Glenn. "A Theory of Vernacular Rhetoric: The Case of the 'Sinner's Prayer' Online." *Folklore* 116 (2005): 174–191.

———. "Toward a Theory of the World Wide Web Vernacular: The Case for Pet Cloning." *Journal of Folklore Research* 42 (2005): 323–360.

———. "The Vernacular Web of Participatory Media." *Critical Studies in Media Communication* 25 (2008): 490–513.

Howard-Pitney, David. *The Afro-American Jeremiad: Appeals for Justice in America*. Philadelphia: Temple University Press, 1990.

Jackson, Ronald L. II, and Elaine B. Richardson, eds. *Understanding African American Rhetoric: Classical Origins to Contemporary Innovations*. New York: Routledge, 2003.

Jasinski, James. *Sourcebook on Rhetoric: Key Concepts in Contemporary Rhetorical Studies*. Thousand Oaks, CA: Sage, 2001.

Jeffries, Hasan Kwame. "SNCC, Black Power, and Independent Political Party Organizing in Alabama, 1964–1966." *Journal of American History* 91, no. 2 (Spring 2006): 171–193.

———. *Bloody Lowndes: Civil Rights and Black Power in Alabama's Black Belt*. New York: New York University Press, 2009.

Jensen, Richard J., and John C. Hammerback. "'Your Tools Are Really the People': The Rhetoric of Robert Parris Moses." *Communication Monographs* 65 (June 1998): 126–140.

———. "Working in 'Quiet Places': The Community Organizing Rhetoric of Robert Parris Moses." *Howard Journal of Communications* 11 (2000): 1–18.

Jewell, K. Sue. *From Mammy to Miss America: Cultural Images & the Shaping of US Social Policy*. London: Routledge, 1993.

Johnson, Susan. "Fannie Lou Hamer: Mississippi Grassroots Organizer." *Black Law Journal* 2 (Summer 1972): 154–162.

Johnson, Thomas A. "Mississippi Poll Watchers Say Harassment Barred Fair Tally." *New York Times*, November 6, 1971.

Jordan, June. *Fannie Lou Hamer*. New York: Thomas Y. Crowell Company, 1972.

Kelley, Robin D. G., and Earl Lewis, eds. *To Make Our World Anew: A History of African Americans*. Oxford: Oxford University Press, 2000.

King, Edwin. "Go Tell It on the Mountain: A Prophet from the Delta." *Sojourner* (December 1982).

King, M. "The Rhetorical Legacy of the Black Church." *Central States Speech Journal* 22 (1971): 179–185.

Kling, Susan. *Fannie Lou Hamer: A Biography*. Women for Racial and Economic Equality, 1979.

Landauer, Megan, and Jonathon Wolman. "Fannie Lou Hamer '. . . forcing a new political reality." *Daily Cardinal*, October 8, 1971.

Lee, Chana Kai. *For Freedom's Sake: The Life of Fannie Lou Hamer*. Urbana: University of Illinois Press, 1999.

Leff, Michael C. "Interpretation and the Art of the Rhetorical Critic." *Western Journal of Speech Communication* 44 (1980): 337–349.

Lerner, Gerda, ed. *Black Women in White America: A Documentary History*. New York: Vintage, 1972.

Leslie, Gay. "Rights Matriarch Pleads for Action Now." *Wisconsin State Journal*, July 19, 1969.

Ling, Peter, and Sharon Monteith, eds. *Gender in the Civil Rights Movement*. New York: Garland, 1999.

Locke, Mamie E. "The Role of African-American Women in the Civil Rights and Women's Movements in Hinds Country and Sunflower County, Mississippi." *Journal of Mississippi History* 53 (August 1991): 229–239.

Lubasch, Arnold H. "Malcolm Favors a Mau Mau in US." *New York Times*, December 21, 1964, 20.

Lucas, Stephen. "Coming to Terms with Movement Studies." *Central States Speech Journal* 31 (Winter 1980): 255–266.

———. "The Renaissance of American Public Address: Text and Context in Rhetorical Criticism." *Quarterly Journal of Speech* 74 (1988): 241–260.

Loftus, Joseph A. "5 Mississippians Seated By House: But Liberals Muster 148 Votes Against Them." *New York Times*, January 5, 1965, 17.

Lynd, Staughton. "A Radical Speaks in Defense of SNCC." *New York Times*, September 10, 1967, 271.

Marsh, Charles. *God's Long Summer: Stories of Faith and Civil Rights*. Princeton, NJ: Princeton University Press, 1997.

McBride, Marian. "Fannie Lou Hamer: Nobody Knows the Trouble She's Seen." *Washington Post*, July 14, 1968, H12.

McGehee, Molly. "'You Do Not Own What You Cannot Control': An Interview with Activist and Folklorist Worth Long." *Mississippi Folklife* 31 (Fall 1998): 12–20.

McGuire, Danielle L., and John Dittmer, eds. *Freedom Rights: New Perspectives on the Civil Rights Movement and the Struggle for Black Equality in the Twentieth Century*. Lexington: University of Kentucky Press, 2011.

———. *At the Dark End of the Street: Black Women, Rape, and Resistance—A New History of the Civil Rights Movement.* New York: Vintage, 2011.

McMillen, Neil R. *Dark Journey: Black Mississippians in the Age of Jim Crow.* Urbana: University of Illinois Press, 1989.

———. *The Citizens' Council: Organized Resistance to the Second Reconstruction, 1954–1964.* Urbana: University of Illinois Press, 1994.

Medhurst, Martin J., ed. *Landmark Essays on American Public Address.* Davis, CA: Hermagoras Press, 1993.

Mills, Kay. *This Little Light of Mine: The Life of Fannie Lou Hamer.* New York: Penguin, 1993.

Mitchell, Henry H. *Black Preaching: The Recovery of a Powerful Art.* Nashville, TN: Abingdon Press, 1990.

Moye, J. Todd. *Let the People Decide: Black Freedom and White Resistance Movements in Sunflower County, Mississippi, 1945–1986.* Chapel Hill: University of North Carolina Press, 2004.

Murphy, John M. "Barack Obama, the Exodus Tradition, and the Joshua Generation." *Quarterly Journal of Speech* 97, no. 4 (November 2011): 387–410.

O'Dell, J. H. "Life in Mississippi: An Interview with Fannie Lou Hamer." *Freedomways* 5, no. 2 (Spring 1965): 231–242.

Ono, Kent A., and John M. Sloop. "The Critique of Vernacular Discourse." *Communication Monographs* 62 (1995): 19–46.

Painter, Nell Irvin. *Sojourner Truth, A Life, A Symbol.* New York: W. W. Norton & Company, 1996.

Parker, Frank R. *Black Votes Count: Political Empowerment in Mississippi after 1965.* Chapel Hill: University of North Carolina Press, 1990.

Parker, Maegan. "Ironic Openings: The Interpretive Challenge of the 'Black Manifesto.'" *Quarterly Journal of Speech* 94, no. 3 (August 2008): 320–342.

Payne, Charles M. *I've Got the Light of Freedom: The Organizing Tradition and the Mississippi Freedom Struggle.* Berkeley: University of California Press, 1995.

Perelman, Chaim, and Lucie Olbrechts-Tyteca. *The New Rhetoric: A Treatise on Argumentation.* Notre Dame, IN: University of Notre Dame Press, 1969.

Peterson, Carla L. *"Doers of the Word": African-American Women Speakers & Writers in the North.* New Brunswick, NJ: Rutgers University Press, 1998.

Peterson, Franklyn. "Sunflowers Don't Grow in Sunflower County." *Sepia* 19 (1970): 8–18.

Pfefferkorn, Robert. "From one who pursued equality, a plea for love." *Wisconsin State Journal* (January 30, 1976).

Pipes, William Harrison. "Old-Time Negro Preaching: An Interpretive Study." *Quarterly Journal of Speech* 33 (February 1948): 15–21.

Raines, Howell. *My Soul Is Rested: Movement Days in the Deep South Remembered.* New York: Putnam, 1977.

Ransby, Barbara. *Ella Baker and the Black Freedom Movement: A Radical Democratic Vision.* Chapel Hill: University of North Carolina Press, 2003.

Reagon, Bernice Johnson. "My Black Mothers and Sisters; or, On Beginning a Cultural Biography." *Feminist Studies* 8, no. 1 (Spring 1982): 81–96.

———. "Let the Church Sing 'Freedom.'" *Black Music Research Journal* 7 (1987): 105–118.

———. "Women as Culture Carriers in the Civil Rights Movement: Fannie Lou Hamer." In *Women in the Civil Rights Movement: Trailblazers and Torchbearers, 1941–1965.*

Edited by Vicki Crawford, Jaqueline Rouse, and Barbara Woods. New York: Carlson, 1990. 203–232.

———. "'Nobody Knows the Trouble I See'; or 'By and By I'm Gonna Lay Down My Heavy Load.'" *Journal of American History* 78, no. 1 (June 1991): 111–119.

Reed, Linda. "Fannie Lou Hamer (1917–1977): A New Voice in American Democracy." In *Mississippi Women: Their Histories, Their Lives*. Edited by Martha H. Swain, Elizabeth Ann Payne, Marjorie Julian Spruill, and Susan Ditto. Athens: University of Georgia Press, 2003. 249–267.

Robnett, Belinda. *How Long? How Long? African Women in the Struggle for Civil Rights*. New York: Oxford University Press, 1997.

Ross, Rosetta E. *Witnessing and Testifying: Black Women, Religion, and Civil Rights*. Minneapolis: Fortress, 2003.

Rubel, David. *Fannie Lou Hamer: From Sharecropping to Politics*. Englewood Cliffs, NJ: Silver Burdett Press, 1990.

Sanger, K. L. "Functions of Freedom Singing in the Civil Rights Movement: The Activists' Implicit Rhetorical Theory." *Howard Journal of Communications* 8, no. 2 (1997): 179–195.

Scott, Robert L., and Donald K. Smith. "The Rhetoric of Confrontation." *Quarterly Journal of Speech* 56 (February 1969): 1–8.

Sewell, George. "Fannie Lou Hamer." *Black Collegian* 8, no. 5 (May/June 1978): 18–20.

Sierichs, Bill. "'Sin-Sickness' Probed at Crime Meet." *Jackson Daily News*, March 24, 1976, B.

Silver, James. *Mississippi: The Closed Society*. New York: Harcourt, Brace & World, 1963.

Smitherman, Geneva. *Talkin and Testifyin: The Language of Black America*. Detroit, MI: Wayne State University Press, 1977.

———. *Talkin That Talk: Language, Culture, and Education in America*. New York: Routledge, 2000.

———. *Word from the Mother: Language and African Americans*. New York: Routledge, 2006.

Springer, Kimberly, ed. *Still Lifting, Still Climbing: African American Women's Contemporary Activism*. New York: New York University Press, 1999.

Stuckey, Sterling, Linda Kerrigan Salvucci with Judith Irvin. *A Call to Freedom*. Austin, TX: Holt, Rinehart, and Winston/Harcourt, 2003.

Sugarman, Tracy. *Stranger at the Gates: A Summer in Mississippi*. New York: Hill and Wang, 1966.

———. *We Had Sneakers, They Had Guns: The Kids Who Fought for Civil Rights in Mississippi*. Syracuse, NY: Syracuse University Press, 2009.

Terrill, Robert E. "Irony, Silence, and Time: Frederick Douglass on the Fifth of July." *Quarterly Journal of Speech* 89 (2003): 224–225.

———. *Malcolm X: Inventing Radical Judgment*. East Lansing: Michigan State Press, 2004.

Torres, Sasha. *Black, White and in Color: Television and Black Civil Rights*. Princeton, NJ: Princeton University Press, 2003.

Walzer, Michael. *Exodus and Revolution*. New York: Basic Books, 1985.

Warnick, Barbara. "Leff in Context: What Is the Critic's Role?" *Quarterly Journal of Speech* 78 (1992): 232–237.

Watters, Pat, and Reese Cleghorn. *Climbing Jacob's Ladder: The Arrival of Negroes in Southern Politics*. New York: Harcourt, Brace & World, 1967.

Watters, Pat. *Down to Now: Reflections on the Southern Civil Rights Movement*. New York: Pantheon, 1971.

White, Deborah Gray. *Too Heavy a Load: Black Women in Defense of Themselves, 1894–1994*. New York: W. W. Norton & Company, 1999.

Wilson, Kirt H. "Interpreting the Discursive Field of the Montgomery Bus Boycott: Martin Luther King Jr.'s Holt Street Address." *Rhetoric & Public Affairs* 8, no. 2 (2005): 299–326.

Wolman, Jonathon. "Mississippi Elections: By Hook or Crook." *Daily Cardinal*, November 5, 1971, 1.

———. "Mississippi Elections: Facing an Old Political Reality." *Daily Cardinal*, November 11, 1971, 1.

Yockey, Roger. "King Co. 'Adopts' Sunflower County." *Progress*, March 7, 1969, 3.

Young, Bille Jean. *Fear Not the Fall and Fannie Lou Hamer: This Little Light . . . .* Montgomery, AL: New South Books, 2004.

Zarefsky, David. "Coming to Terms with Movement Studies." *Central States Speech Journal* 31 (Winter 1980): 245–254.

MISCELLANEOUS SOURCES

Freedom on My Mind. DVD. Directed by Connie Field and Marilyn Mulford. South Burlington, VT: California Newsreel, 1994.

Ginther, Morgan Louise. "From the Closed Society to the Realization of Freedom: Mississippi Delegation Debate at the 1964 Democratic National Convention." Ph.D. diss., University of Memphis, 2011.

Griffin, Farah Jasmine. "DNC Day 4: Remembering Fannie Lou Hamer." From Conventional Wisdom, National Public Radio Transcript, August 29, 2008.

Griffin-Jeuchter, Kay. "Fannie Lou Hamer: From Sharecropper to Freedom Fighter." Master's thesis, Sarah Lawrence College, 1990.

"Key Historic Moments Set the Stage for Obama." National Public Radio Transcript, August 25, 2008.

Reagon, Bernice Johnson. *The Songs Are Free with Bill Moyers*. New York: Mystic Fire Video, 1991.

Sojourner, Sue Lorenzi. *Mrs. Hamer Speaks* photography exhibit within the touring show: "THE SOME PEOPLE OF THAT PLACE—1960, Holmes, Co.: The People and Their Movement."

"Songs My Mother Taught Me." Tape produced by Bernice Johnson Reagon, financed by the We Shall Overcome Fund and the National Endowment for the Humanities, 1980. Songs taped by Worth Long.

Voices of the Civil Rights Movement: Black American Freedom Songs, 1960–1966. Washington, DC: Smithsonian Institution Folkways Recording, 1980.

Index

Acts 17:26, 32, 116, 168, 219
African American Vernacular English (AAVE), 29, 69, 95
"Ain't Gonna Let Nobody Turn Us Around," 39, 224
Allen, Bobbie, 239
Angelou, Maya, 234–35
Atlantic City, New Jersey, 48, 74, 84, 86, 89–91, 94, 105–6, 111, 123, 125, 127, 132, 136, 145–47, 176

Baker, Ella, 35, 41–42, 46, 73, 88–90, 92, 154, 192, 223–24, 228
Belafonte, Harry, 3–4, 30, 127–28, 130, 149, 198, 231
Bethune, Mary McCleod, 99
Bevel, James, 34, 37–38, 61, 223, 232, 241
Bible, 26–28, 33, 137, 160, 168
black Baptist church, 7, 13, 26–28, 30, 42, 44, 51, 117, 187
black empowerment, 24, 238
black equality. See equality
black resistance, 7, 241
black self-reliance, 17
Block, Sam, 35
bottom-up approach to studying black freedom movements, 6–7, 9, 245
boycotts, 26, 34, 88
Brandon plantation, 19
Brooks, Owen, 28, 186, 196, 224–25
Brown, H. Rap, 223
Brown v. Board of Education, 24–25, 124
Burton, Willie, 241, 243

Campbell, Cecil, 38–40, 148, 152
Carmichael, Stokely, 9, 18, 123, 153–57, 223, 225–29, 241
Carter, Hodding, III, 9, 172, 223, 225–26, 230, 242
CEP. See Citizen Education Program
Chaney, James, 77–78, 83, 90–91, 112, 160
cheap labor, 14–15

Chicago Defender, 26
Childs, Jaelyn, 242
Citizens' Council, 25, 34, 36, 53, 55, 101, 124, 129
Citizenship Education Program (CEP), 54–55, 241
civil religion. See religion
civil rights, 3, 38, 60–61, 84, 88, 91–92, 98, 105, 124–25, 130, 139, 142, 145, 153, 170, 183, 189, 193, 209–10, 231–32, 236, 238; abuses, 98, 138; activists, 6, 37, 41, 45, 49, 60, 125, 130, 142, 149–50, 174, 232–33, 245; activities, 34, 39, 41–42, 50, 80, 158; advocacy, 46; cases, 74; history, 6; leaders, 3, 91, 102, 105, 125, 172, 214; legislation, 26, 73, 88; meeting, 50; movement, 7, 28, 30, 42, 65, 158, 184, 196–98, 236, 241, 243; orators, 27; organizations, 24, 34, 48, 66, 84, 91, 94, 100, 119, 124, 142, 156, 158, 196; supporters, 59, 88, 94, 150, 162; violations, 58; workers, 3, 35, 38, 58–59, 61, 75, 90, 112, 224. See also human rights
Civil Rights Act of 1964, 88, 91
Clarion-Ledger, 25
Clark, Septima, 41, 54
clergy, 33–34, 64, 90
Clinton, Bill, 3, 235
community empowerment, 171, 211, 213
community organizing, 7, 14, 154
Congress of Racial Equality (CORE), 26, 34, 55, 91, 122, 142, 154–55, 157, 171
Conyers, John, 231
Council of Federated Organizations (COFO), 34, 36, 41, 45, 66–67, 69–77, 79–80, 82, 84, 87–90, 100, 123, 126, 139–40, 158, 163
Crook, Robert, 178, 181, 242
Current, Gloster, 124, 231

Dane County, Wisconsin. See Wisconsin
Davis, Ossie, 233

Davis, Ruby, 238
Dee, Ruby, 233
Delta Democrat-Times, 153, 209, 225
Democratic National Convention (DNC),
    7, 11, 39, 43, 48, 62, 74, 83, 85–87, 101–2,
    104–10, 119, 122, 124, 130, 136, 144, 172,
    174–75, 177, 206, 208, 226, 232–35, 238,
    241–42
Democratic Party, 3, 8, 45, 87–88, 91,
    93–94, 98, 101–2, 104–6, 123, 125,
    130, 136–37, 169, 173, 175–77, 183, 225,
    234–36, 242
desegregation, 55
Devine, Annie, 76, 104, 137–41, 147–48,
    223, 238
Diggs, Charles, 103, 223
discrimination, 33, 46, 74, 84, 94, 97–98,
    103, 132–33, 183, 235; housing, 245;
    voter, 140–41, 143, 145–46, 148–49, 182,
    235
divine justice, 18, 27, 32, 42
Donahoe, Edgar, 242
Douglass, Frederick, 109, 234

Eastland, James O., 88, 124, 134, 158, 195,
    218, 227, 240
economic equality. *See* equality
economic terrorism, 36
Edwards, Shirley, 241
Ephesians 6:5, 33, 161, 216, 219
equality, 8, 24, 27, 42, 143, 148, 162, 178, 231;
    black, 26; economic, 193; gender, 183;
    racial, 60, 99, 126, 129
Evers, Charles, 151, 172, 222
Evers, Medgar, 60–61, 160, 163, 233
Exodus narrative, 27–28, 46, 49, 110, 117,
    233

Fannie Lou Hamer Memorial Garden, 3,
    238–40, 242–43
Fannie Lou Hamer Recreation Center,
    238–40
Fannie Lou Hamer Statue and Museum,
    3, 9, 236, 238–40, 242, 244
Fanon, Frantz, 131
Farenthold, Francis, 206, 208
Farmer, James, 91, 93

Faulkner, Vergie Hamer, 3, 22, 239
Forman, James, 36–38, 76, 127, 194, 223, 241
Forum, The, 25
Freedom Farm Cooperative, 8, 12, 169,
    194, 196–202, 207, 210–13, 219, 236–37,
    240, 242
Freedom Rides, 26, 35, 55
Freedom Summer, 48, 72–76, 78–83,
    87–90, 96, 99–100, 107, 124, 126, 185,
    224, 230, 232, 240
"Friends of Fannie Lou Hamer" fund, 213,
    219–20
fundraising, 7, 14, 149, 162, 201–2, 205, 238

Galatians 6:7, 27
Garvey, Marcus, 15, 131
gender equality. *See* equality
"Go Tell It on the Mountain," 30–31, 34, 89
Goldstein, Jeff, 198, 200, 202, 204, 211–14
Goldstein, Sarah, 214
Goldwater, Barry, 88, 93, 104, 125
Goodman, Andrew, 77–78, 83, 90–91, 112,
    160
grandfather clause, 38
Gray Adams, Victoria, 79, 238
Great Migration, 13
Guyot, Lawrence, 59–60, 64, 76, 90, 106,
    118, 121, 139–40, 167, 172–73, 184, 193,
    224, 235

Hall, Prathia, 11, 127
Hamer, Dorothy Jean, 22–23, 54, 163–65,
    190, 211, 223–24
Hamer, Fannie Lou: burial, 237; child-
    hood, 16–18, 40, 208; congresswoman
    persona, 144, 146; death, 9, 223, 225–26,
    228–30, 232–33, 237, 244; education, 7,
    19–20, 29, 42–43; empowered persona,
    118, 122; forced sterilization, 22, 72, 189;
    health, 8, 12, 65, 162, 166, 207–8, 214,
    220, 222; intellect, 7, 20–21, 41, 84, 86,
    107, 245; marriage, 21; outsider per-
    sona, 176; persona, 4, 7–8, 28, 48–49,
    84, 122, 162; political persona, 176;
    public persona, 7–8, 162; prophetic
    persona, 28, 233, 244; rebellious nature,
    21–22, 42; sharecropper persona, 7,

16–21, 41, 162, 167, 175, 227, 232–33, 244; singing, 20, 26, 28, 30, 39, 51, 53, 79, 121, 209, 224; symbolic significance, 84, 231; symbolic status, 4, 7, 46, 78, 84, 86, 106, 120–22, 126, 175, 181, 241, 244; truth telling persona, 8, 170, 175, 207–8, 244; vernacular persona, 48–49, 70, 84; warrior persona, 8, 131, 143, 153, 159, 162, 165–67, 228, 244

Hamer, Perry "Pap," 21–24, 37, 40, 49, 51–52, 185–86, 199, 220–21, 237, 241

Hamer v. Campbell, 148, 152

Hanlon, Brian, 238

harassment, 37, 39, 53, 68, 228, 233

Harris, Donald, 127, 131

Harris, Joe, 213

Hayden, Casey, 73

healthcare, 15, 126, 165, 177, 245

Hederman press, 25

Height, Dorothy, 211, 223–24

housing discrimination. *See* discrimination

Hudson, Winston, 90

human rights, 5–6, 99, 106, 166, 209, 230–31, 242. *See also* civil rights

Humphrey, Hubert, 88, 102–3, 106, 136, 145, 241

Hurst, E. H., 36, 160

image making, 29, 61–62

Indianola, Mississippi. *See* Mississippi

integration. *See* racial integration

interracial relationships: audience, 130, 159, 191; coalitions, 166, 170–72, 180, 193; communication, 13; cooperation, 171, 196, 210–14, 218–19, 225–26, 242–43; delegation, 176; love, 220, 225–26, 242; movement, 23, 161, 175, 205, 242; sisterhood, 191

intimidation, 16, 37, 39, 53, 133, 140, 150–51, 153, 181, 235

Jackson, Jesse, Sr., 86, 95, 231

Jackson Daily News, 25

Jeremiad, 7–8, 43, 49, 85–87, 106–7, 109–10, 113, 117, 119, 126, 134, 143, 146, 149, 159, 161, 168, 179, 181, 214, 216, 230–31, 245

Jet, 25

Johnson, June, 53, 56, 221

Johnson, Lyndon, 73, 88, 91, 106

Jordan, Hattie Robinson, 11, 238, 241

Jordan, Vernon, 223–24

King, Coretta Scott, 3, 234

King, Edward, 5, 30–31, 83, 90, 92–93, 100, 102–4, 121, 189, 195, 220

King, Martin Luther, Jr., 34, 57, 60, 91–93, 102–3, 180, 215, 218, 234

Lee, Herbert E., 36, 65, 73, 160

Lewis, John, 127, 154, 173, 177, 209, 234–35

literacy tests, 38, 52, 142, 178, 181, 233

Little Rock Nine, 26

love, 116, 118, 163, 190, 202, 206, 214, 216–18, 220, 224, 231–32; interracial, 220, 225–26, 242; tough, 126, 153, 244; unconditional, 220

Luke, 44

Luke 4:17–19, 31

Luke 12:2, 32

Luke 12:56, 37

lynching, 15–16, 25–26, 83, 90, 111, 133, 233, 237

Madison, Wisconsin. *See* Wisconsin

Malcolm X, 62, 119, 121–22, 131, 137, 153, 156, 180

Malveaux, Julianne, 239, 241, 243, 245

Marlow plantation, 21–24, 40, 42, 49, 52, 72, 96, 132

mass mobilization, 6, 9

Matthew 28:19, 31

McDonald, Joe, 36, 238, 241

McDowell, Cleve, 237

McLaurin, Charles, 35–39, 41, 50–52, 66–68, 74, 108, 119, 154, 179–81, 211, 237–42

McLemore, Leslie, 3, 21, 30, 90–92, 99, 119, 185, 211–12, 221, 223

Measure for Measure, 198, 202, 204–5, 211–15, 219–20

MFDP. *See* Mississippi Freedom Democratic Party

mimicry, 29, 69–71

miscegenation, 25
Mississippi: Indianola, 7, 24, 33, 38–39, 52, 64, 80–81, 86–87, 95, 107–11, 117, 119, 170, 241; Ruleville, 3, 9, 11–12, 14, 21–22, 25, 33, 36–39, 42, 49–52, 58, 68, 72, 74, 79–80, 83, 96, 109, 119, 179, 194, 197, 200–201, 205–6, 209–10, 212–14, 217–23, 230–31, 236–42; Sunflower County, 12–15, 33, 35, 67, 69, 72, 79, 81, 83, 88, 109, 121–22, 125, 148–50, 152, 160, 169, 177–78, 181, 186, 195, 200, 202, 211, 220–21, 245; Winona, 53, 55–66, 72, 96–97, 110, 132, 144, 160, 162, 165, 208, 221, 228
Mississippi Delta, 7–8, 11–14, 16, 25, 28, 34–37, 41–42, 44–48, 50, 53, 58, 64, 66–72, 75, 80–82, 84–85, 108–13, 115–17, 119, 121, 124–25, 129, 136, 149–50, 152–53, 156–57, 169, 177–78, 180, 186–87, 189, 194–96, 199–200, 202–3, 205, 207, 209, 212, 222–23, 225, 229–30, 238–44
Mississippi Freedom Democratic Party (MFDP), 3, 86–94, 96, 98–99, 101–6, 119, 123, 125, 127, 130–31, 133, 136–43, 145–47, 149–52, 157, 167–68, 172–73, 177–78, 182, 224, 233, 235–36, 240, 242
Mississippi "Regular" Party, 88, 92–94, 96, 98, 101–5, 143, 173, 175
Moore, Amzie, 35, 37, 76, 222–23, 241
Moore, Mary, 11
Moses, Bob, 28, 31, 35, 37, 44–45, 51, 73, 75–76, 81, 89, 104–5, 108, 123, 127, 130, 176, 233–34
Muhammad, Elijah, 131

National Association for the Advancement of Colored People (NAACP), 3, 24, 26, 34, 57, 60, 90–91, 100, 123–24, 141, 155, 167, 173, 184–85, 191–92, 231–33
National Council of Negro Women (NCNW), 122, 159, 161, 178, 199–201, 211, 223
National Democratic Party, 88, 104–5, 169, 173, 175, 183
National Fannie Lou Hamer Statue Committee, 238

NCNW. See National Council of Negro Women
New Deal era activism, 24
Nixon, Richard, 177, 210, 215
Nkrumah, Kwame, 131

Obama, Barack, 3, 234–35, 242
oppression, 48, 52, 98, 110–11, 113–14, 116, 119, 160, 169, 191–92, 203–4, 212, 217, 227; class-based, 68; gendered, 186, 190; institutionalized, 203; racial, 72; racist, 44, 46, 186, 192; white, 77
oral histories, 6, 188

Palmer, Hazel, 90
Parks, Rosa, 3, 26, 234, 236
Patridge, Earl Wayne, 55–56, 58, 65
pig bank, 199, 211–12
political power, 40, 82–83, 103, 156, 182, 206
poll taxes, 38
Ponder, Annell, 53, 56–58, 61, 63–64, 97
preachers, 27–28, 30, 32–35, 114, 153, 157, 159–60, 244
Price, Tyler, 242
pride, 13, 20, 75, 146, 199–200, 202, 210; race, 18, 27, 75, 127–28, 130, 156, 188, 197, 202
Proverbs 14:34, 32
Pulliam, Joe, 16

race pride. See pride
race relations, 11, 13, 17, 24, 42, 154, 180, 210, 217–18
racial equality. See equality
racial hierarchy, 15
racial integration, 25, 32, 50, 88, 116, 126, 156–57, 172, 210
racism, 15, 18, 27, 37, 54, 75–76, 100, 156, 171, 180–81, 185–86, 192, 217, 226–27
Randolph, A. Philip, 91, 149
Rauh, Joseph, 88–89, 92–94, 96, 103
Regional Council of Negro Leadership (RCNL), 24
religion, 33–34, 140, 191, 203; civil, 112, 131, 136–37, 146, 234, 241

rhetoric, 4–6, 13, 29, 42, 47, 49, 96, 116, 126, 131–32, 170, 183, 213, 245
rhetorical appeal, 210
rhetorical biography, 4–6, 9, 245–46
rhetorical power, 117–18
rhetorical purpose, 46, 84, 96, 109, 144, 235
rhetorical signature, 5, 7, 43, 61, 72, 84, 87, 107, 119, 143
rhetorical strategy, 49, 69–71, 86, 106, 132, 221
rhetorical structure, 7, 110
rhetorical symbol, 226
rhetorical tradition, 13, 119
Richards, Dona, 73, 127
Richardson-Thomas, Sarah, 240–43
Robinson, Reggie, 37
Ruleville, Mississippi. See Mississippi

Samstein, Mendy, 68, 73
Schwerner, Michael, 75, 77, 83, 90–92, 112, 160
Schwerner Bender, Rita, 75, 77, 90, 92
second-wave feminism, 8, 166, 169, 184–85, 193
segregation, 18, 26, 32–33, 36, 47, 77, 109, 233
segregationists, 24–25, 32, 47, 50, 52, 55, 62, 66, 72, 77, 88, 104, 115–16, 119, 129, 141, 147, 158, 163, 181, 224, 227
self-help, 198, 201, 211–13
self-respect, 18, 27, 222, 228
sharecroppers, 12–15, 19, 21, 26–27, 33, 35, 37–39, 41–42, 44, 48, 53, 64, 69, 102, 119, 125, 178, 194, 244
Simmons, Willie, 239, 241–43
Sisson, Hattie, 36, 50, 238
Sisson, Herman, 36, 50, 238
sit-ins, 26
Smith v. Allwright, 24
social change, 9, 26, 32–33, 35–36, 41, 61, 154, 165, 169–70, 179–81, 183–84, 187, 193, 203–5, 226
social control, 34
Social Darwinist ideology, 15, 17, 25, 129
social movements, 10, 183
southern racial caste system, 17
speeches, 5–9, 26, 30–31, 33–34, 39, 43, 45, 47–48, 61, 64, 68–69, 93, 99, 101, 107,

118–19, 122, 134, 139, 143–44, 153, 161–62, 184, 193–94, 201–5, 215–16, 220, 226, 235, 240
Steptoe, E. W., 76, 90, 125
sterilization, 22, 72–73, 189–90
Story, J. D., 36
Stranger's Home Baptist Church, 26
Student Nonviolent Coordinating Committee (SNCC), 3–4, 6–7, 13, 26, 30, 34–36, 39, 41, 44–53, 58–59, 61, 68, 73–74, 76, 80–81, 87, 91, 96, 99–103, 105–6, 108, 118–19, 122–28, 130–31, 135–37, 139, 141–42, 153–56, 163, 173–74, 177, 180, 182, 194, 223, 228, 235, 241–43
Sunflower County, Mississippi. See Mississippi

Terney, Champ, 218
testifying, 29, 48, 61–62, 64, 72, 84, 92, 101, 132
"This Little Light of Mine," 4, 30–31, 209, 231, 239
Tiggs, Aretha, 241
Till, Emmett, 25–26, 237
Till-Mobley, Mamie, 25
Townsend, James Lee, 12–16, 19
Townsend, Lou Ella, 12–20, 23, 27, 37, 128, 164
Townsend, Nina, 241
Tucker, Mary, 36–37, 49–50, 52, 96, 132, 241
Tucker, Robert, 36

United Negro Improvement Association (UNIA), 15
United States of America v. Earle Wayne Patridge, Thomas J. Herod, Jr., William Surrell, John L. Basinger and Charles Thomas Perkins, 65
US v. Campbell, 148

VEP. See Voter Education Project
verbal wit, 29, 69
vernacular, 29–30, 33, 42–43, 45, 48–49, 69, 81, 84, 86, 94, 99, 104, 107, 110, 112
voter discrimination. See discrimination
Voter Education Project (VEP), 35, 63, 209, 221

voter registration, 7, 14, 24, 34–37, 41, 44–45, 47–48, 50, 52–54, 57–58, 63, 66, 72–74, 80, 82–83, 87, 90, 96–97, 109–10, 117, 127, 144–45, 149, 151, 155, 181, 209, 223, 229, 232
voting rights, 3, 7, 13, 34–35, 52, 60, 84, 101, 105, 122, 142, 145, 149, 222, 233, 235
Voting Rights Act of 1965, 3, 125, 141, 145, 234

"We Shall Overcome," 91, 114, 209
"We're On Our Way," 86–87, 107, 110, 113, 116, 118
white supremacy, 6–7, 24–25, 40, 48, 73, 79, 108, 113, 115–16, 174, 209

Wilkins, Roy, 91, 93, 100, 102, 124, 155, 231
William Chapel Missionary Baptist Church, 36, 38, 49, 52, 223, 228, 241
Winona, Mississippi. See Mississippi
Wisconsin: Dane County, 181, 220; Madison, 16, 32, 170, 181, 184, 194, 197–98, 200–205, 208, 213–14, 216, 218–21
World War I, 13
World War II, 24

Young, Andrew, 9, 41, 51, 54, 61, 96, 101, 107–8, 155, 169, 173, 196, 201–2, 223, 225, 229–31, 239

CPSIA information can be obtained
at www.ICGtesting.com
Printed in the USA
FFHW020603260719
53881120-59586FF

9 781496 807939